INSTRUCTIONAL MEDIA
AND TECHNOLOGY

COMMUNITY DEVELOPMENT SERIES

Series Editor: Richard P. Dober, AIP

CDS/16

INSTRUCTIONAL MEDIA AND TECHNOLOGY:
A Professional's Resource

Edited by

Phillip J. Sleeman
D. M. Rockwell

Dowden, Hutchinson & Ross, Inc.
STROUDSBURG, PENNSYLVANIA

Distributed by
HALSTEAD PRESS
A division of
John Wiley & Sons, Inc.

LIBRARY OF CONGRESS CATALOGING IN PUBLICATION DATA
Main entry under title:

Instructional media and technology.

   (Community development series ; 16)
   Bibliography: p.
   Includes index.
   1. Educational technology--Addresses, essays,
lectures. I. Sleeman, Phillip J. II. Rockwell, D. M.
LB1028.3.I55   371.3'078   75-28118

  0 470-79750-9

Exclusive Distributor: **Halsted Press**
A division of John Wiley & Sons, Inc.

Series Editor's Preface

Some earlier books in the Community Development Series touched on the relationship between information and architecture, suggesting that data, facts, and users' values need to be brought together early in the design process. Fluent communication is essential. Philosophically, then, a reference work that provides professional readers with detailed knowledge as to how to design buildings and rooms for particular forms of contemporary information transfer is especially relevant to our interests.

The Sleeman/Rockwell compendium focuses on multimedia technology. As a source book it deals with theory and application. It will not only assist the everyday practitioner in approaching design problems, but will also inform clients and users as to what expectations they may hold for eliciting constructive solutions.

Here in convenient form is a state-of-the-art book. I hope that it will be the first of several dealing with specialized environments, which together with more general milieus comprise a physical world susceptible to improved planning, programming design, and construction.

Richard P. Dober, AIP   v

Preface

Instructional media and technology has recently weathered severe criticism from individuals within education, industry, and government. The last two decades, however, have witnessed some of the greatest forward strides. Media and technology will reach maturity when (1) the educational community accepts the reality of time, space, manpower, and financial limitations and fully recognizes the importance of full utilization of every resource available for the learning process; (2) local, state, and national governments accept total responsibility for educational funding and reject the idea that warm bodies (teachers) with classroom responsibilities will, of and by themselves, solve the learning problems; (3) students and parents demand and receive better performance from instruction for the time and money spent in the name of education; (4) commercial enterprise is relegated to the role of supplier of media and removed from the consulting and planning of educational systems and programs; (5) state certification procedures are restructured, and required for all professionals working in the field.

Another essential step for instructional media and technology programs and the professionals in the field is the unification of audiovisual, television, library, and data processing areas. This will require aggressive leadership by those in the field and the support of the administration; trends indicate that unification is the direction required for success at the lowest cost. Presently, twelve states have unified programs and fourteen others are soon to follow.

Present-day opportunities offered to learners and the number of institutions offering a full breadth of learning experiences and environments are limited. The traditional excuses of cost and availability are no longer an acceptable reason for the "have nots." Those who are equipped for implementing a unified media program and have not done so, owing to the "time" and "acceptance" routine excuse, are courting a further degradation of the complete learning process and further erosion of present and future support.

We have *not* attempted to be all-encompassing in this book. Rather, we reviewed relevant articles related to core areas of interest and selected one or more thought-provoking concepts for consideration; an annotated bibliography will aid the stimulated reader to further his knowledge of the practices, processes, and achievements of instructional media and technology.

This book is intended as a resource for those who are primarily and/or ultimately concerned about the learner, learner environment, and the processes of learning. We trust that the reader will find it an invaluable document and are indebted to the many contributors who made the publication of such a book a reality at this time.

P. J. Sleeman
D. M. Rockwell

Contents

PART I: HISTORY

What Is Instructional Technology?

Robert Heinich

Ask a representative sampling of Americans to characterize the difference between the United States and underdeveloped countries; a majority are sure to reply "technology." If we were to ask them further to determine the nature of technology, the average American would quickly respond "machines." Yet machines are only visible manifestations of a process so implicit in our society that we take it for granted. We literally use the word "machines" as a figure of speech, as synecdoche, where the instrument stands for the process. Without the process, the machine has little or no meaning.

That this is so is reflected in our humor. All of us have heard and told jokes and anecdotes about people, institutions, and societies eagerly acquiring machinery, then "coming a cropper" while firmly believing that they were getting instant technology. Before we wax too smug, let us take a look at education. Many schools have acquired complex machinery with no commitment to the technological process—no commitment to the implied task of analyzing the other components of the system and synthesizing new relationships. For example, language laboratories and television (particularly

Robert Heinich presently serves as director of Educational systems for Doubleday & Company, Inc., New York, New York.

closed-circuit) were often installed (sometimes as status symbols) with insufficient understanding of their technological potential, resulting in the former being used as ganged tape recorders and the latter as the world's most complicated opaque projector.

Emphasis on machines must not be allowed to obscure the meaning of technology as a process, as a way of going about the solution of problems. Several years ago, Charles F. Hoban called attention to the broader definition of technology as it applies to education:

> The point here is that the term "educational media" does not, in itself, suggest the ramifications for research and for educational policy and operating procedures which are inherent in the term, technology of education. Technology is not just machines and men. It is a complex, integrated organization of men and machines, of ideas, of procedures, and of management. The introduction of this complex organization generates many systematic problems that can be and have been ignored or generally neglected in theory, research and practice in education. The term, educational media, limits, and the term, educational technology, expands the areas of theoretical development, research, and implementation in education.[1]

Galbraith, perhaps the most articulate, and certainly the most widely read economist of our time, extends this definition:

> Technology means the systematic application of scientific or other organized knowledge to practical tasks. Its most important consequence, at least for purposes of economics, is in forcing the division and subdivision of any such task into its component parts. Thus, and only thus, can organized knowledge be brought to bear on performance.[2]

It is in this larger context of technology that the articles that follow are written, even though, of necessity, the word itself may be used to refer to process at one time, instrumentation at another, and, sometimes, to both at once.

By now, it is fairly well accepted that developments in newer media—particularly television, programed instruction, language laboratories, and computer-assisted instruction—permit us to introduce the technological process at the curriculum planning level where we may assign, with confidence, major instructional tasks to mediated instruction. However, the implications of the shift in technological focus from classroom to curriculum planning—from tactics to strategy—are not at all well accepted, particularly as they affect roles of personnel, instructional management rearrangements, budgetary considerations, and research requirements.

Even when we know intellectually that technology makes a range of instructional choices available at the curriculum planning level, we still tend to shoehorn them into traditional management constructs. The inner meaning of the newer media is not that more powerful instruments of instruction have been made available to the classroom teacher, but that curriculum planning and, subsequently, instructional design are thrust into new roles of responsibility, comprehensiveness, and specificity. In traditional practice, when a local curriculum team would undertake to revise, say, fifth-grade social studies, content and materials would be reviewed and suggestions for instructional activities made, but the group would stop short of designing instruments to effect specified student behaviors. The introduction of instructional technology changes all that. The activities of the curriculum teams described by Bolvin, McKeegan, Ogsten, and Conte go far beyond traditional practice. In my own experience, unwillingness of school districts to assign this level of responsibility to curriculum teams, and reluctance on the part of such teams to accept it, plagues many efforts to apply technological concepts to curriculum decision making.

The entry of instructional technology into curriculum planning makes us much more sensitive to theories of instruction as they affect the design of mediated instruction. When the classroom teacher was in charge of the whole instructional complex and was expected to shape materials into appropriate methodologies, we tended to concentrate on the performance of the classroom teacher. With the shift of attention from the performance of the teacher to that of the student, the requisite theories of instruction have to be incorporated more completely into the specific instructional events which the student experiences. We need to experiment with mediated instruction which develops skills in inquiry, problem solving, and the shaping of other complex behavior patterns. The academic disciplines that are involved in curriculum revisions are becoming keenly aware of the viability of using mediated instruction to assure the students' exposure to specific instructional theory. In fact, one of the more refreshing developments of the past several years is the rediscovery, on the part of the disciplines, of some of the better ideas of progressive education. From the other direction, behavioral psychologists have found out that the complex instructional problems of the average classroom generate requirements far beyond descriptions of laboratory-learning situations.

Mention was made of changes in personnel roles. As should be expected, the major share of concern is for the classroom teacher and the new dimensions of his professional activities. A great deal of the discussion over the teacher's new role is exceedingly self-conscious and hypersensitive to a supposed necessity to reassure him about his place in the new scheme of things. We would probably be much further ahead if we simply let the job evolve with the results of curricular and instructional analysis and synthesis. We would also be further ahead if we direct attention to the necessity of training teachers to perform in two capacities, which, because of applied instructional systems, are growing in importance. The first is new wine in an old bottle: participation in curriculum planning. This role is traditional, but . . . few now possess the knowledge and skills to be optimally effective. Anyone who has struggled through the process of getting teachers on a strategy planning level to identify and specify content in behavioral form is well aware of what I mean. The second job has been

such a minor part of professional concern that it might as well be regarded as new: the design[3] of mediated instruction. It is obvious that a great deal of professional time is going to have to be transferred from the use side of instructional media to the design side. Teachers definitely will be "re-placed" to the other side of the macine. Here again, extensive retraining is required.

Characteristic of curricular innovations by the academic disciplines are extensive teacher-training programs designed not only to expose teachers to new content, but also to work out teaching procedures which make media partners in instruction. The financial burden of such programs was, and is, assumed by the federal government. However, the problem of properly orienting teachers to new instructional procedures is so crucial to the success of large packages of media that producers are starting to offer school districts educational services including teacher training. EBEC has established a rather large department, headed by Frank Anderson, whose charge is to help school districts work out newer instructional patterns. A few other companies are doing the same, and more will certainly move in this direction.

While most emphasis on role change has been placed on the teacher, neither a media specialist nor a curriculum director can read this without realizing that his job will never be the same. Curriculum directors are not used to looking as far ahead instructionally as they will need to when instructional technology is part of the curriculum picture. Neither are they used to dealing with instructional events with the [required] degree of specificity and systematization. . . . Evaluation of student progress is a case in point. This is where individually prescribed instruction and continuous progress plans can slip from control. In a number of schools that I have visited, lack of carefully worked out means of constantly appraising student performance has reduced situations to near chaos—or students to invisibility. Yet evaluation lends itself admirably to technological solutions. The techniques have been worked out very well in Pittsburgh, Milton, and Duluth.

As for the media director, he has rarely had the opportunity to participate in curricular decisions to [a great] extent... nor is he used to being in the position of exercising rather tight control over shaping the instructional uses of the materials under his jurisdiction. For example, how many media specialists have experience in supervising the recasting of existing materials into truly self-instructional forms.

For a number of reasons, most of which are related to the traditions of the profession, the topic of cost effectiveness in terms of alternative means of solving instructional problems tends to be shunned. Yet the potential stake that we have in it is great indeed. Programs involving extensive use of instructional technology are expensive if we simply add the cost and do not rearrange the distribution of funds. If we continue to add materials and equipment to the standard budgetary and instructional arrangements, the tendency of superintendents to consider technology as overhead will increase. We need to experiment with instructional management arrangements that permit mediated instruction to pay for itself. Cost-effectiveness information is a first step in buttressing arguments for such arrangements. Much more research, time, and effort are needed in this area.

Hoban has long advocated the use of operations research (OR) as a powerful tool in optimizing the operation of technological systems. By and large, the research in media investigates either how to make a particular medium more effective or how one medium compares with another. Research problems of the system as a whole have been left virtually untouched. I [previously] made the following comment:

> The field may be suffering from an ever-increasing gap between the main concerns of practitioners in reference to the systems approach and the narrower concerns of research workers. If theory and research are intended eventually to influence practice, researchers had best find out what practice is in the process of becoming. (Keynote Address at the Lake Okoboji Educational Leadership Conference.)

While intracomponent research develops technologies of instruction, the system generates requirements beyond that, just as systems engineering goes beyond the individual fields within it. Many factors in the instructional environment determine media use and effectiveness beyond the variables which are examined by the usual research study. Hoban goes a long way in opening up this problem for exploration.

Inevitably the introduction of technology into any process leads to the concept of systems and the systems approach. However, many media specialists have difficulty relating the subsystems within which they operate. More than one media director has told me that he or his district is using the systems approach because a dial-access system has been installed, or because cataloging and booking are accomplished by data processing. The system which should concern media directors is the total instructional system; in such cases they are described as subsystems. The important point is that instructional technology refers to a systems approach to the entire instructional process.

NOTES AND REFERENCES

1. Hoban, Charles F. "From Theory to Policy Decisions." *AV Communications Review* 13: 124; Summer 1965.
2. Galbraith, John Kenneth. *The New Industrial State.* Boston, Mass.: Houghton Mifflin Company, 1967. p. 12.
3. I prefer this designation to the more fashionable "message design." To me, message design belongs to the communications people—particularly Western Union.

What Is a Media Center?

Robert C. Gerletti

A media center is many things. It is called a learning resource center, learning materials center, educational media center, educational resource center, educational services center, educational communication center, instructional technology center, a library, an audiovisual center, or an educational materials center. As Humpty Dumpty has said, "Words can mean whatever we choose them to mean, neither more nor less."

Therefore, a media center is whatever we choose it to be. At the present time it has many forms. The form it takes is based on an idea, a concept, a philosophy held by a person or persons in a school district.

What seems to differentiate one center from another besides the name that is given to it?

When you visit various centers you are interested in what really goes on in the center. This is when you find out what the differences are in various centers.

The key question seems to be, "What do learners do in the centers and how did they get there?" There are at least four reasons why learners are in centers:

Robert C. Gerletti is director, Division of Educational Media, Los Angeles County Superintendent of Schools Office, and adjunct professor, School of Education, University of Southern California, Los Angeles, California.

1. They are in the center on their free time browsing to obtain information in which they are interested.
2. They are there to prepare an individual or small group report. They have been sent there by their teacher or they are in there on their own accord.
3. They are there to sample interest centers established as a result of needs expressed by teachers, students, principals, or coordinating teachers.
4. They are there as an integral part of courses of study in which they are engaged. The student in this case is actually programed by design into the center for information, to learn a skill, to foster an attitude, or all three.

The media center, discussed above, is generally found in an elementary school or a high school. The relationship between the center at the school and the center at the district office or regional center is a relationship which needs to be looked at when you are considering what a media center is. Some school centers exist with a minimum of assistance from a district center. Other school centers exist with almost all materials supplied by the district center. Still others have worked out an arrangement where the district center is an integral part of the school center and acts as a production agency and as a temporary storage agency for excess materials and materials which are not being used in the school center. If we were to describe a function of both centers, we might say they are pumping stations, pumping materials into the educational process as needed.

DESIGN CONSIDERATIONS

What are some of the considerations necessary when you are thinking of building or creating some kind of media center?

It is imperative that you have a large measure of agreement on the educational goals of the school district, the role of each school and each teacher in accomplishing these objectives. Figure 1 indicates how these goal relationships might be charted.

It is apparent that there are four levels of purposes and procedures. There must be a good deal of agreement in the direction these goals take or you will have an uncoordinated, undirected, and fragmented program.

The Fountain Valley School District in California has demonstrated in its publication entitled *A Plan for Educational Reform* how these levels would appear in writing—district goals, district objectives, school objectives, and classroom objectives.

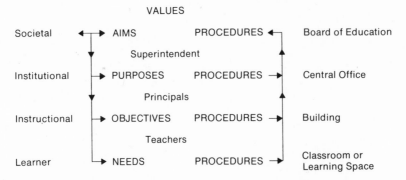

Figure 1
Some relationships of the values, aims, purposes, objectives and procedures to levels of decision making.

District Goal No. 9:
The Constructive Use of Personal Time

District objective   When given unscheduled time blocks, students (institutional objective) will demonstrate their respect for the use of personal time (instructional objective) by their response (behavioral objective) in the learning center.

School objective   Following classroom instruction regarding the use of personal time (instructional objective), students (institutional objective) will demonstrate their response (behavioral objective) to the concept by applying learned skills in the learning centers when given unscheduled blocks of time (evaluative objective).

Classroom objective   When assigned unscheduled blocks of time in the learning centers, students (institutional objective) will demonstrate response (behavioral objective) to the use of personal time (instructional objective) by selecting with greater frequency activities that require independent study rather than activities directed by the coordinating teacher (evaluative objective).

Another factor which you must consider when building a media center is where are you going to focus your effort? Is your effort going to be teacher-centered or learner-centered?

One might call a teacher-centered focus the "Ptolemaic theory." According to Ptolemaic theory, the sun and planets revolved about the earth, which was the center of the solar system. By analogy, the teacher has been viewed as the center of the school system. If you subscribe to the learner-centered focus, you might be inclined to call this the "Copernican theory." In Copernican theory, the earth revolves around the sun, which is a small star in the universe. By analogy, the student is the center, around which the teacher and other members of the school "solar" system revolve.

The activities in a media center at a school and the relationship of the media center of a school and district will be considerably different if your organization is learner-centered. Being learner-centered,

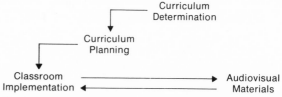

Figure 2

you pay much more attention to the successes and failures of students than if you are teacher-centered. The objectives on all four levels are considerably different. How you plan to integrate instructional materials is also considerably different.

Let's take a look at the place or role of instructional materials in the learning process.

In Figure 2 instructional materials or audiovisual materials were selected by teachers as visual or auditory aids. They were generally appliqued onto the learning process.

In Figure 3 you will note that instructional technology, which is a systematic application of knowledge to the solution of practical problems, has moved up to the curriculum planning level. When curricula are built, materials are considered an integral part of instruction and actually planned for in the curriculum. Philosophically, that is quite a difference from letting the teacher choose from a storehouse or warehouse of materials. (*Note:* Figures 2 and 3 are by Robert Heinich in "The Teacher in an Instructional System," *Instructional Technology*, F. Knirk and J. Childs (editors), New York: Holt, Rinehart and Winston, 1968.)

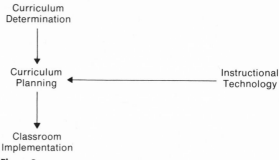

Figure 3

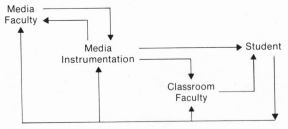

Figure 4

In Figure 4 we have what promises to be a fruitful direction for the application of technology. The media faculty will consist of teachers, student representatives, administrators, curriculum people augmented with specialists such as sociologists, psychologists, anthropologists, and specialists in content areas such as science, mathematics, or social studies. They will plan an entire program for a student or a given group of students. Then they will plan the processes by which the student will obtain the objectives as defined. Note that the classroom faculty members are not necessarily always between the media instrumentation and the student. The classroom faculty will have an opportunity to perform on a much higher professional plane in connection with the learning process than it has up to this time.

A chart for an individual school might look like Figure 5. The media director is a person who may have come through the library, through television, or through the media preparation area or one of any other subsystem. I do not think that there should be

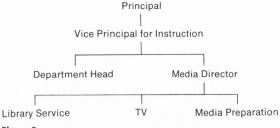

Figure 5

any argument between audiovisual people and librarians over who should head up the programs. There are many factors to be considered when a person is selected to head a unit in a school, such as skill, knowledge, ability, credentials, and even politics. It will take all the skills and knowledges of all people concerned to solve the educational problems. The application of technology requires a major effort with strong leadership in order for it to succeed.

A fourth consideration is the kind of teaching situation in which the materials will be used.

One kind of teaching situation is the self-contained classroom. Students in a self-contained classroom do not all move through the instructional program at the same rate of speed. This has been obvious for many years. Classroom teachers have set up interest centers, divided the class into special groups, and have made many other arrangements to take care of individual differences. There are students whose needs have not been met within the self-contained classroom. Many educators are suggesting other kinds of teaching situations than the self-contained school.

In the self-contained school, students may progress through self-progress or self-direction through an ungraded arrangement. It is possible for students to be at many different places in connection with the learning process with which they are concerned. All the results from experiments in the ungraded, self-progress, or self-directed schools are not in. There are many management and learning problems still being considered and there are many instructional programs not yet available for students with a great variety of needs.

Apparently, even the self-contained school is not a complete answer for meeting needs of all youngsters. In the May 17, 1969, issue of the *Saturday Review,* Donald Cox reported on Philadelphia's new school without walls. In an article entitled "Learning on the Road," Cox reports on one of the most unusual educational experiments now underway. The Parkway Project "opened its doors" to 142 high school students. "There is no single building in which these students learn; instead, they go to nongraded classes in two dozen different public and private institutions located along or near the mile-and-a-half length of the city's tree-lined Benjamin Franklin Parkway."

When you consider the relationship of a media center to this concept, the prospects are staggering. No format or pattern is now available to help identify the kinds of materials required in this new situation.

This discussion raises the question, "Where do we go from here?" How do we organize for the best instruction? What is the relationship of a media center to some of these new ideas? Perhaps we are at a place where the following quotation might be valid: "You must be free to take a path whose end I have no need to know."

PART II: FOUNDATIONS

Educational Technology and Development of Education

Henri Dieuzeide

The activities of International Education Year have enabled us to make an assessment of the spectacular expansion of world education which on the whole is scarcely encouraging. It shows lagging quality in contrast with increasing quantity, inadequate output both internal and external, doubts, and moral crisis.[1] Attention has also been drawn to the growing rift between the educational systems and a society which is breaking the school's monopoly as the source of knowledge, developing through communication media new relationships between man and the world, and obliging all men to continue their education throughout their professional and civic life.[2] It is admitted today that the developing countries, by seeking to multiply indefinitely existing forms of education based on the historic models of the West, are heading rapidly for economic disaster and social bankruptcy.[3] Since the human and financial resources devoted to education have now practically everywhere reached (and often exceeded) their limit in return for inadequate results, it has become evident that improvement in educational output must depend

Henri Dieuzeide is director of the Division of Educational Methods, Materials, and Techniques of the Unesco Secretariat in Paris.

on a distribution of resources geared to a revision of targets.

How can we go about this? First, there is no doubt that the institution of new and more productive educational patterns demands that a certain number of pseudotheorems, which at present block all educational progress, must be strictly and searchingly examined.

One example is sufficient for the moment: educational research has never been able to establish a relation between the *number* of pupils in a class and the *effectiveness* of the instruction they receive. The "ideal formula"—"one teacher for twenty-five pupils"—has no scientific justification.[4] In fact it merely serves as a prop for archaic educational practices, since the sole aim it proposes is to reduce group numbers of pupils *in the hope* of improving efficiency in the educational process. We may ask, for example, whether it would not be more appropriate to try to equip teachers with materials and methods which would increase their efficiency.

The next step, of course, is to seek to incorporate scientific advance and introduce modern methods and techniques into teaching. The ideal of this untouchable sector, the sanctuary of the "direct relationship," has always been widespread adoption of the tutorial principle. There is a current demand everywhere by pupils and students (often supported by teachers) for more human beings and more humanity in relationship. Wherever attempts have been made (even very timidly) to use machines for communication or analysis in education, they have been naively and aggressively condemned as dehumanizing and robot-producing. How many university language laboratories have been abandoned during the last few years, how many television circuits put out of action, and how many computers deliberately paralyzed?

These refusals, fostered sometimes by generous utopianism and sometimes by fear of unemployment resulting from technology, deliberately disregard the importance which the new technologies have acquired, not merely in physics and mechanics but also in human life (through medicine) and social relations (through communications). Need we remind ourselves, for example, of the growing importance of the knowledge industry, which compiles and commercializes knowledge and renews its assimilation in a thousand different ways (e.g., by encyclopedias, teaching machines, correspondence courses, and language methods)? Information, publicity, and political propaganda have devised and brought new and more effective languages of communication into general use. Scientific methods of analysis and organization have developed everywhere; they are transforming industrial organization, political power, and military operations and giving an unprecedented impetus to scientific research.

Even in the most developed countries, however, the world of education still knows nothing about operational research, has only a fleeting acquaintance with data processing, and emphatically distrusts cybernetic models. Following suit, public opinion tends to see in the call for new techniques only manipulation and sterilization of the mind.

The time has come to ask whether education must remain the only major human activity in which technology may not increase man's potential, and to denounce the strange and pernicious paradox whereby education is required to change the world without any concession that it must itself be transformed for good and all.

We have today to agree that the progress of technology has raised a series of fundamental issues among educators and those who depend on them (which means, ultimately, society as a whole). To what extent can present advances in communication and organization technology be used to rationalize and derive the best results from the operation of educational systems, and especially to improve all the processes of learning, memorization, and transfer of knowledge? What patterns of human and material resources will produce better, quicker, and more economical teaching of more individuals? Where positive results have been identified, can they be introduced generally into all educational activities, formal and informal, and in particular be applied to the developing countries? By what strategies could these new technological contributions be introduced into existing educational systems, considering the technical difficulties and human reluctance that they raise?

Innovation and development   We have yet to come to agreement on the still novel concept of educational technology, which produces so many misunderstandings. Recent bibliographies of this subject list hundreds of titles (of treatises, collected articles, publications, and reports) issued during the past 10 years and dealing in particular with the use of audiovisual equipment (from the fixed film to the language laboratory), new methods of learning (from programmed cards to teaching machines), communication networks (including space communication), analysis systems and computers of every kind.[5] However, among these numerous descriptions of what has been done during the last decade to rationalize the learning act within machine–man systems, few models have actually come into widespread use. The report submitted a few weeks ago to President Nixon by the commission of inquiry into instructional technology[6] reveals that even in the United States—the country in which new techniques are more developed than anywhere else in the world—less than 4 percent of educational expenditure is devoted to educational materials, including textbooks, laboratories, and teaching materials of every kind, whereas over 70 percent of the budget is allocated to teachers' salaries. (It should be noted in passing that this proportion of 4 percent is, if we are not mistaken, the highest in the world.)

The issue today is whether the developing countries, whose educational routines have not yet become sacrosanct, may not ask whether six school years are absolutely necessary to achieve the aims of primary education; whether education must be organized on the basis of academic subjects rather than of tasks and problems; whether categories of individual textbooks must be multiplied indefinitely; and whether it is necessary to build and equip school complexes which are unused for almost 6 months of the year, and to run radio and television equipment or computers at a quarter or a third of their capacity.

There seems to be a risk that most of those developing countries which seem willing to skip the stages of the slow educational development of the countries which were industrialized in the nineteenth century will insist on repeating an historical process that will end in a general educational crisis. We should consider whether the introduction of new technologies in education would not enable developing countries to free their schools, while there is still time, from the educational models which belong to the past of the developed countries and of which they imitate, not merely the structure, but also the implicit or explicit objectives.

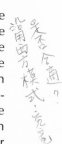

The continuing fragility of the educational systems of the developing countries is an additional reason for inquiring whether they should consolidate organization and equipment which will be obsolete in a few years' time, or should invest in new structures likely to endure and develop. Such a change is urgent and should take place before the systems become blocked by the hypertrophy which is even now appearing in many developed countries.

THE LESSONS OF EXPERIENCE

A survey of the evolution of educational technology in the developed countries should be instructive in this connection as to what tasks need to be accomplished and as to the magnitude of those tasks, the approach to be selected, and the tactics to be employed. Strictly confined at first to marginal and individualized applications, it was subsequently used as a stopgap treatment for deficiencies in the system before resulting in coherent thinking about the scientific organization of the education process.

The "craft" approach   The first point to note is that these new techniques have been very slow in finding their way into schools, and only then after having given long proof of their practical value in daily life (duplication techniques, films, television, tape recorders, and so on). Their increased use has been due, particularly in primary education, to the individual initiative of certain teachers, anxious to establish a new relationship with their pupils, and not to the educational authorities. These techniques have generally been used for fringe activities of extreme diversity. We may quote at random the use of phonograph records and radio in preprimary schools (singing and games), the use of projectors to illustrate history, geography, and general knowledge lessons, use of the tape recorder for improving oral expression, correcting pronunciation, and narrating stories either individually or in groups, the use of films for the teaching of science, technology, and arts subjects, the use of the radio in teaching music, presenting linguistic models, and pronunciation drills, the adoption of television in supervised work, civics, and the introduction of current affairs and contemporary history into traditional education.

Investigation has proved that these activities, at the microcosmic level of the class, have helped in clarifying concepts, stimulating group and individual activities, developing a collective critical awareness, changing attitudes, imposing a new structure or organization on certain subjects, and encouraging originality and creativeness. The use of these techniques has even sometimes made it possible to progress beyond a mere change in the educational climate and, for example, to encourage problem-solving abilities, either collective or individual, or develop self-evaluation processes.

The limits to this approach   All too often, however, it has amounted to nothing more than subjecting the pupils to sporadic bursts of audiovisual information, or the half-hearted attempt to apply the techniques to conventional school activities, and has been based on intuitive judgment rather than measurement of the effects. Use of these aids depends entirely on the teacher and only becomes meaningful when carefully fitted into an educational pattern decided by the teacher himself. In this context, the teacher–"user" tends to be interested only in the "craft" approach to audiovisual methods. Too often his aim is to produce his own documents for his pupils. He prefers using the tape recorder and the overhead projector in his class rather than drawing on documents prepared on a team basis and produced in quantity, such as records, films, and radio and television broadcasts, and thus keeps up the tradition of those generations of teachers who have dictated their lessons, with a sublime disregard for the existence of textbooks.

From the point of view of improving educational output, what hopes does this approach hold out? The strategy of providing each teacher with specialized equipment, maintaining the equipment, and giving the teachers special instruction in its use is certainly a useful way of improving "craft" methods, but a slow and expensive way. The critical mass needed to produce a leap forward in the quality of this output cannot be achieved by injecting new messages in small doses. Economists observe that, since these methods are not financed by a redistribution of existing resources, they can only represent additional costs. There is no certainty that the requisite material will be used to the full, since each teacher decides for himself about using it. If costs per pupil often seem low, it is because they are frequently distorted by the fact that the time taken by the qualified teacher in preparing material (projected visual material, sound recordings) is rarely taken into account. A study of the relationship between the time spent by a qualified teacher on this preparation and the results obtained from a very limited number of pupils might well show that the cost is still high. The development of robust and inexpensive equipment, such as solar projectors and silk-screen printing equipment for the developing countries, cannot disguise the fact that these are again marginal aids to teaching and do not optimize the rôle of the teacher. However interesting such isolated individual efforts may be, it has to be acknowledged that they have not so far resulted in adequate methods for achieving the rapid expansion of education which development demands. All this goes to explain why these methods have been so slow to catch on.

There is, of course, no question of discouraging these experiments, which play their part in the gradual improvement of traditional educational systems, but it would be dishonest to claim that they are among the fundamental remedies for the present crisis.

An exception: the snowball effect   On the other hand, one of the fields in which there seems to be most justification for continuing and developing these experiments, because of their long-term snowball effects, is without doubt that of teacher training: use of language laboratories for modern language teachers, training in programming techniques for use in the arrangement of subject matter, use of the closed circuit for improvement of teacher–pupil communication and relationships (critical study by the student teacher concerned of his teaching performance).[7] Similarly, radio and television can be used to provide teachers with ''remote control'' in-service training. This form of contact helps to avoid the inevitable falling off in the teaching standards of serving teachers and their failure, sometimes, to keep abreast of developments in their profession when they are geographically isolated or become absorbed into the cultural milieu which it is their duty to change. The UNRWA/Unesco Institute of Education in Beirut, which has managed to combine the use of radio, correspondence courses, and programmed instruction for teaching training, constitutes an encouraging example of this use of techniques.

Palliatives and stopgaps   Even more significant is the other tendency, particularly prevalent over the last 10 years, which has sought to use the resources of educational technology—particularly radio and television networks or new learning processes such as programmed instruction—in an authoritarian manner as an emergency treatment for certain defects in the education system, particularly at secondary level.

In certain cases, educational technology has come to be used as a remedy for inherent deficiencies in the system: in one place to offset the teachers' lack of qualifications by regular broadcast demonstrations or drills or by programmed documents for the pupils; in another, to speed up the introduction of new subjects (new mathematics, nuclear physics, data processing) or new education methods (audio-oral teaching or modern languages); and in yet another (still using radio or television), to take over activities on which the schools have fallen down, using informal methods (intensive courses for second examination attempts, such as Radio Télé-Bac in France and the Ivory Coast).

In other cases the aim has been to extend the field of action of the traditional system to cover new sectors of the public who could not be reached by existing institutions, through the création of informal education structures based on the use of radio, television, correspondence courses, and programmed instruction—*extension* courses on the lines of the ''Junior City College'' in Chicago for those not enrolled in schools or *replacement* education in areas where the educational establishments were nonexistent, such as the Italian *Tele-Scuola,* designed to provide the young people in the depressed region of the Mezzogiorno with the rudiments of secondary instruction.

Finally, in other instances the aim has been to eliminate the maladjustments between the school and the social environment by trying, through the use of radio and television in particular, to make up for the cultural handicaps of certain categories of pupils, helping them to learn to express themselves and communicate by familiarizing them with the materials and tools of culture (books, works of art).

These broadcasts to prepare children for school or to make up "cultural leeway" have been developed more particularly in the industrialized nations (socialist countries, United Kingdom, United States of America, France).

There is often a tendency nowadays to pass severe judgment on undertakings of this kind, in which political opportunism has frequently taken precedence over educational needs, and their critics are quick to point out that they are superficial and produce only a temporary respite and false economy.

It is true that they have often been hurriedly improvised and (because of the lack of time and sufficient forethought) have not always made the best of the technical resources and specific potential of the media. With the plea of urgency, they have often been put to uses for which they were not designed: for example, television has often been used simply as a vehicle for a verbal message without any visual content, thus reinforcing old-fashioned practices (authoritarian teaching methods, verbal teaching, stress on learning by heart, encouragement of passive attitudes, glamorization of the television teacher). There has been some justification to speak of "retrograde innovations" which have tended to displace or disguise problems rather than solve them.

It must be said in favor of these operations, however, that their very limitations have given rise to some hard thinking about the impact that the use of communication infrastructures or industrial methods might have on education: education does not mean only the organizing of micro-activities at the level of small groups—it can use the vast resources of radio, television, and programmed material, for instance, to increase its own efficiency. Moreover, the half-hearted combination of technology with a traditional system, by stressing to the point of caricature the worst features of the system, has forcibly emphasized the need to reexamine its aims and methods. It has now been realized, for example, how absurd it is to use television to create a cultural context based on an élitist culture (introducing children to the theater, literature, and works of art) and imposing it on the children of agricultural or urban workers without first giving thought to the cultural aims of education. The most positive result of these experiments has probably been that they have brought educators, administrators and research workers face to face with new concepts and novel technical requirements. They have led—and sometimes compelled—them to take a fresh look at existing systems, their aims and their operation.

Some progressive innovations Last but not least, these experiments have, over the last 2 or 3 years, made possible new and positive lines of approach which go beyond short-term provisional measures. Common features of all of them are that they irrevocably link the use of communication machines with a more scientific organization of school work, they transcend the traditional distinction between school and postschool activities, and they seek to reduce inequality of opportunity.

One of the most obvious examples is the use of inertia-free information networks, such as radio and television. Unlike distribution circuits of the film library type, these networks make possible the industrial-style production of documents by organized teams of education specialists and their instant, widespread distribution. With their aid an average level of educational information and activity can be maintained in schools which do not all enjoy equally favorable circumstances. The programmed and simultaneous introduction over vast territories of identical pioneering models, the distribution of the elements of a coherent collective motivation, and the constant up-dating of instructions for teachers are possible everywhere today by means of radio, and in increasingly extensive regions by means of televisions (Niger, Hungary, Cuba, Singapore).[8]

Another example is the attempt to achieve a combination of various communication networks into more coherent and comprehensive organizations, more responsive to diversified requirements. Instances include the new institutions for technical and secondary education, or even part-time higher education ("second chance" schools) which have been developed during recent years in Western countries and which combine the distribution of programmed documents, the broadcasting of instructions, information models and demonstrations on radio, and models and demonstrations on radio and television, information "feedback" through correspondence courses, the telephone or the duplex system, face-to-face contact provided by traveling instructors, study in small groups and supplementary summer schools ("Tele-Kolleg" in the Federal Republic of Germany, "Tele-polytechnic" in Poland).[9]

Alongside these methods, which combine extremely varied resources, we can also see the emergence of complex arrays of integrated installations designed to provide intensive accelerated courses on an individual basis: learning laboratories, television circuits, teaching machines, individual response control systems, response analyzers, simulation, computers with audio-visual terminals, and so on. This costly apparatus whereby one learns "by appointment" requires, if it is to be an economic proposition, intensive and coordinated collective use; it provides a blueprint in certain developed countries for what great educational centers for intensive courses, on the lines of teaching hospitals,[10] could be like.

It will be noted finally that with the development of research in cognitive psychology and in behavior study laboratories, and more especially the different forms of the programming of learning (operant conditioning in America, learning algorithms in the USSR), the users of the new technologies have been led to state education problems in more precise terms as regards aims, organization of the subject to be taught, nature of the activity of the learner, and evaluation and control methods in relation to these aims and activities.[11] This Copernican revolution in teaching which transfers the center of gravity of educational thinking and research from the teacher's functions and activities (teacher-centered mentality) to the terminal behavior of the pupil (pupil-centered approach) enlarges the prospects opened up by "educational technology."

THE NEED FOR RATIONALIZATION

The technology of education as distinct from technology in education International Education Year probably marks the point at which we can start to move away from thinking about technology in education, that is, thinking chiefly concerned with equipment, the elaboration of ad hoc messages, and the incorporation of technology into traditional teacher-centered activities—to thinking about the technology of education, that is, the systematic application of the resources of scientific knowledge to the process that each individual has to go through to acquire and use knowledge. The aim behind such thinking should be to move away from dispersion of effort and waste (or, worse still, the overhasty adoption of technology as a means of patching up shaky educational systems) to a full and integrated use of all the resources of the technological age. Hitherto, these areas in education to which technology has been applied have all too often resembled patches of ground strewn with machine parts that no one would attempt to assemble. Has not the time now come to put these parts together?

Instead of attempting merely to recruit and train an ever-increasing number of teachers, whose tasks will become increasingly complex, why not analyze the various educational functions with a view to redistributing the various human and material resources available wherever in the educational system their potential can be most fully realized? This implies the acceptance on our part that *instead of continuing to let the machine do only what the teacher cannot do, we should ask ourselves what it is the teacher should do that the machine cannot do.* This further implies the acceptance of far-reaching changes in the organization and hierarchial structures of the educational establishment and in the responsibilities and functions of pupils and teachers alike. There may then be some hope that technology will cease to be a miscellaneous collection of new equipment and methods, designed to lighten some of the teacher's *traditional* tasks, and will offer a coherent set of liberal methods and original concepts of learning and training which will free teachers and pupils from the haunting fear of failure and fear of each other which are characteristics of the traditional, elitist institutions.

New display devices (overhead projectors) and, more important still, image and sound recording and reproduction devices (duplicating machines, tape recorders, video tape recorders, microcards), the storage and collective or individual retrieval, at will, of image and sound (televised films, cassettes, the E.V.R. and Selectavision systems, video discs, etc.), self-scoring and self-assessment possibilities, the feedback facilities and flexibility offered by some techniques (ranging from the individual response control system to the computer) or by particular methods of presentation (programming) are some of the new techniques and methods at our disposal. Modern technology, with its methods of organization and measurement, its evaluation and experimentation techniques, can, it seems, provide education with the *guiding principles* upon which to base a definition of the relationship between these various new techniques and methods and between them and the institutions, content, and existing methods of education. The transition from technology in education to the technology of education involves a thorough reappraisal of the existing educational system, of its objectives and of the means used to attain them, before any decision is reached to employ these new techniques for specific teaching purposes. The teacher-turned-technologist can then gradually assume the functions of an "educational engineer" whose job it is to increase the output of the entire scholastic machine.[12]

The comprehensive approach   Over the past few years experience has shown that educational innovations, technological or otherwise, cannot simply be introduced in the form of a local transplant on to a particular point of the existing educational anatomy. Such innovations are meaningful and effective only *in relation to their effects upon the body as a whole.* We have recently had the opportunity of seeing the futility of introducing school curricula involving, for example, the acquisition of new knowledge or of new methods of teaching (like applied linguistics or new mathematics at a particular level) unless instructors and teachers and the manufacturers of teaching materials are consulted. We have similarly learned the absurdity of teaching a particular section of the population to read and write and then not supplying them with satisfactory printed material (local press, occupational handbooks, etc.). The school today is an organic unit in which the teacher is only one teaching agent among others, just as the school itself is only one component of a larger overall educational activity. The need for technological change bids us today to turn the eye of the biologist or of the mechanic on the educational system and see it is an organism.

The methods of organization which have developed over the past few years under such names as "operational research" or "systems analysis" appear to be suitable intellectual instruments for an overall critical study of existing systems and for suggesting *new educational configurations,* based on scientific principles, in which there would be a place for the resources of technology. Why not apply relevance trees or critical path analysis to the bottlenecks in the educational systems? Would it not be possible to apply the principles of feedback and self-correction to the active functioning of educational institutions? Again, more generally, how can there be any hope of a rational improvement in educational activities without measuring and analyzing their functioning?

We know that by the term *system* analysts mean

the sum of separate parts acting both independently and on one another to achieve predetermined objectives; the system is therefore defined by reference not only to its constituent parts, but to the organization that allows it to function. In any analysis of a system the aim is therefore to measure exactly the objectives to be attained in terms of performance, to define the levels of application, to allow for the constraints under which it operates, and to arrive at rational operating models. Can this effort, the aim of which is to define logical structures incorporating all the constituent parts and to *mar-shal the various agents into a unified process in pursuit of maximum efficiency,* be applied to the educational process?

In human activities other than education these coherent sets of methods have made it possible to detect the weak points and failings in a given organization which need remedying, to choose from a range of schemes for improvement, to rearrange the constituent parts of a body in various combinations, or to add new parts to it in order to secure new results. Systems analysis should make it possible to define for any given organization an optimum structure which maintains equilibrium by means of successive readjustments to the environment. True, the experts are ready to admit that education is too complex an overall process to be analyzed otherwise than in terms of probability: education is an *open* system. However, the thing about systems analysis is that it makes it possible to incorporate uncertainty into action. Since the new technologies are constantly coming up with further sources of information and analysis, increasingly powerful memory units, and increasingly sophisticated control mechanisms, it becomes possible to envisage the development—in some cases still rudimentary and in others already more advanced—of self-organizing and self-regulating educational systems, both at individual level (self-instruction) and at the level of the educational institution (continuous feedback of information permitting continuous adjustment). The educa-

tional system itself could thus steer a more accurate course than at present by means of the incoming reactions and hence be able to evolve, adapt, and grow by mastering change.[13]

An example of analysis: the act of learning   First, however, it must be given the means of establishing correlations among the objectives, the learning processes, the means of instruction, and the teacher's functions. The analysis of the various components and various points in the act of learning will then make it possible to use, on each separate occasion, the situation and means best adapted to the end in view. In the act of learning we can distinguish, for example, an information stage, characterized by research and the collecting together of the data that have to be acquired; an exploitation stage, which involves the marshalling, criticism, and processing of the data that have been gathered; an assimilation stage, in which the knowledge is fixed; a transfer stage, in which the knowledge is applied; and, lastly, an assessment (or self-assessment) stage.

Only the new technologies allow each of these stages to be performed with maximum efficiency. At the first, or "information" stage, technology facilitates individual information by means of visual or audiovisual data banks and documentation and information centers (record libraries, film-slide libraries, etc.) This acquisition of information may be collective in form and involve mass communications (e.g., the cinema and television). The second, or "exploitation" stage, is generally characterized by group work and involves the use, for example, of individual response control systems. The period of assimilation and fixation may be individual and involves the use of programmed instruction, teaching machines, and learning laboratories, but may also involve group work, for example, joint utilization of programmed material or group work or computer terminals. The "transfer" period lends itself to the employment of simulation techniques (closed-circuit television and teaching machines). Response analyzers and testing machines in general can be brought in during the "assessment" period. Recording machines and computers make it possible to keep an individual record of the pupil's progress throughout his school career.

At each point in the learning process and for each application of a particular technique there is a corresponding and different function for the teacher. Before carrying out any educational operation he will have to find the teaching strategy required to apply all the various procedures chosen. During the course of the information phase, his role is that of the guide who prepares the stimulants and supplies the documentation which he has himself prepared or chosen. During the exploitation phase, his role is that of a mediator or group leader who motivates the interactions (and who must, for example, gradually train the members of the group in group leadership). He sees that the ideas which have been acquired are properly understood and helps to discover and correct misunderstandings. During the assimilation and fixation stage, his role is one of diagnosis—he prescribes the treatment best suited to the capabilities of the learner. During the transfer phase, his role becomes that of an adviser-cum-guide. During the last phase of the learning process, his role becomes one of checking, ensuring that the system of marking is uniform and seeing to it that continuity is maintained in the assessment process. At all events, the use of technology will have made the teacher more receptive and will have placed him in a more central position where pupils can more easily approach him with their individual problems. In this connection, we cannot stress too strongly the fact that the use of educational technology—far from implying any qualitative decline in the role of the teacher—frees him from certain purely mechanical tasks of exposition and repetition, thus enabling him to devote himself to the noble and irreplaceable functions of stimulation of interest, diagnosis, motivation, and advice.

This of course implies a fairly radical overhaul of the existing educational and administrative arrangements, which are based generally on the individual unit or class—reorganization of timetables (e.g., so as to fit in joint activities at a particular level), the splitting up of groups of classes, full-time use of schools, continuous assessment, the preparation of educational activities in interdisciplinary teams, dividing and distributing of work among teachers according to their aptitude and experience, adaptation of buildings to give greater flexibility, responsibility of the pupils themselves for discipline, and the production of a considerable amount of teaching materials. Educational technology can help to reintroduce a certain amount of flexibility into the functioning of the school system, which has been in a rut for decades.

Differentiating   However, it should not be thought that there is any single strategy for scientific reorganization of this kind. The point about systems analysis is rather that it helps to define strategies *differentiated* according to the degree of economic development, resources, and type of educational system.

Thus, for example, as far as the distribution of educational information is concerned, it is possible to think of the *dissemination* of information in the form of audiovisual broadcasts, either through a restricting and relatively inexpensive system (radio, television) or through a (more expensive) user-controlled system involving the use of telephone lines and computer networks. Systems for the *distribution* of recordings (films, tape cassettes, teaching-machine programs, etc.) supplied direct either to educational institutions or to individual students at home are another possibility. These systems of distribution, which are more complex and slower than the broadcasting systems, but which are also more selective and better differentiated, can either be centralized (e.g., in the form of film loan libraries and correspondence tuition centers) or decentralized in the form of commercial distribution direct to customers (e.g., institutional tape library or personal record library).

In countries where there are fewer industrial and professional resources, these new systems could be based upon simpler or more cost-effective equipment, taking into account the needs and objectives of the educational system. In a developing country, therefore, if a system of <u>inertia-free instantaneous</u> broadcasting, such as radio or television is chosen, a particular technique must be employed so as to get the best out of it. Where television is available it will be employed *both* for school and out-of-school educational purposes. If it is used to transmit programs for group use, it can also be used to show programmed learning exercises, which would be transmitted by other means (teaching machines) in a country that was better equipped. <u>Television</u> is also used to give instructions to the teacher or instructor as to how he should conduct his teaching and how television can be incorporated in it, and to provide in-service training. The system thus becomes multipurpose. In a number of African countries, however, experience has shown that certain difficulties can arise as a result of combining two different types of transmission network: for example, such a tempting technique as "radiovision" (the projection of slides synchronized with a radio transmission) presents both the disadvantages of being bound by the constraints of broadcasting and the hazards of having to rely on the delivery of the slides.

With a systems approach, it is possible to coordinate uses and techniques and to organize them rationally on a continuous basis for the individual learner but also for the group (class or school grade) and the institution, and at the regional and national level. It is therefore possible, proceeding by analyses, to design a complex set of harmonized functions, ranging from <u>the microsystem</u> of the individual learner to <u>the national macrosystem</u>.[14] Although it is generally accepted that the degree of complexity of systems should increase in proportion to the resources available and the difficulties of the learning process (thus the establishment of a complex technological system will generally be more justified in the case of higher education), in practice there is no reason why such a system should not be applied to functional literacy.

Mass instruction and individualized instruction   Are the methods of strict correlation of edu-

cational objectives with the various technological and human resources available, within the framework of a coherent system, such as can be seen emerging today in the developed countries applicable as they stand to the developing countries? The aims of the developed countries and those of the developing countries do not necessarily coincide with respect to the use of technology. <u>For the developed countries, technology essentially means economies in human resources; for the developing countries technology has other possible functions</u>: true, it means <u>the possibility of better distribution of the available human potential</u>, but above all <u>it is part of the race against time</u>. Educationalists in the developing countries will be more inclined to see educational technology as a means of rapid dissemination of urgently needed education on a massive scale to large groups, whereas the developed countries will see it as a means of increasing the effectiveness of education by <u>making learning a more individual process</u>. This is why there is often a tendency to make a sharp distinction between <u>mass dissemination techniques</u> (the cinema, radio, and television), by means of which it may be possible to solve the tremendous problems of India or Brazil, and <u>individual teaching techniques</u> (programming, teaching machines, learning laboratories, individual response control systems, computer teaching) intended for the "tailor-made," "by appointment" type of education.

This theoretical distinction does not stand up to serious examination, first because the mass media by their very nature make it possible to offer a varied range of means of instruction, and, consequently, to introduce a certain individualization of instruction. Further, the use of individualized techniques such as programmed instruction combined with group techniques, the audiovisual for instance, has already made possible, in Great Britain and France, for example, a fruitful alternation of the global and analytical learning processes. Conversely, we have seen a development in the group use of a single machine (group work with the same programmed material in Central Africa and on a single computer terminal in Spain) for programmed instruction and computers.

It is at the stage of utilization that the difficulties occur, since this approach requires the industrial manufacture of the basic teaching equipment of a standard type but of high quality and capable of being used on a sufficiently wide scale to be economical. It is well known that it requires about 100 hours of collective work by specialists to prepare 1 hour of programmed teaching material and anything up to 200 hours of work by a team to produce 1 hour of computer teaching material. The figures are even higher in the case of film making or the preparation of "prepackaged instruction." Educational technology implies assembly-line methods for the production of teaching material and a division of labor in its use. It involves in particular the development facilities into which these prefabricated elements can be smoothly adapted and integrated. It will inevitably lead the teacher to reconsider his place and functions within the future school system, and no doubt the part played by the school system itself within a developing society based on educational expansion.

The school of tomorrow—factory or self-service establishment? By making it possible to redistribute human and material resources and by lending support to the attempt to find ways and means of increasing the internal output of the educational institution, the development of educational technology opens up the prospect in the years ahead of developing new types of the educational institution radically different in form from the traditional, elitist, and selective establishment.

The establishment in which educational technology (audiovisual communication, learning laboratories, data banks) has been incorporated would, according to one model, tend to resemble an enterprise in which educational technology would be used to reduce wastage to a minimum and to optimize the act of learning by establishing precise mechanisms to produce effective individu-

als by dint of intellectual constraints, fear and the specter of failure having first been banished from their training.

In contrast to this deterministic model based on efficiency, there would be another model, no doubt using similar means but arranged in different configurations. It would offer a community service of individualized self-instruction for safeguarding individual freedom of action—a complete self-service system adaptable to individual needs, to which the pupils would feel an allegiance based on individual involvement.

The first of these formulas would prove particularly useful in immediate vocational training. However, since the society of tomorrow is to be founded on lifelong education and since the spirit of his initial training determines the practical interest subsequently shown by a citizen in his own training, the self-teaching center will, more so than the learning enterprise, be bound up with lifelong education. Teaching will no longer be a matter of forcing information upon pupils (as in the traditional, authoritarian system) or exposing them to knowledge (as in liberal education), but one of instructing the young by the practice of self-teaching—a method calculated to ensure social mobility—how to shape their education by mastering a system and progressing beyond it. Thus educational technology will not be confined to increasing the internal efficiency of the school center; it will also increase its involvement with social reality.

IN FAVOR OF A STRATEGY
OF TECHNOLOGICAL INNOVATION

We shall next have to ask ourselves how the gradual transition from theoretical models similar to those that have just been described to the stage of effective application is to be made. Conversions have hitherto been from one stable system to another. Here, the leap has to be made, under conditions of *permanent instability*, from autocratic, fixed, closed and ponderous systems to planned, open, flexible and self-adjusting systems that will admit of the possibility of forecasting and integration.

Three choices   In theory there are three possible innovation strategies. The first is to change everything at the same time, but so far there has been no instance of this having been done anywhere. The second involves modifying the existing state of affairs by introducing innovation at the lowest level in the system and carrying on from there, the new stem pushing the old one in front of it; such is the case with the gradual introduction of television, year by year, involving, in the case of the Ivory Coast, the transformation of primary education and, in the case of El Salvador, of secondary education. The third strategy involves setting up and developing a new system parallel to the old one and capable of replacing it one day; such is the case, for example, of educational television for elementary schools in Niger, or, at another level, of the Open University in the United Kingdom. In the long term this is no doubt the most effective strategy, although this is not to say that we should not *optimize* right away the use of technology in education such as it is and undertake localized projects, without waiting until all the conditions are right. It is not inconsistent with an attempt to *rationalize* the use of educational technology on the basis of models that combine all the data into an integral system. Planning by segment and long-term planning are only two aspects—strategical and tactical—of the same productive effort.

International Education Year should help to define the new intellectual approaches, the original practical measures, and renewed international contributions called for by these transition strategies.

An optimistic attitude   If we want to apply systems analysis, we should adopt a coherent overall view of the educational situation. We must take action against the fragmentation of schemes and set priorities, ranging from the *project* to the full-scale education *program*. Those microsystems which can be developed first will probably be in

areas less overburdened by antiquated structures and therefore presenting less risk of an abrupt reject—the out-of-school and informal sectors, ''remote-controlled'' education, part-time education, or sectors under review because of strong external pressures, such as higher education or technical education. Even at the microsystem level, care will have to be taken to define an operational *critical mass* that is sufficient to bring about a chain reaction leading to renewal. Such a changeover should be planned in terms of efforts that it is possible to sustain intellectually; a certain degree of flexibility should be observed in calculating the length of the preparatory period that should precede the changeover, so as to avoid the possibility of discouragement. Similarly, within any given program a number of alternatives will be kept open, so that a competitive spirit may be maintained and a process of natural selection may operate. Finally, care will be taken to create a strongly positive climate around the changeover and one that will enable the opportunities for developing the community and improving the lot of individuals to be used to the full. There is nothing more depressing than the gloom surrounding certain innovation schemes in which the difficulties and problems are given undue prominence. Innovative forces should be detected, marshaled, and organized. Properly conducted, *technical innovation should be a focal point for energies,* around which could be grouped efforts at reorganization that could not be undertaken otherwise. There are frequent instances of the catalytic effect of school television or programmed instruction in hastening the reform of school curricula and teacher training.

Decompartmentalizing in order to coordinate   In practice the aim will be to take steps calculated to modify the attitudes of the majority. Experience shows that the first thing to be done is to improve the internal means of communication in educational institutions and to encourage among those concerned a spirit of continuous self-appraisal. Interdisciplinary work at every level

should be used as a means of reducing or eliminating comparmentalization. One of the first stages in this development is to treat as an entity certain problems that are traditionally viewed in isolation or kept artificially apart and, accordingly, to create centers of decision. At the same time an attempt will be made to work out ways in which all those concerned can be associated with the process of innovation; tensions will be resolved by means of participation governor mechanisms. It is not just a question of group therapy: resistance to innovation is an expression of a social reality and it should not be studied in order to circumvent or destroy it, but to use it as a *solid basis* for a collective innovatory endeavor.

At the same time an effort will be made to create the material infrastructure for innovation. One of the first tasks, especially in countries with limited resources, will be to see if there are any technological resources that could be more fully utilized: broadcasting agencies, printing facilities, data-processing centers, and so on. It will be essential to coordinate the use of such resources in the framework of an overall plan. An attempt will also be made to improve cooperation between the various occupational groups concerned with the development of education. To achieve progress in this direction it is essential that the manufacturers of teaching equipment and program producers rally around explicit educational objectives—in some countries electronics engineers and visual aid manufacturers, textbook publishers, and the authors of programmed instruction methods are already trying to combine their efforts (e.g., in the United States and the Federal Republic of Germany). Elsewhere, national agencies for the production and distribution of new teaching materials have been set up (Sweden, Netherlands); also, in some countries (e.g., Japan or the United Kingdom) various authorities or ministries have got together to coordinate their use of the existing communication networks (radio, telephone, transmitted and piped television) for educational purposes.

The institution   Particular care should be taken to develop centers for the promotion of innovation, whose task it will be to produce—or get those concerned to produce—new school curricula, new systems of evaluation and control, and new teaching materials. An effort should also be made to encourage the development, outside the traditional framework, of *"centers of excellence"* and truly experimental establishments based on new organizational principles, to bring them together, to link them, and, if possible, to coordinate them in a flexible manner calculated to ensure mutual benefit and to increase their capacity for innovation and their impact.

Consequently, it is applied research conducted by interdisciplinary teams that should be encouraged. Its results will not be in the form of reports but of *products,* which may be new teaching materials (films, teaching equipment, programmed materials), but also methodological systems or new institutional forms. Research done as a pretext, research of the academic kind with a bias toward theoretical generalization, should be avoided—industry and medicine are standing proof that effective methods can be generally introduced without being given a formal basis in theory.

Finally, the aim will be to inform and to train—to inform the public insofar as it is the customer of the educational system, and especially pupils' families, whose attitude is often wary, and to train the teachers and change the old patterns that they have been used to following in order to prepare them for the new roles that educational technology has marked out for them, especially their role as *in-school and out-of-school leaders.* Such training should be given to serving teachers as well as to student teachers, and this will be possible through the transformation of the professional training institutes into lifelong training institutes having at their command all the resources of modern educational technology. Further, special attention will have to be given to the training of a corps of "educational technologists" (i.e., of specialists of all levels) who, according to some experts, may in 20 years' time account for anything up to 10 percent of the total of all those employed in education. These people will be specialists in the revision of objectives and curricula, testing and measurement specialists, administrators of new systems, communications specialists, production and maintenance technicians, etc.

Preparing the ground   International assistance programs should also be rethought with a view to the systematic development of innovation, taking due care not to spread resources too thinly or to disperse efforts too widely. New avenues are at present being opened up by the tentative start on *integrated* educational planning that has been made in Algeria and Indonesia. Aid should stimulate and not paralyze communication between the motive elements of innovation within the country concerned (research centers and production centers). Consideration should be given to the idea of an international network for liaison between these elements, involving the use of the most up-to-date means of communication and exchange (computers and space communication in particular) and making it possible to achieve a better division of assistance work. Some national centers could be formed into support centers to develop educational technology at the regional level. The one at present being built in Mexico for Latin America (ILCE), or the one planned for Japan to cover the Asian states, should be both information centers using the most up-to-date communication technology and centers for training and research geared to technological innovation. These regional networks and centers should be backed by *task forces* made up of specialists who, at the request of governments, may be called into help fit new educational strategies based on systems analysis and technology to the country's special needs. Finally, it is to be hoped that international assistance agencies may set up an example of the new approach in their own structures by setting up interdisciplinary units entrusted with specific missions in place of the traditional system of compartmentalization by disciplines and techniques.

Of course, such new arrangements only have any meaning if they are supported by appropriate political decisions, as was the case recently when Sweden, Singapore, and Cuba took the decision to bring in educational technology as a means of developing education.

In this connection it should be noted that International Education Year could mark an important turning point. New efforts to think the problem through, combined with new efforts at the organizational level, are being made with Unesco's assistance, with a view to reducing the fatal disproportion between the ever-increasing rate at which technology is advancing and the standstill in educational thinking that we find at the present day.

The Ivory Coast, for instance, has decided to link curriculum reform, the overhaul of teacher training, and the systematic use of television for schools to ensure that its primary education system is better adapted economically and culturally to the environment. India is considering the production of visually based teaching programs suitable for use with the various forms of educational technology as and when they appear, including space communication. Indonesia is employing the systems approach for the first time on a national scale as a means of analyzing the state of its schools and determining what part school radio should play in it. Spain is studying the setting up of a network of computers for the rapid training of a new type of secondary school teacher of the kind that the country will need most urgently in the coming decade. Finally, the states of the Andean region have initiated studies with a view to determining to what extent space communication can be used to speed up educational integration in the region.

In all these cases, an attempt has been made to make an overall analysis of the general state of affairs in the field of education. Projections of the possible futures of education are carried out before any decisions are made on fitting educational technology into the development of education, so that it may play its true role, which is to help transform the very nature of the educational system into which it is to be incorporated.

CONCLUSION

There remains the problem of the price that must be paid for this innovation. It has to be admitted today that innovation is a costly affair and that it is no longer a question of choosing between whether to innovate or not to innovate, but of knowing how to innovate at greater or lesser cost and over a longer or shorter period of time. It is then permissible to look beyond the cost–benefit ratio and to compare costs and performance.

A reasonable proposition It has been established that in most countries educational expenditure is tending to mount regularly, year in, year out, by anything from 5 to 8 percent, depending on the country; most of this increase is accounted for by rising teachers' salaries. The question today is whether priority should not be given to investment that seems likely to have a positive long-term effect on the efficiency of education. *Might not International Education Year be an opportunity for educationalists to ask—and for governments to decide—that some of the increase in national educational expenditure already scheduled for the coming decade (say half) be devoted exclusively to refining the ways and means best calculated to ensure a rapid increase in the efficiency of the educational system and, more especially, the rational development of educational technology?*[15]

Since the purpose of educational technology is not to provide each individual teacher with his own audiovisual outfit, but to reform the functioning of the educational system, and since its introduction provides the opportunity for analyzing—and perhaps for reorganizing—the existing institutions, it is within the available or foreseeable budgetary provisions that educational technology must be introduced, by adjustment of educational practices to resources and vice versa. In a number of European countries the establishment of experimental institutions has been rendered possible by an all-out effort to reorganize teaching spaces and to rethink fittings and equipment. Within a given context this involves a comparison of the effectiveness of the old system with that of the new educational pattern. It is a question of finding out which teaches the greater number of subjects best in terms of quantity and quality, in more places and in the same or less time.

The program that has been undertaken in the Ivory Coast for the incorporation of television into primary education is based on a planned reduction by half over a period of 10 years in the present drop-out rate and on an increase in operating costs in the region of 8 percent, which would be covered by the estimated increase in national revenue. The integration of educational technology is no longer calculated here in terms of *additional expenditure*, but in terms of *overall expenditure*.

We would add that recent studies by economists would seem to indicate that there is an optimum level for the distribution of resources within an education system beyond which there is no longer any improvement in the results. It is this *state of equilibrium* which must be sought and attained. Educational technology first of all provides the opportunity for subjecting education to internal scrutiny and then for measuring it against other human activities.

Technology and machines Such a scrutiny can hardly be put off much longer. This is not to say that laboratory research into the processes of learning have made any particularly rapid progress in this respect—"sleep teaching" and subliminal stimulation, for instance, remain at the stage of working hypotheses. On the other hand, the economic and technical pressures created by the new equipment are mounting: their miniaturization, their reliability, falling costs, and their rapid and widespread introduction are augmenting their educational potential—direct communication links via space, video discs and quarter-inch video tape recorders, desk-top computers, etc.

Countries with limited resources should not

imagine that they are not affected by this: technology is not just a question of hardware but one of man thinking about the nature, function, and rational use of tools. Educational technology is not about how the machine is to be incorporated but how technological principles are to be transferred. Technological invention is not tied to a particular level of GNP.

One major task to which International Education Year should invite the developing countries to address themselves is certainly that of the *acculturation of educational technology*. A particular requirement of the developing countries (e.g., the development of fine motor skills or the learning of the perceptions and associations peculiar to a literate civilization) should be no bar to the adaptation of already proved programming methods. The need to produce educational materials locally should not rule out, but on the contrary justify, the simultaneous appraisal and application of programs and techniques that have already proved their reliability in the developed countries. The combined criteria of educational output and economic viability should soon make it possible to define the proper balance that must be struck between local contributions and outside contributions.

This does not necessarily mean that the key to educational technology is to mechanize schools through and through and transform educators into push-button operators. It is not the teaching machine that is important, but the programming principles which can be deduced therefrom; one could even go so far as to imagine educational technology based on *nonexistent machines* reconstituted from the functions that they are required to carry out. There are no physical, mechanical parts in the "little machines" which the mathematician Dienes uses to introduce young children to modern mathematics—they are merely new "modes of thought" expressed as a game. Similarly, the most effective way of introducing people to the new concepts of information science is to turn a blind eye to the question of how computers function. And it is no coincidence that there is a trend in the most up-to-date forms of educational technology toward simulation, that is, toward devices which seek to deny their own existence. If there could also be in education an *"intermediary" technology* not involving any complex machinery, it is no doubt for the developing countries to discover it and to develop it in the years ahead.

Is it really necessary?   Educational technology does not provide a miracle cure for the world crisis in education, but it does invite us to make a relatively simple effort at rationalization that goes further than the categories and pipe dreams that we have today.

True, education, which is concerned with values, cannot be entirely rationalized, if only because the demand for education is in itself an irrational phenomenon. Education has a great many other functions besides transmitting acquired knowledge and turning out lucid and effective future citizens. Educational institutions, according to their various levels, function as places for child minding and protection, as centers in which national unity may be forged and in which a civic education or a premilitary training may be given, but also as places where the individual learns to find his place in society and as a ritual instrument by means of which the individual is initiated into adult life. The crisis of education is not going to be completely solved by the introduction of technological principles and machinery. But by inducing each educational system to reexamine the functions of production and control, to create for itself a new and more flexible structure, and to generate within itself new rôles and new human relations by making it adaptable and flexible are we not enabling it to fulfill its other functions better and, if need be, to reconsider its ultimate purpose with the requisite lucidity?

NOTES AND REFERENCES

1. See especially International Education Year documents entitled *Reflections on Democratization of Secondary and Higher Education* and *Educating for Development*.
2. See Paul Lengrand, *Introduction à l'Education Permanente*, Unesco-A.I.E., 1970, 100 p.

3. See P. H. Coombs, *The World Educational Crisis—A Systems Analysis*. Paris, Unesco/IIEP, 1967. See review on p. 56.

4. Quite on the contrary, recent research, especially in Canada and the USA, suggests that a reduction in the number of pupils below a certain threshold yields unsatisfactory results. Similarly, the report of the International Association for Evaluation of Educational Achievement in its *International Study of Achievement in Mathematics—A comparison of 12 countries* (1967) shows that, in general, "size of class is not related to mathematics achievement. . . ." When a difference is observed, it will be seen that larger classes operate to advantage for younger children whereas smaller classes suit older students better. "To the average teacher, a class of 25 may mean much the same as a class of 35 or 45. . . ."

5. See, for example, the bibliographies in *Teaching and Learning* (an introduction to new methods and resources in higher education), Unesco, 1970, 210 p., and in *Laboratorio multimedia*, studi e ricerche sulle technologie dell'educazione (Palombi, Roma, 1970, 588 p.).

6. *To Improve Learning*, a report to the President and the Congress by the Commission of Instructional Technology, Washington, D.C., 1969, 248 p. [See also, C. R. Carpenter, "The Commission on Instructional Technology and Its Report," *Educational Broadcasting Review*, IV (Apr. 1970), 3–10.]

7. See Final Report (ED/CONF.14/3) of the meeting on "New Methods and Techniques in Teacher Training," Unesco, Dec. 10–23, 1969.

8. See Unesco Mission Report: Niger, El Salvador, Samoa (Feb.–Mar. 1969) *Collection Programme d'éducation télévisuelle*, Vol. 2.

9. See the Tele-Polytechnic Report, *Television for Higher Technical Education of the Employed*, a first report on a pilot project in Poland, No. 55 in the Reports and Papers on Mass Communication series, Unesco, Paris, 1969.

10. See Report EDS/MMT/CAI-TM, Consultation on computer-assisted instruction for developing countries.

11. See Report ED/ENPRO/17, Seminar on Programmed Instruction, Varna (Bulgaria), Aug. 19–29, 1968, and Unesco/ILO seminar on the application of programmed instruction to technical and science teaching, Turin, July 10–24, 1969.

12. See report on the meeting held to discuss the training of educational technologists, National Commission of the Federal Republic of Germany for Unesco, Constance, June 18–22, 1970.

13. See report of the international study party on educational technology and the learning process, Geneva, May 14–26, 1970.

14. "The only way out of this helpless situation is by helping gradually to develop systems of relationship and negotiation and more complex, more open, more comprehensive and more effective sets of rules and customs and regulatory models . . . by learning to concentrate the resources of the community on the key points of the systems that have to be helped out of the deplorable vicious circle that they are in, *instead of dealing with the adverse effects of the malfunctions and thus contributing to their perpetuation.*" Michel Crozier, *La Société bloquée* (1970), p. 230.

15. The Director-General of Unesco, in his *Long-Term Outline Plan for 1971–1976*, submitted to the sixteenth session of the General Conference, has already proposed (taking an estimated average increase of 7 percent in the Organization's budget) a rate of increase of 15 to 20 percent for curricula and methods.

The Age of Change: A Perspective on Education

Carroll V. Newsom

"This is an age of change"; such is the theme of much that is now spoken and written. But increasingly I find myself disturbed by the fact that there appears to be insufficient comprehension of the profound meaning inherent in the simply worded assertion. For it says that the mores of our society have undergone unprecedented modification in half a century. It says that drastic and dramatic changes have taken place in only a few decades in the demands that are made on human labor, in the implements that man employs in the pursuit of his various activities, and in the attitudes, beliefs, and expectations of men. Consequently the task now confronting all persons, especially educators, who have an active concern for the cultivation of the intellectual processes of men so that they may be prepared for life in the new era must be the most difficult in human history. Possibly a failure to adequately accept the task is a significant factor in the recurrent charge that the present instructional program of our schools and colleges is irrelevant to the needs of the age.

In view of the nature and magnitude of the change that has characterized society of the twen-

Carroll V. Newsom is a retired vice-president for education of the Radio Corporation of America.

tieth century, our generation has been unable to cope with some of the most difficult problems that have resulted. That fact undoubtedly is a significant part of the reason that the major institutions which determine the nature of our society and the kind of life made available to individuals are in a state of crisis. And, it must be emphasized, the church, our political institutions, most of our business organizations, and our educational institutions are in a state of crisis. Yet, entrenched interests persist in fighting the losing fight of trying to maintain outmoded traditions; even people whose background of education and experience should enable them to know better call for a return to the good old days; and most individuals in leadership roles in institutional structures patch and splice in a hopeless effort to maintain functioning organizations. Some of the adjustments in plans and policies that are being made are almost pathetic in the manner in which they "ignore the facts" of present-day society and fail to recognize the proper needs and demands of that society. A few institutions of religion, very few, are beginning to display some understanding of their essential role in modern life; a few businesses and industries, very few, are beginning to develop enlightened leadership; almost no political institution is adapted to the political needs of modern America; and, of the most critical consequence, virtually all educational institutions, to a greater extent than most educators seem to realize, have alienated American society, the very society that in the past has believed in the fundamental importance of education and still wants to believe in it.

It has become obvious to objective observers that the efficiency and the effectiveness of most educational institutions are intolerably low, so educators and their institutions are now being subjected to tremendous criticism; such criticism cannot be eliminated by advancing arguments that support the maintenance of the status quo. Rather, major changes in educational programs and procedures, supported by new understandings of the goals and purposes of education, are required if there is to be appropriate adaptation to the tremendous changes that have taken place in society. This is a time unique in the history of education when courageous and imaginative leadership is required.

About 3 years ago, according to reports, the chief executive officer of one of the largest corporations in the nation, a man not strongly bound to tradition, called his key managerial officers together and, in essence, said, "Fellows, our company is in deep trouble. It is clear to me that we have not kept up with the times. Our poor sales record reveals to me that we are not serving the needs of the marketplace, which has changed drastically in just a few years. We are developing products that may satisfy us, but it is evident that they are not satisfying the wants of our customers. It is my belief that we must move at once to think about the very basis of our existence. We must develop an action program that is founded on an honest evaluation of what our customers have a right to expect from us, what resources we possess or can obtain, and what can be done to use those resources to meet the expectations of our customers." The belief is now common among investors that the competent and determined executive has "turned his company around"; its profit picture has already shown improvement, and its stock is now regarded as a "good buy."

Although some scholars have been making distinctive contributions to curriculum studies and teaching practices and to our knowledge of educational purposes and strategies, necessary progress in resolving the educational purposes and strategies, necessary progress in resolving the educational problems that now confront us will not be made, in my judgment, until more educational executives become educational statesmen and adopt the approach of that particular corporate executive. Too much time and energy have been expended by progressive educators in working with small pieces of the total educational picture. Although ultimately it will be necessary to synthesize small accomplishments to achieve what is necessary to improve the whole of education, we most assuredly are not dealing with a situation where it may be assumed that a solution of the problems of the whole may be accomplished by merely adding the solutions of the problems of its parts. A systematic study of the whole, including the specification of its purposes, a careful statement of the overall problems associated with the achievement of those purposes, and a determination of acceptable boundary conditions associated with the development of solutions to the overall problems must precede any breakdown of the whole into appropriate parts, which is then followed by the attempt to resolve the problems of the parts. The successful moon shots have involved the synthesis of efforts by many subcontractors, each of whom had a concern for solving a particular collection of subproblems of the whole; but every subcontractor was forced to meet certain demands within specified limitations determined in advance by analysts who made pertinent studies of the total project.

The restoration of organized education to its proper place in American society, as conceived by Jefferson, requires, it is evident to me, a systematic reworking of present patterns of educational practices that should be a consequence of a carefully designed program of reconsidering the total educational enterprise. Although no one would deny the probable ultimate significance of the knowledge we have gained from working with such projects as Head Start, the new math, team teaching, computer-assisted instruction, "Sesame Street," and the discovery method of teaching, the necessity now exists for educational analysts to give major attention to the overall problems and policies of education; this, it should be noted, will require a return to some very elementary considerations. Fortunately, substantial knowledge already exists and a philosophy of education has been generally accepted upon which the proposed analyses may be based.

For instance, education, as we all know, is concerned with one of the most natural of phenomena, the growth and development of the human mind. A person's instrument of thought develops or fails to develop in particular ways as a consequence of the use to which it is subjected as the individual grapples continually with problems of his environment. Schools and colleges are not necessary to bring about mental growth and development; in fact, men were educated long before professional educators formalized the processes of education. Even in modern history, "self-made men" have played a significant role. But educators have learned that they can facilitate the development of a person's mind in particular ways by providing him suitable guidance and by introducing him into a proper environment. Consequently, simply stated, the creation and maintenance of special environments in which students will learn and will want to learn, adapted to the needs and intellectual attributes of a student or students, is generally accepted by society as the special task of professional educators.

When creating a learning environment for a student or students, competent professional educators give acknowledgement to the principle that all education is really self-education—an assertion which psychology recognizes as having considerable validity. Through lectures, textbooks, and other educational media, facts can be transferred from one person to another and from one generation to the next; such transmission of information is fundamental to the learning process, but it only provides a start toward a personalized education that will be meaningful. As Paul Weiss has written, "Facts, observations, discoveries, as items, are but nutrients on which the tree of knowledge feeds, and not until they have been thoroughly absorbed and assimilated, have they truly enlarged the body of knowledge."[1] Specifically, each individual must develop for himself, as a result of active involvement in many and diverse experiences, his own laws of adaptation to his environment, his own methods of analysis and utilization of facts, and his own goals and objectives. Since learning cannot be passive, a student develops the powers of his mind by "matching his wits" with problems provided by his natural and teacher-made environments. He must be encouraged to accept the wisdom inherent in the statement, "One learns to think by thinking."

Moreover, the creation of a learning environment appropriate to the needs and mental attributes of an individual student must, insofar as possible, give attention to the fact that there are gross differences in human capabilities and in the ways in which particular individuals may be motivated to want to participate in suggested activities. Upon occasion some particular patterns of intellectual attributes have been characterized as denoting mental inferiority; such a designation is dangerous and is often unfair. The educator must carry out his duties on the assumption that each person's intellect at any particular time in his personal history, as a result of inheritance and especially as a result of the effects of the environment in which the person has spent his life, is a unique composite of abilities, interests, and the other factors with which psychology is concerned. Although such a circumstance adds to the problems of the educator, it must be realized that the very fact of the great variety of human intellects available to society may be most fortuitous as society struggles to meet the great variety of its needs.

It is also important to note that the designer of a learning environment for a group of students must give proper recognition to group differences in both the needs and the mental characteristics common to members of the group when compared with those of other groups. For instance, it is generally true that critical differences exist in informational background, attitudes, and acquired capabilities between the student populations in rural schools and urban schools. Too frequently in the past a learning environment has been developed by professional educators without ascertaining in an adequate manner that the students possess the foundation which the learning program requires. Even greater attention must be given to the fact that

students can become thoroughly frustrated if they do not possess an adequate understanding of the background of a problem or concept in terms of their experience. A very ambitious school boy in an urban community broke down in tears when he was given the problem, "If 95 percent of the 600 eggs in an incubator hatched, how many baby chickens were there?" Through his tears he explained that he didn't understand what was meant by the hatching of eggs and he knew of no connection between eggs and baby chickens. A seventh grade girl in a large city, who enjoyed the poem about "Mary and Her Lamb," explained, when given a problem pertaining to Mary and the Lamb, that she did not understand the problem; it developed that she believed Mary's lamb to be a "fuzzy jacket that Mary always wore"; she had never seen a lamb. Many students in the large cities do not possess the background to understand the setting for a considerable number of problems and common expository presentations, relics of a rural environment, that still appear in widely used instructional materials. A popular television program of the day, designed for young children, contains numerous references that, unfortunately, are meaningless for many children, especially those from the ghettos and from other poverty-stricken areas. Such comments give emphasis to the idea that learning environments must often vary from community to community in some of their most significant aspects. In fact, in view of present knowledge, thoughtful educators can no longer support, at least without significant modification, such concepts as state-adopted textbooks, city-adopted syllabi, even most national testing programs, and some of the certification programs for teachers.

The very fact that the solution of the nation's educational problems must start with a solution of the educational problems of individual communities, following basic analyses of the mores and the social and economic characteristics of each community, actually simplifies the educational challenge with which educators, and the entire nation, is faced. For geography has provided a basis for the creation of comparatively small experimental and pilot endeavors and then makes possible the extension of what has been learned in regard to approaches and methods to other comparatively small endeavors. It may also be noted that efforts by educators in working with the educational problems of an individual community will undoubtedly be more successful and significant and will receive more public acclaim and support if they are properly related to welfare programs, job-training programs, health programs, and a variety of other programs maintained by and for the community. Moreover, in view of educational inequities that exist for students outside of school in every community, in view of present-day problems associated with the fact of the availability of much leisure time for most children and young people, in view of the great demand by our society for citizens with substantial educational accomplishment, and other sociological and economic factors, organized education is slighting its responsibilities if the learning environments that are fostered are designed in such a way that they are restricted in their student applications to only a few hours a day and to specially created facilities. Modern educational programs must have a strong concern for the learning of students outside the school; in fact, home, or a substitute for home, and school must be considered jointly as providing the physical setting for the development of learning environments.

Discussions pertaining to the planned future of education do not proceed very far before the question is raised: What is going to happen to professional educators, including teachers? In truth, a few professionals in the field of education, often revealing concern for their own future, have become irrational opponents of obviously needed improvements in educational policy and procedure. How often in recent years have I heard progressive educational administrators assert, "My problems are teacher problems" or "Teachers teach of change but they are unwilling to change."

The "educational establishment" of the future, it is clear, will require many professional educators who are competent and well prepared. But it is inevitable that there will be some new emphases in professional assignments, and there will be a need for the services of kinds of persons not previously involved in education in any significant way. The actual design of learning environments to meet the new demands will require the involvement of individuals of unusual understanding and imagination, supported by psychologists, sociologists, and many others. And any educational program that is created, it must be emphasized, must be subjected to continual scrutiny and evaluation and probably will be subjected to frequent modification. For reasons of both efficiency and economy, professional educators of the future, as is now recognized in the case of several other professions, must be supported by several kinds of subprofessionals. It is also part of the "wave of the future" that students with the proper mental attributes and the necessary background of understanding will be used, much more than is true at the present time, to make important contributions to educational programs created for other students; instructional strategies that utilize students in significant roles have long been regarded as desirable, based on a variety of satisfactory experiences, but there has been a strange hesitation to experiment with, develop, and employ such strategies.

In the future, the teacher will undoubtedly give up much of his previous responsibility as a conveyor of information; more efficient media that supplement printed materials and the oral presentations of teachers in the communication of many kinds of information are now available, and coming decades will see the development of better and better devices for the communication of information. The teacher of the future must be prepared to provide more and better guidance to individual students, but the chief role of the teacher will continue as in the past to be that of serving as a human model for students in the demonstration of meaningful thought processes. The most effective teacher is the one "who thinks out loud" before and with his students; it can be a thrilling experience for children and young adults to observe the dynamics of the mind of a master thinker as he indulges in a logical analysis and objective interpretation of some situation after he has found his way through a mass of data to select the facts that are pertinent to his analysis.

The present availability of a variety of new technological devices that can be employed to provide great efficiency and effectiveness to a learning environment cannot be ignored by the progressive educational designer. The vast capabilities inherent in the communications media developed in recent decades, in the new audiovisual mechanisms, and in the growing number of important computerized devices and procedures make possible the development of learning resources that enhance in an important way the contributions of teachers. In fact, because of a series of remarkable triumphs of technology, some kinds of student-learning accomplishments are now possible that previously were impossible or were only partially possible when teachers were forced to rely on their own efforts augmented by the limited tools available to them. Consequently, possibly the most difficult task of modern educational designers is the proper blending of "people and things" to create learning environments that will make possible desired kinds of accomplishments in the area of student learning.

But when we consider the educational potentials inherent in some of the new technologies and the present use of these technologies in education, it becomes apparent that a very interesting circumstance is occurring. When the automobile was first developed, the motor was merely inserted into a buggy, which was the traditional and accepted method of transportation. Now the new and powerful educational mechanisms that technology has provided are merely being inserted into the tradi-

tional educational buggy. We squeeze, we pinch, we pull, we tug, trying to make the new fit into the old. It seems to be so very hard for some educators to realize that new and important results in education are now possible if we will only rebuild the learning environments for the citizens of our nation, young and old, in a manner that will take advantage of what is available. Even content and organization of a program of study cannot be considered in isolation from the instructional resources that are now available and should be employed.

In actuality, new-type personnel and new technologies have been introduced into our established learning environments merely as "add-ons" to the traditional. Consequently, there has been little increase in educational effectiveness, and the cost of the "add-ons" has produced a marked increase in some school budgets. Frequently, in fact, I hear the statement, "The new ideas are too expensive; we cannot afford them." It is my considered judgment, based unfortunately on little experience, since almost no acceptable experience is available, that we now have the resources, when properly used, to develop learning environments that will be much more effective than the old in serving the needs of specific student populations and will actually be less costly than the old.

So, it seems to me that the direction in which educators should move and the approach which they should employ to bring about essential adaptations of their endeavors to a changed society are not too difficult to comprehend. But will more than a few educators in positions of responsibility have the will and the courage to move? Will agencies of the public support the initial experimental and exploratory efforts that are a prerequisite to success? Such questions are now being asked with increasing frequency by many concerned citizens.

REFERENCE

1. Paul Weiss, "Knowledge: A Growth Process," *Science*, Vol. LXXXI, No. 3415 (June 10, 1960), pp. 1716–1719.

Planning and Designing a Media Production Facility

Suleiman D. Zalatimo

The basic goal of a media preparation service is to facilitate improved student learning situations by enabling faculty to acquire a variety of visuals and instructional materials that are not readily available. In addition, the service must support all programs and activities undertaken by the institution.

TYPE OF SERVICE

Most educational institutions provide their staffs with some type of media production services to support their teaching needs and the noninstructional needs and programs undertaken by the institution. Traditionally, the approach has been to provide consultants and production staff to produce all types of instructional materials upon order and to deliver the finished product according to the schedule established. This type of service is referred to, in this paper, as "custom service." In my experience, this type of service usually does not adequately support the needs of the institution. Lack of support stems from a deficiency of space, materials, equipment, personnel, or funds. As a result, service is curtailed in many ways. One is the establishment of a schedule whereby orders must

Suleiman D. Zalatimo is associate professor of education at the Center for Instructional Media and Technology, University of Connecticut, Storrs, Connecticut.

be received 2 or 3 weeks before delivery. Another effect is to limit service to selected programs or certain "outstanding" professors. Also, the charges may be set at unreasonably high rates to discourage use of the service and keep demand at a low level. Whatever means are used, the overall result is that custom service does not adequately support the basic intention of its establishment.

To overcome this failing and to provide better service and equal opportunity for all members of the institution, it is recommended here that a self-service facility be established to augment the custom service.

Facilities must be provided in the self-service area for teachers to plan, design, and produce their own materials. Equipment is placed on counter tops with corresponding supplies and materials displayed on shelves above the equipment or under the counters. The quantity of supplies and materials should be adequate for a period of about 5 days; however, since the materials are on display, the person in charge can easily determine when resupply is needed. Thus, the facilities will always be ready with a minimum of effort on the part of the user and the service personnel.

It is helpful to display near each piece of equipment a diagram and step-by-step explanation of the operation of the piece of equipment. It is also helpful to place a sample of high-quality work near each piece of equipment to motivate users to strive for high-quality work.

Establishment of a self-service facility reduces the burden on custom service, and efforts can be focused on large-scale projects such as television programs, multimedia presentations, large-group instruction, individualized instruction, administrative needs, and public relations.

FLOOR PLAN

The floor plan for the media production service includes both the custom-service area and the self-service area. This floor plan is carefully designed to provide maximum efficiency of space for both services. The manager's office is located at the front and housed between the two service areas for convenience. Supplies for both services are centrally located in a storage room directly behind the manager's office for ease in control and distribution to sections and stations as required for daily operation (see Figure 1).

Self-Service Area

There are two studios in this area, the multipurpose studio and the audio studio with the studio control room. The multipurpose studio can be used as a photographic studio, for group activities, film editing, small classroom, or for further expansion of other activities or new services. The audio studio in the self-service area is soundproofed and has an adjoining studio control room for making audio and video recordings, for programming slide and filmstrip sequences, and for producing sound motion picture films and filmclips.

For ease of operation the self-service area has three separate darkrooms. Two are designed for print processing; the third is designed primarily for film processing. The film-processing darkroom can accommodate more than one individual at a time; each print-processing darkroom is designed for use by one individual at a time. All darkrooms must be equipped with revolving doors or special darkroom dividers and drapes to provide easy access without disturbing work in progress.

All interior walls and dividers of the self-service area must be movable panels about 5 feet high with or without glass tops to facilitate quick observation of various activities and allow for quick changes of the floor plan, if necessary. However, darkroom walls and studio control room walls must be permanent floor-to-ceiling panels or dividers. Cabinets or shelves with counter tops provide for storage, and wall shelves are essential for display of

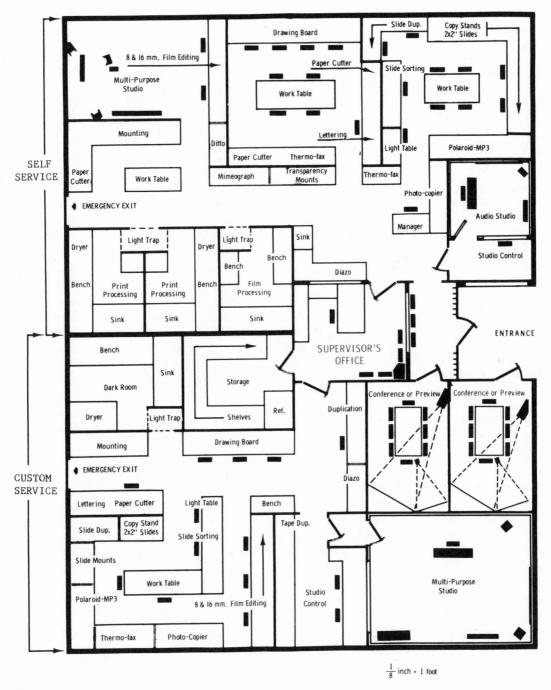

SELF SERVICE

CUSTOM SERVICE

$\frac{1}{8}$ inch = 1 foot

Figure 1
Floor plan design.

needed materials and supplies. One or two sinks with running water outside the darkroom are essential for the operation of the self-service area.

The work space and facilities in the floor plan for the self-service area provide for planning, designing, and producing various types of instructional materials. These areas are designed with multiple stations for various phases of production. To avoid crowding and allow for free flow of traffic, it is essential that equipment and supplies be distributed, not clustered in one area. For example, paper cutters and mounting presses are placed at various locations rather than side by side. Other equipment with the same function should be similarly distributed.

More space and equipment must be provided when planning and designing a floor plan for the self-service area than for a custom-service area, where one piece of each type of equipment will usually suffice.

This floor plan provides for two conference or preview rooms, which can be used by faculty members. The conference room inside the main entrance is designed primarily for those who prepare their own materials in the self-service area.

Custom-Service Area

In the custom-service area the multipurpose studio is soundproofed and has an adjoining studio control room. It is basically designed for producing audio and video recordings, sound motion picture films and filmclips, sound filmstrips, and for programming sound-slide sequences. Only one darkroom is needed in the custom area. Both films and prints can be processed by one or more workers at the same time. Except for the darkroom, the studio, the studio control room, storage, and conference rooms, which have permanent dividers, other work area dividers can be movable panels about 5 feet high. The work space and facilities in this section provide areas for planning, designing, and produc-

ing various types of instructional materials as requested by faculty members.

BASIC MATERIALS AND EQUIPMENT

Figure 2 lists basic materials and equipment needed for production services. The specific needs of the institution must be considered in making the final selection. If the demand is for a large volume of material, high-speed, high-volume production equipment can be added to the custom-service facility. Because of the many types of materials available, selection becomes a lengthy chore. Selecting fewer types and standardizing materials basic to the production needs is recommended. For example, dozens of thermo-copying films for producing transparencies are available; the needs would be met by selecting two or three of the types. Similarly, equipment should be standardized with regard to type to facilitate repair and maintenance and to avoid stocking a large variety of parts, thus reducing the problem of storing and maintaining an adequate supply of each item.

For speed and convenience in maintaining adequate supply and inventory control, a simple file system can be established. Each item is listed on a 5 by 8-inch card containing detailed information concerning the item. The card is numbered and filed according to designated categories. When supplies are needed, the date and the amount required are entered on the card, which serves as the basis for the requisition when given to the secretary. After the requisition is typed, the card is refiled under an "on order" category in the inventory file. When the complete order is received, the card is checked and returned to its proper filing place (see Figure 3).

ELECTRICAL WIRING AND OUTLETS

Frequently, planners give little attention to the electrical power (amperes) needed for adequate use

Lettering

Cutout letters
Dry transfer
Embossograph machine
Mechanical lettering instruments
Inks
Pens and markers
Phototype
Planotype
Primary typewriter
Rubber stamps
Stencil letters

Recording

High-speed magnetic tape duplicator
Magnetic tape
Magnetic tape recorder
Viedotape
Videotape recorder

Duplicating and Reproducing

Diazo
Electronic stencil cutter
Mimeograph duplicator
Spirit duplicator
Thermo-copying equipment

Mounting

Dry mounting press
Dry mounting tissues
Laminating materials
Paper cutter
Rubber cement
Wet mounting

Drawing and Coloring

Adhesives
Airbrush and compressor
Cardboard
Charting tape
Crayons and pencils
Drawing and cutting instruments
Drawing paper
Enlarging and reducing instruments
Inks
Masking tape
Pens and markers
Shading materials
Transparent colors
Watercolors

Photography

Darkroom accessories
Enlarger
Film editing equipment
Light meter
Photographic chemicals
Photographic film and paper
Print dryer
Refrigerator
Slide duplicating unit
Studio lights
Super 8mm camera
Tripod and copy stand
35mm camera
4- by 5-inch press camera
3¼- by 4-inch MP3 Polaroid camera
16mm camera
Vidicon camera
Television port-a-pac unit

Figure 2
List of basic materials and equipment.

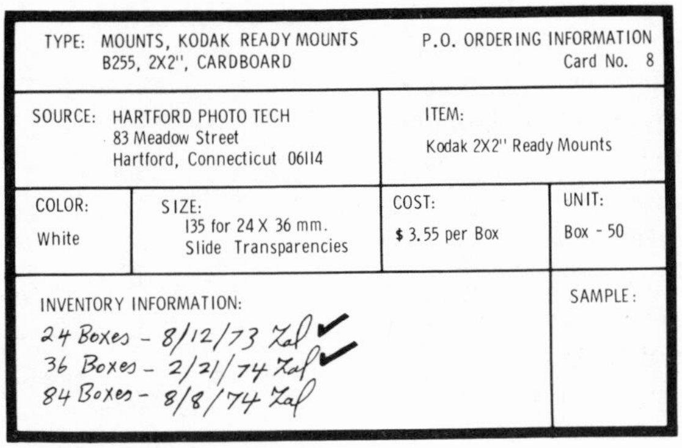

TYPE:	MOUNTS, KODAK READY MOUNTS B255, 2X2'', CARDBOARD	P.O. ORDERING INFORMATION Card No. 8		
SOURCE:	HARTFORD PHOTO TECH 83 Meadow Street Hartford, Connecticut 06114	ITEM: Kodak 2X2'' Ready Mounts		
COLOR: White	SIZE: 135 for 24 X 36 mm. Slide Transparencies	COST: $ 3.55 per Box	UNIT: Box - 50	
INVENTORY INFORMATION: 24 Boxes – 8/12/73 Zal ✔ 36 Boxes – 2/21/74 Zal ✔ 84 Boxes – 8/8/74 Zal			SAMPLE:	

Figure 3
Ordering and inventory card.

of the media production equipment. This oversight results in power failures and interruption of service when more than a few pieces of equipment are in operation simultaneously. These breakdowns are aggravations that can be avoided by providing a conduit and circuit capable of carrying the power required by the combined equipment. For example, if a mounting press (8 amperes), a diazo proto-printer (5 amperes), and a lamination machine (4 amperes) are all connected to one circuit, the power line must be capable of carrying a minimum of 17 amperes. To find the amperage required for a specific piece of equipment, use the following formula:

$$\frac{W \text{ (watts)}}{V \text{ (volts)}} = A \text{ (amperes)}$$

Each piece of equipment is required to carry the wattage needed for operation; most production equipment is designed to operate on 110 volts.

Attention must be given to the electrical conduits to ensure that ample outlets are located immediately behind the equipment and slightly above the counter tops to avoid use of extension cords and the possibility of tripping or other accidents. Electrical outlets must be grounded and accommodate three-pronged plugs.

STAFFING THE FACILITY

The custom service requires at least three full-time media production specialists who, with the help of part-time student workers, should be capable of handling diverse media production demands. These three include a graphic technician who is capable of handling any photographic assignment, including darkroom work and other technical skills that are needed by the service; an artist or illustrator who has a strong background in graphic communication and art and is capable of handling problems of graphics and visual design; and an audio specialist who must be capable of handling problems of sound, sound mixing, and audio systems, in addition to producing the audio portion of programmed materials. The three must be jointly responsible for the total work load and assist each other in whatever capacity the service requires.

For the successful operation of the self-service facility, a highly qualified media production specialist in a professional position (manager) must be employed. This individual manages the self-service facility and must be capable of assisting teachers and faculty in planning and designing media and in the operation of equipment. The manager is also responsible for maintaining inventory and distributing supplies and materials to the stations; he must be capable of determining the skills and needs of the teachers and of maintaining a smooth and efficient operation. Part-time student workers must be trained to assist in the instruction and operation of the facility.

Both the custom-service and the self-service facility are the responsibility of the supervisor who is an experienced teacher and highly qualified in all

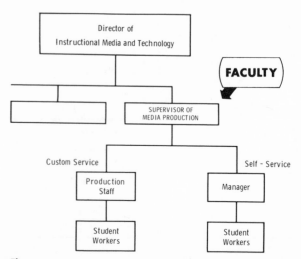

Figure 4
Staff organization.

phases of media production and visual communication. This professional position requires that the supervisor maintain adequate materials and supplies, purchase and maintain equipment in good order, control the budget, seek ways to improve the service, record orders and assign work for production, schedule use of stations of the self-service facility and keep adequate records on this use, and establish and enforce policy in line with the policy of the center. The supervisor also acts as consultant to teachers and faculty members and serves as a professional consultant to the director of the Center for Instructional Media and Technology (see Figure 4).

The supervisor of the media production services and the manager of the self-service facility must be capable of assuming either responsibility so that services will not be interrupted during vacations or other absences.

FINANCIAL NEEDS

The media production service program described here requires separate budgets for (1) materials and supplies, (2) equipment, (3) equipment repair, and (4) part-time staff assistants (student workers). Funds for each category should be allocated directly to the center so that teachers and faculty members may use the facility on a no-charge, first come-first served basis. This system of budgeting is most efficient because it eliminates the need for billing and transfer of funds from one department to another and requires no extensive secretarial work. Furthermore, the allocated monies are spent for the budgeted needs of the service.

Toward a Better Mix of Teaching Resources

Ronald K. Randall

As seen by the social economist, schools are meant to convert limited tax monies into as much learning as possible.

If this is their basic purpose, then so must they be judged. How much learning do they effectively transmit for each dollar spent—not how many bricks and how much mortar. Not how many pupils per class or how high a salary for teachers, but how much learning per dollar.

Buildings, class size, and teacher salaries are but a few of the intermediaries between taxes and learning. Each is important, most are essential, and many are believed critical to educational quality. But none is sacred. Only the tax monies consumed and the learning produced are sacred.

Too often these intermediaries are vested with rights that obscure the subordination to the ultimate purpose of a school. Properly recognizing this subordination, we may view them as no more than alternative uses of the same tax dollars.

This perspective permits us to broaden the search for ways to improve instructional programs. Rather than fixing on the most important element—the

Ronald K. Randall is director of economic analysis, Education Turnkey Systems, Inc., Washington, D.C.

teacher—to the exclusion of others, we must make a more thorough and balanced appraisal of how to allocate tax dollars among educational staff, facilities, and supplies. When we do so, we find that relatively minor changes in school operations can provide financial justification for startlingly large expansions of teaching resources.

If we increase the average class size in a school district, the same number of pupils can be served by fewer teachers and a net savings of funds results. Increasing the average class size from 25 to 26 pupils yields enough savings to pay for a tripling of expenditures for instructional materials in the typical American school.

A tenfold increase in teaching materials can be financed with savings created by an instructional program which allows five-period teachers to teach a sixth period each day. Many of the newer individualized instruction programs reduce teacher lesson planning and other preparatory workloads, making such a change both possible and welcome.

If true educational accountability means producing the most learning per dollar spent, reallocation of funds within the existing budget total is not the only way to justify additional expenditures. Another way is to show that proposed changes in the instructional program yield learning gains that are more than proportionate to their costs.

Since teaching materials represent only about 1 percent of the average school district's budget, increasing the overall budget by only 1 percent allows a 100 percent increase in this category of expenditure. A program innovation which yielded a 10 percent gain in student achievement could, in like manner, justify up to a 1,000 percent increase in teaching materials consumption.

To see how the economics of maximizing learning per dollar can multiply such effects, consider the following example. A new method of instruction which increased class size from 25 to 26, freed teachers for an additional teaching period, and

yielded an additional tenth of a grade-level gain could simultaneously provide enough savings to justify:

1. A tenfold increase in instructional materials.
2. An investment of $9,000 per classroom in instructional equipment.
3. Expenditure of $115 per student for new furniture.
4. Renovation and improvements of $2,000 per classroom.

Would a teacher be willing to add one child to her class and give up her preparation period (and nightly lesson planning at home) to work within a program that offered her these additional resources?

Would local, state, and federal funding agencies provide additional money for the key areas of reading and mathematics if more than proportionate gains in learning could be demonstrated?

The foregoing examples are offered as food for thought. They illustrate the true significance of relating costs not to educational intermediaries, nor to budget years alone, but rather to their true objective—student learning.

Spurred by the profit incentive, and kept accountable by money-back guarantees, several private firms have recently begun performance contracts with schools to teach basic reading and mathematics.

They can succeed only if they can show, on standardized tests, more learning per dollar. In many cases, their allocations of available funds among educational intermediaries are quite different from those of the typical school.

If we have arrived at our present patterns of classroom teaching by selecting the best of all alternatives for spending our tax dollars, we should be pleased. Otherwise, we owe it to ourselves and our students to compare alternatives to present expenditure patterns before feeling satisfied that current policies are the best.

Curriculum Development Through Communications Technology

R. Ross Hempstead

An academic community of 40,000, comprising the nation's third largest campus, generates a multiplicity of curricular needs and recreational interests. In response to many of these needs and interests, the University of Maryland has established a nonprint media laboratory as an integral part of its library operation.

An extensive electronic distribution system, accommodating all nonprint formats, was conceived, designed, and installed during the fall semester, 1972, in a newly constructed building on the College Park campus. Significantly, the facility was developed according to the somewhat unique requirements of this large flagship campus of a state university system; its design should not be transferred intact to another, perhaps dissimilar, institution. In any case, its greater significance lies not so much in its technical detail as in its articulation with the print medium, with instructional programs, and with a pervasive, campuswide effort in active curriculum development.

Accordingly, purely technical descriptions of hardware are less important here than is a func-

R. Ross Hempstead teaches at the University of Maryland, College Park, Maryland.

tional discussion of the potential of the facility as a teaching tool. The latter, presented from a student's-eye view, may well have general application in other educational situations. Similarly, much can be generalized from a broad consideration of the resultant impact of nonprint media upon instruction at this and other colleges and universities. In the course of these discussions, a brief summary of a few logistical details, from a technician's-eye view, may also be of interest to the educator planning a similar installation.

As the College Park system enters its third year of operation, and its first full semester following completion, a significant pattern of development is clearly discernable. The initial, prototype installation reflected a broad survey of electronic formats and a pilot installation of equipment appropriate to them. This first system was conceived, designed, specified, submitted to competitive bidding, its contract awarded, all research and development conducted, the complete installation performed, and the resultant facility opened to the university public—in 6 months. It should be noted that this entire process was greatly compressed in time owing to a certain urgency associated with the completion of an important building 10 months ahead of schedule.

However, more significant is the involvement of a highly useful principle, which has emerged in retrospect and which may be useful to other institutions in different situations. That is, rather than simply contriving a wholly blue sky design in anticipation of campus needs, and setting forth more than very general guidelines for the entire and complete system at the outset, a basic prototype— limited in nature and scope—was ventured during the first installation. Less than one third of the total funds anticipated for the project was committed. Throughout, extensive provision for immediate expansion was inherent in the initial design.

To be sure, simple pressures of time dictated a partial installation at the outset. Important here was a basic principle fundamental to any electronic–

mechanical support of instructional programs: the system must, above all, *work*—immediately, completely, from the very beginning. If failure, real or apparent, is evident when the technique or device is first placed in operation, often irreparable damage is done to its potential for ultimate success. However sound from any technical or pedagogical standpoint, initial fulfillment of its stated or implied function is fundamental to the acceptance and usage of a technological advance in instructional media.

The more significant purpose of a phased installation, however, concerned the complex, convoluted structure of a major educational institution. Far too many variables, many of which were and are changing rapidly, entered into the formula for curriculum development for any facile generalization to be made regarding the ultimate nonprint distribution system. One could not simply presume to know the unique combination of needs and interests that would be most effectively served by such an installation in order to determine the best ways to serve them. To be sure, the designer could draw upon years of personal experience with the educational process—from both sides of the desk—and from largely intuitive judgments about his own academic discipline. Certainly, membership on the faculty of the institution and administrative experience along similar lines are all helpful. However, the final determination of the nature and scope of the system and the relative emphasis upon each of the various subsystems included in it more properly proceeded from actual feedback concerning demonstrated needs.

The first installation, then, represented a cautious investment in each of several major subsystems, with built-in provisions for immediate expansion according to the demonstrated value of any of several areas within each subsystem. Although certain of these areas seemed to have obvious application to the programs of this large campus, none could be installed in its entirety owing to the pressures of time and because of the need to discover its impact upon instruction. The experiences of the first semester of operation (spring 1973) were incorporated into the eventual design of the complete system, fully installed for the fall 1974 term.

Academic year 1973–1974 was devoted to careful observation of system function and its effect upon instructional programs. Both physical facilities and service techniques were refined and expanded as the operation assumed larger scope. During this expansion period, certain areas of several major subsystems emerged as more significant in their contribution to curriculum development.

These areas can be summarized as involving either or both *remote-access* techniques as contrasted with *direct-access* approaches, all of which are supported by extensive *format conversion* capabilities. Each of these is described in brief detail again, their inclusion in the system proceeded from experience with and concern for the instructional requirements of students and faculty, rather than merely from an awareness of technological capabilities or physical resources.

REMOTE ACCESS

When an instructor has assigned a specific selection for listening or viewing, hundreds of students in the course may seek to gain access to that material at one time. The traditional one-copy, one-user approach is woefully inadequate for such a situation. Therefore, a remote-access approach becomes at once more convenient and highly cost effective. The term is derived from the fact that the user gains access to the material from a location which is remote from its source. In the case of the College Park installation, the student can choose from any of hundreds of individual carrels, group listening–viewing rooms, or other stations designed for specific learning situations. These remote-access terminals are equipped with color television monitors and stereo headsets or speakers and with a simple push-button dial pad. The student simply dials in the program number given to him by his instructor, posted throughout the listening–viewing area, or provided by a desk attendant who keeps current with both the library's holdings and the instructional programs. The program begins as he dials (in the case of low-demand tapes) or at scheduled, usually hourly, intervals (in the case of large-class assignments). A third and more frugal hybrid of these basic playback options can be termed timed-on-demand. Rather than start on demand or at a predetermined time, this third technique begins a prescheduled program only if it has been accessed prior to its starting time. Hereby the program source plays only if a student is probably present to hear–view it. A 50-minute selection, then, will begin on the hour if it has been dialed up prior to that time or within approximately 10 minutes after the hour (thus the program will have time to play completely, rewind, and begin again on the next hour). Tape and equipment are conserved, and the student receives better service.

This example of technical operation is included here less for its own sake than to illustrate another important principle. Complexity in the technician's realm is accepted if it achieves simplicity at the student's point of access. That is, the staff is thoroughly trained in the operation of the behind-the-desk equipment and required to exercise a high degree of ingenuity in order to free the library patron to pursue the content of the material and to ignore the format in which it is presented.

For example, the dial pad mentioned is about three sevenths as difficult to use as a telephone. The student may adjust the stereo audio channels to a comfortable level, but need not perform any other technical function. Should he need assistance, an attendant in the area is available to help.

As an alternative, several lounge areas are furnished with upholstered armchairs and provided with ceiling-mounted transmitters broadcasting to wireless headsets. This approach is particularly suitable for extended listening to spoken materials such as lectures and speeches. Like other remote-access techniques, wireless listening provides little control over playback; it does provide comfortable accommodations and relatively economical extension of the number of student stations.

Classes and other groups can access all programs from rooms accommodating up to 50 students; once again, careful provisions are made for various instructional situations. Instructors' consoles contain all audio and video cassette playback capabilities. One of these areas is furnished as a large concert room equipped with a quadraphonic capability for all matrix and discrete four-channel audio programs. Possibilities occur here for simulation of illustrative orchestral effects in the study of music.

Other such examples of special-purpose areas for study can be found throughout the installation. Each is appropriate for one or another instructional situation, particularly in this large, comprehensive educational institution enrolling tens of thousands of students in hundreds of programs of study. Other schools may have particular requirements for certain of these or other subsystems, according to their own unique needs. Again, these remote-access approaches were developed by means of an initial prototype installation, which was expanded and augmented according to the needs of this institution.

DIRECT ACCESS

In other instructional contexts, at the University of Maryland and elsewhere, an invaluable feature of the nonprint media service will generally involve student control of playback. A second group of subsystems, designed to meet this need, can be termed *direct access* insofar as the user is directly and physically in contact with the source of his program. Direct, rather than remote, access to nonprint materials is particularly significant in situations that require careful and repeated study of specific selections or portions of a title. Here the

user greatly benefits from complete control over playback, as he would in the reading of a print volume. Notwithstanding the far greater efficiency of the remote-access approaches, which permit a single copy of a given title to be directed simultaneously to hundreds of listeners or viewers, many students require personal, physical possession of an individual copy of that title. In this mode, the selection can be started, stopped, rewound, or otherwise manipulated according to the student's own rate of progress. He may also follow printed collateral materials, such as musical scores or dramatic scripts.

Accordingly, all materials provided through each of the remote-access subsystems are also circulated in cassette form for individual use. Playback stations are provided in large numbers for audio and/or video cassette study. Again, provisions are made for group listening–viewing and for instructor control of playback. As in the case of the remote-access approaches, programs are played in color and in stereo, if appropriate to the content. Automatic loading and threading are inherent in the cassette formats utilized and minimal adjustments are necessary. The student's concern is with content, not format.

FORMAT CONVERSION

To achieve this objective of relieving the user of any concern for the multiplicity of competing formats, important technical provisions were included from the outset. These included *format conversion* capabilities, which serve the function of changing any electronic or projected format to the basic cassette. Regardless of the form the original material might have taken, it is converted to either the standard Norelco or U-Matic format for circulation—copyright restrictions permitting. In the process, the remote- and direct-access areas of service are effectively articulated; both cassette format have been interfaced with the dialed and broadcast systems. It need be of little importance to the library public that the original material was originally produced on 8 or 16 or 35mm film, or recorded on helical scan or quadraplex video tape, or that it was creation of the still photographer, the cinematographer, or the videotographer, or that it was the result of any of dozens of other processes and techniques. It can all be converted to the easy-to-use, simple-to-operate, automatic-threading cassette. In those cases in which the inherently superior resolution and clarity, particularly in a large-screen situation, of the film formats is preferred—as in the case of students of art or architecture—such facilities are provided. All standard projection devices are included in the nonprint media service operation.

As in the areas of remote and direct access, format conversion capabilities were expanded and developed during the second year of operation. Such specialized techniques as alphanumeric titling of videotapes by means of a video character generator were added. Speech compression and expansion capabilities were included, and disc-to-reel, reel-to-reel, reel-to-cassette, cassette-to-cassette, cassette-to-reel, and disc-to-cassette dubbing facilities were expanded. Format conversion services operate in color and stereo or quadraphonic modes, as well as monochrome and monaural formats.

CONTROL ROOM FUNCTIONS

To separate this technical operation with its inherent complexity from the user areas of the library, a glass-enclosed control room was provided directly behind the charge desk. A bay of a dozen electronic racks was installed, and subsequently expanded, to vertically mount all program transports for the remote-access subsystems. Format conversion equipment and a technician's workbench occupy this area, together with a small computer system to monitor system operation.

This last aspect of the control room operation, that of continuous and precise system monitoring, is

particularly significant in its potential contribution to curriculum development. Every 4 hours of every 16-hour day, instructors have an opportunity, and the staff the obligation, to gain and act upon immediate feedback on program usage. The number of times each source is dialed, and eventually the mean, median, and mode durations of those accesses, may be of very great significance to the instructional process. If, for example, students are dialing out of a 50-minute demonstration at 37 minutes on a recurring and frequent basis, the instructor may wish to alter his presentation. Valuable insights, otherwise not readily apparent, may become immediately obvious. In addition, such data are useful in devising daily or weekly remote-access schedules to assure that program space, always in high demand, is devoted to those courses which make greatest use of it. Although quality of usage is much more difficult to assess, at least the quantifiable aspects of student behavior are potentially discoverable. Potential for other computer functions is endless: preventive maintenance schedules can be prepared as system function and transport operation are continuously monitored; various interactive processes can be introduced for programmed instruction. These examples of control room operation are becoming increasingly complex, as system potential increases during the second and third years of operation.

At the other end of the distribution system, by contrast, the student can ignore such technical concerns. His interest should be with the content of the lecture, demonstration, experiment, musical or dramatic performance, historical event, or other curricular material. Once he has dialed in the appropriate program number or checked out the audio or video cassette, he need only concentrate on content. Components in terminals are flush-mounted with tamperproof screws; tuning controls are covered by protective plates; electrical power is controlled from the technician's station.

During the second year, or phase two, installation, the student terminals were greatly increased in number and in function. By far the most effective in usage, and therefore the most extensively expanded, subsystem was the dial-access operation. In this case, the original 8 terminals were increased to 114. These include 96 carrels, 9 instructors' consoles in enclosed rooms (including the quadraphonic concert room, served by several mobile consoles), 4 display cases throughout the building, 4 wall stations against which wired tables can be placed as needed to provide 200 additional terminals, and 1 test station in the control room. These dial-access stations can be combined with an expanded wireless subsystem to air a single copy of a program to nearly 500 patrons at one time.

However, the more significant expansion of this subsystem lies in its enlarged capacity to provide varied and timely programs. The number of these programs was increased from 22, including 2 video, to 36, including 10 video. All additions were in color and stereo, with audio fidelity comparable to the conventional phonodisc recording and video quality at least equal to commercial broadcast levels.

But hardware characteristics are at most only a small part of any effort in instructional development through communications technology. Most important is the collection of nonprint materials for which the entire system was installed. This rapidly growing collection of commercially prerecorded and locally produced titles is interfiled with the print materials in the library's main catalog. Although the primary emphasis is upon curricular materials, enrichment and recreational titles are also included. These materials will eventually circulate in conventional library fashion or electronically through an expanded remote-access subsystem throughout the campus. Audio and video playback units are being installed in many locations, and cable installations are planned.

In building a substantial and effective collection of nonprint titles, and in articulating that collection with the instructional programs of the campus, a number of significant and challenging issues have emerged. The remarkable technological advances in this field offer only the opportunity, not the assurance, of making a significant contribution to the educational process. It should be noted here that no definitive precedents exist for many of these collection-building activities.

For example, frequently the sole source for a title occurs in a format that is not appropriate for library use. In such cases, it becomes necessary to negotiate the purchase in terms of conversion rights. Perhaps the work is offered for sale in the 16mm film format and must be dubbed to video cassette. Frequently, copyright restrictions exist in connection with such dubbing or with closed-circuit broadcast. Occasionally, private agreements must be made with other electronics facilities on or off campus to process unusual or obsolete formats. Increasingly, entire film catalogs contain alternative provisions for purchase in the video-cassette form, with considerable savings. In these and in many other unique situations, progress must be made not only in building the collection of a particular institution, but also in helping to establish precedents for such work throughout the library profession. Pending copyright legislation and litigation must be carefully followed and observed, and great care exercised to avoid any infringement of legal restrictions. Several important lawsuits are currently in the courts; hopefully, a long-awaited and sweeping copyright reform bill will soon bring some guidance to both producers and consumers in this field.

In any event, many titles will remain by their very nature highly restricted in their usage and must be purchased at relatively high cost with all restrictions intact. By contrast, many educational institutions and public-service organizations permit free use of their materials. Generally, titles produced in-house by faculty are available for multiple-copy or closed-circuit broadcast applications, although careful agreements must be concluded even in these situations.

Between the high-cost video recording of a feature film and the no-cost duplication of a copyright-free tape or broadcast is a much larger group of titles that can be acquired for somewhat less than the cost of an average print volume. Recordings of musical works, for example, constitute a major source for many of a large library's holdings. Collateral materials, bound as necessary, can be open-shelved by the same catalog number as the recorded material. Libretti, scripts, musical scores, and many other printed items should be available to library patrons. Charts, diagrams, lecture notes, check sheets, and many other instructor-produced materials should also be shelved in the nonprint area.

All these materials can have an increasingly significant impact upon instruction. Certainly, dramatic presentations were never meant to be studied exclusively in their written forms. Poetry and plays take on added or entirely different meanings in their aural and pictorial versions. Recent historical and scientific events are recorded as a matter of course, and are available for careful and realistic study.

To satisfy countless other instructional needs, the addition of sound and motion to the silent, static print medium can be invaluable in the educational process. Particularly by use of emerging electronic formats, these nonprint materials can be readily applied with high efficiency and important cost effectiveness to curriculum development.

Nontraditional Study: Emergence Through Social Change

Eugene E. DuBois and Frederick A. Ricci

The current state of American higher education has caused administrators to again reexamine their educational role and the manner in which they impart their commodity to their clientele. The social forces that have made an impact upon institutions were not generally foreseen by administrators and planners—for all of their sophistication and computers. It is probably axiomatic that every institution that claims to be continually in the quest for truth and meaning has not been looking at itself to develop new designs or approaches on any significant scale. Not until pressured by a changing society or the clamorings of the youth culture for new and more meaningful experiences did the house of learning begun to examine itself in any major way.

EMERGENCE OF RECOGNITION

In America, higher education in the 1960s brought about recognition of minority students, blacks, chicanos, Puerto Rican, American Indians, and others. These students, as administrators recognized, had new needs and demands on higher

Eugene E. DuBois is an executive associate, American Association of Community and Junior Colleges.

Frederick A. Ricci is assistant professor of education, University of Maryland, College Park, Maryland.

education. Emergence of the career education concept, education for life, and special higher education increased the need for new programs and nontraditional study. Although society has played a significant role in changing education, one must remember that it is education that changes society. For example, college graduates tend to act more effectively in the care of their health, in the purchase of goods and services, in the investment of their money, and in the care and education of their children.[1]

Today nearly 20 percent of an average lifetime in the United States is spent in substantial attention to formal education, 12.6 years out of 71, and the percentage has risen rapidly during the past century.[2] Higher education will continue to be more and more capable of exercising leadership in all phases of education and in our society.

Bernard Luskin, in a telephone discussion with journal editors, stated that the time is closely approaching when we need to bring the experiences that have been gained so far together into forces for those who would like to take advantage of them. New ways must be developed to deliver education to the students. One cannot do new things very differently with traditional mechanisms. We must provide new, high-quality materials. He concluded by stating that what is really needed are new methods, not new institutions.[3]

MODEL FOR NONTRADITIONAL DESIGNS

It would be impossible to include here all the current attempts at nontraditional study or innovative designs; others have prepared descriptive reports, and references for a select few are given at the end of this paper. The situations cited here have been selected for illustrative purposes only, for certainly other designs are equally meritorious.

A simple model that appears to be recurrent in nontraditional designs might be the following:

Establish objectives
Examine constraints →Determine alternatives
Prepare learning design or learning activity

The various formats range from modification of individual courses, to the use of simple programmed materials, to the more sophisticated learning packages and computer-aided designs. By simple we do not mean to infer that time, energy, and testing must not be employed; simple might represent a low level of learning such as in elementary arithmetic with a teacher-prepared exercise.

After having established objectives for the learning experience, an examination of the constraints is usually employed. The constraints may be minor or rather formidable, and might involve time, money, or resources. Teaching an alternative design might be determined and examined. These alternatives would then have variations or levels of acceptability that result in one or more preferable alternatives. The result would be the actual development or implementation of a new learning design or learning activity.

This rather simplistic model obviously requires considerably more testing and retesting than this short description would imply. However, it does serve as a generalized construct with which one might examine new designs or nontraditional study.

AN ANDRAGOGICAL DESIGN FOR LEARNING

Another design used to deliver education to students is the concept of andragogy: "the art and science of helping adults to learn has attracted considerable attention in recent years."[4] Andragogy is based upon four assumptions about the characteristics of adult learners: (1) the adult enters the learning experience with a concept of himself as a mature human being with values and an adultness unique to himself; (2) as an adult, he has a body of past experiences that he may utilize in determining what is relevant to his learning needs; (3) his readiness to learn is modified by his developmental tasks and his social role; (4) and, unlike the youth, his time perspective is one of immediacy and not future oriented. Thus his learning shifts from subject centeredness to problem centeredness.

The design of learning experiences for adults obviously has implications for youth learners. The humanizing of the classroom, through which the student becomes an active participant responsible for his learning, encourages self-direction in the student and thus instills independence, rather than his remaining an apathetic receptor of learning.

SYSTEMS APPROACH TO INSTRUCTION

The field of systems development has taken on wider implications in recent years. Long utilized in government and industry, educational planners and administrators have determined that there is a place for systems approaches in education.

Mager and Beach say that

Systematic course development is no different than systematic development of an airplane, or systematic design and construction of a building. . . . The tools are different, but the procedure is the same.

Essentially, the three phases of the procedure ask us to:

1. Determine and describe what it is we want to achieve.
2. Do what is necessary to achieve the desired result.
3. Check to see that we have succeeded in what we set out to do.

In developing instruction, this means:

1. Deriving and describing the objectives in meaningful form.
2. Developing lessons and materials designed to meet these objectives and trying out the course.
3. Determining how well the objectives were achieved and improving the course to improve the results.[5]

The systems approach to instruction received its greatest impetus from Samuel Postelthwait of Purdue University in the field of botany. Here the systems method was utilized to decrease the number of students failing botany and, eventually, biology courses.[6]

When Oakland Community College in Michigan opened in the fall of 1965 under the leadership of President John E. Tirrell, that institution initiated one of the largest experiments in nontraditional study. Oakland enrolled almost 4,000 students that fall, and all the students were exposed to instruction through the systems approach or an audio-tutorial plan of teaching.

Features of audio-tutorial teaching at Oakland Community College were the following:

1. A degree of flexibility in the relative emphasis given in various courses to general assembly sessions and to small assembly sessions.
2. A degree of flexibility in the relative emphasis given in various courses to required attendance at general assembly sessions and at small assembly sessions, as well as to scheduled attendance at individual study sessions.
3. The development and use in all learning laboratories of "Oakland-designed" study carrells, specifically planned for audio-tutorial teaching and providing facilities for the use of varied audiovisual materials by individual students.
4. The use of "functional teaching teams" in various courses—consisting of a coordinator, associated instructors, tutors, materials experts, and laboratory assistants—with every team member having specific responsibilities appropriate to his background of education and experience.

Table 1 further describes the rationale and functioning of audio-tutorial teaching there as compared with "conventional" teaching.[7]

Whereas at Purdue the audio-tutorial approach to instruction was limited to individual courses, the unique feature at Oakland was that it involved the entire college, and only those prospective faculty that indicated a desire to teach in this innovative

Table 1
Audio-Tutorial Teaching at Oakland Community College Compared with Conventional Method[8]

Teaching Element	Conventional	Oakland Community College
Objectives	Nonbehavioral, generalized. Student guesses or assumes.	Behavioral, specific, detailed. Given to student at start of term for each unit and study period.
Course outline	Chapter, topic, textbook, test dates.	Detailed, step-by-step objectives and media chains to be used.
Course conduct	Three weekly lectures, outside reading, "trouble conferences" arranged.	One weekly assembly, independent self-study, multimedia, small seminar groups, much tutorial assistance.
Grading	Twice a year.	Weekly at least, twice a year, and summary reports.
Knowledge of results	Twice a semester—long delays. Formal faculty test, written by students in a group.	Weekly, immediately. Self-testing. Written, oral, group, and individual examinations and quizzes.
Emphasis	Teacher	Learner
	Text	Multimedia
	>Instructional	>Learning
	Test	Feedback
	Grades	Achievement

manner were eventually appointed. The college turned to industry for assistance in initiating its plan. Litton Instructional Materials provided a 2-month workshop for the faculty to instruct them in determining behavioral objectives and in designing materials and instructional aids.

More recently other institutions have attempted to utilize the audio-tutorial approach to instruction. Although the time, money, and effort required for this nontraditional approach are considerable, its proponents believe that the desired results are worth the expenditure.

NONDEGREE SPECIAL PROGRAMS

The need of today's society for "more relevant learning experiences" is being responded to, and change is taking place primarily in the junior and community college phase of higher education. Estimates indicate that special and internal degree programs are emerging each week. The commission on nontraditional study conducted a survey which indicated that 1,000 to 1,400 nontraditional study programs now exist in institutions of higher learning, most having emerged during the past 2 years. The new degree programs confer college credit for one or many of the following elements: (1) life experiences and accomplishments, (2) learning occurrences in industrial and/or business settings, (3) proficiency demonstrated by examination in subject matter, (4) correspondence courses, (5) computer- and media-assisted instruction, (6) independent study, (7) regional counseling and learning centers, (8) seminars, (9) utilization of community resources, and (10) traditional classroom learning.[9]

Special degree programs thus allow great flexibility for the student and permit a wide range of field experiences, thus not necessarily confining the learning experience to the traditional classroom.

The Bachelor of Liberal Studies and the Master of Liberal Studies degrees have thus provided a refreshing alternative to the traditional educational experiences in higher education.

New degrees in the community and junior colleges may be looked upon as pioneers in the nontraditional era. The Technical Institute at Memphis inaugurated an Associate of Independent Studies Degree with majors in each of the areas offered. The degree will indicate that the recipient has been certified through testing and evaluation to possess abilities normally required by the graduates. These abilities, however, are acquired primarily on an independent basis. At Spoon River College in Illinois an Associate Degree in Liberal Studies is offered for students 25 years or older who have pursued their studies independently through an 8-week seminar consisting of 2-hour weekly sessions. The 12 learning centers of the Vermont Regional Community College Commission can meet student needs for instruction anywhere within the state.

SPECIAL DEGREE PROGRAMS

Special degree programs are relatively new. They are a departure from the traditional academic experiences provided by institutions of higher education. Most authorities in the field believe that as more adults return to the university or colleges the need for special degree programs will be recognized, and that the number of institutions providing these nontraditional degrees will increase.

The first special degree program began in 1954 at Brooklyn College. Eventually, a host of other institutions recognized the special or unique learning needs of adults and instituted similar programs with various modifications.

The early institutions to initiate programs were Syracuse University, University of Oklahoma, Queens College, Goddard College, Johns Hopkins University, San Francisco Theological Seminary, New York University, Boston University, the University of South Florida, Roosevelt University, Brigham Young University, and the State University of New York, College at Brookport.

These degree programs evolved out of several working conferences; however, considerable effort by the now defunct Center for the Study of Liberal Education for Adults gave impetus to the establishment of several specific degree programs.

Although there are several differences in individual programs, Liveright categorized them according to four variables:

1. The amount of credit that must be earned through regular on-campus classes.
2. The total residence requirements.
3. The extent to which special methods and media are utilized.
4. The extent to which the credit hour system is replaced by other means of measuring and reporting progress.[10]

In addition to the objective of providing liberal education, most of the programs have other common objectives, such as the following:

1. They attempt to instill a desire for learning and to provide skills of independent study so that students may continue self-enrichment study beyond the degree.
2. The curriculum is interdisciplinary, emphasizing broad knowledge and understanding of basic concepts and the interrelationship of knowledge, rather than the accumulation of factual information.
3. They attempt to develop skills and habits of study and research in a particular discipline or problem area.
4. They are designed to meet the special needs and interests of adults.
5. They permit adults to pursue a degree program in a manner and under circumstances convenient to them.
6. They provide opportunities for student evaluation, program evaluation, and educational research.

Guided independent study is a major element in most special degree programs. Typically, the independent study program is planned by a faculty member in conference with the student, and the two continue to work together throughout the period of independent study in a given area or on a given topic. The importance placed on independent study is appropriate. Experience and research indicate that many adult students are willing and able to assume large responsibility for their learning through guided independent study. With reasonable guidance and proper materials, adults easily learn through various techniques and procedures.

Independent study is a convenient means of learning since it permits the student to pursue his studies at a time and place of his choosing. It also permits flexibility in his rate of progress, allowing him to proceed at his own pace according to his ability, initiative, self-discipline, desire, and time available for study.[11]

THE UNIVERSITY WITHOUT WALLS

The University Without Walls (UWW) is a program of the Union for Experimenting Colleges and Universities located at Antioch College, Yellow Springs, Ohio. A consortium of 25 institutions joined together to encourage research and to experiment in many aspects of higher education.

The Union began with a grant of $415,000 from the U.S. Office of Education. The Ford Foundation gave an additional $400,000. Recently, Unesco gave an additional grant of $10,000 to begin plans for a University Without Walls abroad.

Currently, the participating institutions in UWW are the University of Minnesota, Minneapolis, Minnesota; the University of Massachusetts, Amherst, Massachusetts; Antioch College, Yellow Springs, Ohio; New College at Sarasota, Sarasota, Florida; Shaw University, Raleigh, North Carolina; the University of South Carolina, Columbia, South Carolina; Roger Williams College, Bristol, Rhode Island; Bard College, Annandale-on-Hudson, New York; Chicago State University, Chicago, Illinois; Goddard College, Plainfield, Vermont; Howard University, Washington, D.C.; Friends World College, Westbury, New York; Northeastern Illinois University, Chicago, Illinois; Stephens College, Columbia, Missouri; Loretto Heights College,

Denver, Colorado; Staten Island Community College, Staten Island, New York; Skidmore College, Saratoga Springs, New York; Morgan State College, Baltimore, Maryland; New York University, New York, New York; Westminster College, Fulton, Missouri.

In general, the plan of UWW is based on flexibility and individual responsibility or self-direction. The UWW's annual report reflects this flexibility as it relates the general plan.

In the course of planning, each University Without Walls institution agreed to develop its UWW program around certain key ideas which constitute the basic components of the UWW plan. These included:

1. *Inclusion of a broad age range of persons (16 to 60 and older) so as to provide an opportunity for persons of all ages to secure an undergraduate education and to make for a new mix of age ranges in our programs of undergraduate education.*
2. *Involvement of students, faculty members, and administrators in the design and development of each UWW unit.*
3. *Development of special seminars and other procedures to prepare students to learn on their own and to keep students and faculty in touch with each other; development of special training programs to prepare faculty members for the new instructional procedures to be used in the UWW plan.*
4. *Employment of flexible time units so that a student could spend varying periods of time in a particular kind of program experience. Programs were to be individually tailored by student and adviser. There would be no fixed curriculum and no uniform time schedule for the award of the degree.*
5. *Use of a broad array of resources for teaching and learning, both in and out of the classroom. Development of the Inventory of Learning Resources as a guide for program planning.*
6. *Use of an adjunct faculty of government officials, business executives, persons from community agencies, scientists, artists, and others as a regular part of the UWW's instructional staff; development of an extensive seminar-in-the-field program to draw on skills and experiences of this adjunct faculty.*
7. *Opportunities for students to use the resources of other UWW units.*
8. *Concern for both cognitive and affective learning; development of new assessment procedures, with periodic evaluations to include both students and their advisers.[12]*

Students proceed at their own pace at UWW and the graphic representations[13] shown in Figure 1

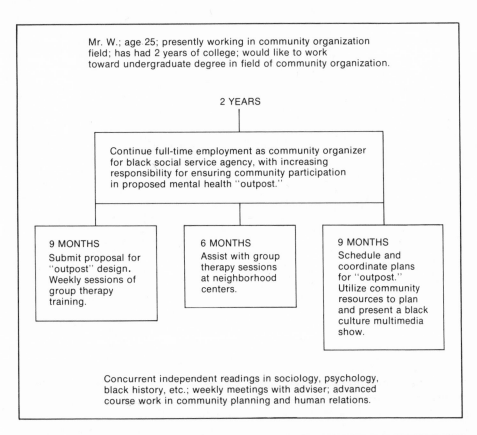

Mr. W.; age 25; presently working in community organization field; has had 2 years of college; would like to work toward undergraduate degree in field of community organization.

2 YEARS

Continue full-time employment as community organizer for black social service agency, with increasing responsibility for ensuring community participation in proposed mental health "outpost."

9 MONTHS
Submit proposal for "outpost" design. Weekly sessions of group therapy training.

6 MONTHS
Assist with group therapy sessions at neighborhood centers.

9 MONTHS
Schedule and coordinate plans for "outpost." Utilize community resources to plan and present a black culture multimedia show.

Concurrent independent readings in sociology, psychology, black history, etc.; weekly meetings with adviser; advanced course work in community planning and human relations.

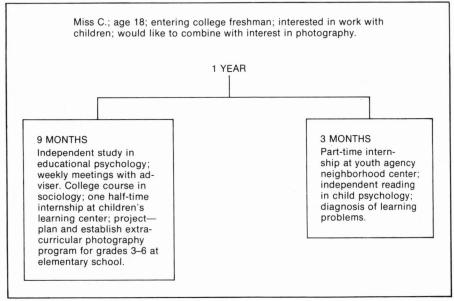

Miss C.; age 18; entering college freshman; interested in work with children; would like to combine with interest in photography.

1 YEAR

9 MONTHS
Independent study in educational psychology; weekly meetings with adviser. College course in sociology; one half-time internship at children's learning center; project—plan and establish extra-curricular photography program for grades 3–6 at elementary school.

3 MONTHS
Part-time internship at youth agency neighborhood center; independent reading in child psychology; diagnosis of learning problems.

Figure 1

(continued on next page)

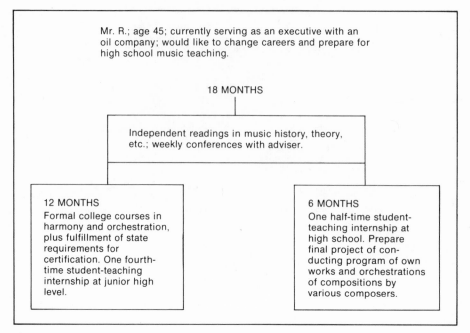

Mr. R.; age 45; currently serving as an executive with an oil company; would like to change careers and prepare for high school music teaching.

18 MONTHS

Independent readings in music history, theory, etc.; weekly conferences with adviser.

12 MONTHS
Formal college courses in harmony and orchestration, plus fulfillment of state requirements for certification. One fourth-time student-teaching internship at junior high level.

6 MONTHS
One half-time student-teaching internship at high school. Prepare final project of conducting program of own works and orchestrations of compositions by various composers.

Figure 1

illustrate various stages and sequences of learning experiences in which a student might engage.

It has not been easy for these institutions, each with a history of independence, various tuition rates, and programs to cooperate and work as a unit. It is firmly believed that the UWW benefits from its very diversity. The role of the central office located at Antioch has been one of catalysis, or a coordinating agent.

The UWW has been very successful, and already spin off or ancillary projects have emerged, such as the following:

Drug and Alcohol Rehabilitation

At the initiation of the National Institute for Mental Health (NIMH), the Union has held several meetings with staff members of NIMH about adapting UWW to the rehabilitation and staff development needs of drug and alcohol abuse centers. As a result, the Union has submitted a proposal for joint funding by NIMH and the U.S. Office of Education.

Under the plan, Northeastern Illinois University and Chicago State University would collaborate with the Illinois Drug Abuse Center in a UWW program designed to meet program and educational needs of staff members and patients at the Illinois Drug Abuse Center. A similar program is contemplated in Philadelphia, where the Urban Education Center, an affiliate of Antioch College, would collaborate with the Eagleville Drug Abuse Treatment Center and other agencies in the development of a comparable UWW program for patients and staff at the Eagleville Center. The Union would be the accountable agent and would co-ordinate and evaluate the project, attempting to determine whether it should be replicated with other drug abuse centers.

Penal Institutions

Northeastern Illinois University is negotiating with the State Corrections Department to establish UWW programs in various corrections units. Programs might include both inmates and prison guards. (The University of Minnesota already has four students pursuing programs from behind bars.) Loretto Heights College, Shaw University, Antioch, and other institutions intend to work with local corrections units.

University Year in ACTION

The Union was among the first organizations invited by ACTION (formerly the Peace Corps agency) to discuss possible affiliation with its University Year for ACTION program. Several UWW institutions have received grants from ACTION. One of the most interesting is at Morgan State College, where 25 black students are working for a year's worth of credit with community organizing groups in Baltimore.

Technology

The Goddard Space Flight Agency and the National Aeronautics and Space Administration, located in Greenbelt, Maryland, held a two-day workshop at the Goddard Agency where UWW Project Directors and several information and communications specialists from Goddard discussed ways in which new technological developments might relate to the educational program needs of the UWW. The Space Agency is preparing a position paper on some initial steps that UWW institutions might take to use computer-based information systems in dealing with UWW program needs. The Union envisions a continuing and collaborative effort with the Space Agency to discover ways by which technological advances can be used in the UWW program.

Other Colleges and Universities

Over 100 colleges and universities (a number from outside the United States) have asked the Union for further information on the UWW plan.

About 40 of these are interested in developing their own UWW units and in joining the network of UWW institutions. During the coming months, the Union plans to hold a series of one-day workshops in different parts of the country to acquaint institutions with the UWW plan and to explore plans for the establishment of UWW Regional Centers. The U.S. Office of Education is currently studying preliminary proposals for such Regional Centers.

International Component

In addition to a network of institutions in this country, the original proposal of the University Without Walls contemplated the development of UWW units in other countries. A grant from the United Nations Educational, Cultural and Scientific Organization will enable the Union to undertake conferences with institutions abroad as potential UWW units. The first conference will be held in the late spring and summer, 1972.

UWW as a Model for Teacher Preparation

As previously mentioned, one of the UWW units has just received a Title VII bilingual education grant to assist Navajos, working as aides and trainees in two Navajo schools to acquire an undergraduate degree and teaching certificates. The program being developed for these persons builds on the basic ideas of the UWW model.

More recently, the Commission on Undergraduate Education and the Preparation of Teachers brought together several presidents of UWW institutions and other educators to explore new ideas for the preparation of elementary and secondary school teachers and implications that the UWW model might have for such teacher-training programs. A number of ideas emerged from this conference as to ways in which the University Without Walls model might be more directly applied in the preparation of elementary and secondary school teachers. These ideas included (1) local communities might take initiative in recruiting, training, and accrediting the teachers and school administrators they desire; (2) potential good teachers might be identified in early adolescence and given guided experience in teaching projects; (3) pairing students well-versed in theory with para-professionals rich in experience may be educative for both; and (4) a new professional role in education, the street worker, employed by schools, is emerging.

A proposal is now being prepared on how UWW units might test these ideas.[14]

Programs for Para-Professionals

Since most para-professionals have to moonlight to acquire a degree and rarely receive any credit for what they learn from their jobs, the UWW is useful to them. A number of para-professionals are already enrolled in UWW programs, and the Union is exploring with several community agencies, hospitals, and school groups ways by which the UWW might be more fully related to their educational and program needs.

High School–College UWW Model

As a result of inquiries from several superintendents of schools, high school teachers, and principals, the Union is contemplating a high school–college unit where students might begin UWW programs early in high school and move directly from there into a college UWW unit. Initial discussions have been held with Dr. Harvey Scribner, Chancellor of the New York City school system, and the Union hopes to evolve a proposal in cooperation with Dr. Scribner's office in the near future.[15] A meeting is also being planned with a committee of school superintendents (a subcommittee of the Commission on Education and the Preparation of Teachers) to explore such ideas.

SUMMARY

American higher education is presently on the threshold of a new era. The costs of education have encouraged the emergence of new forms of management and nontraditional programs. The flexibility and independent study inherent in the nontraditional programs cited in this chapter provide the educational benefits that occur from self-directed learning, as well as cost savings.

The nontraditional movement is one response to the influence of current social forces in American society, but one must be aware that evaluation on a continuous basis is needed.

Thurman White, a pioneer in nontraditional education, has presented 12 quality indicators that could be used for examining nontraditional educational programs.[16] These are as follows:

A Concern for Quality

1. Builds on the previous learning of the student.
2. Allows students to proceed at their own rate of learning.
3. Encourages students in their systematic study of individual concerns.
4. Places heavy responsibility on students for independent effort.
5. Satisfies special requirements of external bodies.
6. Has standards and responsibilities set by a responsible faculty.
7. Brings professors into contact with students at convenient times and places.
8. Provides extensive individual student guidance.
9. Assessment procedures include appropriate national norms.
10. Employs teaching talents of external colleagues.
11. Uses a rich variety of delivery systems.
12. Admits and enrolls students every day.

If a man is to become a continuous learner throughout his life, through self-direction and the knowledge of how to obtain those resources which will enable him to continue his necessary learnings, the independence fostered by the nontraditional approaches discussed here will have positive results for American higher education. The important factor is to discover new techniques and for administrators to discover new educational patterns, designs, and other possibilities to bring to the attention of their own institutions.

NOTES AND REFERENCES

1. *Chronicle of Higher Education,* Oct. 9, 1973, p. 7.
2. *Chronicle of Higher Education,* Oct. 9, 1973, p. 7.
3. *Community and Junior College Journal,* Open Education, Mar. 1973, pp. 12–14.
4. Malcolm S. Knowles, *The Modern Practice of Adult Education,* New York, Associated Press, 1970, p. 38.
5. Robert E. Mager and Kenneth M. Beach, Jr., *Developing Vocational Instruction,* Palo Alto, Calif., Tearon Publishers, 1967, p. 2.
6. For a more generalized discussion see Samuel Postelthwait, Planning for Better Learning, in G. Kerry Smith (ed.), *In Search of Leaders.* Washington, D.C.: A.A.H.E., 1967.
7. B. Lamar Johnson, *Island of Innovation Expanding*: Changes in the Community College, Beverly Hills, Calif., Glencoe Press, 1969, p. 100.
8. *The University Without Walls: A First Report,* Yellow Springs, Ohio, Union for Experimenting Colleges and Universities, 1972, p. 101.
9. Lee J. Betts, *Nontraditional Education and the Community College* (draft).
10. Roy Troutt, *Special Degree Programs for Adults: Exploring Nontraditional Degree Programs in Higher Education,* Iowa City, Iowa, American College Testing Program, 1971, p. 10.
11. *Ibid.,* p. 13.
12. *The University Without Walls: A First Report,* Yellow Springs, Ohio, Union for Experimenting Colleges and Universities, 1972, p. 12.
13. *Ibid.,* p. 11.
14. *Ibid.,* pp. 43–46.
15. Dr. Scribner is currently a professor at the University of Massachusetts.
16. Lee J. Betts, *Nontraditional Education and the Community College, A Concern for Quality,* p. 14 (draft).

ADDITIONAL READINGS

Ashby, Eric. *Any Person, Any Study.* Berkley, Calif.: Carnegie Foundation for the Advancement of Teaching, 1971.

Gould, Samuel B., K. Patricia Cross (eds.). *Explorations in Non-Traditional Study.* San Francisco: Jossey-Bass, Inc., 1972.

Immegart, Glenn L., and Francis J. Pilecki. *An Introduction to Systems for the Educational Administrator.* Reading, Mass.: Addison-Wesley Publishing Company, Inc., 1973.

Knowles, Malcolm S. *Higher Adult Education in the United States.* Washington, D.C.: American Council on Education, 1969.

Milton, Ohmer. *Alternatives to the Traditional.* San Francisco: Jossey-Bass, Inc., 1972.

Rosecrance, Francis C. *The American College and Its Teachers.* New York: Macmillan Publishing Co., Inc., 1962.

Sanford, Nevitt (ed.). *The American College.* New York: John Wiley & Sons, Inc., 1962.

Smith, G. Kerry (ed.). *New Teaching, New Learnings.* San Francisco: Jossey-Bass, Inc., 1971.

Vermityne, Dyckman W. (ed.). *The Expanded Campus.* San Francisco: Jossey-Bass, Inc., 1972.

PART III: CURRENT RESEARCH

Teacher Attitudes to Media Teaching Environments

Charles C. Aquino

This research, sponsored by State University of New York Research Foundation and Manitoba Teachers' Society, was a follow-up to an earlier study (Aquino, 1970). As such, its objectives sought to determine: (1) If teacher attitudes toward audiovisual instruction were influenced by the period of time which had elapsed since they studied a formal course in that area; (2) If specific factors within the population's educational media teaching environments were related to attitudes toward audiovisual instruction. These factors were availability of audiovisual equipment, availability of audiovisual materials, accessibility of audiovisual equipment and accessibility of audiovisual materials.

SUMMARY OF PREVIOUS RESEARCH

The previous research project had as its population 40 teachers who had studied an audiovisual education course and returned to teaching during the semester immediately following that course. Through dual administrations of the *New Media*

Charles C. Aquino is associate professor of instructional resources at State University College, Buffalo, New York.

Attitude Scale (NMAS) (Ramsey, 1961) the researcher had been enabled to divide that population into subgroups based upon positive or negative direction and intensity of changes in attitudes toward audiovisual instruction which had occurred over a single teaching semester. A prior investigation (Aquino, 1968) had allowed the researcher to assume that attitudes would improve during the course of formal studies, and this assumption had been supported by others reporting on student attitudes toward other academic areas (Jones, 1963; Munger, 1963).

Having divided the population according to the above criteria, relationships between changes in direction and intensity of attitudes toward audiovisual instruction and the teaching environment factors noted within the second objective for the current study were investigated. Statistical analysis revealed positive and significant relationships between direction and intensity of attitudinal changes with accessibility of audiovisual equipment, accessibility of audiovisual materials, and availability of audiovisual materials. Little relationship was discovered for the factor involved with availability of audiovisual equipment.

Thus, it was concluded that the population's attitudes toward audiovisual instruction were not influenced by the amounts of audiovisual equipment which their schools owned, as long as that equipment was accessible when it was needed. On the other hand, the population attached great significance to the amount of audiovisual materials their schools owned as well as to the accessibility of those materials.

During recent years, several researchers had investigated attitudes toward audiovisual instruction and factors which influence those attitudes. Grant and White (1970) studied a population of secondary school teachers who had experienced a specific audiovisual education demonstration unit and related various personality characteristics to changes in attitude toward newer media. Teacher perceptions of environmental conditions within schools which influence utilization of educational media were investigated by Miller (1970), who concluded that organized audiovisual programs supervised by audiovisual coordinators were related to significantly superior audiovisual educational climates. Lewis (1970) tested 15 questions in an effort to determine teacher perceptions relative to educational media. Among his findings were conclusions that teachers perceive educational media as being readily available and that they perceive formal training in the area of audiovisual instruction as being necessary.

Tobias (1966, 1968) investigated educational media factors and terminology which threaten teachers and concluded that threats of automation influence teacher attitudes toward educational media. Finch, Gustilo, and Wiersteiner (1970) reported findings indicating that availability of instructional resources leads to increased utilization of such media, but that teacher attitudes have little influence upon availability–use relationships; Guba and Snyder (1964) found users of media within their population to possess more favorable attitudes toward newer media than did nonusers of those media. Increased utilization of audiovisual materials was identified by Eboch (1966) as being related to increased availability of such materials, and Godfrey (1965), reporting upon availability of educational media in schools, identified teacher requests as being among the more influential channels for having school authorities provide greater amounts of audiovisual equipment and materials.

Among earlier researchers of teacher attitudes toward educational media were Kelley (1959), who identified 16 factors related to that construct, Ramsey (1961), developer of the NMAS, and Brown (1965), who tested that scale with a large population of educational media institute participants and found it to be a suitable indicator of attitudes toward educational media. Knowlton and Hawes (1962, 1963) concluded that negative teacher attitudes toward educational media are related to utilization barriers, and that increased utilization of educational media by teachers following their participation in an audiovisual education course is the result of improved information rather than improved attitudes.

FOUNDATION FOR THIS RESEARCH

As noted, the population for the 1970 study was comprised of 40 educators who had returned to teaching immediately following formal study in the area of audiovisual instruction. The NMAS was administered at the conclusion of the audiovisual education course and again at the conclusion of the population's first semester of teaching following that course. Thus, changes in attitudes were based upon a period of 6 months which had elapsed between the two administrations of that instrument, and the population's perceptions of their audiovisual education environments were restricted to observations made during that period of time.

This gave rise to questions which led to the research reported here. Specifically, (1) Was the period of time which had elapsed of sufficient length to offset the improvement in attitudes which had occurred during the audiovisual education course? (2) Would a population who was further removed by time from formal study in audiovisual instruction possess different attitudes toward that construct because of a greater period of elapsed time? (3) Would a population react differently to factors within their audiovisual education teaching environments if a lengthier period of time were allowed to elapse between formal study of audiovisual instruction and the gathering of data concerning those environments?

POPULATION AND PROCEDURES

The population for this study was made up of 156 educators who resumed teaching duties following participation in an audiovisual education course at the University of Manitoba, Winnipeg. Of these, 96 had completed the course during summer 1968 and were designated as study group A. The remaining 60 persons had completed the audiovisual instruction course during summer 1969 and were designated as study group B. Both groups had completed the same course with the same instructor, possessed similar educational backgrounds and experiences, and expressed similar motivations for studying audiovisual instruction.

The *Media Attitude Profile* (MAP) was utilized for collecting data indicating teacher attitudes toward educational media. That instrument, developed by Dawson (1971), was designed to measure attitudes toward eight areas of educational media. The "general" category of the MAP was used for this study.

Data relating to educational media teaching environments were self-reported by responses to 5-point rating scales for each of the factors tested. As in the previous study, specific operational definitions were provided to respondents to eliminate ambiguity between availability–accessibility and equipment–materials factors.

Mailings, which included the MAP rating scale, and cover letter, were sent to each member of the population during January 1970. Of the 156 initial mailings, returns were received from 141 of the intended population. Of these, 26 were unlocated by postal authorities, 10 were no longer teaching, and returns were invalidated because of respondent error. Thus, the final population totaled 102 individuals or approximately 70 percent of the possible population. As noted, the final population was divided into study groups on the basis of elapsed time since formal audiovisual education study. Study group A, which had completed the audiovisual education course 18 months prior to the measurement of attitudes, numbered 58 individuals or 60 percent of those eligible. Study group B, whose members had completed the audiovisual education course 6 months prior to the measurement of attitudes, included 44 persons or 73 percent of those eligible.

During February 1970 the researcher held personal and telephone interviews with randomly selected members of the population. These interviews, conducted with 40 percent of the population, established that self-reported data were free of ambiguity and in accordance with directions for completing the environment data questionnaire.

ANALYSIS, FINDINGS, AND CONCLUSIONS

Raw scores for the general category of the MAP were divided into subgroups and subjected to standard descriptive analysis. Means for groups A and B, respectively, were 162.6 and 166.2, with 16.8 representing one standard deviation for group A and 14.4 for group B.

A t test of means was computed with $t > 1.99$ as the criterion for rejecting the null hypothesis that no difference in attitudes toward educational media existed between groups A and B at the time of the study. The resultant $t = 1.14$ dictated acceptance of that hypothesis.

As results of the t test made it apparent that little difference in attitude toward audiovisual instruction existed between the subgroups, subsequent attitude–media environment analyses were extended to include groups A and B combined, as well as independent analyses for group A and group B.

Relations between attitudes and educational media environment factors were tested by means of a Pearson product moment correlation. Results of that examination are shown in Table 1.

Analysis of factor–attitude data revealed a negative and significant relationship between availability factors for both audiovisual equipment and materials and for the equipment segment of the accessibility factor. These relationships were consistent for groups A and B separately and for groups A and B combined. The only deviation from these findings was the attitude–accessibility of audiovisual equipment relationship for group A, which maintained a negative relationship but did not meet the criterion for significance.

As the MAP data revealed no significant difference between attitudes toward audiovisual instruction between groups A and B, it was concluded that difference in time which had elapsed since formal study in audiovisual education for groups A and B did not influence the population's attitudes toward audiovisual instruction. Hovland (1953), commenting on the retention of attitudes, stated that various researchers differ widely in their conclusions and that some have reported a continued change of attitudes in the direction favored by the researcher with the passage of time. The implication is that the determination of factors which cause attitudes to change or be maintained is necessary before general inferences may be made from such findings.

Several considerations are germane to the finding that attitudes between groups A and B were not

Table 1
Relationships Between Teacher Attitudes and Educational Media Factors

Group	Availability Factor		Accessibility Factor	
	AV Equipment	AV Material	AV Equipment	AV Material
A	−.28[a]	−.32[a]	−.15	.05
B	−.43[b]	−.29[a]	−.33[a]	.19
A & B	−.35[b]	−.30[b]	−.24[a]	.05

[a]P .05 for one-tailed test.
[b]P .01 for one-tailed test.

related to time which had elapsed since study in audiovisual instruction. Hovland (1953), commenting on the retention of attitudes, stated that various researchers differ widely in their conclusions and that some have reported a continued change of attitudes in the direction favored by the researcher with the passage of time. The implication is that the determination of factors which cause attitudes to change or be maintained is necessary before general inferences may be made from such findings.

Several considerations are germane to the finding that attitudes between groups A and B were not related to time which had elapsed since study in audiovisual instruction. The first, and most obvious, is that the periods of time encompassed by this study may not have been sufficiently lengthy to have a measurable influence upon attitudes. This question was also posed by the previous study and, while suggesting an avenue for further research, a valid inference cannot be provided within this report.

Two considerations which do warrant further attention are (1) that the population may have found the formal audiovisual education experience stimulating to the extent of overcoming a tendency for attitudes to decline over the period of time that they were measured, and (2) they may have found sufficient opportunities within their teaching environments to apply and practice those methods and techniques which had been learned during the audiovisual education course.

There is some subjective evidence to support the former of these considerations, although the nature of that evidence is incidental rather than a result of this study. The population's MAP scores, when compared with Dawson's test groups (1971), were found to be more favorable toward audiovisual instruction. While Dawson's developmental research did not determine an arbitrary MAP score which would distinguish between positive and negative attitudes toward educational media, the comparison indicates that the population for this study was generally favorable in their attitudes

toward audiovisual instruction. Therefore, it might be assumed that attitudes toward audiovisual instruction which were developed during the audiovisual education course were of sufficient strength to resist negative influences which the population experienced during the time which elapsed since that course and the measurement of attitudes.

It is the latter consideration, however, which is of major relevance to this study, for factor–attitude analysis refuted the consideration that the population's audiovisual education teaching environments encouraged applications of audiovisual education methods and techniques which they had learned. The negative relationships shown in Table 1 indicate, of course, that the more favorable attitudes toward educational media were matched with more negative rating of educational media teaching environments and vice versa. Since the population for this study appeared to be generally favorable in their attitudes toward audiovisual instruction, it would be whimsical to conclude that those negative relationships implied that a further decline in the quality of educational media teaching environments would lead to greater improvements in attitudes toward audiovisual instruction. Rather, it was concluded that those members of the population who exhibited more favorable attitudes toward audiovisual instruction were also more inclined to be critical of the educational media environments within which they were employed. Teachers who possess extremely positive attitudes toward audiovisual instruction are apparently those who suffer the greater frustrations when their efforts to utilize educational media are rebuffed by environmental conditions which do not provide audiovisual equipment and materials at the times they are required. Furthermore, these teachers presumably develop many plans which require the utilization of educational media, thereby exposing themselves more frequently to disillusionment when they are not able to implement their plans. Conversely, those who are less favorably disposed toward educational media probably use and plan for educational media presentations less often and do not feel as sharply the disappointment of not being able to bring their plans to fruition. Such persons would be less likely to notice faults within their audiovisual education teaching environments and would be more inclined to overlook defects which did attract their attention.

These conclusions support the need for additional research to be directed toward determining if teachers with positive attitudes toward audiovisual instruction are indeed more often frustrated by and therefore more critical of their educational media teaching environments. Such an investigation might be accommodated by first identifying those within a population of teachers who are users or nonusers of media and relating the use factor with attitudes toward educational media. Available evidence indicates that a positive and significant relationship would be the outcome of that analysis (Guba and Snyder, 1964). In that event, the total user–nonuser population could be observed within a common educational media teaching environment. Changes in attitudes and use of educational media by both groups could be measured over varying periods of time during which additions to or deletions from the educational media environment made it more positive or negative for the application of audiovisual instruction. As a result of data analysis for that study, the researcher could tentatively identify specific satisfaction–frustration conditions which seem to influence teacher attitudes toward educational media, insert various of those conditions into different educational media teaching environments, and seek data which might reveal more specifically their impact upon teacher attitudes toward audiovisual instruction. The outcome of such research would provide educational media supervisors and coordinators with specific conditions to implement or avoid in their efforts to assist teachers in utilizing educational media toward the improvement of instruction.

REFERENCES

Aquino, C. C. "Teacher attitudes toward audiovisual instruction as they are influenced by selected factors within teaching environments." *AV Communication Review,* 1970, **18** (2) 187.

Aquino, C. C. "A study to determine educators' attitudes towards audiovisual instruction following study in that area." Ph.D. dissertation, Syracuse University, Syracuse, N.Y., 1968.

Brown, J. "Educational media institute evaluation project." Washington, D.C. United States Office of Education, 1965.

Dawson, P. "Teacher militancy and instructional media." *AV Communication Review,* 1971, **19**(2), 184–197.

Eboch, S. "Implementation of research strategies and tactics for demonstration," Ohio State University, Columbus, Ohio, 1966.

Finch, C., Gustilo, T., and Wiersteiner, "Instructional resources for vocational–technical education: teacher attitude, resource availability and resources utilization." Pennsylvania State University, University Park, 1970.

Godfrey, E. *Audiovisual media in the public schools, 1961–64.* Washington, D.C.: Bureau of Social Science Research, 1965.

Grant, A. and White, F. "A study of the personality characteristics of the acceptor and rejector of the newer educational media among secondary teachers of Wisconsin." Stanford, Calif.: ERIC Research Abstract for AECT Convention, 1970.

Guba, E., and Snyder, C. "Instructional television and the classroom teacher," Ohio State University, Columbus, Ohio, 1964.

Hovland, C., Janis, I., and Kelley, H. *Communication and Persuasion.* New Haven, Conn.: Yale University Press, 1953.

Jones, V. "Attitude changes in an NDEA institute." *Personnel and Guidance Journal,* 1963, **42,** 387–442.

Kelley, G. "A study of teachers' attitudes toward audiovisual materials." *Educational Screen and Audiovisual Guide,* 1960, **39** (3), 119–121.

Kelley, G. "An analysis of teachers' attitudes toward the use of audiovisual materials." Ph.D. dissertation, Boston University, Boston, Mass., 1959.

Knowlton, J. "Studies of patterns in influence in the school situation as they affect the use of audiovisual materials." Indiana University, Bloomington, Ind., 1963.

Knowlton, J., and Hawes, E. "Attitude: Helpful predictor of audiovisual usage?" *AV Communication Review,* 1962, **10** (3), 147–157.

Lewis, E. "A study to determine teacher preceptions in relation to educational media." Stanford, Calif.: ERIC Research Abstract for AECT Convention, 1970.

Miller, P. "The relationship of teacher perceptions of a school's audiovisual climate to the organizational structure of its media programme." Stanford, Calif.: ERIC Research Abstract for AECT Convention, 1970.

Munger, P., Myers, R., and Brown, D. "Guidance institutes and the persistence of attitudes." *Personnel and Guidance Journal,* 1963, **41,** 415–419.

Ramsey, C. "A research project for the development of a measure to assess attitudes regarding the uses of newer educational media." George Peabody College for Teachers, Nashville, Tenn., 1961.

Tobias, S. "Dimensions of teachers' attitudes toward instructional media." *American Educational Research Journal,* 1968, **5** (1), 91–98.

Tobias, S. "Lack of knowledge and fear of automation as factors in teachers' attitudes toward programmed instruction and other media." *AV Communication Review,* 1966, **14,** 99–109.

Why Educational Research?

Boris Blai, Jr.

The purpose of educational research may be simply stated—to develop *specific findings* upon which to base educational decisions. In the final analysis, educational research is nothing more than a means for systematic, empirical, observations resulting in the generation of a limited amount of data or set of facts. In its broadest implications, such research considers the impact of one set of conditions or events upon another. This, in the classically defined "scientific experiment," consists of changing the "independent variables.. (such as different intensities, amounts, or kinds of things) and then carefully noting the effects on the "dependent variables" (such as behavior, reactions, or thoughts).

In sound programs of educational research, conducted systematically and on a continuing basis, there is much of potential value. Such research provides information about (1) students (demographic characteristics, areas of growth and development, academic achievement, etc.), (2) learning processes, (3) educational practices, and (4) the institutional environment, to help determine the effectiveness of the various educational endeavors

Boris Blai, Jr., is director of research at Harcum Junior College, Bryn Mawr, Pennsylvania.

which presumably are the reasons for the existence of the educational institution. Wherever possible, emphasis in such research studies should be upon those designed to provide a *factual basis* for consideration of educational questions relevant to the institution.

Properly applied, in the decision-making process, research data will enable the institution to fully utilize its resources (manpower, money, methods, and materials). Also, long-range planning can be improved through the use of sound research-derived data upon which to base projections and forecasts of the institution's future. Conversely, the absence of "good" research-based information can result in the use of linear, status quo projections of growth and change. These can easily lead to absurd or economically unsound estimates of quantitative measures, which are often essential for sound planning.

The following elements are to be found in any program of sound research. It is

1. Based upon theory and, when available, previous research findings.
2. Ingenious, creative, and timely.
3. Rigorously and carefully conducted with due respect to the importance of controls.
4. Identified as having rigorous standards to follow to ensure that the research design tests the hypothesis it sets out to test, not something else!

In connection with item (4), sound research makes use of carefully formulated hypotheses. A hypothesis may be conveniently defined as a tentative generalization calling attention to fundamental relationships or possible solutions that may help guide the research inquiry. There are two types of hypotheses:

1. *Statistical null hypothesis,* which says that any difference or departure from normal, or other predetermined state, can be attributed to sampling errors. If the difference or departure is greater than one would expect by chance, the null hypothesis is rejected. One may then look to the second type of hypothesis.

2. *Nonstatistical, descriptive hypothesis,* which is simply some tentative formulation about causes, relationships, or possible solutions to posed problems.

It is well in this connection to note that the student, what he is, what he experiences, what he becomes, is a centrality for meaningful educational research, for this provides facts for understanding, managing, and/or changing educational practices. In the final analysis, planned education consists of contrived learning experiences, and by means of educational research we take a more active and conscious part in the contrivance.

The functional or practical utility of educational research depends upon (1) the technological adequacy of the instruments used, and (2) the specific methodological design of the study, which includes a careful statement of hypothesis, a careful determination on selection of individuals and/or records contributing the data to be collected, and application of appropriate statistical techniques to the data collected. (This is the critical step of data quantification in order to draw conclusions from them.)

Speaking of statistics, two broad categories are suitable for utilization in educational research:

1. *Descriptive statistics:* embrace the various methods for summarizing and communicating results, such as statistics from samples which describe specific characteristics of data, and may serve the function of summarizing important aspects of controlled observations of individuals or analysis of records, that is, measures of central tendency (mean, median, mode), measures of variability (standard deviation, average deviation, variability or coefficient of variation), and degrees of interacting relationship between two or more items of data (coefficients of correlation).

2. *Inferential statistics:* involve the making of generalizations from a given set of observations to a larger set of potential observations.

And perhaps the most significant item to remember about statistics is the fact that a statistical relationship between two variables does not necessarily indicate that one variable causes the other!

For convenience, educational researches may be grouped into three broad categories:

1. *Survey research:* This type of investigation may include the collection of data by questionnaires, analysis of records, and interviewing of either specific samples or total populations.
2. *Experimental research:* Here the general procedure involves manipulation of selected variables and the use of experimental and control groups to study the effects of such manipulations upon selected criterion variables.
3. *Historical research:* This involves the use of historical data to answer specific questions by attempting to research historical records to secure valid and reliable information through careful examination and statistical treatment of the data.

In summary, the elements of "good" education research embrace the following:

1. Careful formulation or statement of problem.
2. Meticulous definition of both technical and nontechnical terms.
3. Careful formulation of hypotheses.
4. Careful selection of population or sample for investigation.
5. Careful attention to how the data are collected.
6. Accurate analysis of data.
7. Carefully formulated inferences or generalizations (conclusions).

We therefore conclude—in answer to the question "Why Educational Research?"—that through educational research an increasing number of educational institutions are learning to find ways and means of identifying and analyzing some of their problems—of knowing themselves better—*in order that they may improve their programs and operations, and plan intelligently for the future.*

Instructional Media Research: Past, Present, and Future

William H. Allen

When Hoban and van Ormer's comprehensive review of instructional film research appeared in 1950, educational television was still a dream, the term *programed instruction* was not even coined, and such esoteric instructional forms as simulations, games, and computer-assisted instruction was beyond comprehension. The name of the game then was "evaluation"—how film use compared with some intangible entity called "conventional instruction."

In the last two decades, both the state of the art of mediated instruction and the research with such media have matured. And this journal has spanned the greater part of the change, serving as a transmitter and interpreter of that knowledge. It may be helpful to review what has happened during the past 20 years, to assess the present state of research, and to make some projections into the future.

BEFORE 1950

With some notable exceptions, instructional media research prior to 1950 was characterized

William H. Allen is professor of education and director of cinema research at the University of Southern California, Los Angeles, California.

by a preoccupation with what Lumsdaine (1963) called "evaluative" comparisons. In other words, learning from some unspecified film or other medium was compared with learning from some unspecified presentation by an instructor or other medium. This was the predominant type of research for over 30 years, and the results of hundreds of such studies furnished the base upon which the entire audiovisual movement was justified (Hoban and van Ormer, 1950; Allen, 1960; Saettler, 1968). For the results of these studies showed, almost without exception, decided advantages for films and other audiovisual materials over the usual kinds of classroom instruction. Even though this research is of questionable value, the reasons for conducting such studies at the time (and their counterparts with television and programed instruction in more recent times) are apparent: the educational establishment demanded proof of the effectiveness of these innovative techniques, and the baseline for comparison was clearly the current teaching practices. As a consequence, the general perception of instructional media research even today is in these terms.

But some important exceptions to this research pattern existed in the early days. As a matter of fact, the first respectable study to be conducted (Lashley and Watson, 1922) set a standard for the conceptualization of research variables that was not to be duplicated until recently. Similarly, the research conducted by F. Dean McClusky (Freeman, 1924) investigated theoretical variables that were not to surface again for several decades. But these types of studies proved to be but historical forerunners of a research direction that was to arise much later and even then independently of its precursors.

Several other strands of research effort began in this earlier period, but their influence on the main thrust of instructional media research is uncertain. The first of these was research with educational radio, which was largely evaluative in the earlier period and later merged with communication research in its concern with listener measurement

problems. By the end of World War II instructional radio research was virtually dead. A second strand was the broad field of communication research, centering largely on propaganda studies, public opinion polling, content analysis, and audience measurement. Social psychologists played a distinctive role in these studies as the psychological and persuasive aspects of communication were emphasized. Somehow the results of this research never became integrated with the mainstream of instructional media research, and to this day these two related disciplines are taking different routes. A third strand of research was associated with investigations of reading skills and included studies of readability, vocabulary difficulty, and typography as they related to textbook writing.

In retrospect, it is tempting to point up the inadequacies of much of the early research and to deplore the failure of the different communication disciplines to unify their findings. Yet this criticism hardly does justice to the intensity of effort expended and the residue of results that affect current instructional practices.

The first 30 years of instructional media research made a number of contributions. First, evaluative and nonscientific though the research may have been, it focused the attention of educators and the public on instructional media as legitimate and viable channels for the transmission of educational content and confirmed their overall effectiveness. Second, it supplied a base of suppositions and hypotheses regarding the unique attributes of instructional media which can be studied under controlled experimental conditions. Third, by trying many forms of presentation and organization it revealed the richness and diversity of the utilization of media. Fourth, a body of measurement, audience-learner analysis, and content analysis techniques evolved out of communication research. Fifth, a beginning was made toward the understanding of the persuasive and motivational aspects of communications.

Let us now turn to that transitional period, when

some of the old values of research were being discarded and new approaches and problems were being investigated.

MILITARY STUDIES

The 10-year period immediately following World War II was a pivotal one for instructional media research, and the lead was taken by the military services. Their research programs, two conducted during the war and two after, studied critical theoretical problems and made use of precise evaluative techniques. They heralded a new age of instructional media research and involved prominent experimental and educational psychologists.

The most extensive wartime study was conducted in the Army and reported in a series of studies by Hovland, Lumsdaine, and Sheffield (1949). Not only did *Experiments on Mass Communication* make intensive evaluations of the "Why We Fight" series of orientation films prepared to explain the background of the war, but it reported on an extensive group of studies employing controlled variation and investigating such problems as the short-time and long-time effects of such films, the effects of presenting one or both sides of a controversial subject, and the effects of audience participation upon learning. Aside from the reported findings from these studies, the program's greatest value was in its theoretical discussions of the factors involved in film effectiveness and the sophistication of the measurement techniques employed in the analyses. One of the authors, A. A. Lumsdaine, was to investigate some of these hypotheses and employ these techniques later in his research at Yale University (May and Lumsdaine, 1958), and C. I. Hovland was to carry on the work in the Yale studies in attitude and communication (Hovland, Janis, and Kelley, 1953).

Another product of the Army's research efforts during the war was J. J. Gibson's *Motion Picture Testing and Research* (1947), a report of the Army Air Forces Aviation Psychology Program, in which studies were made of the motion picture medium for purposes of psychological testing, the problem of effective instruction by means of still and motion pictures, perceptual learning, and the representation of three-dimensional space by means of pictures. Out of the study emerged a number of generalizations relating to the characteristics of motion pictures as a method of instruction. This report, edited by one of the leading perceptual psychologists in the country, has been largely neglected, yet both the research reported and the theoretical insights discussed make a significant contribution to our knowledge of instructional media and their effects.

The first of the two major postwar military research programs was the Instructional Film Research Program conducted by C. R. Carpenter at Pennsylvania State University from 1947 to 1955 under the direction of the Navy's Special Devices Center (Carpenter, 1953; Carpenter and Greenhill, 1956). The results from this extensive program of instructional film research are too numerous to detail in this brief overview; however, over 80 studies dealt with many variables important to the production and use of instructional media: motor skill training with films, film utilization, structuring attitudes, evaluational techniques, pictorial testing, techniques of film production, development and use of film research tools, and theoretical and practical considerations in film research and application. Some studies from this program are occasionally cited, but the full impact of the program has yet to be realized.

The second major postwar military research program was conducted by A. A. Lumsdaine for the Air Force Research and Development Command from 1950 to 1957, the major results of which were published in the symposium report, *Student Response in Programed Instruction* (Lumsdaine, 1961). This series of film studies in such broad areas as learning complex sequential tasks, academic subject-matter learning, and paired-associate material was conducted by prominent experimental psychologists and had significant implications for the design of mediated instruction. The only attempt to integrate the results into a rationale for media use and design was by Lumsdaine (1963) himself.

The importance of these military studies should not be underestimated. They constitute virtually the only attempts to approach problems in instructional media with a systematic programatic research effort. They dealt with a number of psychological, production, and utilization variables at a level of sophistication and precision. Yet, as Saettler (1968) pointed out, none of the results have been implemented in the instructional films produced by the military services, much less the commercial producers of instructional materials. This problem of translation of research findings into practice is one of the major problems needing solution in the future.

TELEVISION RESEARCH

The period from the mid-1950s to the mid-1960s could be appropriately labeled "the decade of educational television." With enactment of legislation allocating television channels to education, the emphasis in instructional media research switched dramatically from film to television. And with this change the cycle of "evaluative" research was repeated; television researchers almost totally disregarded the findings from previous film research in their enthusiasm for the new medium. Leading this parade was the Ford Foundation's Fund for the Advancement of Education, which supported an extensive program of research of very dubious quality aimed at proving the value of television as a substitute for conventional teaching. The emphasis was on development rather than research.

Despite the fumbling of these early attempts to assess the values of instructional television (reported by Reid and MacLennan, 1967, and Chu and Schramm, 1967), some serious research attempts were being made to understand the nature of

television as an instructional tool. The series of studies conducted by Kanner and his associates (Kanner, 1957, 1958) probed in depth the use of television in the Army; Carpenter and Greenhill (1955, 1958) investigated a number of instructional variables in a university setting; and Gropper and Lumsdaine (1961) studied the relationship of student response in a programed instructional mode to televised instruction.

The predominant finding from the hundreds of evaluative studies in instructional television is its overall equal effectiveness when compared with face-to-face instruction. That students learn from televised teaching cannot be doubted, but the conditions under which such learning takes place and the specific characteristics of televised presentations that bring this about are yet to be determined, and most research ignored such questions.

RESEARCH ON PROGRAMED INSTRUCTION

When programed instruction burst onto the educational scene a little over a decade ago, the same "evaluative" research cycle was repeated, and promoted not only by educational proponents, but by commercial interests as well. However, programed instruction had the additional support of those educational psychologists who saw it as a tool for studying the learning process. Thus, while the more public aspects of the programed instruction boom came to flower and faded quickly, a base of solid research was being established, and many insights relating to the design, sequencing, and structuring of media emerged. Unlike research with other instructional media, some of the experimental results from programed instruction are being translated into practice, and guidelines for materials design have evolved (Lange, 1967).

Perhaps the most important outgrowth of this research, however, is the impetus given to the study of the individualization of instruction. Whereas in the past, instructional media were usually considered useful in one-way mass communication or for group instruction, attention has shifted to the use of media in individual teaching modes. The intensive studies of programed instruction, and the learning principles represented, are largely responsible for this change, with individual student response becoming a key factor in the design of instructional procedures.

FEDERAL RESEARCH SUPPORT

With the enactment of the National Defense Education Act of 1958, and the provisions under Title VII of that Act, the most extensive support of instructional media research in the nation's history was instituted. For a period of over 5 years hundreds of media research studies were funded on a variety of topics, and attempts were made to disseminate research results.

When one evaluates the overall effectiveness of this program, however, no clear pattern of accomplishments emerges. What becomes apparent is that many isolated and independent studies were conducted that made distinct contributions to our understanding of instructional media. Yet, the nature of the support program made it virtually impossible to carry out "programmatic" research that would have permitted the investigation of particular problems in depth, but instead required the precise specification of each analysis to be made in advance of funding. Consequently, generalization from one study to another, or to past research, is almost impossible. Except for an occasional grant (e.g., Gropper and Lumsdaine, 1961; Carpenter and Greenhill, 1963; Schramm and Oberholtzer, 1964), which permitted some flexibility in the research to be conducted, tight control was exercised over the design of the specific studies, and each stands as a unique experiment. Therefore, this mass of research, much of it worthless, some of it highly significant, has yet to be synthesized with earlier efforts into a set of operational generalizations.

PRESENT STATE OF THE ART

Where does research on instructional media stand today? Federal and foundation support has dried up. Interest in studying the effectiveness of television, programed instruction, and computer-assisted instruction as self-contained and exclusive instructional systems has declined. Educational voices are raised in lip service to the need for more research, but the words are backed by little overt effort to answer the need. The objective observer can't help but feel that media research today is in a state of tense suspension, ready to move but lacking an activator. Yet some important efforts are being quietly made that may have some implications for future progress in the field.

There is a consistent attempt by a number of researchers and theorists to discover the unique attributes of instructional media and their relationships to the performance of particular psychological functions with different kinds of learners. The study of this three-way interaction of stimulus, task, and learner is extremely complex, but some evidence is building up that could lead to a more precise understanding of the place of media in the instructional process. In particular, the discussions of this problem by Gagné (1965), Briggs, Campeau, Gagné, and May (1967), Salomon and Snow (1968), Briggs (1970), Allen (1970a), and Salomon (1970) have sharpened our appreciation of the implications of such research and some of its dimensions. The time is far off, if in fact it ever arrives, when we can identify an instructional problem and then faultlessly select the proper instructional mix to solve it. Yet the significance of the present research is that careful investigation of the design elements in mediated instruction are being made and that these searches are being conducted within a theoretical framework, thus laying a foundation for a theory of instructional media.

There is a second related development, rising largely out of the research with programed instruction, that is contributing to our knowledge of the proper use of instructional media. This is the research on the structure and sequencing of instruction with particular emphasis on the hierarchical characteristics of the content, the use of advance organizers, the degree of control exercised over the presentation of content, and other factors relating to learner actions that lead to increased learning. The study of these variables is still in its infancy, but insightful reviews of the progress to date have been made by Briggs (1968), Gagné and Rohwer (1969), Frase (1970), and Rothkopf (1970).

We also know a great deal more than we did a decade ago about the individualization of instruction and the factors that are involved in it. As pointed out previously, one major focus of research with media today is on the relationships of stimulus and task to the characteristics of the learners. It would appear that this emphasis is a direct result of the developments in programed instruction and the consequences of such attention by investigators into the psychology of learning and teaching. In a recent paper Snow and Salomon (1968) have considered the nature of learner aptitudes and its relevance for instructional media design and selection. Gagné (1967) has edited an imortant group of papers discussing the problem of individual differences as they relate to evidence from studies in different types of learning, problem solving, attention, and mental retardation. The present interest in individually prescribed instruction has centered more on development than on research, but the resultant attention has opened up the possibilities of a more precise investigation of the variables identified by such efforts.

In another area, the perhaps promising current concern with the identification and preparation of instructional objectives by diverse groups has resulted in both the accumulation of a vast amount of information about behavioral objectives and the emergence of a cult. The extensive literature on this topic has not been supported by research that probes the nature of the objectives and their application. Rather, their acceptance is one of faith and logic, and we might hope that this approval will be backed up with some disciplined analysis of the characteristics and effects of these objectives so that we will be able to predict their specific advantages when applied in particular instructional situations.

Some of the same observations may be made about the present enthusiasm for the systems approach to instruction. There is much interest, many models and flow-chart representations, but little tangible systematic research. The very logic of the approach as a technique sanctions its use in education, and it has been widely embraced as the answer to how to solve almost any problem. Its latest manifestation, the concept of "instructional development" (wherein the technique is used by an instructional team to solve instructional problems, develop curricula, and mediate specific courses) is a potentially powerful tool (Briggs, 1970). Yet apparently little effort is being made to submit the procedures evolved through verbal explication and practice to rigid and objective evaluation or to determine the effectiveness of alternative forms of the technique for particular problems or goals. Of course, the question of whether or not such techniques as the systems approach and the development of instructional objectives *can* be studied under such controlled conditions needs to be answered. It may be that they are not susceptible to this kind of assessment. The fact remains, however, that there is little evidence that such research is going on.

Finally, we need to look at the state of the art of research on factors that are external to the direct instructional situation but which influence the overall impact of media in the schools—factors such as the administrative procedures used in the organization of the school itself and/or the media program within the school, cost-effectiveness benefit considerations, the nature of innovative practices and their effects, the applications of media to teacher education, psychometric applications, and the design and development of equipment. With some notable exceptions, these areas have yet to be studied in a systematic way.

It is apparent that some sound foundations have been laid for future research efforts. Five decades of instructional media research have resulted in a mass of results still waiting for synthesis and interpretation and a knowledge about the media and their use that will be useful in accomplishing this task. Taken with the theories of learning and teaching that have evolved and the research in such areas as human information processing, perception, and human development, it may be possible to evolve a true theory of instructional media.

A LOOK
AT THE FUTURE

It is hazardous to try to look into the educational future. Too many unknown forces operate to make such predictions unreliable. Yet there may be some trends in the present that point the way to future research approaches and developments. The possible directions and probable research needs are not necessarily compatible.

There is some indication that the current thrust of federal and foundation research funding will emphasize larger-scale applied and developmental projects at the expense of the more carefully controlled and circumscribed basic experimental studies (Allen, 1970b). We might expect that these projects would be directed toward the solution of problems of a social rather than a theoretical nature in such high-commitment areas as the preschool child, disadvantaged learner, reading, and vocational education. If it is true that "the research follows the money," this redirection of research emphasis could well take place. Such an occurrence would probably put more emphasis on teams of researcher–developers that would produce generalizations and products of immediate usefulness.

There is reason to expect that the present growing attention being given to the study of the unique attributes of instructional media and their relationships to the characteristics of the learner and the nature of the instructional task will be increased in the future. The folly of assigning generalized and all-inclusive attributes to specific classes of media (e.g., television, film, print, computer-assisted instruction) under all conditions is finally being appreciated, and we should observe more intensive research efforts to discover how to design and manipulate the media so as to enhance their effectiveness under specified instructional conditions. Such research will occupy our attention for some time, leading to the evolution of taxonomies of unique media effects so that we can predict that the use of a particular instructional medium will lead to specified learning outcomes with different kinds of learners.

Going hand in hand with such objectives will be research on the development of a theoretical framework that will concentrate on "laying the foundations for a theory of instructional media" (Salomon, 1970), or an "optimal way of presenting and arranging information, which can be carefully controlled and managed." Lumsdaine (1963, 1968) has also made this point, stressing that the important problems of media research are the broader, theoretically oriented problems that are closely related to research on learning and, thus, must become a part of that discipline. There is every indication that efforts toward this goal will be implemented in the future.

Somehow our research must be directed to the problem of how we put together optimum instructional systems for meeting different objectives. As noted earlier, we are advocating the use of something called "the systems approach," but this is still only a verbal construct of steps to be taken in the solution of problems. We need to find out the best ways of implementing this system so that the choices made at each decision stage are the proper ones. So far, researchers have not come to grips with this problem.

Finally, it appears that we will need to spend

more time on the formulation of appropriate questions to ask and on the generation of hypotheses to test. Too often our research is based on expediency, the pursuit of a particular interest, or the attack on an inconsequential issue. Only by some systematic approach to the problem of what questions warrant research effort of what kind and with what payoffs can we best conserve and utilize our human research resources.

REFERENCES

Allen, W. H. Audio-visual communication. In C. W. Harris (ed.), *Encyclopedia of educational research.* (3rd ed.) New York: Macmillan, 1960. Pp. 123–130.

———, Categories of instructional media research. In G. Salomon and R. E. Snow (eds.), Commentaries on research in instructional media: An examination of conceptual schemes. *Viewpoints: Bulletin of the School of Education, Indiana University,* 1970, 46, 1–13. (a)

Allen, W. H. *Trends in instructional technology—the ERIC at Stanford 1970 planning report.* Stanford, Calif.: Stanford University, ERIC Clearinghouse on Educational Media and Technology, 1970.(b)

Briggs, L. J. *Sequencing of instruction in relation to hierarchies of competence.* Pittsburgh: American Institutes for Research, 1968.

———. *Handbook of procedures for the design of instruction.* Pittsburgh, Pa.: American Institutes for Research, Sept. 1970.

———, Campeau, P. L., Gagné, R. M., and May, M. A. *Instructional media: A procedure for the design of multimedia instruction, a critical review of research, and suggestions for future research.* Pittsburgh, Pa.: American Institutes for Research, 1967.

Carpenter, C. R. (Program Director). *Instructional film research reports.* Vol. I, NAVEXOS P-1220 (Technical Report No. SDC 269-7-36). Port Washington, L.I., N.Y.: U.S. Navy, Special Devices Center, 1953.

———, and Greenhill, L. P. (Program Directors). *Instructional film research reports.* Vol. II, NAVEXOS P-1543 (Technical Report No. SDC 269-7-61). Port Washington, L.I., N.Y.: U.S. Navy, Special Devices Center, 1956.

———, and Greenhill, L. P. *An investigation of closed-circuit television for teaching university courses.* Report No. 2. University Park, Pa.: Pennsylvania State University, 1958.

———, and Greenhill, L. P. *Comparative research on methods and media for presenting programed courses in mathematics and English.* University Park, Pa.: Pennsylvania State University, 1963.

Chu, G. C., and Schramm, W. *Learning from television: What the research says.* Stanford, Calif.: Stanford University, Institute for Communication Research, 1967.

Frase, L. T. Boundary conditions for mathemagenic behaviors. *Review of Educational Research,* 1970, 40, 337–347.

Freeman, F. N. (Ed.). *Visual education.* Chicago: University of Chicago Press, 1924.

Gagné, R. M. *The conditions of learning.* New York: Holt, Rinehart and Winston, 1965.

——— (Ed.). *Learning and individual differences.* Columbus, Ohio: Charles E. Merrill, 1967.

———, and Rohwer, W. D., Jr. Instructional psychology. *Annual Review of Psychology,* Vol. 20. Palo Alto, Calif.: Annual Reviews, 1969.

Gibson, J. J. (Ed.). *Motion picture testing and research.* Army Air Forces Aviation Psychology Program Research Report No. 7. Washington, D.C.: U.S. Government Printing Office, 1947.

———. A theory of pictorial perception. *AV Communication Review,* 1954, 2, 3–23.

Gropper, G. L., and Lumsdaine, A. A. *The use of student response to improve instruction: An overview.* Report No. 7. Pittsburgh, Pa.: Metropolitan Pittsburgh Educational Television Stations, WQED-WQEX, and American Institutes for Research, 1961.

Hoban, C. F., and van Ormer, E. B. *Instructional film research: 1918–1950.* Technical Report No. SDC 269-7-19, Instructional Film Research Program. Port Washington, L.I., N.Y.: U.S. Navy, Special Devices Center, 1950.

Hovland, C. I., Janis, I. L., and Kelley, H. H. *Communication and persuasion.* New Haven, Conn.: Yale University Press, 1953.

———, Lumsdaine, A. A., and Sheffield, F. D. *Experiments on mass communication.* Princeton, N.J.: Princeton University Press, 1949.

Kanner, J. H. Future trends in television teaching and research. *AV Communication Review,* 1957, 5, 513–527.

———. Teaching by television in the army—an overview. *AV Communication Review,* 1958, 6, 172–188.

Lange, P. C. (Ed.). *Programed instruction.* 66th Yearbook of the National Society for the Study of Education, Part II. Chicago: University of Chicago Press, 1967.

Lashley, K. S., and Watson, J. B. *A psychological study of motion pictures in relation to venereal disease campaigns.* Washington, D.C.: U.S. Interdepartmental Social Hygiene Board, 1922.

Lumsdaine, A. A. (Ed.). *Student response in programed instruction.* Publication 943. Washington, D.C.: National Academy of Sciences–National Research Council, 1961.

———. Instruments and media of instruction. In N. L. Gage (Ed.), *Handbook of research on teaching.* Chicago: Rand McNally, 1963. Pp. 583–682.

———. Instructional research: Some aspects of its status, defects, and needs. In H. J. Klausmeier and G. T. O'Hearn (eds.), *Research and development toward the improvement of education.* Madison, Wis.: Dembar Educational Research Services, 1968. Pp. 95–101.

May, M. A., and Lumsdaine, A. A. *Learning from films.* New Haven, Conn.: Yale University Press, 1958.

Reid, J. C., and MacLennan, D. W. *Research in instructional television and film.* Washington, D.C.: U.S. Government Printing Office, 1967.

Rothkopf, E. Z. The concept of mathemagenic activities. *Review of Educational Research,* 1970, *40,* 325–336.

Saettler, P. *A history of instructional technology.* New York: McGraw-Hill, 1968.

Salomon, G. What does it do to Johnny? A cognitive-functionalistic view of research on media. In G. Salomon and R. E. Snow (eds.), Commentaries on research in instructional media: An examination of conceptual schemes. *Viewpoints: Bulletin of the School of Education, Indiana University,* 1970, *46,* 33–62.

_____, and Snow, R. E. The specification of film attributes for psychological and educational research purposes. *AV Communication Review,* 1968, *16,* 225–244.

Schramm, W., and Oberholtzer, K. E. *The context of instructional television: Summary report of research findings, the Denver–Stanford project.* Denver, Colo., and Stanford, Calif.: Denver Public Schools and Stanford University, 1964.

Snow, R. E., and Salomon, G. Aptitudes and instructional media. *AV Communication Review,* 1968, *16,* 341–357.

Learning as a Communication Process

Hower J. Hsia

LEARNING AS A COMMUNICATION PROCESS

> *Learning is the modification of a behavior pattern on the basis of experience so as to achieve specific antientropic ends. In these higher forms of communication organisms the environment, considered as the past experience of the individual, can modify the pattern of behavior into one which in some sense or other will deal more effectively with the future environment. In other words, the organism is not like the clockwork nomad of Leibnitz with its one-established harmony with the universe, but actually seeks a new equilibrium with the universe and its future contingencies (p. 48). . . . The physiological condition for memory and hence for learning seems to be a certain continuity of organization, which allows the alterations produced by outer sense impressions to be retained as more or less permanent changes of structure or function (p. 56).*
>
> Wiener, 1954

Amid many controversial learning theories, many who are not well versed in learning seem to be at a loss to understand simple concepts such as whether learning is "all or none" or "incremental" (Jones, 1962; Estes, 1960) and whether learning must be a conscious effort or a homeostatic function (Young, 1964, p. 299). Since "no single universally accepted 'basic' learning theory exists" (Hunt, 1962, p. 47), learning may be termed the acquisi-

Hower J. Hsia teaches at Texas Technological College, Lubbock, Texas.

tion, retention, and transfer of information, all involved in an antientropic process. Acquisition is

the primary phenomenon of learning, is a progressive, incremental change in the proficiency of performance by an organism. The direction, rate, and extent of change in the proficiency of performance are functions for continuous presentation of the conditions under which measurement of the change in performance is made (Brogden, 1951, p. 569).

Learning, put more simply, is "the change in performance, associated with practice and not explicable on the basis of fatigue, of artifacts or measurement, or of receptor and effector changes" (Hovland, 1951, p. 613). Or, learning is the process by which an activity originates or is changed through reacting to an encountered situation, provided that the characteristics of the change in activity cannot be explained on the basis of native response tendencies, maturation, or temporary state of the organism (e.g., fatigue, drugs, etc.). Thus, for psychologists, learning is concerned with how behavior patterns are established and changed; for students of communications, all changes are the results of information processing, and learning is a process of receiving, storing, and transferring information embodied in any communication, processed by any modality or modalities, with a resultant modification of existing behavior. Hunt (1962) specifies concept learning as (1) any situation that involves the "acquisition or utilization, or both, of a common response to dissimilar stimuli," (2) concept formation, (3) concept selection, and (4) concept identification. All these may be termed as outcomes of information processing. Hovland (1951) was perhaps the first to analyze learning as a communication process.

From a cybernetist's point of view, learning is the reduction of entropy or uncertainty (Wiener, 1954) in the communication process. For Wiener, the very purpose of processing information is for an organism to adapt to the environment—a process of biological survival. Every bit of new information creates a disturbance within the organism. To

reestablish equilibrium after the absorption of new information, some kind of strategy is called for. The strategy varies in accordance with a host of factors, but the general procedure is usually the same, for example, the TOTE unit, which stands for test, operate, test again, and exit (Miller, Galanter, and Pribram, 1960). The very notion of TOTE unit involves selection, and the notion of selection involves strategy. " 'Information' in most, if not all, of its connotations, seems to rest upon the notion of selection power" (Cherry, 1957).

As man is immersed in information, selection is also a homeostatic function against information overloading, as James Miller (1963) demonstrated.

The selection power is determined by the strategy a student adopts, and the adoption of any strategy is decided largely by the consideration of the cost involved in information processing. To explore information processing strategy, we may use the entertaining question posed by Ashby (1956):find a particular atom in the universe, which contains about 100,000,000 galaxies; each galaxy contains 100,000,000,000 solar systems, each solar system contains about 300,000 bodies like the earth, the earth contains about 1,000,000,000,000,000,000,000,000 dust particles, and each particle contains about 10,000,000,000,000,000 atoms.

The student can proceed, Ashby suggests, in one of two ways: (1) he can examine one atom at a time; even with the fastest computer, he would have to spend a century to find the atom; or (2) he can divide the number of atoms in half each time, and ask the question, "Is the atom in this half?" He can find the exact atom in about 4 minutes. This is precisely the strength of information theory; but, of course, few worldly phenomena are arranged in the best possible dichotomous order within an unidimensional system that can be consistently divided by two.

Not only is the selection power manifest in the encoding and decoding processes but, in most cases, it determines the acceptance or rejection of information. The rarity, exclusiveness, or surprise value of information, all of which can be expressed in terms of information or uncertainty, determines how information is to be processed. The exclusiveness of information can be seen in a news "scoop" or an invention. Exclusiveness based on the rarity of information has greater surprise value. Selective power is dependent upon exclusiveness and prediction power (Gabor, 1951). These are actually two sides of a coin: exclusiveness indicates uncertainty and prediction implies redundancy.

Many principles propounded in information theory (Shannon and Weaver, 1949) with only slight modification seem eminently suitable for the formulation of a general communication theory. Information theory, which has had worldwide impact in many diverse disciplines (Dahling, 1962), is derived from several branches of science, notably cybernetics, a synthesized theory of society—human, animal, and machine (Wiener, 1948). It may also prove to be a means of solving many fundamental problems in human communications and learning.

Controversy Over Information Theory

MacKay (1952) points out that general information is concerned with the problem of measuring changes in knowledge, and communication is the activity of replicating representations.

> Amount of selective information is evidently a measure of the statistical rarity of a representation and has no direct logical connection with its form of content, except in cases where they affect its statistical status. One word which was unexpected could yield more selective information to a receiver than a whole paragraph which he knew he would receive.

Precisely because information theory is based upon the statistical rarity of elements in any sign, symbol, or signal system, it is both versatile and handicapped: the versatility of information theory in communication and other research has been clearly demonstrated; its handicaps include tedious computation and the complete separation of information from the idea of meaning or significance.

Attneave (1959, p. 88) has warned that information theory is "useful in the study of the organism's information-handling processes, [but] other techniques may often be more useful and more appropriate." Mandelbrot (1965) has commented on its inconvenience, too.

But the usefulness of the theory to communications research lies in the possibility it affords of producing a general, systematized communication theory dealing with information processing. It is not, as G. A. Miller (1953, p. 119) points out, a panacea: the deficiencies in its practical application are fairly well known. Cronbach (1955) seems to offer more despair than hope:

> The power of information theory to stimulate scientific thought, and psychological thought in particular, is simply demonstrated by the number of projects and publications which Shannon's work has inspired.... Many studies begin with insight obtained by looking on a certain psychological process as a communication system. These analogies from the information model lead very often to significant generalizations. The language of information theory has been suggestive in our studies of theory of mental tests, for example, but when we attempted to formulate our generalization in the Shannon mathematics rather than simply as analogies, we ran into difficulties. Some results were unreasonable. Others were reasonable, but we could not defend them as more correct than alternative results derived from other mathematical formulation (p. 14).

Notwithstanding all these limitations, the application of information theory to communication research is primarily based upon the following assertions: first, information theory offers the best possibility of formulating a general, systematized communication model and theory, universally applicable. Second, by employing information theory it is possible to determine an optimal information level for any given individual, or any system under a given condition and at a given time; such knowledge can make it possible to curtail the effort, cost, and time involved in information processing.

Learning Theories and Information Theory

The concept of learning is closely related to information theory, if learning is represented by orderly changes resulting from occurrence of events. To illustrate, we choose two major psychological theories of learning: reinforcement theory derived from Thorndike's law of effect, and contiguity theory based upon association. No reinforcement or association is possible without information processing; therefore, information, or rather, communication is the foundation of any learning theory and learning as well.

Information theory is also consistent with the fundamental assumptions of learning theories. To further illustrate it with Thorndike's law of learning (Thorndike, 1932), (1) the law of effect—a connection between a stimulus and response; whether it is strengthened or weakened is primarily determined by a subsequent satisfying or annoying state of affairs—describes the resultant behavior as changed by input information; (2) the law of exercise—the connection is strengthened with use or weakened with disuse—describes the functions of information redundancy; and (3) the law of readiness—readiness of neurons to conduction in order to make connections—describes the initiating function of the central nervous system, analogous to clearing the memory in a computer. (Thorndike's notion on "readiness of neurons" is questionable for neurons are charged and discharged in a fraction of a second, although they may be fatigued. Thorndike might have suggested the mental state of readiness.)

At this stage, it may be desirable to compare further some other learning theories with information theory. Hilgard, who examined the differences in learning theories, dealt with environmentalism–nativism, the part–whole problem, the emphasis upon reaction or cognition, the selected physical model, and the problem of historical versus contemporary explanation. None of the issues raised by Hilgard can be divorced from information processing. Thorndike's connectionism (1932), as we have seen, is strictly an information-processing model. Hilgard's estimate of Thorndike's position on typical problems of learning in terms of capacity, practice, motivation,

understanding, transfer, and forgetting are, in terms of information theory, information processing, transformation, and equivocation. Guthrie's continuous conditioning (1952), dealing primarily with the principles of association, discrimination, reinforcement and cue, is directly transformable to information-processing terms. Hull's systematic behavior (1943), although not strictly a learning model, is primarily based upon four fundamental variables: drive, cue, response, and reward. Drive is concerned with prestored information, both cue and response are communication, and reward is the reinforcement information. The Carr–Robinson laws of association of modern functionalism in the form of instigating and instigatable processes are easily recognizable as information processes.

The Gestalt law of Pragnanz (Hilgard, 1958) postulates that a "good" gestalt has such properties as regularity, simplicity, stability, and so on, which are almost identical to information theory properties. By varying the entropy and redundancy, the major Pragnanz laws (the laws of similarity, proximity, closure, and good continuation) become simple. The Gestalt main contention of the trace theory features past experience, selectivity, reactivity, recall or recognition, "insight," and so on, which are all within the domain of information theory. Kurt Lewin's topological and vector theory (1936) exemplifies to a certain extent the basic assumption of information theory, the quantification of information, and, furthermore, the direction of the vector force. According to Tolman (1932) only organisms can learn, evidently because only organisms can process and store information. The summarization of Tolman's laws (capacity laws, laws relating to the nature of the material, and laws relative to the manner of presentation) presents a nearly complete summary of information theory in learning, or at least the analogy of information theory and learning. For example, the list of capacity laws is (1) formal means–end capacity; (2) discriminating and manipulating capacities; (3) retentivity; (4) means–end capacities needed for alternative routes, detours, and so on; (5) ideational capacities; and (6) creative instability. All these are entropic properties in different channels with different capacity and at different stages.

Taking the laws relating to the nature of the material, the list consists of (1) togetherness, (2) fusibility, (3) other gestalt-like laws, (4) interrelations among the spatial, temporal, and other characters of the alternatives, and (5) characters in the material favoring new closures and expansions of the field. In the terminology of information theory, all these are the variation of entropy and redundancy, that is, correlational, distributional, sequential entropies and redundancies. Even Piaget's (1975) work on problem solving and Skinner's (1957) on conditioning can be interpreted in terms of information theory.

Furthermore, the laws governing the manner of presentation consist of (1) frequence and recency, (2) revival after extinction, primacy, and distributed repetition, (3) motivation, (4) no "effect" but "emphasis," and (5) temporal orders and sequences in the presentation of certain of the already given alternatives and the true solution. Each is a manipulation of information and/or redundancy in an attempt to reduce equivocation and noise, thereby cutting down the cost of information processing.

This exposition may very well overgeneralize many schools of learning theories. However, the great need for information theory in the field of education seems to be a sufficient justification for at least a concerted effort to unite the two. Information theory, as Muses (1958) says of another topic, "represents a type of thing in which brilliance, validity, and constructive values all combine to yield an approach of significant synthesis and catholicity—an approach increasingly observable, the spirit of which can well become what future historians may finally deem the finest overall contribution to humanity's advancement by this technological twentieth century."

Application of Information Theory to Learning

"Information theory has subtly influenced the thinking of many behavioral scientists. Not only has it affected their analysis of certain kinds of data, but also their choice of experimental problems. Such influences cannot be succinctly described or tabulated" (Luce et al., 1960). But our problem remains: how to apply information theory to the teaching–learning situation? The application of information theory can best be illustrated with the popular "Twenty Questions" TV show, implicitly suggesting the existence of 2^{20} states. Since the answer is either yes or no, 20 well-phrased questions can provide 20 bits of information, or 1,048,576 possible outcomes. An experienced questioner could reduce the uncertainty to half with each question. In Garner's (1962) terms, information is obtained by a reduction of uncertainty, which is the potential information.

Ashby (1956) demonstrates the application of information theory with traffic lights: if traffic lights show the combinations of red, red–yellow, green, and yellow with a duration of 25, 5, 25, and 5 seconds, respectively, a motorist would find the lights in various states with frequencies of 42, 8, 42, and 8 percent, respectively. By using Shannon's formula, entropy (H), the information presented, would be $-\Sigma P_i \log P_i = 1.63$ bits of information. Miller and Selfridge (1950) made what is believed to be the first attempt at using the information theory concept in the study of learning. Lists of words are constructed by the Shannonian procedure with various orders of approximation to English; the orders of approximation are found to affect the ability in learning the lists. Immediate recall for lists for fixed length is found to be affected by the similarity of the lists to actual English (Van de Geer, 1957). Immediate memory span increases linearly with the increased order of approximation (Marks and Jack, 1952). Control of sequential constraints of letter sequences is said to facilitate the learning rate to a greater extent than control of either meaning-fulness or pronunciability (Carterette and Jones, 1962). These are, without exception, examples of the effective use of redundancy principle (Hsia, 1973). In the traditional concept of learning, the order of approximation is an association ex-perimentation. The order of approximation to En-glish has a linear function with association—the more it resembles English, the easier it is to retain and recall.

In a number of studies, uncertainty prior to the response is found to be an important variable; greater response uncertainty leads, as expected, to slower learning (Riley, 1952; Brogden and Schmidt, 1954; Adelson, Muckler, and Williams, 1955; all cited by Garner, 1962). In a recognition experiment with respect to learning and perception in which the subjects are to learn lists of monosyllables either 8, 16, 32, or 64 words long (corresponding to 3, 4, 5, and 6 bits), it is found that learning is a function of the length of list; the longer lists would be less well learned and recognition would be poorer (Bruner, Miller, and Zimmerman, 1955). All these experi-ments support the idea that the quantity of informa-tion is inversely proportional to recognition or learning. When information exceeds the information-processing capacity of an individual, poor learning results. It is, however, not necessarily true that less uncertainty or information always leads to better learning when time is taken into consideration for learning also obeys the law of diminishing return (Thurstone, 1930). "In the majority of learning curves, the amount of attain-ment gained per unit of practice decreases as practice increases." When the input information is reduced to a minimum, which would appear to make the learning task easy, learning is likely to suffer because of the waste of information-processing capacity. Demonstrably all learning theorists work on the concept of information con-trol and manipulation. The traditional conditioning, reinforcing, and stimulus–response concepts are a classical example of information control. To

achieve the most efficient learning requires only subtle and sophisticated manipulation of informa-tion. Evidently, all learning theories deal with the optimal amount of information that can be pro-cessed through various channels and the central nervous system (CNS), stored in the memory sys-tem, and retrieved (Hsia, 1968a, 1971).

Control of Information in Learning: The Teaching Information Output

Learning and teaching are the controlled form of information processing. The efficient control of information results in efficient learning. To what extent information should be controlled to produce the best learning is of primary importance. To control is partly to select, and the selective process is forever at work; for example, a teacher selects teaching materials and the best method of presenta-tion, and a student selects from the presented instruction to his best advantage. The question is then, "What are the criteria for selection?" At a fundamental level, for example, no one memorizes prose by starting at the beginning and going through it line by line. "More often we repeat lines in small groups or skip from one part to the next" (Deese, 1958). This suggests that the units of information carry different weight, and the CNS has bias in its selection of both input and output information. Generally, the more associable, redundant, and novel information can be memorized more readily.

Controllability is based upon the following as-sumptions: (1) any meaningful set of signs or sym-bols can be optimally coded; (2) any information can be differentiated; (3) the channel capacity of any modality can be known; (4) any information processing is a continuous process, assuming that "action upon the environment is regulated by a continuing process of perception in which the perceived external reality is compared with an end state to be achieved" (Dechert, 1965). This is particularly true with learning, for learning is a continuous process without bound and with the end of life as the ultimate limit. (5) Information redundancy can be varied in accordance with a student's capacity and condition to achieve maximum efficiency. These assumptions are more or less substantiated facts, except for the differentiability of information, for which many writers have attempted to work out some reasonable categorization schemes. The implication of these assumptions is clear: Learning is not an all-or-none process but a gradual increment of information. Although studying all-or-none processes, Estes (1960) points out that learning appears sometimes to be an essentially continuous and sometimes a sharply discontinuous process. Recent studies have further supported the claim of the continuity of learning, and repudiated the "path independent" theory of learning; that is, the probability of success at trail n is independent of success on trail $n - 1$ (Hunt, 1962; Anderson, 1959, 1960; Suppes, 1960). Since learning in its simple definition is only the additive information in the CNS, instrumental teaching is likely to be the ideal method to carry out the teaching task, in view of the fact that the probability of eliciting a correct response increases with successive trials (Atkinson and Calfee, 1965). The controlling process starts at the very beginning of teaching information coding in the appropriate sign, symbols, and/or signal system, presented through a variety of forms of transmission to be readily processed by the student. The interplay of the feedback information and new information makes it a never-ending process.

Teaching and Learning Processes

This fundamental model of teaching–learning is no different from the basic communication system model (Rothstein, 1958). Based upon a number of communication models (Broadbent, 1958; Chase, 1967; Norman, 1969, pp. 34, 90, 154; Roy, 1962; Sperry, 1967; Welford, 1965, p. 6; Westley and MacLean, 1957; Zemanek, Kretz, and Angyan, 1961), teaching–learning as a communication

model can be worked out (Fig. 1). The teacher, seeking information from all available sources, has access only to information of a very limited scope in the information universe. He must select, in terms of not only his time, efforts, and objectives, among others, but in terms of the reception, retention, and logicalization, among others, of his student. Since any communication suffers from noise, internal or external, and equivocation (loss) (Hsia, 1973), the teacher must develop an an adequate protection for his instructions; therefore, he must work out a redundancy system (Hsia, 1973) to ensure the passage of information between transmission and reception in the predictably noisy channels without too much loss. For the most efficient communication (information transmission and reception), it is imperative to devise a code system that presumably takes care of all the problems briefly expounded above. Encoding thus is the most important factor in all communication (Garner, 1970) and, in fact, holds the key to the success of teaching and learning.

The variation in the mode of presentation is but the combination of a variety of different redundancies. The encoding of teaching information within each sign, symbol, or signal system has internal redundancy; within each channel, within-channel redundancy; and between two channels, between-channel redundancy (Hsia, 1968a, b). The choice of the form of transmission is assumed to present the information in the most advantageous manner; for example, one never presents a building blueprint in the oral form. Information is coded in such a way as to facilitate the information processing in both the student's audiovisual modalities and the CNS, to be readily absorbed, processed, and retained by the student. In any form of student feedback, it is safe to assume that the teaching information has been at least partially processed. This suggests the existence of information stored and retained in the CNS. Any feedback information coming from the student is, to a certain extent, redundant with teaching information.

Information processing is subject to a number of environmental, social, physical, and cognitive factors that may facilitate or hinder the orderly flow of information. Environmental factors such as room, light, seating, and temperature affect information processing to varying degrees. It can be very well assumed that optimum environmental conditions would facilitate information processing. For example, a sound-insulated room would constitute a better environmental condition than would a noninsulated room; a room of moderate temperature is better than a hot or cold one. The control of environmental factors is to insulate external noise from information processing or to render it harmless. With respect to cognitive factors, the same principle applies. Propositions such as "the student is motivated to learn" and "he loves to study" are the internal mechanisms that clear the internal information path. They serve to either eliminate all noise factors entirely or at least to suppress or control them, thus making the normal or optimal information processing possible. These factors would affect not only the modalities, but also the CNS.

Physical factors such as fatigue, the biological cyclic functions of working efficiency (Luce, 1971), health, body functions, and modality, among others, influence information processing; however, social factors, as shown in Figure 1, have only indirect effects upon information processing and are mostly in one way or another related to cognitive factors. Cognitive factors are generally a problematic area for information theory to deal with, as cognitive and psychological factors are not readily quantifiable.

Student Thought and Output Processes

Only in the permanent memory system do thought processes take place. The thought process is defined as the active association, discrimination, and selection of information to determine its relevancy, meaningfulness, and signification in a logicalizing operation of induction, deduction, and evaluation. It implies also the retention and transfer of information when the need arises. The whole processing operation may only take a fraction of a microsecond, and may be assumed to take place simultaneously. The difference between the information perceived (at the receptor level, Fig. 1) and the information that actually reaches the long-term memory is readily seen, and indicates the inequality of teaching information and learned information. In the very process of association, discrimination, and selection, and the later operation of logicalization, the information is changed rapidly as it is internalized or fantasized. The overlapping of new information upon existing information and memory decay, which supposedly takes place immediately upon arrival of information in the permanent system, introduce noise, error, and ambiguity.

In the permanent memory system, it is assumed that the information retained can be recalled whenever the demand for it is received. Such a demand activates the high command (Hernandez-Peon, 1961) to engage in a memory search, to retrieve information from the permanent memory system, and to reconstitute all information, including new information sought from other sources. Finally, the high command in a reverse process of input mobilizes appropriate effectors to respond— that is, the feedback for the teacher.

Natural Adjustment in Information Processing

The selective mechanism in each level of the CNS prompts Broadbent (1958) to advance his "filter theory," which presupposes the existence of a filter at the entrance to the nervous system that passes some classes of stimuli but rejects others. Since man's information-processing capacity is limited, he argues, a filter placed early in his nervous system selects only part of the information. The filter tends to show preference on channels carrying novel events. Broadbent is essentially arguing the assumption that "a nervous system acts

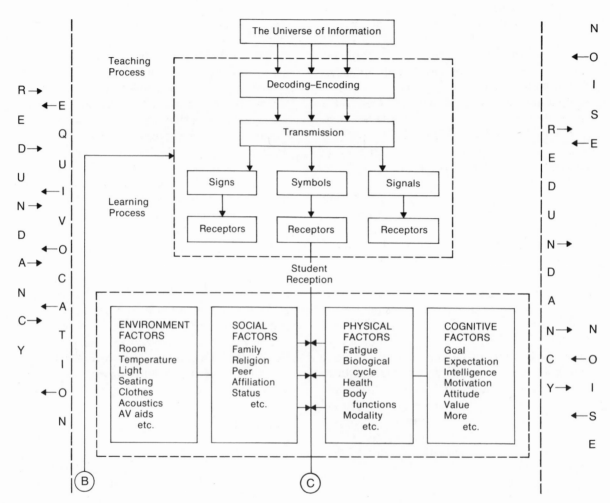

Figure 1
Teaching–learning as a communication process.

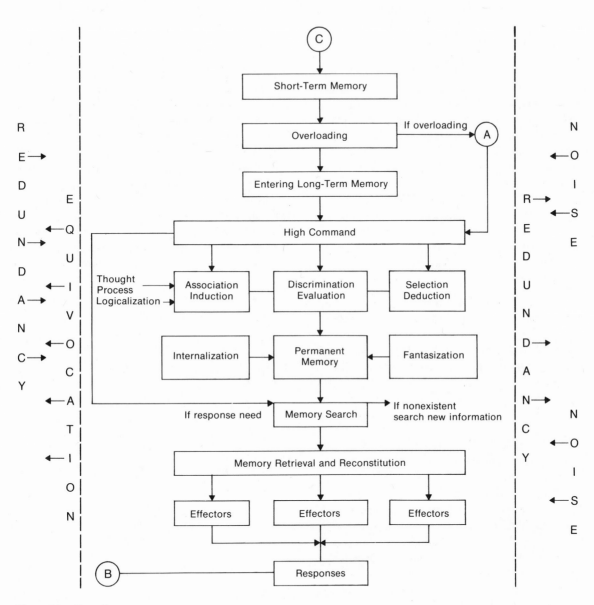

Figure 1 *(continued)*

to some extent as a single communication channel." From the viewpoint of information theory, it may be safe to conclude that the output of information is the linear function of the input until the channel capacity is reached. When input information is overwhelming the organism or institution with an oversupply through either one channel or a combination of channels, the CNS with its limited information-processing capacity is unable to process the vast amount of information in spite of the individual's conscious effort to process it. Then natural adjustment mechanisms, many of them homeostatic in nature, take over the processing operation, in whole or in part. For any organism or organization, the defensive mechanisms, triggered by information overloading, bring forth a number of phenomena in the order of the amount of overloading (Miller, 1963).

1. Omission: an organism simply stops processing information periodically whenever there is overloading.
2. Error: an organism processes information incorrectly, and does not make the necessary adjustments.
3. Queuing: an organism delays responses during the peak load, and places information in temporary storage.
4. Filtering: an organism systematically selects (or omits) certain categories of information according to some priority scheme or bias.
5. Approximation: an organism approximates information in order to process it, whereby precision and accuracy of information suffers.
6. Utilization of multiple channels: an organism instinctively utilizes all available channels to process information.
7. Escape: an organism mentally leaves a situation entirely or takes other steps to effectively cut off the flow of information.

How the adjusting mechanism works is not all very clear. Presumably, overloading of information, based on incomplete experimental proof, will immediately trigger the natural adjustment mechanism into operation, unconsciously or consciously (Fig. 2).

No scholar would ever claim that all the information-processing phenomena are known or can be manipulated; however, information, input or output, (teaching and learning), can be controlled at every stage of the information processing except the physiological systems (modalities and the CNS). Since learning is a permanent operation, that is, man never ceases to receive information, it is clear that the information retained in the CNS changes all the time; therefore, the rate of, and the ratio between, redundancy and noise change as well. To sum up, this much can be said: control of information is possible, because learning information can be broken down into

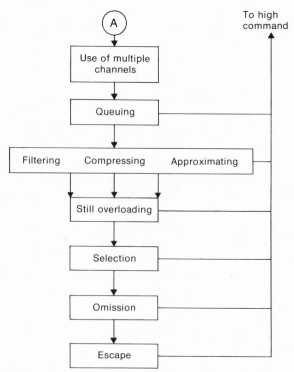

Figure 2
Defensive mechanism against information overloading in the memory system.

segments to be processed at a given time. That is exactly what information theory can be assigned to do and can do effectively.

Trade-off in Teaching and Learning

One of the most important concepts in education must be explored first before we examine the fundamental communication laws implicit in any information processing. This concept can be simply stated as follows: education is a coalition in which members—teachers, students, students' parents, and taxpayers—all have conflicting demands and interests; they must be reconciled to reach an idealized but somehow compromised situation where the payoff in terms of learning can be kept at the maximum while the cost involved can be kept at the relative minimum.

Conflicting demands and interests exist even though teachers and students may have a common set of goals. Teachers frequently require a student to spend more time and effort than the student thinks desirable.

A student would normally desire to expend less effort and time (both may be expressed in terms of cost). The conflict between teachers and students is not necessarily limited to this factor. Teachers often attempt the output of as much teaching information as possible because it is his duty or obligation; students, with the possible exception of a few who are highly motivated, often try to process as little information as possible. The "conflict of demands" is not necessarily limited to the amount of information, either, but may also include the interest, value, and significance of the information as judged by teachers and students from different perspectives and vantage points.

One attribute of learning is the student's allocation of time, which is another variable or concept frequently neglected. Time determines the information-processing rate and amount, which are directly related to learning. The allocated time for studying is predetermined, but subject to adjust-

ment under various learning–teaching or communication situations. Generally, the student assesses the interest and difficulty of the learning task and determines the level of attention and the length of time that he needs to attend to the task. Time allocation is just as important as allocation of funds for any organization; only the payoff in this case is learning, and the cost is effort and time. Effort can be termed as a time factor, too, assuming that the more difficult the task, the more time necessary to process the information (Hsia, 1968a, b). The evaluation of the task for which the length of time is determined can be probed with some known attributes. Usually, the student measures the value and interest of the information, determines its difficulty level against his goal, aspiration, or expectation, and then decides how much time he needs for study or how much attention he must pay if he is in a classroom situation.

Utilization of Information Theory in Learning

Information theory consists of five major concepts, which can be taken also as variables or attributes for learning: (1) the amount of information in terms of entropy or uncertainty; (2) equivocation in terms of the loss of information; (3) noise in terms of error or unwanted information; (4) redundancy in terms of relative information as the ratio between the maximum possible uncertainty and actual uncertainty; and (5) cost in terms of the time and effort that are needed to process information. The basic idea expounded is almost too simple to be true; the mathematical formulation of the theory is simple but sound, the fundamental concepts are easy to grasp; and the information-processing model seems to be logical, parsimonious, efficient, economic, and predictive.

The prevailing criticism of information theory is concentrated upon its inapplicability to the theories of personality, ability, motivation, and attitude. According to popular belief, the fitting of information theory into learning seems highly unlikely, if not impossible. Addressing ourselves to this problem, we wish to make some further exploration of the relations between information theory and the psychology of learning.

"By definition all human abilities are learned. Beyond this, the learning of certain abilities makes possible the learning of other abilities. For example, speaking words normally precedes reading words, and reading normally precedes spelling the words" (Klausmeier, 1961). This statement assumes the existence of prestored information in the memory; therefore, learning is information acquired in the human permanent memory storage system. Any acquired information has to be processed first before entering the permanent system; within the system information processing is continuous, as new information keeps coming in from all information-processing modalities that an organism possesses. Furthermore, to use Klausmeier's term, information processing involves three key items— "ability, capacity and learning." Ability is further subdivided into cognitive, psychomotor, and affective domains. Within the cognitive domain there are processes of perceiving, remembering, discriminating, integrating, abstracting, generalizing, evaluating, imagining, thinking, problem solving, inventing, and creating. Within the psychomotor domain there are processes of strength, speed, impulsion, precision, coordinates, flexibility, vocal–circulatory–respiratory endurance, and muscular endurance. Both domains are information processing in various stages or all stages. Within the affective domain there are some "unknown" processes—"unknown" because the outcomes of the affective domain are mainly in the forms of feelings, attitudes, values, and motives, personality and character. In the terminology of information theory, they are all, in one form or another, feedback information. For information theory does not confine feedback information to verbal or written responses only, but defines it as all sorts of reactions, responses, and information-seeking be-

havior generated by the input information. In other words, feedback is the output caused or generated by the input information.

This may seem to be an oversimplification of learning, one of the most complex of human behaviors. However, from a theoretical point of view, information theory is a concise, compact, and coherent theory that comprises both traditional and modern theories of learning; from a practical point of view, information theory presents a manageable, feasible, and highly sophisticated model for the measurement and explication of learning behavior. One must realize that information theory is void of discussion of personality, motivation, value, and attitude; yet clearly the quantity of uncertainty, the loss of information, the added, unwanted information, relative information, and cost are integral parts of the attributes of the learning process. Unrefutably, the gradual evolution of personality, motivation, value, and attitude formulation involves information processing. In other words, what brings about a certain personality characteristic is a matter of information transference from the outside world to the permanent memory system, where personality, motivation, and attitude are germinated and stabilized. Again, information processing is a dynamic, never-ending process. To a great extent, the possible building of personality, motivation, attitude, and value can be explained through the use of the theory of information processing. Many educational psychologists object to the application of information theory to learning. At best, they claim, the use of information theory is an oversimplification, dealing only with probabilistic learning; at worst, the more vehement objectors assert, the two are entirely unrelated. A clear understanding of the true nature of information theory, however, reveals the close connection that does indeed exist. Take motivation for example: explained in terms of information theory, it is information generated from the permanent memory system to match with information existing and/or possibly realizable in the outside world. The theoretical aspect of this concept is beyond the scope of this paper. However, taking again Klausmeier's major topics in motivation for example, the relations between information-processing motivation may be made clear. These topics are all information-processing, information-seeking, and information-gaining behavior. Individual personality, attitude, and intelligence can be treated in the same manner. Within each space or domain, every attribute within the framework of information theory can be finely differentiated, quantified, and weighted; this has been propounded extensively in the previous sections.

Unquestionably, information theory can be used in education, in addition to the function it performed in the fields of biology, engineering, chemistry, physics, psychology, and other sciences. The simplicity of information theory is its strongest merit, yet also its weakest point. Probably, Hunt (1962) and Garner (1962) to a great extent laid down the foundation of information theory for education. Yet much more work needs to be done if information theory is to claim a legitimate place in education and learning theories. If optimism is permissible, we feel that information theory may even have a greater objective, the synthesization of learning theories. Before joining the battle, we can probably view the diversified theories of learning with objectivity. Conflicting learning theories have indeed precipitated the boom of research papers, many of which have intensified the war between rival learning theorists. The adoption of the information theory concept may resolve some of the differences between learning theories of different schools, and pave a way, if possible, for the integration of learning theories. A general learning theory may emerge as a result of using the information theory approach to teaching–learning.

Research findings in learning have grown to such proportions that even the use of computer information retrieval methods has not kept pace with the documentation problem. And findings regarding learning efficiency associated with various charac-teristics and functions of teaching and learning methods simply produce a chaotic world of learning. Research efforts seem to be directed increasingly toward diversified objectives, as is evidenced by the number of theoretical expositions and experiments conducted on divergent theoretical bases.

Any comparison on the basis of categorized findings is meaningless unless the exact quantity of teaching–learning information is known; more such studies can add but little to the controversy already supported by masses of experimental evidence produced on both sides of the issue. An attempt will be made to simplify the description of the whole teaching–learning process. When learning is viewed as information processing, some fundamental principles of information processing must be observed. These principles are derived mainly from information theory and physiological theories; they are intended to explain communication phenomena in all phases of information processing.

1. Capacity principle: any information-processing organism, modality, channel, or medium is subject to the limit of capacity.
2. Redundancy principle: the redundancy law specifies the optimum rate of redundancy for any information-processing organism, modality, channel, medium, and content with all its semiotic properties.
3. Equivocation principle: there is information loss in any information-processing channel. This principle is similar, if not identical, to the second law of thermodynamics with all its essential characteristics.
4. Ambiguity principle: there exists noise in any information processing, and it can be self-generating or caused by some outside sources.
5. Cost principle: the cost principle specifies the effort and time that are needed for information processing.

These fundamental laws of information processing have been to a large extent disregarded in much research. Many researchers, probably trying for simplicity, treat the information process as unidimensional and discrete. This is never an accurate appraisal of the communication process, either practically or theoretically. Information processing is a very complicated process with all these communication laws at work simultaneously in a fast-changing, volatile state.

CONCLUSION

The fundamental problem in communication and learning is to achieve maximum communication efficiency and dependability. Perfect information transmission and reception (perfect communication) is only theoretically possible; by perfect communication is meant that in which the information being transmitted, processed, and fed back sustains no equivocation or error.

The rationale for employing information theory principles in basic communication and learning research seems to be justifiable on these grounds:

1. The basic concepts of information theory are applicable to the quantitative aspect of communication and learning. Yet they are also highly general. Wiener (1948) regards all systems as information-processing mechanisms. History, culture, and civilization may be thought of as societal information processing. An excellent indicator of cultural achievement, for example, is a person's vocabulary (Meier, 1962, p. 116), and the expansion of vocabulary appears to obey information-processing principles precisely.

2. From a universalistic point of view, information theory is not restricted to any particular language; it deals with basic communication elements rather than the structure of particular communication systems; it is adaptable to any sign, signal, or symbol system.

3. From a physiological point of view, information theory works in a manner similar to the assumed functions of the central nervous system, in which neurons appear to function exactly as information theory predicts (Von Neumann, 1958; Bell, 1962).

4. From a pragmatic point of view, only information theory endeavors to quantify information of various kinds in a systematic way; thus, it is capable of dealing with all possible communication functions, including information exchange, storage, and transfer.

5. From a scholarly point of view, only information theory, of all other theories in communications, offers a unified, standardized terminology with appropriate measures, rules, and functions. There is reason to hope that a set of communications laws based upon information theory principles may eventually be developed.

Any purposive communication has an intrinsic objective: it is what Weaver calls "the effectiveness problem" (Shannon and Weaver, 1949, p. 96). Its prerequisite is, however, "the technical problem," to obtain maximum communication efficiency and dependability; the former indicates minimum equivocation (information loss) and the latter signifies minimum error in information transfer from the communicator to receiver. How to arrive at maximum communication efficiency and dependability is a crucial matter in the study of communication and learning. In any information transfer, particularly in human communication, principally because of man's limited capacity in information processing together with other physio-psychological factors, both equivocation and error are inevitable. The inevitability of equiovication and error demands a remedy, and redundancy is probably the most effective means man has found to reduce equiovication and error in information transmission and reception.

The function of redundancy is to curtail equivocation; to reduce error to a tolerable level in both encoding and decoding processes; to lessen the effects of noise, interference, and distortion; to facilitate information association and discrimination; and to reduce forgetting. But the introduction of redundancy into sign systems and channel systems invariably raises the cost of information processing in terms of time and space, as redundancy has to take away message space that information might otherwise occupy. To reduce equivocation and error, it is necessary to increase redundancy; but to increase redundancy is to decrease information. This is the dilemma of communication and learning.

The existence of equivocation and error renders perfect communication impossible. By manipulating redundancy in a message and/or between channels, it appears possible to achieve relative maximum information transfer, taking into account entropy, equivocation, error, and redundancy. In other words, information and redundancy must be maintained at an optimal ratio to keep equivocation and error at a relative minimum, and to keep the cost of information processing to a minimum. The maintenance of an optimal ratio between information and redundancy is of fundamental importance in communication and education, for it can increase "selection power." Although "selection power" may not be exactly equal to "intellectual power," as Ashby (1956, p. 272) suggests, it may very well be the first step toward achieving maximum communication efficiency and dependability.

REFERENCES

Adelson, M., Muckler, F. A., and Williams, A. C., Jr. Verbal learning and message variable related to amount of information. In H. Quastler (ed.), *Information Theory in Psychology*. New York: Free Press, 1955, 291–305.

Anderson, N. H. Effect of first order conditional probability in learning situation. *Journal of Experimental Psychology*, 1959, 59, 73–93.

_____, and Whalen, R. H. Likelihood judgments and sequential effects in a two-choice probability learning situation. *Journal of Experimental Psychology*, 1960, 60, 111–120.

Ashby, W. R. *An introduction to cybernetics*. New York: John Wiley, 1956; Science edition, 1963.

Atkinson, R. C., and Calfee, R. C. Mathematical learning theory.

In B. B. Wolman (ed.), *Scientific Psychology*. New York: Basic Books, 1965, 254–275.

Attneave, F. *Application of information theory to psychology*. New York: Henry Holt, 1959.

Bell, D. A. *Intelligent machines*. New York: Lexington, Mass.: Xerox College Publishing, 1962.

Broadbent, D. E. *Perception and communication*. Elmsford, N.Y.: Pergamon Press, 1958.

Brogden, W. J. Animal studies of learning. In S. S. Stevens (ed.), *Handbook of Experimental Psychology*. New York: Wiley, 1951.

_____, and Schmidt, R. E. Acquisition of a 24-unit verbal maze on learning and serial position errors. *Journal of Experimental Psychology*, 1954, 48, 335–338.

Bruner, J. S., Miller, G. A., and Zimmerman, C. Discriminative skill and discriminative matching in perceptual recognition. *Journal of Experimental Psychology*, 1955, 49, 187–192.

Carterette, E. C., and Jones, M. J. *Contextual constraints in the language of child*. Prouect English Newsletter, Issue 2, OE30006-2, U.S. Office of Education, 1962.

Chase, R. A. Verbal behavior: some points of reference. In K. Salzinger and S. Salzinger (eds.), *Research in Verbal Behavior and Some Neurophysiological Implication*. New York: Academic Press, 1967, 441–457.

Cherry, C. On human communications: a review, a survey, and a criticism. New York: Wiley, 1957; Science edition, 1961.

Cronbach, L. J. On the non-rational application of information measures in psychology. In H. Quastler (ed.), *Information Theory in Psychology*. New York: Free Press, 1955.

Dahling, R. L. Shannon's information theory: the spread of an idea. In E. Katz et al. (eds.), *Studies of Innovation and of Communication to the Public: Studies in the Utilization of Behavioral Science*, Vol. 2. Stanford, Calif.: Stanford University Institute of Communication Research, 1962, 117–140.

Dechert, C. R. The development of cybernetics. *American Behavioral Scientist*, 1965, 8, 9–14.

Deese, J. *The psychology of learning*. New York: McGraw-Hill, 1958.

Estes, W. K. All-or-none process in learning and retention. *American Psychologist*, 1960, 19, 16–25.

Gabor, D. *Lectures on information theory*. Cambridge, Mass.: MIT Press, 1951.

Garner, W. R. *Uncertainty and structure as psychological concepts*. New York: Wiley, 1962.

_____. The stimulus in information processing. *American Psychologist*, 1970, 25, 350–358.

Guthrie, E. R. *The psychology of learning*. New York: Harper & Row, 1952.

Hernandez-Peon, R. Reticular mechanisms of sensory control. In W. A. Rosenbilih (ed.), *Sensory Communication*. Cambridge, Mass.: MIT Press, 1961.

_____. A "communication analysis" of concept learning. *Psychological Review*, 1952, 59, 461–472.

Hovland, C. I. Human learning and retention. In S. S. Stevens (ed.), *Handbook of Experimental Psychology*. New York: Wiley, 1951, 613–689.

Hsia, H. J. On channel effectiveness. *Audiovisual Communication Review*, 1968, 16, 245–267. (a)

———. Output, error, equivocation, and recall information in auditory, visual, and audiovisual information processing. *Journal of Communication*, 1968, 18, 323–353. (b)

———. The information processing capacity of modality and channel performance. *Audiovisual Communication Review*, 1971, 19, 51–75.

———. On redundancy: a theoretical exploration on redundancy in human communications. Paper read at the Association for Education in Journalism Convention, Fort Collins, Colo., 1973.

Hull, C. L. *Principle of behavior.* New York: Appleton-Century-Crofts, 1943.

Hunt, E. B. *Concept learning: an information processing problem.* New York: Wiley, 1962.

Jones, J. E. All-or-none versus incremental learning. *Psychological Review*, 1962, 69, 156–160.

Klausmeier, H. J. *Learning and human abilities: educational psychology.* New York: Harper & Row, 1961.

Lewin, K. *Principles of topological psychology.* New York: McGraw-Hill, 1936.

Luce, D. R., et al., *Developments in mathematical psychology.* New York: Free Press, 1960.

Luce, G. G. *Biological rhythms in human and animal physiology.* New York: Dover, 1971.

MacKay, D. M. In search of basic symbols. In H. Von Foerster et al. (eds.), *Cybernetics: Circular Causal and Feedback Mechanisms in Biological and Social System.* New York: J. M. Macy Foundation, 1952, 181–184.

Mandelbrot, B. Information theory and psycholinguistics. In B. B. Wolman (ed.), *Scientific Psychology: Principles and Approaches.* New York: Basic Books, 1965, 550–562.

Marks, M. R., and Jack, O. Verbal context and memory span for meaningful material. *American Journal of Psychology*, 1952, 65, 298–300.

Meier, R. L. *A communication theory of urban growth.* Cambridge, Mass.: MIT Press, 1962.

Miller, G. A. Information theory and the study of speech. In G. McMillan et al. (eds.), *Current Trends in Information Theory.* Pittsburgh: University of Pittsburgh Press, 1953.

———, Galanter, E., and Pribram, K. *Plans and the structure of behavior.* New York: Holt, Rinehart and Winston, 1960.

———, and Selfridge, J. A. Verbal context and the recall of meaningful material. *American Journal of Psychology*, 1950, 63, 176–185.

Miller, J. The individual as an information processing system. In W. W. Fields and W. Abbott (eds.), *Information Storage and Neural Control.* Springfield, Ill.: Charles C Thomas, 1963, 301–328.

Muses, C. A. Forward. In J. Rothstein (ed.), *Communication Organization and Science.* Indian Hills, Colo.: Falcon's Wing Press, 1958.

Norman, D. A. *Memory and attention: an introduction to human information processing.* New York: Wiley, 1969.

Piaget, J. *Logic and psychology.* New York: Basic Books, 1957.

Riley, D. A. Rote learning as a function of distribution of practice and the complexity of the situation. *Journal of Experimental Psychology*, 1952, 43, 88–95.

Rothstein, J. *Communication, organization and science.* Indian Hills, Colo.: Falcon's Wings Press, 1958.

Roy, J. E. Some speculations on the psychophysiology of mind. In J. N. Scher (ed.), *Theories of the Mind.* New York: Free Press, 1962, 80–121.

Shannon, C. E., and Weaver, W. *The mathematical theory of communication.* Urbana, Ill.: University of Illinois Press, 1949.

Skinner, B. F. *Verbal behavior.* New York: Appleton-Century-Crofts, 1957.

Sperry, R. W. Cerebral organization and behavior. In T. K. Landauer (ed.), *Readings in Physiological Psychology: The Bodily Basis of Behavior.* New York: McGraw-Hill, 1967, 314–334.

Suppes, P., and Atkinson, R. *Markov learning models for multiperson interaction.* Stanford, Calif.: Stanford University Press, 1960.

Thorndike, E. E. *The fundamentals of learning.* New York: Teacher's College, Columbia University, 1932.

Thurstone, L. L. Relation between learning time and length of task. *Psychological Review*, 1930, 37, 44–53.

Tolman, E. C. *Purposive behavior in animals and men.* New York: Century, 1932.

Van de Geer, J. P. Psycholische toepassingen van de information theorie. *Ned. Tijdschr. Psychologie*, 1957, 12, 295–328.

Von Neumann, J. *The computer and the brain.* New Haven, Conn.: Yale University Press, 1958.

Weiner, N. *Cybernetics.* Cambridge, Mass.: MIT Press, 1948.

Weiner, N. *Human use of human beings.* New York: Doubleday, 1954.

Welford, A. T. Performance, biological mechanisms and age: a theoretical sketch. In A. T. Welford and J. E. Birren (eds.), *Behavior, Aging and the Nervous System.* Springfield, Ill.: Charles C Thomas, 1965, 3–20.

Westley, B. H., and MacLean, M. S. A conceptual model for communication research. *Journalism Quarterly*, 1957, 34, 31–38.

Young, J. A. *A model of the brain.* New York: Oxford University Press, 1964.

Zemanek, H., Kretz, H., and Angyan, A. J. A model for neurophysiological functions. In C. Cherry (ed.), *Information Theory*, Fourth London Symposium. Washington, D.C.: Butterworth, 1961, 271–284.

Limitations of Systems Analysis

Systems analysis has shortcomings in its application to education. But an increasing number of educators are making use of sophisticated planning procedures that will help them exert control over their schools' future instead of merely reacting to events and being controlled by them. A question that confronts many officials today is not *whether* systems analysis should be used in schools and universities, but *how* it can be used most effectively. We live in a time in which student revolt, black separatism, teacher power, and public disaffection for educators are growing movements. To improve planning and offset the sense of powerlessness felt by school officials caught up in radical change, more sophisticated policy-making tools have been developed and phased into specific activities such as curriculum design, instructional media usage, pupil evaluation, facilities design, racial balancing, budgeting, personnel management, and general long-range planning. Many observers tell us that education is on the threshold of a "systems era."

What is systems analysis?   A *system* consists of two or more parts and their relations which together form a single identifiable entity. Analysis provides

Harry J. Hartley is Vice President for Finance and Administration, University of Connecticut, Storrs, Connecticut.

glimpses into the parts and operations of the system. The notion of a system is certainly not new. Frequently, we have spoken of a social system or an economic system or an educational system when we wished to simplify what would otherwise be a maze of complex relationships. Because of the propensity of the human mind to impose order on what actually may be random events, individuals tend to associate their observations with some sort of system. Systems analysis is a mode of thinking. It provides a framework that permits the judgment of experts in numerous fields to be utilized so as to yield results which transcend individual judgment. It enables persons to achieve solutions and raise probing questions in a universal language, that is, systems analysis.

The systems approach, which is a composite of a number of planning, procedural, and allocative strategies, has spread from industry and the federal government to local school districts. It includes the four major areas of educational application noted in Table 1. We may view schools as an open system; identify the properties of various subsystems; analyze processes such as instruction, budgeting, and negotiations; and evaluate performance of the school system with the help of specific concepts such as the planning–programming–budgeting system (PPBS), which is being adopted by local school districts in more than 20 states.

It is beyond the scope of this article to offer comprehensive definitions and varied illustrations of systems analysis. The current literature devoted to this topic is extensive and easily available. But as

might be expected, most of the literature describing this new generation of interrelated management processes is rather long on persuasion and short on critical appraisal. The net result is that educators often do not have sufficient information with which to judge the relative worth of competing systems techniques.

My basic objectives, then, are to consider some of the major limitations of systems procedures for education and reduce the gap between expectations and achievement. This focus on shortcomings, offered by one who is strongly committed to the systems approach, should not be interpreted as a rejection of the emergent techniques. Rather, it is intended to call for even wider usage of systems analysis in schools after educators and the public have a more realistic understanding of the benefits to be gained. The 25 limitations I describe are not listed in order of priority. They fall under three basic categories: (1) *conceptual* (problems of theoretical definition); (2) *operational* (problems of administrative execution); and (3) *societal* (problems of environmental relevance). Some of the limitations may fall within all three categories, and thus no simple taxonomy is offered.

Confusion over terminology The term systems analysis possesses nearly as many definitions as there are persons who advocate its use. One indication of the confusion that surrounds the topic is the fact that there are at least 60 different code names and acronyms for approaches or management controls, such as systems analysis, operations research, operations analysis, PERT, PPBS, program

Table 1
Four Areas of Application of Systems Analysis in Education

Area	Activity	Example
1. Policy formulation	Strategic planning	PPBS
2. Management	Administrative execution—control	MIS
3. Instruction	Learning and evaluation	CAI
4. Research	Pure and applied projects	PERT

budgeting, cost-effectiveness, input–output analysis, cost–benefit analysis, modular scheduling, computer-assisted instruction, and so forth. . . . Systems analysis is more than computer-based techniques. It subsumes an outlook, or mode of thinking, by which a particular organization may be defined, examined, evaluated, and improved.

Problems in adapting models Generic models should be altered to fit specific situations. Models and procedures formuated in one context may not be transferable to another. One should be aware of the possible loss inherent in the adaptation process. Subclasses of systems possess a narrow scope of applicability and thus policy makers should be apprised of what borrowed models can do and cannot do. The pathetic fallacy of the expert is to believe that his technical concepts and language can be used to explain the universe. In terms of quantitative analysis, schools are much more complicated than any system yet devised by the military, which is where systems analysis was largely developed. There appears to be a more clear-cut mission and decision process for defense than for education.

A wisdom lag The quantum jump of technology and science far transcends any comparable advance in human wisdom. A wisdom lag is apparent. We can analyze intricate educational problems with computers, but oftentimes we cannot estimate the value and relevance of data. The tragedy of our era is that human intellectual capacity, as addressed to problems of human relationships, seems, if anything, regressive.

Illusions of adequacy by model builders Too strong confidence in mathematical models of schools may bring a condition in which far from adequate models are taken too seriously, for want of better models which remain tractable. Operations researchers, in particular, seem to suffer from "illusions of adequacy" in their modeling of educational systems. Elaborate analysis may be based upon poor data or questionable premises.

Inadequate impetus from states Systems analysis is not going to be adopted in the many smaller school districts until state departments of education increase their support for it. It is my opinion that individual states will not increase support until at least six conditions are met: (1) existing experimental projects of higher priority are completed, (2) regional data-processing centers are established on a time-shared basis, (3) mandatory consolidation reduces the total number of districts, (4) the advantages of systems procedures to local schools are specified in a convincing manner, (5) pilot programs are designed and conducted, and (6) the U.S. Office of Education demonstrates that its involvement with operations analysis is a success.

Centralizing bias As many local districts have grown and increased their complexities with data banks, information centers, and other computerized devices, decision making has become much more centralized within a tightly defined chain of command. The distance between the leader and the led has been increased, thus reducing the individual's democratic rights of decision, dissent, and deviation. How to balance the advantages of efficiency obtained from centralized decision making against the human survival values of individual decision making at the "point of stress" is a basic problem of public school governance in our time.

Unanticipated increased costs New systems procedures, including the planning–programming–budgeting system (PPBS), are not designed to reduce spending per se. Program budgeting, for example, is neutral on the issue of cost reduction. In fact, it may actually accelerate school costs because of requirements for additional personnel, equipment, and material. There is nothing inherent in program budgeting to enable it to avoid at least one pitfall of conventional function–object school budgets, that is, "worse than the last, but not as bad as the next." The basic advantage of PPBS lies in its attempt to shift the budgetary focus from objects to be bought to programs to be accomplished.[1]

Goal distortion   Systems analysts do not suggest that the entire output of an educational organization can be quantified and measured. Unfortunately, there is a tendency for organizations to place greater emphasis on those goals that are most easily measured, such as cognitive mastery, and to neglect more important goals that cannot be quantified and measured, such as moral perspective. This is called goal distortion.

Measuring the unmeasurable   The matching of educational program objectives and performance measures is much more complex than some systems analysts seem to believe. In a decentralized, open system such as a local school, objectives may be matters of rigorous public debate. There is remarkably little unanimity regarding objectives and effective ways to attain and measure them. We may be trying to measure the unmeasurable. Presently, systems procedures and available mathematical instruments are appreciably more elaborate than educational measurement criteria. Performance indicators are needed.

Cult of testing   Standardized tests of academic achievement have long been used as indicators of systems performance, although they may have created more problems than they resolved. There is danger that a cult of testing may be created. Testing that is based upon poor instruments, disputable assumptions, incorrectly interpreted data, and purposely manipulated data can offset the advantages afforded by systems procedures. Organizing education in terms of the economic theory of input and output is rather dangerous at a time when our evaluation methods are so primitive. It tends to minimize those significant school activities, especially in the affective–moral–aesthetic realm, that do not lend themselves to the crude instruments now available for testing. It is easier to assert that anything which can be described can be quantified than it is to develop acceptable measures.

Cult of efficiency   Systems analysis may place too much emphasis upon economic savings. As a result, preference is given to *saving* at the expense of *accomplishing*. Critics of economic policy point to current urban wastelands as examples of how humane concerns often give way to economic efficiency with disastrous results. The need exists in local schools for occasional *uneconomic* allocations of resources.[2] In this way, schools will benefit from money being "wasted" on noneconomic values that mirror our social conscience.

Spread of institutional racism   Because systems analysis is a means rather than an end in itself, it may be used to perpetuate the subtle institutional racism that threatens to divide this nation permanently. Violent black–white confrontation will increase in intensity if our planning strategists do not actively seek to destroy the seeds of both institutional and private racism. Tactics of dissent can lead to strategies of reform, but success of systems strategies is dependent ultimately upon the social conscience and talent of their proponents.

Political barriers[3]   Schools are not politically unencumbered. Because public education is public policy, the schools are directly responsive to political elements that may serve as roadblocks to systems procedures. The "politics of education" is still in a formative stage of development and thus lacks sufficient critical study. The introduction of systems procedures, such as program budgeting, may cause school officials to choose political feasibility in preference to economic desirability. The budgetary process takes place in the political arena, and many persons may not wish to expose their values and to make visible in the program budget some of the items that can be somewhat camouflaged at present. Even though education is amenable to some amount of systems analysis, members of the power structure may view economic rationality as an infringement upon their domain.

Conventional collective negotiations procedures   A major limitation involves the topic of teachers' negotiations and the inherent struggle for economic–political power. Each school year since 1965 has brought a record number of teacher strikes, and no end is in sight. In spite of new, systematic approaches to resource allocations, collective negotiations for the immediate future will continue to be based upon the conventional, function–object type of budget. This condition will also exist in those institutions that claim to be using program budgeting and other systems concepts.

Lack of orderliness for data processing As part of their preparatory program for educational administrators, several universities have attempted to develop elaborate data bases. The primary difficulty in adapting an information storage and retrieval model in educational administration, as in the behavioral sciences, is one of orderliness of content. Information retrieval usually implies organized information so that discrete data may be easily located. Educational administration presently lacks a comprehensive theory, and thus it also lacks the orderliness of a uniform scheme for classification, storage, and retrieval of information. A taxonomy, or extensive classification scheme, should serve as the point of departure for the data bases to be developed.

Monumental computer errors Computers have been represented as infallible, impartial, and indispensable machines. At times they have been oversold by their zealous proponents. There is increasing evidence that computers may be erratic and easily made inoperative, in some cases by a mere speck of dust. A new business has even been developed to provide insurance against computer-inflicted disasters. Because of the speed of computations, even normally trivial mistakes which can be blamed on human programmers become monumental when put onto punch cards. In short, when data-processing errors occur, they can be extremely costly and difficult to remedy. In addition to the error factor, additional long-range costs may be incurred because of the high obsolescence rate of computer hardware.

Shortage of trained personnel Local schools generally have inadequate staffs for systems planning. This problem is compounded by the fact that many districts do not have the financial resources that might be needed for a full-scale installation. Deficiencies exist in the training programs of school administrators, the usage and number of administrative personnel, and the usage of electronic data processing. The result is that the approach of a number of school districts, particularly in cities, has been deliberately opportunistic, rather than systematic and comprehensive. They have phased in specific systems elements without installing comprehensive procedures. The focus of these districts is upon sectors, or areas, of high apparent yield.

Invasion of individual privacy Unless there is some sort of model regulatory code, the computer could endanger individual privacy rights. If lifelong computer dossiers are to be used, then a comprehensive set of rules on information gathering, disclosure, and confidentiality should be enacted. Otherwise, computers could turn schools and society into a transparent world in which every indiscretion of an individual could be evaluated by others. Similar arguments at the national level have been put forth in the attempts to develop a national data center. Disagreement exists over whether such a center would be a purely statistical data bank or an "intelligence center."

Organizational strains Systems procedures tend to put organizational dynamics into the spotlight, and this may create conflicts and pressures. With the introduction of concepts such as PPBS, it can be anticipated that there will *not* be a disappearance of bureaucratic inertia, vested interests, old prides, honest differences of opinion, and political activities. In fact, such procedures may initially serve to accentuate conflicts and engender antagonisms as the schools' objectives are exposed in analytical terms. Measuring school performance quantitatively may irritate those who are value oriented, emotionally oriented, politically oriented, or just do not understand.

Resistance to planned change It is possible that some of the new systems procedures may encounter opposition from classroom teachers who view operations analysis as an encroachment upon their professional activities. Impersonal efficiency measures may be incompatible with the human subtleties of education. Opposition of some degree to any kind of planned change or innovation exists in education. In the case of systems analysis, some teachers may resist the new procedures, not because they are stubborn, but because their pride causes them to be fearful of failing at something new.

Antiquated legislation Legislative appropriations for education continue to be based on an object-of-expenditure basis rather than a program basis. This tends to restrict the extent to which programmatic priorities can be determined with analytical tools. It also tends to perpetuate meaningless truisms and clichés such as "meet the needs." A well-informed political representative of the future will no longer be content to know, in mere dollars terms, what constitutes the abstract "needs" of the school. He will be unimpressed with continuing requests for more input without some concurrent explanation of the schools' output.

Doomed to success It is likely that some new systems procedures will be "doomed to success" in local schools. The reason is that evaluation of an innovative technique may be conducted by the very same persons who originally installed the new device. It is unlikely that such officials will claim that their modern technology is anything less than a smashing godsend. The success of a number of the systems concepts has never really been measured. Instead, most of the descriptive literature pertains to the potential value of new concepts, but does not validate them.

Imagery problems The value of new approaches will depend in part upon their acceptance. A serious impediment to an early achievement of widespread approval could be the sophistication of the image imparted to systems analysis. The image of systems procedures may include a belief that they can be operational only with a staff of highly specialized systems experts backed by an expensive computer installation. Such misconceptions arise because many of the systems procedures are used primarily in large city school systems and in government agencies that possess such facilities and trained personnel.

Defects in analysis It is admitted that every systems analysis has defects. Some of these are limitations inherent in all analyses of choice. Others

Table 2
Limitations of Systems Analysis in Education

1. Confusion over terminology	14. Conventional collective negotiations procedures
2. Problems in adapting models	15. Lack of orderliness for data processing
3. A wisdom lag	16. Monumental computer errors
4. Illusions of adequacy by model builders	17. Shortage of trained personnel
5. Inadequate impetus from states	18. Invasion of individual privacy
6. Centralizing bias	19. Organizational strains
7. Unanticipated increased costs	20. Resistance to planned change
8. Goal distortion	21. Antiquated legislation
9. Measuring the unmeasurable	22. Doomed to success
10. Cult of testing	23. Imagery problems
11. Cult of efficiency	24. Defects in analysis
12. Spread of institutional racism	25. Accelerating social change rate
13. Political barriers	

are a consequence of the difficulties and complexities of the particular question or issue. Still others are blunders or errors in thinking which hopefully will disappear as specialists learn to do better and more complete analyses.[4] The human mind possesses what has been called a "rage for order." It means that man may attempt to impose order on what are simply random events. If we interpret random events as nonrandom, our analysis is likely to be defective and produce no predictive value.

Accelerating rate of social change Some cynics claim that the future has become a thing of the past. They seem to be indicating that the increasing rate of social change makes long-range planning impossible. Others claim that a modern social system, such as a school, actually may not be a system. The New York City schools, for example, possess little of the arrangement and almost none of the harmony that are necessary if a system is defined as a "harmonious arrangement or pattern." Hydraheaded social problems seem to defy systems analysis. The president of the 7,000-member Operations Research Society of America stated the issue succinctly: "We're very good at hardware and tactical problems and starting well-defined research and development programs. But we're lousy at strategic and philosophical problems. I see a very long and difficult road ahead."[5] Actually, modern social systems are a type of "conflict system," and they may be examined by means of numerous models developed in the areas of national security research and peace research.

CONCLUSION

It is easy to exaggerate the extent to which the 60 or more different systems concepts can assist educators. The purpose of this article was to identify a number of current shortcomings in the methodology of systems analysis. It should be emphasized that systems procedures are a means, not an end, for achieving educational equality and excellence. I am aware that some persons believe that in education there are no ends, only means. Although preceding paragraphs emphasized the defects of systems procedures, it is my opinion that the limitations outlined in Table 2 are far outweighed by the potential advantages to be gained. It is probable that many of the present limitations can be overcome as more persons apply their talents to this topic. In the final analysis, the success of systems procedures is dependent upon the artistry of the user.

REFERENCES

1. Harry J. Hartley, *Educational Planning–Programming–Budgeting: A Systems Approach.* Englewood Cliffs, N.J.: Prentice-Hall, Inc., 1968.
2. Harry J. Hartley, "P.P.B.S.: The Emergence of a Systemic Concept for Public Governance," in *General Systems,* Yearbook for the Society of General Systems Research, Vol. XIII, 1969.
3. Harry J. Hartley, "Twelve Hurdles To Clear Before You Take on Systems Analysis," *American School Board Journal,* July 1968, p. 17.
4. E. S. Quade, *Systems Analysis Techniques for PPBS,* P-3322. Santa Monica, Calif: RAND Corporation, Mar. 1966, p. 19.
5. Joseph H. Engel, "Systems Analysis and Social Change," *New York Times,* Mar. 24, 1968, p. 28.

PART IV: DESIGN AND PRODUCTION

Modular Approach
to Curriculum Design
Using the Systems Approach

Thomas E. Cyrs, Jr.

The purpose of applying the systems approach to curriculum design is to individualize, personalize, and humanize the teaching–learning environment.

The concept of "system" found in the military and business communities can be extrapolated to the educational enterprise in many different ways. Its application to curriculum design will be the major concern of this paper. We shall demonstrate how the concept of system can help us make decisions about the choice of learning alternatives and how to individualize instruction through the design of small sequences or modules of instruction.

A *system* is an identifiable entity consisting of parts that are distinguishable from but closely related to each other and to the entity. These parts function in such a way as to attain a specific goal or produce an output. The entity (wholeness) is highly organized and complex. This concept of wholeness is central to the study of systems. The latter, in whatever form it may be, must be seen as an entity.

All systems have *boundaries* or parameters within which they exist. When defining a system these boundaries must be made explicit. The boundaries are conceptual rather than being a physical

Thomas E. Cyrs, Jr., is Director, Division of Instructional Systems Development, Office of Educational Resources, Northwestern University.

reality. There is no *one* system. There are many different types of systems that will always constitute a higher-order system. In fact, anything can be treated as a system.

A system is designated by what we say it is. All systems are made up of parts called *sybsystems* and are part of a higher-order system called the *suprasystem:*

```
            SUPRASYSTEM
      System      │    System
      Subsystem   │    Subsystem
      Subsystem   │    Subsystem
      Subsystem   │    Subsystem
```

There are *physical systems* such as thermostats, biological systems such as the nervous system and circulatory system, psychological systems, information systems, cultural systems, economic systems, instructional systems, and many other forms of systems. Systems may be *natural,* such as those found in nature—solar and environmental. They may be *man-made,* such as those found in society—political and educational. Within the perspective of natural and man-made systems a hierarchy is identifiable. Systems can encompass something as large as a whole social environment or something as small as a lesson of instruction. These hierarchies, respectively, are referred to as *macrosystems* and *microsystems.* The microsystem maintains all the characteristics of a macrosystem.

The purpose of viewing something as a system is to understand the entity and the relationships of the parts. How do the parts affect each other and the entity under investigation, and how would the entity be affected or altered if any of the parts were changed?

"Systems approach" suggests a methodological approach to problem solving that is explicit, objective, and comprehensive. When applied to educa-

tion, a systems approach is a "... rational problem-solving method of analyzing the educational process taken as a whole, incorporating all of its parts and aspects, including the students, and teachers, the curriculum content, the instructional materials, the instructional strategy, the physical environment, and the evaluation of instructional objectives."[1] The ultimate objective of a systems approach is the effective *control* of the component parts of the system.

The type of system that we shall deal with in this paper is *closed,* which means that it is self-contained and, through feedback, self-regulatory. Feedback is defined as the return of output (usually in the form of information) to the system. All change within the system is generated through this feedback principle. Applied to the educational enterprise, a *closed-loop system* could be presented in the following model:

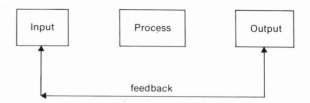

The *input* represents uneducated students who spend 12 or more years going through a *process* called education. Inputs also include buildings, instructional materials, faculty, and expenses. The effect of the *process* is shown in the output of the system, which purportedly represents educated students. The total instructional system would be held accountable for producing the types of skill and human relations development called for in the instructional objectives. If the student did not meet the requirements or minimum standards of the system, he would then be recycled through selected parts of the system until he overcame the deficiencies. Control points to monitor effective learning are provided by continuous feedback of information about student progress. Unfortunately, education has not concentrated on the outputs of the system. The tragic national dropout rate is evidence of this in the public schools, and the high attrition rate during the freshman year in higher education. Emphasis seems to be placed on the inputs rather than on the outputs.

If applied to education, the systems approach would demand that all output specifications (learning objectives) be specified so that appropriate inputs could be selected. The systems approach when applied to education places prime emphasis on the learner as central to the educational process. This process necessitates four identifiable steps that will have to be accounted for in the total instructional system:

1. Specification of all outputs or objectives in a precise and measureable form relating to the learner.
2. Identification of many alternative learning strategies in a variety of media and methods.
3. Design of evaluation procedures that reflect the intent of the stated learning objectives.
4. Provision for immediate feedback to both the learner and instructor of all vital information relative to the student's progress.

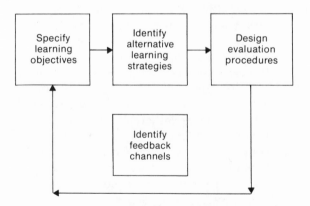

When applied to *curriculum* design the instructional system can be defined as an integrated arrangement of equipment, personnel, instructional materials, subject matter, presentation form, and learning environments that functions in such a way as to lead to the achievement of predetermined learning objectives. The total instructional system is the curriculum. When the end product or learning objectives are clearly defined, the instructional system designer retraces his steps to develop an instructional system that will lead the student to achievement of the objectives. He uses all the tools of behavioral analysis in seeking the best combination of media and methods to effect learning. The designer must identify the most effective way for the student to *interact* with the subject matter in some mediated form.

An instructional systems approach demands this *interactive approach* to learning. The interaction could be between pupil and instructor; pupil, instructor, and media; or possibly pupil and media without the direct intervention of the instructor. The student cannot be a passive assimilator of information but rather must be actively involved in the learning process.

How can this theoretical construct be put to practical use for everyday classroom instruction? The analysis and development of instruction and classroom management procedures will be considered in the design of learning modules that afford a feasible means to manage students through a curriculum. A learning module is a *self-contained* set of teaching–learning materials in form. Completion time varies from a few hours to a few weeks. It is *predesigned* as a classroom management strategy to help the student achieve specified performance objectives. It is *self-directing* and *self-correcting* and provides for a wide variety of learning styles by incorporating a range of commercially available or locally produced *multimedia* instructional materials. The module allows the student to pace at his *own rate of speed* so that learning progress is known to both student and instructor at all times and is based on *measured understanding*.

This approach will provide the beginning of an individualized and humanistic approach to instruction where student pacing is dependent on performance and measured understanding rather than group instruction where discrimination is between high and low achievers. An instructional systems approach will attempt to provide a design for instruction so that all students achieve to the fullest extent of their abilities. A major advantage of the systems approach is its flexibility in absorbing the best features of newer curriculum programs and technologies as they are developed. When a system is learner-centered, it is maintained only if it produces the appropriate learning. Instructors teach to achievement of 100 percent of the specified learning objectives—a mastery learning system.

CHARACTERISTICS OF LEARNING MODULES

One might say that textbooks were initially conceived as modules, providing a student with all the structure and information he needed to know. Although many good texts are available, they still do not contain the design characteristics proposed here. Instructional modules contain specific characteristics that make them distinct from conventional textbooks or multimedia kits. Regardless of the physical format of the individual modules, the following characteristics will be found:

1. *Defined population.* Each module is designed for a specific population of students having particular or general characteristics.
2. *Single or multiple concepts.* The module format facilitates easy identification and management of each concept or procedure to be learned.
3. *Specified performance objectives.* Information within the module indicates specifically what the student is expected to do.
4. *Relevant content.* Content or subject matter is selected only as it relates to the achievement of the performance objectives.
5. *Variety of media.* The media is selected on the basis of performance objectives. The use of the media is completely integrated into the module rather than supplementary to it.
6. *Integrated or supplementary instruction.* Instructional modules can provide remedial or enrichment instruction depending on the particular situation. They may form the entire curriculum or any part of it.
7. *Self-directing.* The module provides any information or directions that the student needs to achieve the objectives. It is basically a classroom management device.
8. *Various strategies.* The module might direct the student to work alone, in small groups, or attend large group presentations and lectures.
9. *Self-pacing.* Students move at their own rate of speed depending on the nature of the module. The student is not forced to keep up with the class when he does not understand. The student's progress is based on his measured understanding of the topic, skill, or procedure.
10. *Continuous reinforcement.* The student as well as the instructor knows at all times how well the student is doing.
11. *Adequate practice.* The student is given the opportunity to practice the skill, principle, or rule in a variety of different applications. This is accomplished through a series of self-tests imbedded into the module. The learning blueprint of the student indicates need for remediation or faster pacing.
12. *Relevant evaluation.* All guesswork in testing is removed. The student knows exactly how he will be evaluated and is able to distinguish relevant from irrelevant subject matter. Evaluation is based on the criterion specified in the performance objectives and is in the form of tests (pre-, post-, self-), observation, projects, and any other form that adequately reflects the objectives.
13. *Field tested.* The instructional module should be tried out on an adequate sample of the user population to determine if the activities and resources will, in fact, help the student to

achieve the objectives. The field-test results should be made available in the case of commercial modules.

These criteria distinguish instructional modules from textbooks and most of the available multimedia kits. We can expect the market soon to be flooded, and such criteria should be used to judge the validity of commercially available materials purporting to be self-instructional learning modules.

MODULE SIZE AND LAYOUT

Learning modules can require any length of time to complete and can take on any physical form. A total curriculum program (macrosystem) would be composed of smaller individual modules (microsystems). Nothing prevents individual modules from being developed at random within an existing curriculum structure as supplementary or enrichment units. This is most commonly done by individual instructors. These individual modules could take anywhere from 1 hour to several weeks to complete. The physical layout of individual modules can assume any form, ranging from student learning contracts printed on individual 8½- by 11-inch sheets to the larger instructional packages that contain all necessary information and run from 5 to 50 pages in length. An instructional module might consist of a combination filmstrip–audiotape and worksheets or might include videotapes tied in with interactive response textbooks. Regardless of format or specific components, if a unit utilizes the elements of systems design we have been discussing, it qualifies as an instructional module.

Steps in the Design of a Learning Module

The actual design of a learning module involves 12 distinct and sequential steps, which are shown graphically in Figure 1. Each major step or function

is numbered 1.0, 2.0, and so on. Subfunctions within each step are numbered 5.1, 5.2, and so on. Each arrow represents the flow of information from one step to the next. Information that is returned or fed back causes us to reexamine what we did in that step. The steps in module design are presented numerically. Each number corresponds to the exact number on the flowchart. Detailed expansion of each step will follow this brief outline.

 1.0. Identify user population.
 2.0. Select concept, principle, or skill.
 3.0. Specify terminal performance objective(s).
 4.0. Identify all constraints.
 5.0. Conduct behavioral analysis.
 6.0. Design criterion tests.
 7.0. Select teaching–learning strategy.
 8.0. Select content.
 9.0. Select media alternatives.
10.0. Assemble module.
11.0. Field test module.
12.0. Produce final module.

Step 1.0: Identify user population The user population comprises the group for which the instructional module was designed. Some possible characteristics of the user population might include grade level, achievement level as determined by standardized tests, background of students, motivational factors, and special considerations such as reading problems.

Step 2.0: Select a concept, principle, rule, or procedure Once selected this should be broken down into subparts and a limitation placed on the analysis.

Step 3.0: Specify the terminal performance objective (TPO) The TPO specifies the final performance requirement and is, therefore, the highest level of intellectual development in the module.

Step 4.0: Identify all constraints All those things that would inhibit the design and implementation of the module should be identified. These could be physical (lack of equipment), environmental (no adequate place to study independently), and

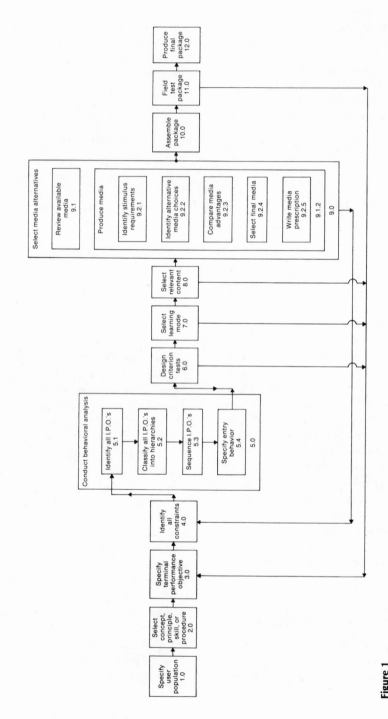

Figure 1
Designing learning packages.

personal (not enough time to complete the module).

Step 5.0: Conduct the behavioral analysis

5.1. *Identify all intermediate performance objectives (IPO).* The IPO's include all transitional steps toward achievement of the TPO.

5.2 *Classify all IPO's into hierarchies.* Classify all IPO's as cognitive, affective, or psychomotor, and if cognitive into a hierarchy.

5.3. *Sequence IPO's.* Examine the cognitive classification of the IPO's and sequence into a learning hierarchy. More IPO's will probably have to be added as transitional steps toward achievement of the TPO.

5.4. *Specify entering behavior.* These include all prerequisite skills that you expect the student will already have mastered *prior* to beginning the module.

Step 6.0: Design criterion tests   Criterion tests are designed to evaluate the achievement of each performance objective. They include preassessment, postassessment; and self-assessment such as progress quizzes. Criterion tests include anything that provides a numerical index of performance.

Step 7.0: Select the teaching–learning strategy   Strategies include all grouping patterns and are based on the types of responses called for in the performance objectives.

Step 8.0: Select the content   Only that content or subject matter relevant to the achievement of the objectives is selected. The "nice-to-know" and "need-to-know" is clearly distinguishable.

Step 9.0: Select media alternatives   Commercial media may be available for objective achievement. If not, the media will have to be developed locally. As many different media as possible should be selected in order to accommodate a wide range of learning styles.

Step 10.0: Assemble the module   Many different physical formats are available for the module design. These include unipacs, learning activity packages, teaching–learning units, differentiated learning packages, interactive learning packages, learning contracts, and a host of others.

Step 11.0: Field test the module   The completed module should be used with one to three students who represent the user population. Observe these students working through the module and note all questions and points of difficulty. Note the feedback points throughout the flowchart. Continue to redesign the module until your specified criterion level is reached.

Step 12.0: Produce the final module

SUMMARY

The nature and characteristics of a "systems approach" have been defined and applied to instructional systems. A practical approach for implementation of these principles has been proposed in the form of learning modules. The steps for module development have been specified and elaborated upon. A great deal of research remains to be done to validate the proposed procedures. The future proliferation of predesigned learning modules is inevitable. Banks of validated modules will be available in the future from which a variety of objectives, learning activities, and evaluation procedures can be mixed and matched for different populations of students. A beginning has been made to truly individualize and humanize education.

REFERENCE

1. Cyrs, Thomas, and Lowenthal, Rita, "A Model for a Systems Approach to Curriculum Design," *Audiovisual Instruction*, Jan. 1970.

Target:
Rational Design

Ted C. Cobun

A profession, worthy of the privileges and obligations of the designation, must conduct its operations to meet the highest standards possible to it. Professional conduct presumes the use of techniques of the highest quality, the greatest possible sophistication, and of optimally effective production.

In contribution to advancement of the profession, members are obligated to develop, refine, and validate new and more productive techniques. When innovative techniques are not available, professionals refine currently used methods to achieve the greatest possible effectiveness.

Research is being accomplished in several advanced areas of transmitting information to learners. The use of chemicals, hypnosis, radiation, and certain psi phenomena have been tested. Results of such tests are not yet conclusive enough for general application. Unless a breakthrough is made in one or more similar areas, or other equivalent areas as yet unconceived, teaching and learning will continue to be implemented by procedures that use more or less traditional methods.

Today, most educators are familiar with varieties of programmed instruction, message designs, team

Ted C. Cobun teaches at East Tennessee State University, Johnson City, Tennessee.

teaching, individualized instruction, and game theory activities. Media have been arranged for transmission as paper sheets, rolls, cards, in pamphlet, booklet, magazine, and book formats, by many kinds of display machines, by computers and, otherwise, electronically.

All contemporary systems have one element in common. They all require some form of media to contact the learners. Media that support any of the systems are effective in relation to the characteristics which determine their design. Without rigorous design, influenced by the nature of the learning event and the characteristics peculiar to the learner, no system can be predictably more effective than any other, except as affected by factors of chance. Thus, no contemporary system can be said to be any more significantly effective than any traditional learning mode, or vice versa.

Pending desirable breakthroughs, resulting from extensive research, it is reasonable to develop and refine selected methodologies. It is predictable that no amount of physical arrangement, logistical legerdemain, or pedagogical gymnastics will convert a monolithic technique to guaranteed effectiveness. No amount of exterior superstructure will strengthen invalid interior frameworks.

For the teaching–learning process, professional accountability is the product of validatable learning events. Validatable learning events are the products of rigorous design. Rigorous design is controlled by and generated from the following:

1. Relevant curricular decisions.
2. Comprehensive learner analyses.
3. Design of the learning event.
4. Selection of pertinent media.
5. Media design and production.
6. Developmental testing and validation.
7. Logistical arrangements.

Such design does not occur in a situation that is not organized, manned, and tooled to support it. It does not occur with professionals whose training has not included such practices. It does require professional support personnel, extensive intensive periods of in-service education, materials, media, and hardware.

STATUS QUO

It is a euphonious, debilitating platitude to say that there is more than one way to educate people. Of course there is more than one way! There are as many ways as there are people, but, in practice, we tend to gravitate to a single way and use it with everyone. In present practices, most of the time we do not know whether the way we gravitate to is a good way or not. And our evaluation devices are usually only as good and effective as each other, with none being certainly valid.

Saying that there is more than one way does not lead to better ways. It gives no clue for prescription. It does not take one step toward rational design. It seems to give license to the procedurally inept and the unwittingly inconsiderate. It gives no help to the concerned. It leaves the learner at status quo, however that was for him. Contemporary literature and public opinion shows that for many the status quo is not good.

MEDIA

There are floods of media and all kinds of hardware available for instruction. I am under constant persuasion from salesmen to buy this or that. Their efforts are reinforced by a barrage of propaganda from the parent companies and franchisers. Salesmen and propaganda suggest that their wares are high in potential value and success. Of course, they say, in the end, it's up to me. If the process fails, it is because of something I did or did not do, and not the fault of the hardware or the media.

They're right, you know! They may not know why they are right or what to do about it, but the hardware and the media cannot absorb the professional responsibility.

I have nothing against salesmen. Some of my best friends are salesmen. Occasionally, salesmen perform useful services for my program. I need hardware, and some media are laden with values. But having the right items, at the right place, for the right persons, at the right time becomes a great deal more than a casual, offhand choice. And the personality of the salesman does not have much to do with it, either.

It is my privilege to teach all kinds of educators. Some have more responsibilities than others. Almost all are proud of their stables of hardware and collections of media. And most still use the obsolete term "audiovisual," as though to be able to hear and see in a learning situation was something unique requiring sophisticated equipment and media. Some of them act as though they believe that possession of a trove of resources is a guarantee of sure success for all but the most recalcitrant or unfortunate learners.

"G"-Forces

But some of the hardware is still in the original shipping boxes. Since about 1965, their seals have never been broken nor their contents operated.

Media, produced commercially, must be designed to suit a large potential market. Each must be as many things to as many people as possible. Consequently, they cannot have the kinds of individual impact needed, except as we are willing to ignore the needs of individuals and compromise required emphases. Artistic production, logical arrangement, and technical effects are available for the asking. What is far less available—hardly ever—is validation. Not many media producers validate their products. Not many educators demand validation. Some educators do not even know about validation, or, perhaps, care about it, one way or another.

Too Often, Too Little, Too Late!

Students call projectors "sleep" machines. It is easier to sleep in a dimly lighted room than in a bright one. They are so saturated by high-impact commercial radio, television, and magazines that the comparative impact of instructional media leaves all but the devoted turned off.

I have heard teachers, making "jokes," I presume, say that they never use a medium for teaching that does not last for 45 minutes, at least, in running time. Of course, this comment was made by only a few teachers, in one way or another, in five or six states, in five or six different kinds of schools. And there are still some schools where a teacher can attain professional prestige by being the one who can operate a motion picture projector!

"J"-Curve Generation

Hardware, media, and systems of any kind are not omnipotent in their own rights. Mere presence of hardware and media is not a guarantee of successful learning or teaching. Hardware is neutral. It is inert until it is loaded and displays its companion medium.

A medium is anything that carries a message. Until the message is carried, the medium is only paper, plastic, glass, or whatever. There is nothing magical about a medium. The magic is created by

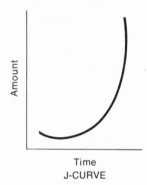

Time

J-CURVE

the effect of the message. A message that creates no reaction, or a reaction that is not sought, may be magical in a sense, but it is not very useful for learning.

A medium is effective when the message it carries produces a reaction that is predictable within some kind of perimeters. Effectiveness is brought about through the skillful use of verbal and pictorial symbols that learners can interpret as they were intended, by levels of content and paces of display that match and stimulate the learner's capacity, and by generated responses and practice that reinforce his behavior. None of these characteristics can be produced with certainty by a message of casual design that places content or attractiveness before the peculiar reception capacities of the learner.

It is counteropposed to the rational process of developmental learning, by about 180 degrees, to presume that hardware and media assure success. If you owned the finest stable of hardware and the most extensive library of media in the world, it would be antithetical to design a learning event based on the ownership, unless you had taken into account other critical elements.

For one thing, since most media are not validated, you would need to validate them yourself. In the absence of validation, not even entertainment can be assured for a medium. With validation, a presumption of success may be expected, but the validation of a medium occurs as a result of what the learner is stimulated to do. A validated medium becomes a successful learning event.

INITIAL POINT

At the initial point, the designer of the learning event assumes that he cannot presume learning by chance. He must design the event so that it generates the kind of learning he seeks. Thus, the initial point is when the decision is made to teach whatever is supposed to be learned.

Decisions about learning may be made by learn-ers. They may, of course, be made by teachers. They may also be made, in concert, by learners with teachers. In the latter case, conditions are condu-cive for the production of long-term memory and high cognitive objectives. At the same time, affec-tive and psychomotor objectives may be targeted in the design.

At the initial point, the decision about what is to be learned is only a decision. It should define and describe what an acceptable product is to be like.

Once made, the decision implies further proces-sing for rational development of the learning event.

ANALYSIS

One of the reasons—only one—why some lear-ners learn less ably than others is because they are exposed less often to events designed to suit their peculiar characteristics. Seldom, if ever, are learn-ers adequately analyzed in relation to their learn-ing requirements. Seldom, therefore, are learning events designed to correspond to requirements of specific learners.

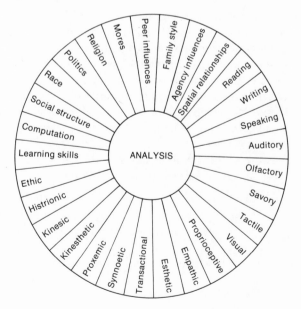

Commercial media are most often designed for mass audiences. And most commercial media are not validated. It is to those kinds of media that learners are most often exposed. And most of the time exposure is the only treatment the learner gets!

To design a learning event and to arm it, eventually, with a medium that can be validated requires analysis of the learner. Analysis of the learner is the second step in the rational development of the learning event.

It is presumptuous to assume that

1. A learning event that produces predictable behavior can be designed successfully in the absence of adequate learner analysis.
2. Analysis of massed groups will provide data for adequate analysis of individual learners.
3. Simple observation can provide adequate data for learner analysis.
4. Intuition is adequate as a technique to provide data for learner analysis.

Variables

The variables that control learner success are powerfully influential. Each varies in required amounts. One may act as the catalyst for others. The absence of treatment for any single variable may be enough to neutralize or even wreck the learning effect. Except by chance, at fantastic odds for failure, no single treatment of a learning event of significance can have optimal effects for more than a given learner.

Some of the variables that control the achievement of learner successes are the following:

1. The ability to hear clearly and listen skillfully.
2. The ability to see, clearly, all significant details.
3. The ability to receive and interpret appropriate aromas.
4. The ability to receive and interpret appropriate tastes.
5. The ability to feel and interpret appropriately tactile stimuli.

6. The ability to detect and interpret, for appropriate applications, degrees of bone–joint angulations, change of angulations, muscle stretches, and tendon tensions.
7. The ability to receive, interpret, and identify with the feelings, ideas, emotions, and purposes of others.
8. The ability to receive and interpret situations, products, and ideas in terms of the beauty or pureness of their character.
9. The ability to receive, interpret, and commit to a describable set of values or moral principles, obligations, or duties.
10. The ability to observe, interpret, or perform a staged behavior, or a deliberate exhibition of emotion or temperament, apparently intended to have a deliberate effect on others.
11. The ability to receive, interpret, and use nonverbal language intended to create effects.
12. The ability to perform and develop in a relevant set of motor skills.
13. The ability to judge and respect, perhaps tactfully penetrate, the critical physical and social distance fields of others, and to extend one's personal fields to optimal limits.
14. The ability to interpret one's relationships to environment and to revise and refine either, or both, optimally.
15. The ability to maintain an interaction of influence with a variety of others.
16. The identification and interpretation of functional patterns of mores as they influence the behavior of a variety of others and as they relate to one's own.
17. The identification and interpretation of the influencing religious concepts and practices of others as they relate to one's own.
18. The identification and interpretation of the influencing political concepts and practices of others as they relate to one's own.
19. The identification and interpretation of the influencing racial concepts and interactive behavior of others as they relate to one's own.

20. The identification and interpretation of the influencing aspects of membership in an identifiable social structure as they relate to one's own.
21. The identification and interpretation of the influencing peers of others and the relationships of those peer members to one's own peer group.
22. The identification and interpretation of the family organization and practices of others as they relate to one's own.
23. The identification and interpretation of agencies that influence the behavior of others as they relate to agencies which influence the analyzer.
24. The ability to read with optimal speed and comprehension at pertinent levels.
25. The ability to write efficiently and expressively at pertinent levels about pertinent matters.
26. The ability to speak efficiently and expressively at pertinent levels about pertinent matters.
27. The ability to use techniques to learn with efficiency and effectiveness.
28. The ability to compute relevant problems involving quantities or qualities that can be symbolized numerically.
29. The ability to rank high in contact ability as indicated by a variety of sociogrametric techniques.
30. The ability to conceive and interpret spatial relationships.

It is probable that flash analyses and intuition "guesstimations" are inaccurate and ineffectual most, if not all, of the time. Learning variables impinge on learners in so many indeterminable combinations that a system of coherent and continuous analysis is mandated.

Artistic design, literary style, and technical workmanship are expectable characteristics of professionally designed learning events. Notice that a commercially designed learning event is implied to be not necessarily professional in design. But artistic design, literary style, and technical workmanship are characteristics that are considerable only after learner analysis has been accomplished.

Unavailable media may implement a learning event (if they ever reach the learners) if treated with consummate skill and, perhaps, serve somebody, someplace, well. A learning event that is a product of rational design resulting from the data from adequate learner analysis has more chances of serving identified learners well than learning events designed by means of the shotgun, broadside, run-it-up-the-flagpole-and-see-who-salutes technique.

Levels

Motivated learners who seek a broad goal may undertake any kind of a learning event that constitutes a step toward their goal. If such learners have a history of success, it is probable that they have learned some technique which helps.

Much of what most learners learn is on the level of short-term memory and simple recall. If short-term memory and simple recall is claimed to be a desirable product, then any design that gets it, in whole or in part, can be considered successful. It is difficult to believe that the true intent of the process of education accepts such ends.

Education becomes economical and professionally successful when significant information, concepts, skills, and attitudes are learned for application, analysis, synthesis, and evaluation. Added to this must be the generation of attitudes, values, and psychomotor skills on the level of successful practice. As practice of these ends is continued and refined, and as varieties of applications increase insights for transfer, learning becomes long-term in nature.

At the level of long-term learning, disregard of the process and product of learner analysis in the design of the learning event is sheer audacity. It is horrendous, but true, that currently there is no comprehensive, valid, more or less convenient way to analyze learners. There are pieces and parts here and there, now and then, but there is no coherent technique that is adequate for prescription and design.

IQ

Currently, when it exists at all, the analysis of learners is made on several important but rather obvious characteristics. The intelligence quotient (IQ) and, consequently, something called mental age (MA) and chronological age (CA) are computed. IQ has long been a controversial matter. Intervening variables have modified IQ's to make them unpredictable and by no means static over periods of time.

It is more or less common practice to test the ability of learners to see and to hear. In the area of vision, visual span, peripheral vision, and eye movements are sometimes measured. These are valuable for analysis. They can be critical determinants for learning event design. It is more or less common practice to test the ability of learners to read with speed and comprehension at a variety of levels. This kind of testing does much to influence the design of learning events. The ability to hear is sometimes tested. But the ability to listen is not commonly measured!

Achievement testing is practiced by many schools. Some special attention has been given to characteristics such as ability to perceive spatial relationships and the size of informational bits that can be spanned.

Cognitive Mapping

As concerns the needs of individuals for learning, little other analyses have been commonly practiced. Cognitive mapping, preceded by comprehensive testing, has been practiced by Oakland Community College at Bloomfield Hills, Michigan, under the presidency of Joseph E. Hill. Cognitive mapping is subsequently used for prescribing con-

tact modes to bring the learner to the subject matter; but the design of learning events with which to contact the learner has not yet been exercised to its optimal potential.

One attitude frequently found in schools is that learners are exposed to events under assignment. Success is a sign of skill and good attitude. Moderate success is a sign of teacher skill and less desirable student attitudes. Failure is often taken as being unquestionably the result of the student's characteristics.

STATUS QUO, ERODING

That there are more ways than one to educate people is a sign of an active and versatile profession and a repertoire of alternatives. The question is still whether we use the alternatives of the repertoire in the right ways, with the right learners, at the right time.

It is important to know which alternatives, or which combinations, influence the rational design of learning events. The repertoire is noneffective if a single way is chosen to be used with a massed group, unless the group is almost totally equated. For any given learner with any given learning event, it is probable that there is one better way for him to learn; but that way is more likely to be different from the ways that other learners may learn than it is to be the same.

If we are really sincere about developing learning successes as a guarantee, at some level, for all learners, we need a means for determining which of the many possible ways are better for everyone. We need, then, a means of rational design, including pertinent modes of display, reaction, practice, and performance, criterion checks to diagnose progress, and evaluation techniques to signal success.

Process, in General

We can analyze learner characteristics. When learner characteristics are identified that require analysis, we can design analyses if they do not already exist. As a practice, consistently, we do not use analysis techniques and the data they produce to diagnose and prescribe. What is needed is to

1. Identify and classify the learning characteristics that apply to specific persons for specific learning events.
2. Test the degrees of possession, or absence, of the learning characteristics of each person.
3. Design techniques of analysis and treat the data accumulated by the tests.
4. Design a means of expository summarization of the data. The purpose is to make the summary useful for diagnoses.
5. Make prescriptions of learning events for specific learners based on diagnoses.
6. Design and produce learning events that implement prescriptions.
7. Developmentally test and validate learning events.
8. Design criterion checks to monitor progress in learning at critical checkpoints.
9. Generate appropriate remediation, repetition, or advancement in scope and/or depth.

PLANNING

Without data, the designer operates with the sheerest fabric of guesswork. An adequate analysis of the learner provides the orientation and specific characteristics to be applied in the design of the learning event.

Analogically, planning without analysis data is the same as starting to cook a meal (a general goal) without deciding that the product will be a cake (a specific objective). And not having a recipe for the fruitcake is the same as not knowing the ingredient characteristics of the design of the specific learning event.

The elements of a learning event may have a sequential order. A sequential order may also be unnecessary. Analysis data direct the designer to engage the learner at some point in the order or to ignore order as a requirement.

Except for the most obvious kinds of conditions, specific objectives should have the following as their consistent format:

1. An action verb that is semantically stable.
2. The conditions with which the learner must work.
3. The standards of performance called successful.

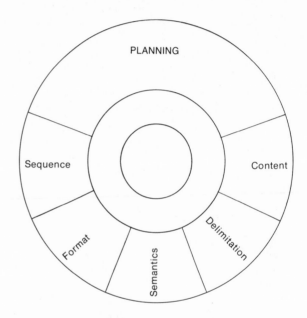

Process, in General

To serve the purposes of a definitely written objective, the designer must identify the content that supports it. The designer takes into account the following.

1. Entry information, concepts, skills, and attitudes brought to the event by the learner.
2. Point at which the content must begin.
3. Level at which the content must proceed.
4. Pace that is most acceptable to the learner.
5. Relevance that makes the content worthwhile to learner.

6. Point at which the content must end to ensure closure for the learning event.
7. Removal of elements that are not pertinent to the stated objective.
8. Design of one or more enrichment activities to satisfy the potential of unexpected learner interest and success.

Formats of planning

Format is a consideration in the planning of a learning event. Some formats, by the nature of their content, are rigorously structured. Rigorously structured formats, when they are prerequisite, require almost no decisions other than assuring that the rigor of development is accomplished.

Other formats have no such rigorous destiny. The object is for one element of such content after another to contact and complete exposure to the learner. When formats have no predetermined destiny, the designer is enjoined to do the following:

1. Arrange a sequence in the most apparently logical way, for example, from the easy to the difficult, from the simple to the complex, from the concrete to the abstract, or from the naive to the sophisticated.
2. Design the mode, or combination of modes, which appear to implement the presentation of the content so that it will be expeditiously exposed to the learner, for example,
   a. lecture or recorded sound, including,
   b. visualization in any of the available forms,
   c. printed matter, including the obvious, and worksheets, enrichment matter, maps, charts, and diagrams,
   d. tools, materials, and facilities indigenous to the event.
3. Check the general design for semantic content. Design the event as much as possible in the idiom of the learner without sacrificing rules of

acceptable grammar or principles of communication.
4. Keep in mind that visuals require semantic editing, too. For both verbal symbols and pictorial symbols, establish definitions with learner, or replace the symbols with others that have previously been defined.

SELECTION

After a learning event has been planned, there are several ways to treat the media that potentially support it:

1. Do not use any media. Now, this sounds easy, but you must remember the definition of a medium. A medium has been defined to be anything that carries a message. By that definition, even the voice becomes a medium. So to decide not to use any media becomes an irrelevant decision.
2. Select relevant commercially prepared media. If you find such media that truly and accurately serve your purposes, they are actually less

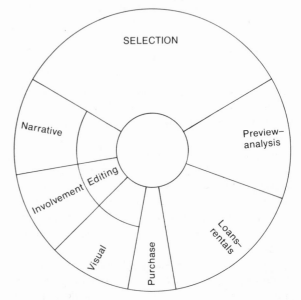

expensive of money, effort, and time than to produce your own media.

3. Produce your own media. In fact, unless a commercial medium can be located that fits the objective of the learning event and the requirements of the learner, you should produce your own.

At its most realistic level, educational philosophy continuously extols the worth and dignity of the individual. At some point in the statement of philosophy of almost all schools, a declaration can be found that describes, to some degree, concern for the individual differences among learners and the consequent differential in needs for learning. In practice, this philosophy should convert to action. The action implies that different learners need different treatments and media for learning events which arrive at their moment of attention.

Money, Time, Effort

Acquiring media for learners is implicitly expensive of money, time, and effort. Providing remediative media for learners is additionally expensive in no lesser way. Repetition media, media that provide a variety of experiences in a variety of situations related to common elements, thus developing transfer, and media for enrichment in scope and depth are all expensive in the same way as any other media. There is really no alternative to expending such resources, however. The choice, if there is any, is between accountability and sophistication as opposed to geometrically increasing degrees of mediocrity and obsolescence. And, thus far, we have been talking about acquiring commercially produced media.

To produce one's own media also takes money, effort, and time if an acceptable product is to meet reasonable standards. It takes even more if the media is to be developmentally tested and validated.

Production Ratio

A ratio of, minimally, 100 : 1, expressed in man-hours, is needed on the average to produce the media for learning events with quality of acceptable standards. Developmental testing and validation might easily consume another 50 : 1 man-hours.

The development of validated learning events is obviously expensive. But invalidated learning events, whatever their structure, have developed a history that shows them to be expensive, too. What matters is what we accept as our values. It matters what kind of a product we want, and who wants it, for whom.

Are we in the business of educating all learners to the limits of their apparent capacities? Or are we, as educators, involved in the management of a competition, where the losers gain only our sympathy—and not much of that? Do we design learning events to produce successful learners, whatever it costs? Or do we organize groups called "classes," expound, display, and expose as we choose, and let the educational casualties drop out as they may?

Validated design is expensive in terms of time, effort, and money, but it is economical in terms of success and the generation of appetites to continue. Any other techniques may be economical of time, effort, and money, but they are expensive in terms of people who become educational casualties.

Media are highly complex instruments. They are laden, sometimes jammed, with signals, cues, and other message elements. To know a medium well enough to apply it to a learning event requires intensive preview. This is axiomatic. It is ignorable, but at a price. The price is loss of learner effect.

It can never be construed to be enough information, for the design of learning events, to proceed on what one might find in a catalog blurb, a teacher's guide, or even the written or spoken professional opinions of colleagues. Professional selection is the reactive yield resulting from the requirements exposed by analysis of the learner. Quod erat demonstrandum, you have to look at the medium yourself, carefully, perhaps more than once, with details in mind!

Logistics

To make use of a medium in all its potential, several logistical considerations are necessary:

1. Can you own it, and, obviously, do you?
2. Or can you rent it for periods of time long enough to be useful?
3. Or can you borrow it, if it is a free-loan item, for long enough periods of time to be useful?

Editing

There are three kinds of editing that a professional educator will want to exercise on a medium, unless the medium is designed to precise specifications for the learning event:

1. Visual editing.
2. Narrative editing.
3. Involvement editing.

You must own a medium to edit it visually. It is not considered good practice to cut up rental media or free-loan media. You might need to get permission from your administrators to edit a medium visually, even if you do own it.

The purpose of visual editing is to eliminate superfluities, redundancies, and distractions, or anything else not to the point. Many media have title and credit leaders, an introduction, a body of message, a summary, and trailer credits and leaders. Not seldom, the body of the message makes the point. When it does, the rest can be ignored, even removed, without essentially affecting the message.

In the other direction, the message of a medium may need additions for it to meet the required standards. To name a few, such additions may be added to

1. Provide clarifications.
2. Make transitions.
3. Make reorientations.
4. Demonstrate examples.
5. Demonstrate applications.
6. Develop relationships.

Such developmental editing, advisedly accomplished, can make the difference between no significant effects, mediocrity, and an optimal quality of success.

When existing narratives on recordings or sound tracks are at inappropriate levels, editing can be done to bring them to desirable standards. Narrative editing would be desirable when

1. Expository pace is too fast or too slow.
2. Pace of development is too fast or too slow.
3. Idioms are inappropriate.
4. Level is inappropriate.
5. Audio symbols need definition.
6. Timing, especially for response, is inadequate.

Audio tapes can be edited by excision, insertion, or dubbing.

Excision   Excision means that you cut out what you do not want and splice the tape together at the cutout point.

Insertion   Insertion means that you cut the tape at a logical point and splice in a piece of tape which contains whatever you want it to contain.

Dubbing   Dubbing is a corruption of the word "duplication." As you duplicate a tape, you can eliminate whatever you want from the original simply by not recording it on the copy. You can insert whatever you want during dubbing by means of either a physical splice and addition or by stopping the original, recording the addition, and then continuing with the original at whatever point you choose.

The general purpose of narrative editing is to make the narrative appropriate to the needs of the learner and the objectives of the learning event.

Involvement

Involvement editing is a technique used to include learner activities within the message of a medium. Such inclusions would be any one or combinations of the following examples:

1. To stimulate commentary, questions, and the like.
2. To seek applications for message content.
3. To react to direct questions.
4. To practice skills.
5. To complete notes.
6. To provide timing cues to signal stopping points. This would allow the learning event to undertake any desirable activity and return to the medium when appropriate.

Involvement editing can be implemented by the following:

1. Timing cues and subsequent verbal direction.
2. Visual supplement, slides, overhead transparencies, for example, charts, diagrams, or posters.
3. Multimediation.

A medium, otherwise untreated, may or may not be optimally effective. A simple display of any medium may be an inadequate use of a relatively expensive item.

People are complex. Learning is complex. The adequate design of a learning event that is validatable is a complex process. Media are complex. The production of a validatable medium is complex. Adequate application of validatable media to successful learning events requires the complex synthesis of analyses and treatments.

DESIGN

Considerations for design of a learning event include the following major elements of concern:

1. Message design.
2. Modalities design.
3. Medial design.
4. Control techniques design.
5. Feedback search design.
6. Developmental testing design.
7. Validation design.

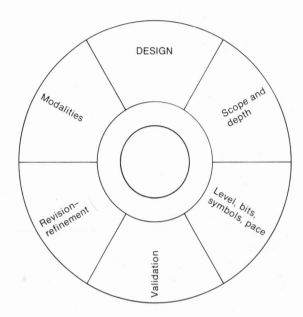

Process

Message design is a product that results from data and selections from earlier parts of the design process. The product of design comes from synthesis of the following:

1. Curricular decision.
2. Selection of content.
3. Delimitation of content.
4. When available and appropriate, media selection.
5. When appropriate, editing of media.
6. The main subject of this segment, message design considerations.

Considerations for Design of the Message

The considerations of message design include the following:

1. What is the scope of the message?
2. What is the depth of the message and its elements?
3. What entry level skills are required to learn the message content?
4. At what level will the verbal and pictorial parts of the message be designed?
5. What verbal and pictorial symbols will be used?
6. What limits of verbal bit lengths will be used?
7. What limits of eye span will be used for pictorial bits?
8. What techniques of eye scan will be used for pictorial bits?
9. At what pace will the message be exposed?

All messages should have a level of optimal reception. Learners vary in their abilities to receive messages. Messages should also conform to the abilities of various learners to comprehend them.

Reception and comprehension are controlled to various degrees by the size of the informational bits that are exposed to learners. The pace at which bits are exposed also influence the success of reception and comprehension.

Pictorial Elements

With pictorial elements of message, eye span is also important for reception and comprehension. Too many pictorial symbols presented at once, or over an area that is wider than the learner can effectively span at one glance, tend to create confusion, frustration, and loss of learning.

Verbal Elements

To some extent with verbal symbols, and always with pictorial symbols, it is important to consider eye scan. The direction that is taken by the occidental eye is from a starting point at the upper left part of visual image moving to the right, and increasingly downward. It behooves the designer to place attention-getting symbols with appropriate location and intensiveness, and to include appropriate recycling devices at strategic points.

Entry Points and Entry Behaviors

The message of a learning event begins at some starting point. Logically, the message ends at a point where the objective of the learning event is accomplished.

Not all learners can enter a learning event at the same point. Any given message may be designed at just the right starting point for some learners. Other learners will need to learn relevant preliminary matters before they can begin. Still others may already know parts of the learning events that are more suitable for advanced conditions. These kinds of considerations constitute the process of delimitation in message design.

The human voice is a medium. The human voice is carried by the air in the form of waves. When the waves strike the ear of a receiver, they may be interpreted as being a message. If the receiver has meaning for the symbols he interprets from the air waves, he may comprehend the message. If the meaning he has for the symbols is the same as the meaning the sender intends for them, the learner may comprehend the messages as the sender expects he will.

Modalities

No matter what medium is chosen to carry the message, it must be exposed so that the learner can receive it as it is intended. The arrangement chosen to expose the learner to the message is called a modality. The following are examples of modalities:

1. Formal lectures, informal lectures, extemporaneous lectures.
2. Chalk talks, illustrated lectures, presentations.
3. Demonstrations, participatory instruction.
4. Seminars, forums, panels, symposia.
5. Experiments, investigations, conferences, workshops.
6. Tutorials.
7. Independent learning activities:
   a. Individually prescribed instruction.
   b. Independently guided education.
   c. Programmed education prescriptions.
   d. Competency-based education.

Hardware such as projectors, television monitors, and recording playback units, individually or in any combination, are basically inert until they are loaded with an appropriate medium. A medium is basically irrelevant unless it carries a message that generates the responses intended by the designer of the learning event.

The message must be such that the learner has meaning for its symbols and their interactive intent. When it is exposed, the learner must interpret the exposure as the designer intended or the message is unsuccessful. It is naive to presume that any message can be successfully carried in optimal quality of characteristics by any medium.

Media Characteristics

Figure 1 shows characteristics possessed by a wide range of media. Combinations of media, used in multimediated learning events, may be able to provide learning experiences that could not be achieved by a single medium. The chart describes the characteristics possessed by the medium for carrying and exposing the message. Where obviously necessary, it is presumed that the appropriate hardware is also used.

Explanations of some of the terms used across the top of the chart are as follows:

1. *Mass instruction:* the message must be large enough and loud enough to be seen and heard by all learners. Significant details in words, numbers, and other pictures must be distinct and clear.
2. *Individualized instruction:* learners should not need to cope with heavy, numerous, or complicated items of equipment. The message should be designed so that all necessary information is inserted as it becomes relevant, and means of responses and practices should be provided along with adequate time.
3. *Shift of levels:* the medium should be flexible so that when one level or another is discovered to be inadequate for the learner, an appropriate one may replace the inadequate one.
4. *Details of symbols:* some symbols are more detailed than others. When perception of details is pertinent to learning, those details should be clear and distinct.
5. *Details of staging:* some learning events develop a continuum that is related to the nature of the learning objective. When such development is a characteristic of the event, the event should progress through a series of stages. Some events require such staging in more detail than others. The medium should be able to tolerate staging in whatever detail is required.
6. *Additive:* some learning events require that the learning be provided with a base from which to begin. As the event progresses, elements are added when they become appropriate. The medium should permit additions of elements when they are required.
7. *Subtractive:* some learning events require the removal of elements from an event. An example would be the disassembly of machinery or the dissection of animals and plants. The medium show allow such progressive display.
8. *Timed exposure:* motion pictures, video tapes, and audiotapes, even filmstrips and slide sets accompanied by audiotaped sound, run through their respective hardware at constant

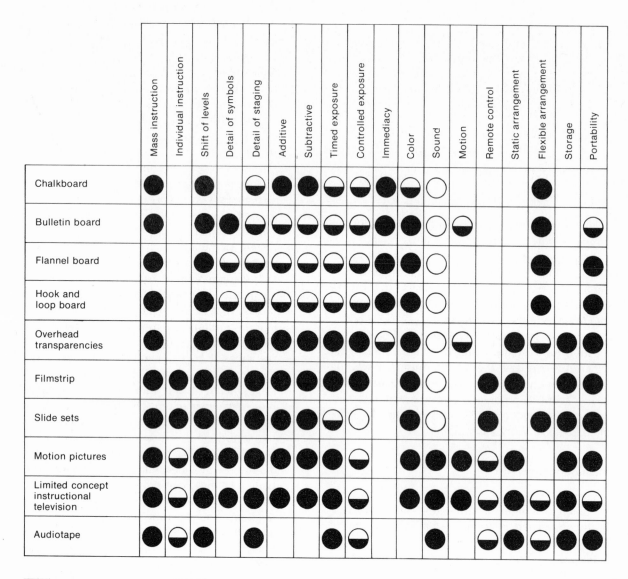

Figure 1

rates of speed. This characteristic may or may not be desirable, depending on the nature of the learning event. The medium should be able to tolerate necessary basic designs or modifications to provide timed exposure, or to eliminate such timing, as appropriate.

9. *Controlled exposure:* some learning events, and some learners, require different exposure times than others. The medium and its hardware should be adaptable to requirements. It should be possible to hold or to proceed with any given segment of the medium.

10. *Immediacy:* by diagnoses of learner needs and progress, specific experiences may come to be relevant for learning. It should be possible to design a medium that can be provided as needed. Media that have such characteristics can provide learners with learning support with more or less immediacy.

11. *Static arrangement:* some learning experiences need to be displayed to learners in a specific sequence for optimal learning. Media which are arranged so that only one sequence is effectively possible are said to have static arrangement.

12. *Flexible arrangement:* a medium that can be arranged in different ways with convenience.

Learning Events

A learning event consists of the following fundamental parts:

1. A rationale that describes to the learner the reasons why it is desirable to expend the energy, time, and perhaps money to learn a particular objective.

2. The broad goal to which the learning event contributes.

3. The specific objective of the learning event, including the action, the conditions of practice and performance, and the standards of successful performance.

4. The scheme of participation and progress.
5. The medium that supports the scheme, which may include media.
6. Criteria checks to diagnose strategic points of progress or breakdowns in learning.
7. The appropriate performance that exposes success.

When a learning event is designed, using the framework of fundamental parts, it is possible to exercise a degree of control over each. Criterion checks are designed to provide the learner and teacher with means of diagnoses for learner successes, progress, or specific points of difficulty or breakdown.

When a rationale is presented, especially when it is from the learner's point of view, the learner is more likely to spend energy and time leading to long-term learning. Such learner acceptance of what he perceives to be worthwhile learning may also lead to increased versatility of transfer and applicability.

The broad goal to which the learning event contributes helps the learner to perceive the larger picture into which the specific objective fits. It assists in making relationships, syntheses, generalizations, and evaluations.

The specific objective informs the learner about his immediate learning target. When the objective describes action, the learner knows what kind of behavior is expected. When it describes conditions, the learner knows the environment, tools, and materials with which he must perform. When it describes standards, the learner knows that when he is able to perform at identified levels of quality and quantity he is successful.

The terminal evaluation is made using the objective criteria. More often than not, learners become successful, some earlier than others, but eventually successful at expectable levels.

A learning event can be said to be appropriate when the learner for whom it is designed can perform as described by the standards of performance. Of course, this is also, *prima facie,* valid and reliable evidence of the success of the learner, as well.

Validation

If a learning event is designed to accommodate more than one learner, it becomes increasingly difficult to validate the event as successful for all the learners in the group.

Validation is a two-stage process: (1) developmental testing, and (2) validation. Validation is an expensive process if one considers the energy, time, and money involved. The skill necessary for design and validation is an axiomatic prerequisite. But to achieve acceptable accountability at the definition of learner success per educator effort, there is no other route. If the difference between whether or not a learner learns to the limits of his developable capacities is a function of the adequacy of the learning event, measured by its productive effect, then there is no other route.

Developmental Testing

Developmental testing is a process of revision and refinement. The data that direct the apparently needed changes are produced by five stages of testing:

1. The learning event is tried out by a student selected from the more rapid learners of the target group. In the presence of the developmental tester, who may or may not be the designer, this student does what he is directed to do by the design of the learning event. In addition, because he is informed, he knows that he should ask any questions he wants to ask that are related to the event. During the tryout, the tester makes notes about whatever the student says or about any points at which learning seems to diverge from the path of smooth success. Using these data, the learning event is revised.
2. Then the revised event is tried out by a student selected from the more ordinary learners of the target group. He, too, is informed that he is, in fact, testing the event. Notes are kept in detail, as before. Revisions are made as indicated by the accumulated data.
3. The same process is repeated with a student selected from the slower learners of the target group. He is treated just like the other two. Data are collected, and revisions made as indicated.
4. After the third-stage revisions have been made, three to six students, other than the first three, are selected. They are selected to represent each of the kinds of learners as characterized by the original three. The small group tries out the event. They, too, ask any questions or make any comments they deem useful. Detailed notes are kept by the tester. Revisions are made on the basis of the notes. By this time, the revisions should be few in number.
5. The last stage is validation. At this point, the design is used under conditions directed. It is used with the target group. It should be, by this time, effective. It is, therefore, validated. If any problems arise, revisions should be made accordingly. There is, probably, no learning event that will ever be without revision-preference for some learners. After validation, however, such revisions should be rare to few in number and easy to provide.

PLANNING

The emphasis in this part of the rational design of learning events is on planning for production. That is, the emphasis is on designing what will be produced. There is little or no attention given to the technical process of production in this segment.

Certain technicalities of planning are unique to the production of specific media. A motion picture script or scenario is somewhat different from the script for a narration or audioplay recorded on audiotape. Either scenario or script are different from the plan for a graphic display, or the text and content plan for a programmed instruction item.

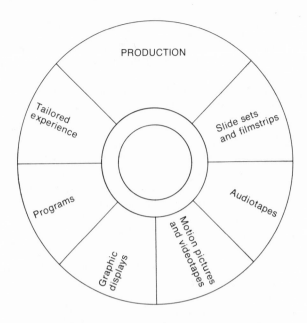

PRODUCTION

Tailored experience

Slide sets and filmstrips

Audiotapes

Motion pictures and videotapes

Graphic displays

Programs

Data Sources

In general, all the data from the foregoing pages impinge upon the plan for production. The data sources include the following:

1. Curricular decision, including a statement of relevance for each learning event, and a plan for motivation to be developed from later data.
2. Analyses of learners.
3. Components of planning.
4. Selection of media or rejection.
5. Design of learning events.

Levels of Production

The objective of planning is to organize the elements that can predictably generate the expected behavioral outcomes. Organization of elements occurs on the following levels:

1. Specifically relevant learning at a basic level.
2. Enrichment learning at a level advanced in scope and/or depth.

3. Levels, apparently repetitious, for the purpose of developing versatility in application, or for recouping otherwise unobtained details of information, or for reinforcing learning.
4. Remediative levels for the purpose of bringing the learner to the proper abilities of learning that enable him to enter successfully the original learning event.

Intent of Planning

The intent of planning is to organize for production the message, the mode of exposure of the message, the medium(a) to carry the message, supplementary items for response and practice, and a testing device. A medium is produced to show something or to say something. The emphasis on showing, or on saying, may be total or partial. Decisions about which, or in what combination, are made by the producer as a result of his analysis of what will efficaciously produce the intended behavior outcome(s).

To develop the intended behavior outcomes, plans are made for means, including supplementary items as required, for (1) response participation, (2) reinforcement techniques, and/or (3) practice events.

Basic Items

The following are the basic items to be treated in planning for production:

1. The objective to be developed and attained as a result of exposure to the medium(a) and its supplements.
2. The format of the medium(a) and its supplements.
3. The structure of the content of the medium(a), that is, the terms and symbols to be used and the ways in which they are to be arranged.
4. The physical specifications of the medium(a), that is,

a. Color or black and white.
b. Sound or silent.
c. Length in feet, minutes of exposure time, frames, slides, or whatever.
d. Features of the target audience that influence production aspects of the medium(a), such as
    (1) Rate of development.
    (2) Pace.
    (3) Level of content.
    (4) Size of images.
    (5) Intensity of detail.
    (6) Size of informational bits.
5. The nature of the supplemental media required for appropriate involvement, responses, and practices.

Purposes of Motion Media

Except for apparent motion effects, the only media that can provide motion for learning events are, obviously, motion pictures and instructional television. Motion pictures and television can also display still images. The advantage, when it is relevant, of using motion media to display still images is in the timing of exposure that they can provide.

The use of motion media is thus pertinent only when motion and/or timing is a critical element of the learning event. It is critical when it affects whether or not the learner learns what he is expected to learn in the ways he is expected to learn it. It is also critical when it affects or reinforces the attraction, retention, guidance, or recycling of attention.

Formats

Media can be produced in specific formats or a combination of them. The format of an event is selected for planning for only one reason, that is, because it appears to be the most desirable to expose the content which proposes to generate the intended behavioral outcomes.

The following are some formats that are successfully applied to learning events:

1. *Documentary event:* an event that is recorded as it occurs. It is, in a sense, history as it happens. It can be a record of any kind of happening, including all the events of the universe—the action of stars, the eruption of a volcano, the birth of an infant, the election of a president, the construction of a machine, the creation of a work of art, and so on.

2. *Reconstructed event:* an event of unrecorded history recorded as reconstructed because the event was missed as a documentary. Missing the documentary recording of an event may be because of timing or because, when the actual event occurred, appropriate recording technology was not available. A reconstructed event can be accurate and precise when data allow, or it can be more or less imaginative in nature.

3. *Contrived event:* an event produced to display what might have been under conditions which did not prevail but might have. It can also be used to display predictions about what might be, presuming the existence of certain conditions and certain interactions. It is to some extent imaginative in nature. On the other hand, it might approach acceptable plausibility, depending on what is displayed and how it is arranged.

4. *Logical situation event:* an event produced to display the actual or predicted outcomes from a variety of variables in interaction. It is based on facts, generalizations, hypotheses, axioms, principles, and the like. It is as close to plausibility as possible.

5. *Inductive situation event:* an event designed to portray and display circumstances which lead to the question, "Given these circumstances, what if. . . ?" It is a form of problem situation.

6. *Deductive situation event:* an event that presents data or variables for learners to deduce solutions to problems.

7. *Open-ended situation event:* an event that presents a situation which does not necessarily lead to a clear-cut solution or answers. The

classic example of this kind of event is given by the story "The Lady or the Tiger?"

8. *Demonstration event:* an event designed to demonstrate step by step any process or the development of any product. It can have characteristics of the documentary event, and it may have characteristics of the contrived event. It can also be used for presentation of problems, experiments, skills, or attitudes.

9. *Expository event:* an event that may have the characteristics of several of the foregoing. Its specific purpose is to display, from beginning to termination or logical conclusion, any event that normally has closure. It is used, designed with acceptable detail, to show structure, format, organization, process, growth, erosion, chemical reaction, logic, historical development, and so forth.

10. *Participatory event:* an event that is structured to present its content in whatever form seems most productive for the objective. Woven into the content at strategic points are devices to cause the learner to respond and to practice the behavior that are the objective. Criterion check items may also be woven into the event, especially at points where enroute behaviors produce closure on subobjectives.

11. *Theatrical play event:* an event designed, mainly, for entertainment. It may be adapted, however, as psychodrama, sociodrama, or as any of the various situation events. It can be structured to allow audience participation, both directly and in response. It is a good technique for developing moral points, attitudinal points, and insights related to the point of view of "the other."

12. *Fantasy event:* an event designed, intentionally, to distort normality. It is an imaginative application of reality, and can serve to emphasize important elements and issues. It can be used to make otherwise dry and technical matters palatable.

13. *Animated event:* an event that uses animation as a vehicle to portray any of the other kinds of formats. It can be used to display the otherwise inaccessible. It can be used to display "plausible impossibilities" when they become relevant to making a point that is part of the objective.

14. *Data event:* an event designed to display data to demonstrate logical developments, statistical treatments, or in accumulative trends. It can be used to present problems, and provide response, discussion, and solution time for learners. It can use documentary, contrived, demonstration, fantasy, or animation techniques.

15. *Programmed event:* an event with visualized programming techniques. It makes use of these techniques for providing stimuli, getting responses, reinforcing, and application. It can make use of the techniques of any other event, when appropriately arranged.

Sound Track

The production of media resolves, eventually, into the planning for one or both of a visualized portion and a sound, or audio, portion. The audio portion of planning can be (1) expository or (2) personalized.

An expository audio medium is formalized. Some may be more formally presented than others, but they are, basically, impersonal.

The personalized audio medium is informal. As their designation implies, they are presented in a style which seeks to make the learner feel that the narrator is talking to him, personally.

It is conceivable that an audio portion of a medium might make use of both, the expository style of narration and the personalized style, in appropriate combinations. Research has shown that younger learners tend to prefer and learn more effectively when audio portions are personalized. As learners become older and gain more learning experience, they tend to prefer and learn more effectively when audio portions are more increasingly expository.

Film Techniques

Depending on what is being visualized and how it must be displayed, a number of techniques are useful in planning. One basic finding of the Pennsylvania State Studies was that, for skill development, the objective angle was better. The objective angle means that the visual image is produced from an angle of view of the learner, as though the learner was actually practicing, or performing, the skill under consideration.

Other techniques that may be planned in the production of visuals are the following:

1. *Cowcatchers:* a technique often used in commercial production. It takes its name from the device on the front of a locomotive that is intended to remove obstacles from the track. In practice with media production, it means
   a. The display of content usually begins with some attention-getting effects designed to be as impactive as possible. This part often establishes the intent of the production.
   b. At a logical point following the introduction, titles, credits, or any printed messages relating to the production are given. Often, the development of the main theme continues under the titles, credits, or printed messages. Sometimes the audio effects are used to hold the basic theme in the mind of the learner.
   c. When titles, credits, or other printed messages are finished, they fade out, and the main theme continues in development.

   The object of the cowcatcher technique is to engage the attention of the viewer, get him involved, and present a message deemed to be essential in a way that is likely to require his presence and hold his attention.

2. *Overprints:* an image displayed over the main image. Sometimes, the main image is faded under the overprint. In such cases, the overprint is bold and with high contrast. An overprint may be a pictorial image or a verbal image. The purposes of overprints are to define or clarify terms, to establish relationships, to show processes and flows, or to demonstrate organizational hierarchies.

3. *Pop-on:* a picture, word, or phrase that is essentially a modified overprint. Overprints usually fade in and fade out with motion media. With still pictures, except in rare cases, fade in and fade out are not as practical. The pop-on, by comparison, is the instant appearance of a label, detail, definition, highlight, or any device having the purpose of bringing a specific element of information, relevantly, to the immediate attention of the viewer. Pop-ons may also pop off when they are no longer pertinent.

4. *Highlights:* a technique used to emphasize a part or a segment of a visual. The technique may be employed by dimming the main body of the visual with gray film or with a darker-colored film than the background of the visual. The portion of the visual of the highlight is cut away, bringing the detail up to normal brilliance. The technique is used to bring the detail to the viewer's attention while keeping it in relationship to the larger image. Highlighting may of course be an accumulative and progressive, bringing the whole image to the forefront of viewer attention in relationships and relevant stages.

5. *Exploded views:* a technique used to show the relational positions of an image composed of more than one part. The complete image has all parts in the positions they would be at a point of intention to assemble. The technique is used to show "what goes where," "which comes first," and "how it's supposed to look."

6. *Multiple exposures:* a technique that uses a main image, a series of secondary or tertiary images, and, sometimes, the apparent blur of motion leading from one significant movement to another. It is used for motion analysis. It usually includes the progress of motion from a

completely stationary beginning point to a completely stationary terminal point, showing a detail of all movements between the points. The technique can also be a transitional effect, attention getter, attention director, or recycler.

7. *Selective coloration:* a technique that is more or less the reverse of highlighting. Using selective coloration, the chosen detail is colored in a contrasting hue. The technique specifies the detail expected to be under attention.

8. *Distinctive coloration:* a technique that enlarges on selective coloration and uses a variety of colors to enable the learner to distinguish between two or several details, units, components, systems, and so on. Any number of colors may be used, but a single color is assigned to one class of details and another distinctively different color is used for another class of details. Care must be taken to avoid colors that may be within a spectrum of color blindness afflicting certain learners.

9. *Technamation:* a process that uses polarized light and certain transparent materials which respond to polarity. It creates an apparent motion of images. The motion can be linear, radiating, concentric expansion, curved, or somewhat kaleidoscopic. It is used to indicate process flows or growth lines, to direct attention, and to provide apparently animated symbols.

10. *Slow motion:* a technique that uses high-speed photography which, when displayed at normal speeds or slower, provides a possibility of perception of details of motion that would not be possible under life conditions at normal speeds.

11. *Time lapse:* the reverse of slow motion. It is used when processes, growth, and the like, happen at a slow rate of speed that prohibits perception or makes it difficult. The process is one where camera and object are held in the same relative position over the time of recording. Images are recorded, measured time is allowed to pass, then other images are recorded. When displayed at normal speeds, the result is a speeding up of the otherwise slow process.

12. *Stop motion:* in this technique the speed of the camera brings the swiftly moving image to an apparent full stop. It is a process like slow motion except that the intervals between stops are actually absent. It is used for motion analyses, erosion analyses, and for situation–condition analyses.

13. *Photomicrography:* photography of magnified images and their details, which are normally too small to be seen without magnification to some relevant power.

14. *Photomacrography:* photography of image details when the image itself is visible to the unaided eye, but the details require magnification for perception.

15. *Cinefluoroscopy:* a motion picture made of an image in motion by means of xrays. It can be used to show motion in parts that are obscured by other opaque parts.

There are several ways of planning for a production. Whatever format is eventually selected, in general planning consists of three basic stages:

1. Story boarding (5- by 7-inch card planning).
2. Working scripting.
3. Finished scripting.

Story Boarding

Story boarding is a process that uses cards or pieces of paper for development of the following three components of a production:

1. The content outline, conforming to the basic items for consideration.
2. The narrative, which consists of
   a. Content and its details.
   b. Devices designed for response, participation, and practice.

3. The visual images, still or motion, that present content, support and supplement the narrative, and provide data for response, participation, and practice.

A card size that is useful and convenient for general handling and storage is 5 by 7 inches. One way to arrange the card is to make lines on one face of the card. Dimensions that have proved to be applicable are:

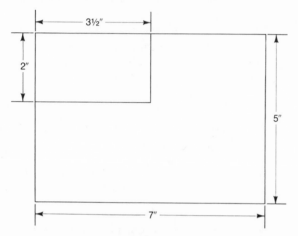

In use, the card provides spaces for the content outline, the narrative, and a suggestion for the visual image. For use with motion pictures or television, the suggestion for visual image is accompanied by a shot direction (long shot, medium shot, close-up, etc.) and any visual effects directions (fade in, fade out, dissolve, wipe, cut, etc.).

Content outline The content outline is developed, first. One element of the outline is placed on a single card. It is written in the upper right corner. Any amount of detail can be added to the outline simply by adding another card with the desired item of detail. Items can be deleted from the outline, when desired, by withdrawing any card and discarding it.

When arranged in sequence on a cork board, the content outline is convenient to inspect visually. It can be added to or subtracted from for purposes of

tailoring and refinement. The following main kinds of items should be arranged in their most apparently desirable strategic positions.

1. Objectives.
2. Subobjectives and interim objectives (when useful).
3. Criterion checks.
4. Supporting details.
5. Participation devices.
6. Reinforcement items.
7. Application items.

Narrative When the content outline is refined to its apparent limits, the narrative is written. Each item on each card is included in the narrative. It may be presented in whatever simplicity or detail seems to be most potentially effective.

The narrative portion of the card is the lower half. This space should be adequate to make most points. When it is not enough space, the reverse side of the card may be used in whatever part is needed.

Planning cards make it possible to edit a narrative by (1) addition, (2) subtraction, (3) modification, and (4) replacement.

Cards are added for the following purposes:

1. Transition between two related elements.
2. Bridging between apparently unrelated elements.
3. Supplementation when elements need
   a. Clarification.
   b. Definition.
   c. Expansion of content to complete required details.
   d. Coordination when several elements need to have relationships illuminated.

Cards are subtracted for the following reasons:

1. Narratives are at levels too high or too low for the audience.
2. Narratives are excessively wordy.
3. Restructuring is needed for development of better generation of meaning.

4. Elements need to be divided or subdivided for better development of content.

Cards are modified for the following reasons:

1. Grammatical improvement is needed.
2. Editorial restructuring is indicated.
3. Opportunities are induced for better visualization.

Cards are replaced whenever changes make the need for replacement obvious and imperative.

Visual treatments   When the narrative is completed in the best discernable context with the content outline, visualization is designed for each card. Visualization may be, of course, by means of any visual image, such as the following:

1. The words of the content outline.
2. Appropriate lists, charts, or diagrams.
3. Appropriate outline drawings, maps, or plans.
4. Sketches of any relevant item.
5. Photographs of models, mock-ups, or realia.
6. Symbols that have meaning to learners.

At this point in story boarding, executing the graphic work for visuals is accomplished. When still pictures are required, transparencies for overhead projection may be desirable. Or they may be committed to flip charts, slide sets, or further processed into filmstrips. Motion pictures can be recorded by means of motion picture photography or by video taping televised camera work. The decision about which kind of treatment to use for what kind of production is based on analyses of the requirements of all the variables. The veracity of the analyses can be proved only by eventual validation.

The narrative is also a focus for a decision. The decision to be made is to determine how the narrative is to be presented. Presentation of the narrative can be done "live" when the presenter reads the script aloud as the visuals are exposed at points of control, called cues. The narrative may become a sound track on a motion picture or an audio track on a video tape. Audio tape recording is also a means of control and presentation of the narrative.

Plan cards are an excellent system for designing programmed instruction. Whether linear or branching, programmed instruction has several parts:

1. An information base.
2. A stimulus.
3. An opportunity requiring a response.
4. A reinforcement.

Branching programs also provide

5. Remediation.

In effective programs, remediation may never be used. If needed, however, it is there. In linear programs, the need for remediation is not recognized. It is presumed, for linear programs, that if remediation is needed the program needs revision.

For branching programs, the first three parts constitute an information–response frame. The fourth part is the format of the reinforcement frame. The fifth part is a remediation frame.

Frames may be designed, developmentally tested, and validated by means of planning cards.

Multimediation Planning

Under some conditions, combinations of narrative presentation methods and visual presentation methods may be required. When more than one medium is used for any presentation, the presentation is known as a "multimediated" presentation or learning event.

In a multimediated learning event, control is a factor of planning. The need for control is centered around presenting to the learner the appropriate visual, or combination of visuals, together with its related narrative. In effect, to reduce confusion to a minimum, the designer of the learning event should plan so that only one component of hardware (loaded with relevant media) needs to operate or be controlled by a presenter (live, electronic, or mechanical) at any one time.

Planning for such presentational control can be accomplished efficiently by means of a planning sheet. In its final forms, the planning sheet provides the following:

1. Information about content and objectives of the learning event.
2. Author and date of completion.
3. Pagination.
4. Narrative, including exposition, directions for response or practice, reinforcement, and application devices.
5. Cues to indicate, more or less precisely, where visuals are to be exposed, changed, or removed from attention.
6. Control channels to indicate the kind of hardware required at any given cue mark, and what the action of the hardware is supposed to be.
7. The channel content, which describes what is to be exposed to the learner when the hardware presents any visual, or when any visual mode is presented.

Like any other element of production, developmental testing that proceeds to validation will disclose needs for refinement of the multimediated plan and any or all of its associated elements. Before achieving validation, the multimediated plan may be changed a number of times, usually in the direction of clarification and definition, and often in the direction of simplicity.

Figure 2 shows a multimediated plan sheet. In practice, the multimediated plan sheet is used by writing the title of the subject-matter content across the top of the sheet. This title can be in whatever detail is needed to maintain the orientation of the designer.

Title section   Immediately beneath the title, the objective of the learning event is written in behavioral form, as follows:

1. Use an action verb that is semantically stable.
2. Provide the conditions under which behavior is to be performed, including
   a. Cognitive.
   b. Psychomotor.

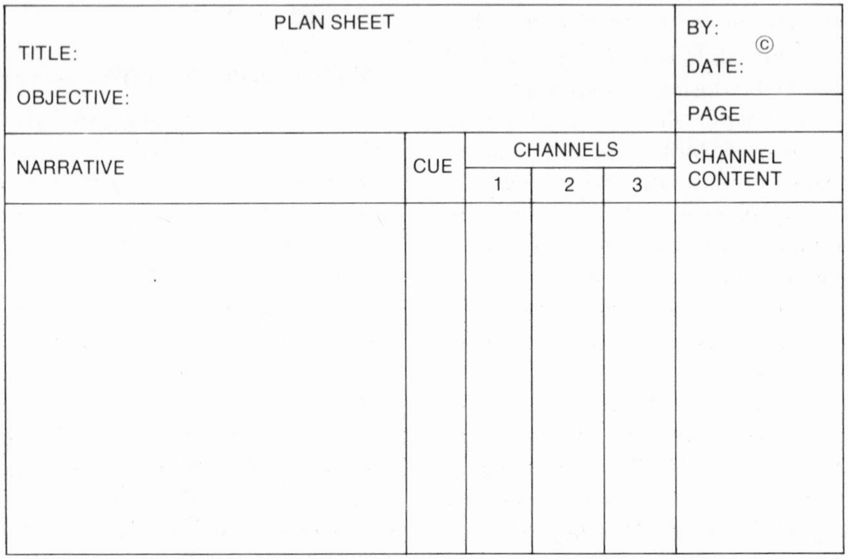

PLAN SHEET					BY: ©
TITLE:					DATE:
OBJECTIVE:					
					PAGE
NARRATIVE	CUE	CHANNELS			CHANNEL CONTENT
		1	2	3	

Figure 2

c. Affective.

d. Verbal.

e. Discriminating.

3. Provide standards of performance that are acceptable as being satisfactory.

```
┌──────────────────────────────┬─────────────┐
│ TITLE:                       │             │
│ OBJECTIVE:                   ├─────────────┤
│                              │             │
├──────────────┬──┬───┬────────┴─────────────┤
│              │  │   │                      │
│              │  │   │                      │
│              │  │   │                      │
└──────────────┴──┴───┴──────────────────────┘
```

In the right corner block of the plan sheet, four items of information are recorded:

1. Name of the designer (author).

2. The word "copyright" or the abbreviation "copr." or the symbol "©," to indicate that the design has statutory copyright benefits.

3. Date of completion, that is, the year.

4. Pagination.

```
┌──────────────────────────┬────────────────┐
│                          │ BY: NAME     © │
│                          │ DATE:          │
│                          ├────────────────┤
│                          │ PAGE           │
├───────────────┬──┬───────┴────────────────┤
│               │  │  │  │                   │
│               │  │  │  │                   │
│               │  │  │  │                   │
└───────────────┴──┴──┴──┴───────────────────┘
```

Narrative column   The narrative is, preferably, typed in the left column on the lower part of the page. The area of the column is designed so that when elite type, single spacing between lines, and double spacing between paragraphs are used, and the column is read at about 120 words per minute, the column will take about 2 minutes to read. Obviously, this rate and density per sheet provides a convenient means for timing the presentation.

When pauses in the narrative are required for any purpose, such pauses can be timed by showing a series of dots following the word at which the pause begins. Each dot stands for one second of pause time. If pauses are to be longer than 10 seconds, the paragraph of narration is triple spaced at the pause point, and the required length of pause is indicated in parentheses, for example, (15 seconds) or (2 minutes) or whatever is necessary.

If, during the multimediated presentation, a segment of a motion picture, or a video tape, or an audio tape is used in place of the narrative, the narrative paragraph is given five lines of spacing. In parentheses, conveniently within the five lines, the title of the recorded medium is given, plus its running time, for example, (Maurice Evans—Hamlet's soliloquy—3 minutes).

Cue column   The column labeled CUE is used to indicate points in the narrative where a piece of hardware or an element of media that does not require hardware will be operated or otherwise manipulated. At the point of decision to operate or manipulate, an asterisk or other emphatic mark is used. The cue mark indicates the line of narrative on which the operation or manipulation is relevant.

When it becomes important to operate hardware or manipulate a medium for display at a specific word in the narration, the word is circled, and a line is drawn in the space between lines of type to connect the circled word with its companion cue mark. The circled word, connected with the cue mark, indicates that the display should appear to the learner at that specific word.

Channel columns   On the multimediated plan sheet, there are three columns labeled CHANNELS and numbered 1, 2, and 3. Channels are used to indicate what hardware will be used and what it will be doing. For purposes of expedition, a medium that requires no companion hardware is treated the same as a piece of hardware in the channel columns.

Hardware abbreviations Abbreviations that indicate the companion hardware or media that are not hardware-bound will save a great deal of writing or typing time. The following are examples:

M/P	= motion picture projector
M/P8	= standard 8mm motion picture projector
M/P8+	= super 8mm motion picture projector
F/S	= filmstrip projector
S/S	= slide projector
T/R	= tape recorder, reel to reel
CT/R	= cassette tape recorder
P/T	= phonograph
O/H	= overhead projector
O/P	= opaque projector
C/B	= chalkboard
B/B	= bulletin board
RLA	= realia
MAP	= map
CHT	= chart
DIA	= diagram
F/C	= flip chart
VTR	= video tape recorder
CVTR	= cassette video tape recorder
EVR	= electro video recorder
MDL	= model
H/O	= hand out
?	= time to ask, or answer, questions
T/M	= tools and materials
FWD	= filmstrip, or slide set, advance one forward
BWD	= filmstrip, or slide set, retreat one frame backward; when more than one frame or slide is to be advanced, the symbols would be

FWD+3 or BWD−3

+1	= add one overhead overlay, #1
+2	= add one overhead overlay, #2
−1	= withdraw one overlay, #1
−2	= withdraw one overlay, #2

Hardware notations Whether the medium requires companion hardware or not when it is cued is noted in the channel columns. Whenever the medium is brought to the attention of learners, it is recorded as ON. When removed from learner attention, it is recorded as OFF.

The symbol ON is considered to block the channel. That channel can be used for nothing else until the symbol OFF appears in it. Any further media use is recorded in channels which happen to be free, that is, not blocked. Whenever the symbol OFF does appear, the channel can be used for any other medium or item of companion hardware.

The ON, OFF rule can be modified when filmstrips, slide sets, overhead transparencies, flip charts, or any other medium that develops progressively by addition, subtraction, or change remains in the constant attention of the learner. A filmstrip or slide set may move forward or backward one or more frames or slides. The symbols FWD, to mean move forward, and BWD, to mean move in reverse (or backward), are used. A numeral, for example, FWD+1, is used to indicate the number of frames or slides to move forward. Or BWD−1 means to reverse the direction of movement by the number of frames or slides indicated. The same would be true for flip chart pages.

Overhead transparencies often have overlays designed for random or sequential addition or removal. Removal or addition of overlays is indicated by numerals, for example, −1 or +1. The numeral refers to the number of the overlay to be added or removed.

Channel content column The last column, the channel content column, is used to describe the medium to be used. It can show media that need to be produced or media that are already in a collection.

If a medium is already in a collection, a bibliographical reference is recorded in the channel content column. This enables librarians to support the design of the learning event by acquiring the necessary reference.

If the medium needs to be produced, reading across the plan sheet discloses what kind of medium it is. Reading the notation in the channel content column shows what the content of the medium is, specifically, supposed to be.

Channel content notations may be taken directly from the left corner block of the plan cards. In transfer, the notation may be refined.

Multimediated Plan Sheet as a Televised Lesson Plan

The multimediated plan sheet can also be used as a televised lesson plan. The only differences in use technique are found in the channel columns. Everything else is used as described before.

The channel columns 1, 2, and 3 are used to indicate television cameras 1, 2, and 3. Usually, camera 3 is a fixed overhead camera and is used to transmit charts, diagrams, logos, and the like.

In the channel columns, since channel 1 is for camera 1, and channel 2 is for camera 2, and so on, no reference is made to hardware. Instead, the space is used to make camera position references like long shot (LS), medium shot (MS), or close-up (CU). It is also used to refer to camera movement, such as dolly (D), pan (PAN), truck (TK), or pedestal (P). The space also used to indicate effects, such as fade in (FI), fade out (FO), dissolves (⧖), cuts (H), and so on.

Multiscreen Planning

The multimediated plan sheet can also be used to plan the form of multimediated presentation that is known as multiscreen, in which several projectors are used to project images on several screens, either simultaneously, in developmental support, or to achieve affects.

The channel columns are the only places on the multimediated plan sheet that are treated differently when using multiscreen. The channel columns are used to represent the screens. It is assumed that channel 1 is the left screen, channel 2 the middle screen, and channel 3 the right screen. All items of companion hardware are aimed at screens that will contain their images.

Presuming that the learning event is basically presented by means of slides, no symbol is used when slides are shown. The designated abbreviation symbols are used in the channels whenever any medium other than the base medium (in this case, slides) is used (□ M/P8+). A frame symbol, by the way, always holds a dot, as described in the next paragraph, but there may be dots without frames.

In a multiscreen learning event, a screen either contains an image or it does not. When it does not contain an image, the screen is either black or it is illuminated with color. In the channel columns, a large black dot (●) means that the screen is black. A large shaded dot, with a designation beside it indicates no image, but a color screen (◎ red). A large dot with a square around it means that the screen holds an image (⊡).

Presuming that the hardware of a multiscreen presentation is under remote control, each time a black, shaded, or framed dot appears a control button is pushed. Retreats are indicated by (⊡ BWD). If more than one frame or slide is retreated, the designation would be (⊡ BWD–3). If advances were to be made past several filmstrip frames, for any reason, the designation would be (⊡ BWD + 3).

By reading a finished script, the producer should be able to discern whether the screen is to be black, colored, or contain an image. He should know how far each advance or retreat should be to the next image to be displayed. He should know when any screen is to move from image or color to black.

The multimediated plan sheet can also be used for motion picture production. The technique is the same as for televised learning events.

CONTACT

Considerations for contacting learners with media are part of the terminal planning. Contacting the learner should be a consideration that influences, and is influenced by, all parts of the rational planning process. There are three large concerns for planning learner–media contact: (1) packaging, (2) hardware, and (3) environment.

Packaging

Packaging is the manifestation of the plan for arranging the medium(a) and its supplements so that the learner–medium contact can be

1. Established early in the learning event.
2. Maintained for periods of time long enough to develop optimal effects.
3. Repeated with learners upon disclosure of need, or on request, as often as appropriate.

Package components   The following are the package components:

1. The medium(a) relevant to the learning event.
2. The supplements that provide for response, reinforcement, practice, application, and transfer; for example,
   a. Worksheets.
   b. Checklists.
   c. Materials and tools.
   d. Programmed events.
3. The hardware needed to display the medium(a) and to support the conduct of the learning event.

Package characteristics   The characteristics of optimally designed packages are as follows:

1. Portability, including weight limitations, compactness, and toughness for protection of items of value within the package.
2. Manipulation, including convenience and effectiveness of setup of equipment, relationships of media and supplements, successful directions for use of supplements in relation to medium(a), and ease of repacking.
3. System compatibility, concerning whether the package is totally self-contained and can, effectively, be taken anywhere and used by the learner, or whether the items of the package are enslaved by a larger system, for example, a closed-circuit television system, an audio tape dial access system, a "teaching" machine, or a computer.
4. Maintenance, including the expedition with which expended supplements can be replaced and refurbished, the medium(a) can be reprocessed (including refinements when they are disclosed) for continued use, and the hardware treated for effective function.
5. Storage, including package shapes for shelving, boxing, filing, or whatever, cataloging, and record keeping.
6. Basic expense of production of all package components, which controls concerns such as
   a. Can the items of the package be revised and refined as necessary?
   b. Can more than one package be afforded for use by several learners at the same time?
   c. Can each learner be assigned his own package?

Selected criteria   The following are criteria for selecting a previously produced package or for determining which elements of a package need revision and/or production:

1. Is the medium at the necessary level?
2. Is the message pertinent?
3. Is the style of presentation suitable?

4. Is the rate of development appropriate?
5. Do the supplements call for overt responses?
6. Do the supplements provide opportunities for practice?
7. Do the supplements provide opportunities for practical applications?
8. Do the supplements provide opportunities, when possible and appropriate, for generalizations?
9. Do the supplements provide opportunities for making transfers to other relevant subject-matter areas?
10. Is the hardware needed to display the medium(a) diversified? Is the diversification inconvenient?
11. Can the medium(a) be revised to more nearly standardize the required hardware?
12. Are components of the package expendable?
13. If not expendable, can components be reused?
14. If components are reused, do they require extensive maintenance to restore them to useful conditions?
15. If components are expendable, are they easily duplicated and in numbers large enough for complete dissemination?
16. Can components be expeditiously revised?
17. Is revision expensive?
18. Can learners produce components?
19. Can learners own components reasonably?
20. Have validatable media and/or supplements been developmentally tested?

Hardware

Certain media do not require companion hardware. Certain media are modifications of formats that do require hardware, such as microforms of printed texts. In the latter case, the cost and relative inconvenience of hardware is traded for storage space and convenience of media manipulation, and, perhaps, for duplication capabilities.

Other media, in original formats, imply the use of hardware. In general, there are two categories of hardware: (1) image display and (2) recording–playback devices.

Hardware Applications: Environmental

Items of hardware can be used as follows:

1. In auditorium situations, in which case they are usually heavy, high-powered, expensive, and more or less complicated.
2. In classroom situations, in which case they are transportable by means of carts. This kind of hardware is less expensive, uses household current electricity for power, and is not as complicated. To some extent, expense, weight, and complexity are functions of the degree of automation that is added to each item.
3. In carrels in libraries. In some cases, the carrel is equipped with built-in, bolted-down hard-ware. This is a good situation when the hardware is relatively heavy, specialized, or more or less delicate. It also is convenient because it saves set-up and coordination time. In other cases, the

carrel is equipped only with power outlets. Hardware is brought to the carrel as needed by the learner. This arrangement makes hardware more flexible. It also eliminates conflict of interests when carrels are not equipped with the hardware needed by the learner at that instant of learning experience. But it adds some wear and tear to items. It also reduces working space because the hardware and its parts require table space.

4. Carried by the learner to wherever he wants to study. If the learner chooses to go where there are no power outlets, the hardware must be internally powered by means of batteries. Hardware that is loaned to learners should be durable. It should not be excessively heavy. It should have systems which can provide images of illuminations equivalent to real conditions and amplifications similar to real situations. It must be easily maintained. Wear and tear is likely to be more than ordinary. Especially for playback hardware, it should be possible for a number of learners to listen at one time. This might mean, under certain conditions, that the hardware could be equipped with multiple headsets. It would also mean that the hardware had enough driving power to make the headset useful.

Companion Media

Hardware is usable for displaying images to learners and for recording and playback of actual or contrived audio events. Basically, hardware is the companion of the medium that carries the message. More often than not, when there is no suitable message recorded on a medium, the hardware is not useful at that point.

The requirements imposed by the terminal behavior defined, and intended as the product of a learning event, mandate the following:

1. Specificity of relevant content.

2. A mode of presentation designed to generate
   a. Responses.
   b. Reinforcement.
   c. Practice.
3. Opportunities for applications of cognitive, psychomotor, and affective elements, especially at levels of
   a. Analysis.
   b. Synthesis.
   c. Evaluation.
   d. Generalization.

To achieve such lofty goals and precision of purpose, it may probably and often be necessary to find, select, define, and use portions of messages on a variety of media, linked together, to achieve and complete exposure to one or more learners.

The obvious way to circumvent the need for a variety of media items, and, consequently, a variety of hardware items with all the implicit need for a system of control, is to plan and produce a standardized version of both the required plan and the required message. Standardized version, in this case, is intended to mean a reduction in the kinds of media that can be found to carry the message. The presentational modes for mediated presentations begin with the human voice, otherwise unsupported, and proceed through a variety of phases of increases in media and companion hardware uses, to complex systems of multihardware, remotely controlled, with learner–responder-modified learning.

Presentational modes   Some of the more complicated techniques are the following:

1. *Multihardware systems* are contrived to allow the use of different kinds of media in a controlled presentation. The idea assumes remote control, because the alternative is audiovisual gymnastics, which may prove to be more engrossing than the message.
2. *Learner–responder systems,* which have a number of possible features:

a. Capability for multihardware display, more or less limited in variety and numbers of items.

b. Capability of remote control of hardware items activated by electronic triggering recorded on audio tape.

c. When optimally designed, the media may present stimuli, get responses, and provide reinforcement.

d. Instructors and message designers may get feedback from the response integration system, presumably allowing for remediation, when necessary, by manual means or by means of auxiliary systems. It should not need to be pointed out that such sophisticated usage will certainly increase the planning–production ratio in man-hours significantly. It does, however, provide a technique applicable to developmental testing and validation.

e. When linked to appropriate computers and related to a seating position encodement, responses of learners can be recorded and accumulated, weighted or unweighted (and weighting can even be revised in the middle of a presentation), and subjected to statistical treatment.

f. When linked to appropriate printout devices, instructors can obtain means, medians, modes, rankings, standard deviations, and a variety of statistically processed scores within seconds or minutes after the data are accumulated, and the process signal is sent to the computer.

3. *Multimediated systems.* This term is really contrived to make a distinction between the unlimited varieties of hardware required by multihardware systems, and the controlled and limited hardware types required when messages are designed to be carried by a mediated form standardized for the purpose. One kind of multimediated system, in practice, would be when slide sets of pertinent design are displayed by means of an appropriate number of slide projectors and accompanied by an audio-taped narrative. Another kind might include several overhead projectors and an audio-taped narrative. Other varieties are, of course, possible and practical, depending on the availability or produceability of media standardized to the necessary requirements.

4. *Multiscreen systems* may employ elements of hardware that have the characteristics of multihardware systems, learner–responder systems, or multimediated systems. There are, however, sound purposes for the employment of multiscreen systems:

a. To provide a panoramic view or vista.

b. To provide progressive development with lingering establishment of basic cues or frameworks.

c. To demonstrate growth patterns.

d. To provide a parallel to motion.

e. To extend listings, charts, and diagrams.

f. To synchronize stimuli, response modes, and reinforcement.

5. *Quasi-programmed, self-contained media* are usually found as printed media, like workbooks, or as filmstrips. They could be found in motion picture formats or as video tapes when the medium selected seems useful for optimal dissemination. As an example, either the workbook or the filmstrip would be structured with the following format characteristics:

a. There would be no sound.

b. All images would be verbal or pictorial.

c. All directions would be appropriately and strategically included on the selected page or frame.

d. All directions, stimuli, response opportunities, reinforcements, and even remediation (with directions to ignore and pass over when not pertinent) would be included in required sequences.

e. Supplemental materials, tools, and equipment would be furnished in kit, by direction and learner procurement, or by the learner as the need arose.

f. Pretests, criterion checks, and posttests would be included as a part of the message of the medium.

g. The learner would require the ability to read and no hardware if the medium was a book. Writing would also be needed for some forms of learning.

h. The learner would require the ability to read, to write when pertinent, and a simple filmstrip viewer, powered or daylight, if the medium was a filmstrip.

i. A simple motion picture viewer could display the companion media to the learner. If reel size is a limiting factor, the event could be reeled and packaged appropriately.

j. A video-taped event requires a video-tape playback device. Usually, the system requires, at least, a closed-circuit system, for example,

    (1) Video-tape recorder and a monitor.

    (2) Transmission system cued by manual request.

    (3) Dial access system.

    Obviously, such events might be broadcast by means of standard, limited range, or microwave methods.

Environments

Economy of time, effort, and money are attained when learning is long-term and generalizable. Quality results are more likely to occur when environments correspond more closely in reality to learning objectives.

Environments in which learning might occur, more or less successfully, may be arranged as a kind of continuum, as follows:

Typical, traditional classroom This environment consists of desks and chairs, which are, not infrequently, bolted to the floor, a teacher's desk and chair, a chalkboard, perhaps a bulletin board, charts, maps, and little else. Much of what occurs in such rooms is based on the notion that the teacher is the information source and the authority figure. The information flow is from the teacher to the learners, with occasional called feedback to the teacher.

This is the reading, writing, listening, and answering-when-called-upon situation. It does not lend itself to ideation, interchange, innovation, and creativity, if used in its more sterile forms.

Modified traditional classroom This environment consists of movable desks and/or chairs. In other respects, it is the same as the typical traditional classroom. The teacher is still the information source and authority figure, but, by movement of chairs and/or desks, part of the function is tentatively transferred to learners. To reading, writing, listening, and answering-when-called-upon is added discussion and reporting. As a function of discussion and reporting, individual research and projects may be undertaken. Materials, tools, and references are usually found in limited, relatively restrictive kinds and amounts in the classroom. Any variations from the theme are imported, when available. Ideation, interchange, innovation, and creativity are more present than in the typical traditional classroom, but are still somewhat limited.

Open classrooms In this environment, the cubicle arrangement is eliminated because walls are absent in areas where they are not functionally contributive. Carpets, rugs, and even functional cushions may be found in use. Tables, desks, study carrels, and comfortable seating is the usual style of work area, but floors, risers, and platforms are also used.

Teachers may be responsible for classes of learners, or learners may be free to consult any available and appropriate teacher. Learners may organize as small groups for certain kinds of learning situations. Teachers may or may not meet with small groups. Teachers may assemble large groups for special learning events.

The open classroom situation presupposes individualized and independent learning to some degree. It also presumes that, for extraordinary events, there is opportunity for some learning en masse. In either, an assumption is that, while standard references and media are useful, sooner or later the learner will need media designed to specifications supporting his unique needs.

The teacher is designer, referent, guide, and synthesizer. To use a phrase that is in common use in some professional literature, the teacher becomes a manager of learning events. The open classroom lends itself to validation of learning, accountability of the kind which means that learners become successful as a result of their participation in the process, ideation, interchange, innovation, and creativity. Learners learn on a long-term basis and can use what they learn applicatively, in transfer, in synthesis, in evaluation, and to generalize.

Open schools   These are, environmentally, like open classrooms. In their extreme forms, a school per se may not be needed. Teachers are available in a central building. The central building may have specialized spaces to be used as required. Laboratories of all kinds, workshops, conference rooms of various sizes, large and small auditoriums, wet and dry carrels, libraries, supply rooms, gymnasiums, playing fields, automotive driving ranges, and such specialized conditions may be provided.

In the largest part, the open school presumes that its learning events will be provided by the community and the city. Depending on the age, the learning sophistication, and the purpose of the event, learners may experience purposeful events that are parts of the continuing functions of society and its installations and intercourses.

Electronic learning events   With the invention and implementation of electronic transmissions and recording techniques, it is possible that learning may be transferred in significant parts to the home. Electro video recording, in at least one of its present forms, makes it possible to record, re-record, store, recover, transmit, copy, and play back any event that has been, is, or can be recorded.

Electronic learning presumes that learning events can be designed to make use of actual events or contrived events to provide learner successes. This means that the central installation, such as with the open school, would still be available and useful. It also means that teachers, the managers of learning events, would be designers of learning events. The products of design would be stored after recording for recall, synthesis, modification, validation, or any other continuing use. Obsolete materials would be erased or discarded.

A vast and growing accumulation of recorded learning events could be exchanged electronically throughout the world among any number of participating installations. The following would be needed:

1. Strategically placed learning centers. Placement would depend on population numbers and geographical conditions.
2. Satellite relay transmission systems. This would allow any stored event or any event in progress to be transmitted and relayed to any other point in the world that possessed a receiver.
3. Cable and/or laser antenna television networks, linked and interconnected by means of satellite relays. In effect, this would make a worldwide antenna television network, and would allow transmission and reception of video and/or audio signals.
4. A worldwide telephone network with a touch-tone dial system. This would allow contact for ordering transmissions from any of the learning centers or transmission points.
5. An electro video recorder with a high-speed recording capability. This would allow making copies of anything existing as part of the collections of learning centers. Since the learning centers would be computer-controlled, collection keys, special catalog data, bibliographies, or schedules might be transmitted and recorded in minutes. This would allow the receiver to

study and select pertinent references. Encodement by the dial system could call up any specific references for recording.

6. The recorder would also be a playback unit. Recordings would be displayed by connection to an ordinary television receiver in both audio and video signals.

EPILOGUE

The process of design of learning events is greatly sensitive, complicated, and time consuming. It is also expensive. It requires skilled personnel. Considering the amount of designing to be done, the process will require many such personnel, much of their time, and the time of others, as well.

To round out and complete the design of a learning event requires that the event pass through several processing steps:

1. Message design.
2. Media design.
3. Media production.
4. Assembly and supplementation.
5. Developmental testing.
6. Validation.

It is not practical to presume that any one person can be and do all these things. The various steps require a particular kind of person having particular kinds of training, and even a special trend of professional application.

Yes, the process is expensive. But meeting its requirements with money is far less potentially expensive than failing to do so. Educating people for continuous reeducation is a societal mandate. It is becoming more important to have such skills with every passing day. The alternative to success in developing continuous reeducation skills and techniques is a caretaker society, or a welfare state, or a benevolent paternalist dictatorship, to name a few of the more pleasant ones.

The effective and successful design of an effective and successful learning event is not a process of intuition. It is not a matter of "feelings" and guesses. It is a matter of applying a message, tools, materials, and situations to a learner who is ready to learn, and knows and believes in why he must learn. It is a matter of information, reaction, practice, application, transfer, synthesis, evaluation, and generalization. Learning must be this if it is to be more than short-term, persisting only under the onus of some kind of Damoclean sword.

Student candidates for certificates as teachers need training for expertise in their subject-matter fields. But expertise is only a beginning. It is shortsighted to presume that such expertise makes anyone an effective teaching professional, or amateur for that matter.

It is reasonable to assume that competent learners can learn much from a subject-matter expert. It is also reasonable to presume that competent learners might learn a great deal more from a subject-matter expert who is also trained and competent in the rational design of learning events. Even more, the latter kind of professional can provide learning experiences of an effective nature for learners who are not so competent. And, in the process, the not-so-competent learner might become even more competent in specific subject-matter conditions, as well as psychomotor skills, and affective behavior.

Teachers who possess skills in the rational design of learning events should, certainly, be involved in the process of message design and related media design. But the purpose of teachers, especially when they are intensively committed to and involved in the management of learning events, is to interact with learners. Sensitive response to the changing characteristics of the learner is the most valuable contribution to maintaining a continuous growth in scope and depth by any learner. Therefore, beyond contribution and direction in message design and media design, the teacher is stringently limited in his time to contribute to further processing.

The production of media and its subsequent assembly and packaging are vital roles in the existence of an effective learning event. But the actual performance of these tasks is a role for a specialist. Approval of product is, finally, with the teacher, but the teacher has little or no time to carry out production, especially at the level of quality necessary for optimal effectiveness. Because of the nature of their basic or even graduate training, teachers have only limited skills in such work.

Finally, a learning event can be said to be effective only when it accomplishes what it is supposed to accomplish and that for which it was designed. Again, a time factor enters the process. Except over long periods of time, which involve too many learners in superficial, unrelated, and possibly lower quality learning experiences, the teacher is not the professional who should undertake developmental testing. Another reason is that there is too much possibility of bias entering the situation.

Developmental testing should be a role for a specialist. It is important enough. It is a task of sufficient density and intensity to suggest and require a specialist's role. Its purpose and product are, in fact, vital enough to persuade that it should be implemented.

Validation is the last step in rational design before the learning event becomes a permanent component of the resources for learning. Validation may also be a role for a specialist. It might be a continuing part of the assignment of the developmental tester. Since, however, validation is a task that is accomplished with the individual learner, or the small group, or the specific mass of learners, the responsible teacher might undertake the role. But only when a teacher is trained and is competent should he be involved in validation. Subtle signals, feedback from learners, subtle changes that show growths and regressions are too vital to the learner's success to allow any but the best to conduct validation.

Public accountability demands that schools and professional teachers be able to describe the product which they intend to develop. The product is an outgrowth of what the patronage of the school wants it to be—or, at least, it ought to be.

Once described, together with input from client students, the appropriate learning events are designed, produced, validated, and administered. At that point, the product of learner behavior should be, within reasonable degrees of freedom, at reasonable limits of confidence, what the school, its faculty, its patronage, and the acceptable input from its client students described that it would be.

Professional accountability demands that professional teachers be able to provide validated learning experiences for client students with a supporting framework of relevance and motivation patterns. All elements of a curriculum that are effectively experienced by client learners, to generate a perimeter and contents of behavior growth, should be of optimal quality and quantity. Effective learning events are accompanied by enrichment, entry behavior essentials, and remediation.

Personal accountability demands that a professional teacher remain abreast of his field, which implies both content upgrading and technique revision, when either or both are available. It implies the ability to design and provide learners with learning events when and how they are needed. At a high level of personal accountability, the professional teacher makes useful and frequent professional contributions.

Administrative accountability demands that the entire environment of the school be marked by the provision of adequate and appropriate staffing, materials, and time, so that accountable results can be obtained from public, professional, and personal accountability efforts. It needs to be recognized that for specific results specialized staffing, materials, and programming are requirements.

Rational design can accomplish a great deal on the road to successful accountability. Without rational design, randomness, chance, speculation, bias, emotion, and unpredictability will all effect the product.

BIBLIOGRAPHY

Carrison, Muriel P., et al. "A Kappan Pro/Con Series," *Phi Delta Kappan,* LIV, 9 (May 1973), 593–601, Phi Delta Kappa, Bloomington, Ind.

Cobun, Ted C. "Educational Consumerism," *International Journal of Instructional Media,* 1973, Storrs, Conn.

Faure, Edgar, et al. *Learning to Be: The World of Education Today and Tomorrow,* 1972, UNESCO Publications Center, New York.

Fleming, Malcolm L., and Mehdi Sheikhian. "Influence of Pictorial Attributes on Recognition Memory," *Audiovisual Communication Review,* XX, 4 (Winter 1972), 423–441, AECT, Washington, D.C.

Haavelsrud, Magnus. "Learning Resources in the Formation of International Orientations," *Audiovisual Communication Review,* XX, 3 (Fall 1972), 229–251, AECT, Washington, D.C.

Hack, Walter G., et al. *Educational Tuturism 1985,* 1971, p. 225, McCutchan Publishing Corporation, Berkeley, Calif.

Heinich, Robert, ed., et al "Instructional Development," *Audiovisual Communication Review,* XXI, 1 (Spring 1973), AECT, Washington, D.C.

Hill, Joseph E. *The Educational Sciences,* 1972, p. 21, Oakland Community College, Bloomfield Hills, Mich.

Hitchens, Howard B., Jr., ed. *Audiovisual Instruction,* XVII, 8 (Oct. 1972), AECT, Washington, D.C.

Hull, Ronald E. "Selecting an Approach to Individual Education," *Phi Delta Kappan,* LV, 3 (Nov. 1973), 169–173, Phi Delta Kappa, Bloomington, Ind.

Landers, Jacob. "Accountability and Progress by Nomenclative," *Phi Delta Kappan,* LIV, 8 (Apr. 1973), 539–541, Phi Delta Kappa, Bloomington, Ind.

Maeroff, Gene I. "The Traditional School," *Phi Delta Kappan,* LIV, 7 (Mar. 1973), Phi Delta Kappa, Bloomington, Ind.

McMurrin, Sterling, et al. *To Improve Learning,* 1970, p. 124, U.S. Government Printing Office, Washington, D.C.

Mielke, Kieth W. "Renewing the Link Between Communications and Educational Technology," *Audiovisual Communication Review,* XX, 4 (Winter 1972), 357–399, AECT, Washington, D.C.

Neill, S. D. "McLuhan's Media Charts Related to the Process of Communication," *Audiovisual Communication Review,* XXI, 3 (Fall 1973), 277–297, AECT, Washington, D.C.

Pearson, Betty D. "Applying Learning Theory and Instructional Film Principles to Films for Learning Observational Skills," *Audiovisual Communication Review,* XX, 3 (Fall 1972), 281–295, AECT, Washington, D.C.

Salomon, Gavriel. "Can We Affect Cognitive Skills Through Visual Media?," *Audiovisual Communication Review,* XX, 4 (Winter 1972), 401–422, AECT, Washington, D.C.

Silvern, Leonard C. *Systems Engineering Applied to Training,* 1972, Gulf Publishing Company, Houston, Texas.

Smith, Earl P. "The Effects of Filmstrip/Tape Program on Teacher's Attitudes Toward Behaviorally Stated Objectives," *Audiovisual Communication Review,* XX, 4 (Winter 1972), 443–457, AECT, Washington, D.C.

Suessmuth, Patrick. "Can You Trouble-Shoot This Lesson Plan?," *Training,* 1973, pp. 42–45.

Tracy, William. "Goodbye IQ, Hello EI (Erth Index)," *Phi Delta Kappan,* LIV, 2 (Oct. 1972), 89–94, Phi Delta Kappa, Bloomington, Ind.

Yacasua, L. T. "Intelligence," *Phi Delta Kappan,* LIV, 10 (June 1973), 689–691, Phi Delta Kappa, Bloomington, Ind.

PART V: CONTENT AND OBJECTIVES

Systematic Approach to Developing Curriculum in the Domain of Instructional Technology

Margarete N. Butz

What is instructional technology? What does an instructional technologist do? What does he do to get that way? This particular session tried to disseminate in 1½ hours the work of 15 people at Syracuse University who have worked for 6 months on this problem under the auspices of the U.S. Office of Education, plus the work of the 80 various department chairmen from all over the country who worked diligently for 2 days in preconference sessions.

Chairman for this session, Donald P. Ely, Syracuse University, Area of Instructional Technology, introduced Kenneth Silber of the national staff of the Division of Educational Technology, National Education Association; John Johnson and Dennis Myers, interns in Instructional Technology at Syracuse University and members of the research team of 15 people. After brief comments they put the entire group into action.

In the domain of instructional technology (DIT), we should not base what one does on the job title, for this differs from place to place as well as by size of the organization. Instead, we must base it on task

Margarete N. Butz is on the staff of the Indiana School Libraries Association, Indianapolis, Indiana.

analysis. This research team drew upon a list of 2,000 tasks which technologists do.

Competencies are listed under nine functions in the domain of instructional technology developed by the Jobs in Instructional Media Study and Media Guidelines Project. These functions are not job titles and they are not people. They are broad areas of performance in instructional technology.

The nine functions are as follows:

1. Organization management, with competencies related to structure, budget, and so on, of organizations performing DIT functions to ensure the effective operations of the organizations.
2. Personnel management, with competencies related to interaction with and/or supervision of personnel performing DIT functions.
3. Research–Theory, with competencies related to obtaining empirical evidence to generate and test facts, theories, and methodologies related to instructional technology.
4. Design, with competencies related to translating general and theoretical knowledge about learning and instruction into specifications for instructional materials, devices, or settings.
5. Production, with competencies related to translating specifications for instructional materials into prototype, final version, or mass-produced products.
6. Evaluation–selection, with competencies related to the assessment of instructional materials, devices, and settings.
7. Utilization, with competencies related to bringing learners into contact with instructional materials, devices, and settings.
8. Utilization–dissemination, with competencies related to informing others of instructional technology and how it may be used.
9. Support–supply, with competencies related to obtaining, cataloging, and distributing materials and devices.

How do we get people to match tasks in the various DIT functions? One approach is to define jobs in terms of the types and complexity of the tasks performed. They can be classified according to what workers do—through functional job analysis (FJA) scales, and according to what gets done—the domain of instructional technology (DIT) functions. This gives us two ways of looking at the same class.

Believing that we learn by doing, the meeting was divided into four small groups. Group 1 examined functional job analysis—especially worker instructions. The FJA technique measures the workers' involvement with a task according to three dimensions: (1) Worker functions—what workers do, the levels on which they function in relation to data, people, and things. (2) Worker instructions—what workers are instructed to do to get the job done. (3) General educational development—what reasoning, math, and language skills workers need to know to carry out instructions. Figure 1 represents a breakdown of the definitions of the worker instruction scale according to levels and categories. At level 1, the simplest level, the worker is given on the job all he needs to know to perform the task. At level 7–8, the most complex, the worker must not only determine what needs to be done, how, why, when, but is also responsible for assigning work to others.

There are three major levels of personnel. The distinctions among the three levels of personnel are in the areas of the focus of the worker's attention, and the procedures for task performance. Entry level personnel are concerned with "the tasks they perform, though the tasks may be only a part of a process." Their procedure is to follow instructions. Middle level workers deal "more with a cluster of tasks leading to a specified output." Their procedures involve the selection and use of standards and procedures. Advanced level personnel are "responsible for a general problem." They must determine the problem as well as the purposes, outcomes, standards, and procedures to solve it.

W1 Scale
Level

1	ENTRY (aide)		
2			
3	(overlap area)	MIDDLE (technician)	
4			
5		(overlap area)	
6			ADVANCED (professional)
7, 8			

Figure 1
Level of personnel.

Group 2 studied the domain of instructional technology—a way of looking at tasks in terms of what gets done. It provides another dimension to the notions of task type and classification. The field of instructional technology deals with (1) the organization and (2) the application of (3) resources—men, materials, messages, techniques, settings, and devices—in a systematic manner in order to solve instructional problems. The resources are actually the components which can make up an instructional system from which students learn. It makes sense, therefore, to call them instructional system components. The application phase, when applied to instructional space systems, is instructional development. The organization phase relates to the organization of instructional development, and therefore can be called instructional management. Figure 2 shows their interrelationship.

Group 3 concentrated on instructional development functions—functions which have as their

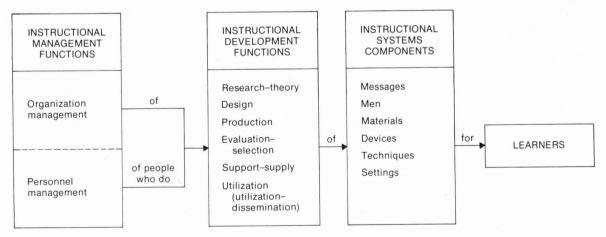

Figure 2
Domain of instructional technology—summary.

purpose the application of instructional systems components to solve instructional problems. Figure 2 shows the complete domain of instructional technology, including the instructional systems components, the instructional management and development functions, the relationships among the three, and the scope of the model. The definitions for each function include its purpose, outcome, and activities.

Group 4 was concerned with a general model for curriculum development. This new approach built upon two concepts: First, the tasks which were to be taught were derived from a data bank which also held additional information about the complexity of the task, the worker instructions, and what other tasks might be related through the DIT. Second, the training methods should be appropriate to the task levels themselves. Training, then, for entry levels, should be of a different nature from that for middle or advanced levels, since the approach to the tasks is different. For example, since the worker instructions for low level tasks stress that all the information needed to complete the task is within the parameters of the task, we can assume that in most

Table 1
Procedures for Training (What the Learner Needs to Be Able to Do or Know)

Entry *Follows specific instructions to perform discrete procedures (Activities)*	*Middle* *Selects/uses standards to perform a sequence of procedures to produce an outcome*	*Advanced* *Determines purposes/outcomes/ standards and procedures to fulfill purposes*
What are the standards/criteria/ requirements (DIT)	What are the standards/criteria/requirements (DIT)	How to recognize problems (WI)
How to follow instructions (WI)	How to synthesize or select the appropriate standards (WI)	How to define problems (FS)
What are the discrete procedures for performing activities (DIT and FS)	What are the procedures for applying the standards to produce an outcome (DIT)	How to select/devise standards/ parameters for solutions to the problem (DIT)
How to perform the procedures (DIT and FS)	How to select or synthesize these procedures (WI)	How to select/devise solutions (WI) (DIT)
	How to carry out the procedures (FS and DIT)	How to select/devise procedures for implementing the solutions (WI)
		How to carry out the procedures (FS and DIT)
		How to assign work to others (WI)
		What are the standards for evaluating outputs (DIT)

DIT = domain of instructional technology
WI = worker instructions
FS = functional skills from functional job analysis

cases on-the-job training would be appropriate, and actual hands-on experience (as opposed to extensive theory) would work best. Table 1 gives a rough overview to the different approaches. Full information about the detailed sequence for curriculum development, including unit objectives and subobjectives, will be found in the final report of the Jobs in Instructional Media Study, tentatively scheduled to be released sometime late this summer through Educational Resources Information Center.

As Silber, Johnson, and Myers pointed out, this is a new approach to our field. It questions some of the basic tenets and procedures of the field, and will undoubtedly be the subject of some controversy. But it does seem to be a significant step forward for instructional technology. In conclusion, this was a session well worth attending.

Improving the Quality
of Instructional Materials

C. R. Carpenter

The problem of how to build high quality in instructional programs has been explored both theoretically and by extensive research and development efforts. These efforts have been financed by federal agencies and foundations. A great effort has been made by the U.S. Office of Education, Bureau of Research, which has conducted research and dissemination activities authorized by NDEA–Title VII for 10 years, 1958–1968. This program has been recently reviewed and evaluated by Filep (1970) and by Filep and Schramm (1970).[1] The definition and delineation of all factors, conditions, and determinants of quality, effectiveness, or excellence have largely eluded the grasp alike of investigators and practical educators. The investigators' disturbing and ubiquitous findings of "no *statistically* significant differences" have arisen by the hundreds to smite those who have sought to compare variables or factors which relate to quality. For the practical educators, there remains the difficult and frustrating task of developing ordered conceptual and operational systems which will yield instruction materials of high excellence.

C. R. Carpenter is research professor of psychology and anthropology at the University of Georgia, Athens, Georgia, and professor emeritus of Pennsylvania State University, University Park, Pennsylvania.

There are two intersecting trends relative to the quality problem. The research and development projects and programs on the use of new mass media for education, instruction, and training are one trend that began during and following World War II. This trend was accelerated by private foundations and the Title VII of NDEA enacted in 1958. The other interacting trend was extensive and persisting attempts to formulate and apply "learning principles" to instructional processes by means of the media and complex media assemblies. Included are computers for regulating learning behavior and systems of instruction which use a plurality of training devices.

Two subordinate developments contributed to an increasing interest and awareness of the quality problem. First, many efforts were made, about 400 for television alone, to answer the question of what medium or patterns of media are most effective, practical, and economical. Here emerged the effectiveness, productivity, and cost–benefit ratio considerations about instruction and media. Second, programmed instruction and teaching machines swept into the educational bivouacs, disturbing their structure while at the same time contributing to the art of writing specifications for instructional materials and for formulating the criteria or objectives for learned performances.

Efforts were made to organize and synthesize converging trends of thought, effort, and information using the concepts of combinations of selected media to provide favorable conditions for learning and instructional-learning systems. There were other orienting concepts.

METHODS AND PROCEDURES

Initiation of the study of instructional quality or excellence raised many questions: What orienting concepts, approaches, methods, procedures, and techniques could possibly make *new* contributions to thinking about and research on this problem? What could be gained that has not already resulted

from extensive effort and sustained research and application work to improve the quality of instructional media programs? What conventional and unconventional methods might be used to collect useful information and to formulate significant conclusions for the Commission on Instructional Technology? What evidence in what form would affect the recommendations that the commission could make to the president and the Secretary of Health, Education, and Welfare? How could a broad and rational perspective be developed from the results of research and experience that, when accepted by the commission, would make a significant practical difference in the extent of use and the effectiveness of instruction in the whole educational system of the nation? How are these questions to be answered?

Consideration of these questions and hypothesis about answers clearly indicated that this must be a practical study appropriate to important decisions at the federal level of government. The study could not be a purely academic exercise of limited scope. Methods and procedures were required, therefore, which would yield this kind of relevant information in brief and clearly presented form.

Study of the complex problem of instructional media quality, the rational analysis of alternative approaches, general orienting concepts, and professional viewpoints indicated that methods and procedures very different from the traditional were necessary for the conduct of the study. Clearly, limitations of both time and funds precluded the use of research and development methods, nor was this expected by the sponsors. However, the anticipated needs of the commission were that the results of research and development investigations and studies in brief useful form were urgently required. Therefore, a first and very conventional procedure was indicated; namely, the collection, abstraction, and production on McBee edge-punched cards of abstracts of the current literature pertinent to the problem of instructional quality, much of which was not available in abstracts and reviews. The developing Educational Resources Information Center Clearinghouse on Educational Media and Technology at Stanford University was not yet in a position to be of much assistance to the commission by providing abstracts and digests of the literature. Furthermore, media literature is so scattered and varied, characterized by limited and special publications, that it is extremely difficult to survey the published information in an orderly manner and make it usefully available. It was *not* proposed once again to make a review of the heterogeneous research literature on the effectiveness of instructional media. As a source of identification of the most valuable background information for the staff of the Academy for Education Development and the members of the commission, a bibliography was compiled consisting of over 800 titles. A first selected bibliography was also prepared.[2]

It was decided that the main procedure would be to confront directly small groups of selected, informed, mature, and experienced professional men with the problems of defining or specifying the factors, conditions, requirements, and variables and contingencies which they judged would affect the quality of complex learning mediated by instructional materials.

In the early plans and discussions emphasis was put on television programming for instructional purposes. However, as the project evolved and conceptualizations deepened and broadened, the study came to include references to a very wide spectrum of instructional materials including both "new" electronic media and print. The same evolution and broadening occurred as the task of the commission was successively defined.

Nine locations were selected in the eastern part of the United States where it would be practical to have small groups of educators and media professionals assemble in information "harvest" or "delphian" seminars for intensive discussions and decisions about the variables and contingencies of instructional materials that defined the quality problem. Men and women were invited who were

well known in their professions, who held real responsibilities in the media field, and who had extensive research and practical experience. They were recognized for their interests and competencies in research, development, and the application of instructional media to the many varied problems of education, the sciences, engineering, and to the arts. A total of about 100 professional people were invited to contribute to the thinking, deliberations, and decisions on central questions of how to achieve high-quality instructional materials that are produced for schools, colleges, universities, continuing education, and professional training programs.

The early seminars were exploratory and yielded information on how best the other seminars might be conducted. The first was a seminar held at Indiana University at which I, as project director, served as chairman. The second was held at Notre Dame with John W. Meaney as chairman. This later seminar was composed of faculty members from both the University of Notre Dame and Purdue. From these seminars it became evident that due to the high-level generality of deliberations, the broad perspective involved, and the complexity of the judgments and decisions required, an outline or framework was necessary for guiding the discussions. Consequently, I designed Figure 1 for the purpose of having a general frame of reference for subsequent seminar discussions. The outline was planned to be incomplete and suggestive of possibilities rather than complete and closed.

The general expectation was that intelligent, experienced professional men when freed from the pressure of daily routines to work in a situation favorable for concentrated thought could define the most important contingencies to high-quality instructional materials. The appeal was to the mature judgment of people operating at the same levels as those who make practical decisions.

To have focused discussions, attention was sometimes directed to particular media like instructional films, television, or computers as they might be

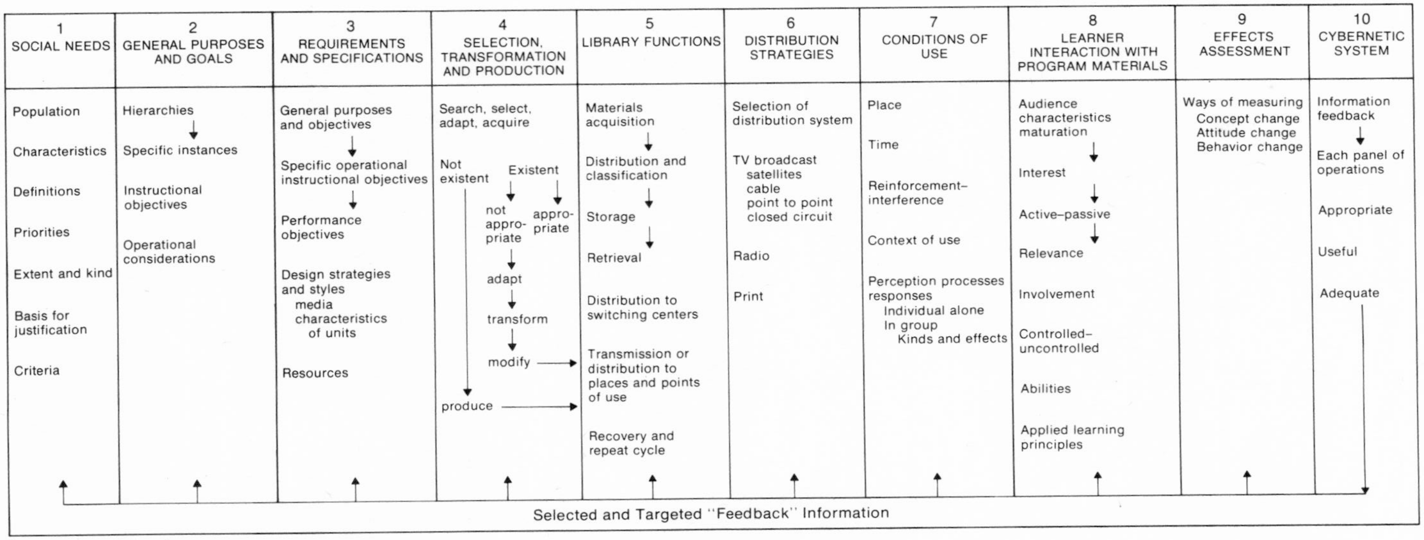

1 SOCIAL NEEDS	2 GENERAL PURPOSES AND GOALS	3 REQUIREMENTS AND SPECIFICATIONS	4 SELECTION, TRANSFORMATION AND PRODUCTION	5 LIBRARY FUNCTIONS	6 DISTRIBUTION STRATEGIES	7 CONDITIONS OF USE	8 LEARNER INTERACTION WITH PROGRAM MATERIALS	9 EFFECTS ASSESSMENT	10 CYBERNETIC SYSTEM
Population	Hierarchies → Specific instances	General purposes and objectives	Search, select, adapt, acquire	Materials acquisition	Selection of distribution system	Place	Audience characteristics maturation →	Ways of measuring Concept change Attitude change Behavior change	Information feedback →
Characteristics		Specific operational instructional objectives	Existent → appropriate	Distribution and classification	TV broadcast satellites cable point to point closed circuit	Time	Interest → Active-passive →		Each panel of operations
Definitions	Instructional objectives		Not existent / not appropriate	Storage →	Radio	Reinforcement–interference	Relevance		Appropriate
Priorities	Operational considerations	Performance objectives	adapt → transform → modify → produce	Retrieval	Print	Context of use	Involvement		Useful
Extent and kind		Design strategies and styles		Distribution to switching centers		Perception processes responses Individual alone In group	Controlled–uncontrolled		Adequate
Basis for justification		media characteristics of units		Transmission or distribution to places and points of use		Kinds and effects	Abilities		
Criteria		Resources		Recovery and repeat cycle			Applied learning principles		

Selected and Targeted "Feedback" Information

*A tentative incomplete chart

Figure 1
General sequential operations of an instructional system.

brought to bear on problems of teaching and learning in a course of instruction, or in a more limited or more general area of a curriculum. However, the perspective was always broad and references were made to all media and to a wide spectrum of their uses throughout the educational systems, formal or informal.

The settings and conduct of the seminars were planned to yield unrestrained and imaginative thinking about the quality of instructional materials. The seminar members were encouraged to bring to bear their best focused judgments on the problem. Freedom of thinking and conceptual explorations were encouraged while critical, restraining reactions typical of academics were discouraged. Members were challenged to condense and to present information pertinent to the problem in direct, practical, and clear language.

Not only were the seminar settings arranged to be out of the mainstream of activities and away from distractions, but also sufficient time was provided for reorientation and disengagement of seminar members from concerns about their regular work. Time was provided for members to become personally involved in the issues of what is meant by high-quality instruction and how excellent media can be produced for a very broad spectrum of educational requirements in this nation. The seminars were in session for from 1 to 2½ days.

Orientation of the discussions, including the stating of the problem, was most important. Discussion group leaders challenged the members at once to define and understand the general quality problem and to formulate realistic expectations of results from the extended and intensive discussions. Participants were challenged to make substantive, significant, and realistic recommendations for the proposed Commission on Instructional Technology on what needs to be done throughout this country.

At the beginning of a seminar, furthermore, each member was told that near the end of the seminar he would be asked to make for the record one, two, or three of the most important statements that he could formulate on the general question of how best to improve the quality of instructional materials for use in a wide range of available technologies and media at specified levels of education or for a defined instructional task.

Simulation and role-playing techniques were used in some of the seminars. Members were instructed to assume realistic decision-making roles in areas of responsibility for which they believed themselves most competent. This was done in some instances by asking the question, "Suppose that you were responsible for drafting the recommendations to the President of the United States for the commission on how adequate instructional programs for the media are to be produced on the highest possible levels of quality and effectiveness, what would be the content and form of your recommendations?" Or, again, "What are the most important requirements and conditions for producing instructional programs of the highest quality in your field of teaching?"

Early in the first seminar the issue arose of how quality was to be defined. To expedite discussions, it was decided to define quality operationally for all succeeding seminars as being synonymous with effectiveness, and therefore meaning the instigation, stimulation, and assurance of the production of intended specified changes in the behavior of defined populations of learners.

There are two subordinate concepts to this definition: *first,* quality or effectiveness is a continuum of degrees that invites measurements and not an absolute quality or quantity, and, *second,* the intended or proposed changes in behavior must be specified and clearly expressed so that the instructional objectives can be known by all those responsible for the management and regulation of the teaching and learning operations, and especially including learners themselves.

Discussions were recorded on audiotape, transcribed, analyzed, and written up. Both the audio recording and the typed abstract of discussions became the main products and primary data base for this study.[3]

SPECIAL STUDIES

The basic seminars, the literature searches, and contemporary practices suggested the need for special studies, two of which were speedily undertaken, subject to the limitations of time, funds, and staff assistance. First, it became abundantly clear that the current prescriptions and formulas that are offered for the production, testing, revision, and retesting cycles of operations in the preparation of instructional materials cannot only be done in complex and expensive centers which provide the necessary conditions, characteristics, and funds. Therefore, practical and shortcut procedures will continue to be required. Once again it was emphasized, also, that tested forms for guiding the making of *informed human judgments* about instructional units, lessons, and programs will continue to be needed and will serve useful purposes. Another attempt was made, therefore, to revise, make useful, and test a judgment guidance form by program professionals who used it to aid in judging television programs and films which had been nominated as being superior. This form[4] has been revised many times, and it is believed now to be a useful and practical means short of actual testing for getting judgmental assessments of the quality of instructional materials.

A second problem emerged for study. It has been evident for many years that it is necessary to have a national complement of instructional material production centers or laboratories. These are required especially for production of nonprint materials. In some respects, the research and development centers and regional educational laboratories sponsored under Title IV of the Elementary and Secondary Education Act of 1965 served as models for developing, creating, producing, and testing in-

structional and experimental materials. It was expected, therefore, that the Commission on Instructional Technology would need to consider whether or not to recommend federal support commensurate with the needs for a national complement of production and testing centers. Consequently, a special study was made of the places and facilities known to be producing instructional programs of high quality for the electronic media. Also, inquiries were made of all National Educational Television (NET) stations. From this information a special report[5] was written. The objective of this study was to begin to develop planning and evaluating procedures on the basis of direct observations of existing facilities.

Television was assumed to be a multimedia information originating and distribution system and as such it was viewed as a good model of the kinds of demands and requirements for future new and advanced instructional material production centers.

A fifth substantive document[6] was prepared from the clear, succinct statements seminar members offered of how to solve the quality of instructional materials.

RESULTS

It became evident early in this study that a large number of approaches, orienting concepts, bodies of evidence, theories, and practical considerations is relevant and contingent to the problem of instructional quality of media programs. The problem becomes one of selecting pertinent elements from arrays of contingencies and of integrating these into a meaningful configuration. Toward this end it was very useful to define seven orienting concepts.

The concepts of systems, the systems approaches, operational systems, and systems analysis emerged as a kind of catalytic organizing theme. However vague and general, systems concepts did orient discussions to complexes of factors and contingencies and their interactions. Single elements and little variables in larger wholes became subordinated, although for theoretical and experimental purposes such elements remained important for the functional system.

Clearly a key orienting concept is one of functions, interactions, and processes. The oversimplified expression of "the learning process" was rejected in favor of a plurality of functioning, interacting processes which are goal oriented. Closely related is the concept of identified operations that are traced and related to both intermediate or terminal states, conditions, or objectives. While accepting the operational behavioral procedures for designing learning strategies, the specifying of limited and particular overt responses as the end products of learning was put into a more balanced perspective with a large number of other requirements and contingencies of complex teaching and learning operations.

Activities of teaching and learning grow out of prior states and merge into present states that are oriented to future conditions. Therefore, learning and its regulation require the control of many sequential operations over time. Prior states and operations shape, determine, limit, facilitate, and interfere with subsequent configured events. Furthermore, the time span of contingencies varies from brief moments to long periods of time. Thus, instructional learning operations are sequential and interactional over varying time spans.

Learning may be visualized, also, as involving cycles of behavior, events, and processes. This concept is consistent with depicting learning as having cybernetic regulation and control. Feedback loops from intended or expected end states to behavior which is sequentially related to these organic states are essential to the regulation of goal-oriented adaptive behavior.

The crucial importance of defining or specifying overt performance criteria or behavioral objectives for learning involves this feedback directly in the learning cycle. The knowledge of results or effects of efforts to learn is most important for the learner himself and only of secondary use to the experimenter, observer, teacher, or record keeper. This direct feedback to the learner *is* reinforcement. Reinforcement can be positive or negative, either facilitating or inhibiting.

The concepts of media and modes of the communication processes and materials were differentiated. The *medium* is the base carrier of the information, whereas the *mode* is the form of the signs, signals, or symbols. The mode is the form of encoded messages. In stimulus–response terms, the medium is the material carrier of the stimuli, while the mode is the form of the stimulus, that is, the voice, the image, and the photograph, graphic, or printed word. The problem of selecting and using multichannel instructional communication is more easily solved for media, which are primarily practical, economic considerations, than for the modes. The selection and use of the most appropriate mode or combination of modes are fine arts. This is what is truly meant by the often-stated "multimedia" approach to instruction and learning.

There was another orienting concept for the seminar discussions, that of the relative importance of micro- and macro-variables or contingencies in a total operational frame of the practical uses of media for instruction. The concept can be dramatically and briefly defined by the statement that, however refined and perfected a media-carried unit of instruction, it is practically useless unless the materials are properly presented for learner interactions. However splendid and excellent the units of instruction, they are useless unless managed by effective library methods and presented in a mode available for appropriate uses.

This point illustrates the mood of almost every seminar. Members were generally impatient with theory and with small but practically insignificant experimental results. They were interested in pragmatic operational materials and procedures which would lead to an observable educational change and development.

MISCONCEPTIONS AND BARRIERS

The information-yielding seminars often broached definitions of factors and contingencies which have had *negative* or adverse effects on the quality of instructional media. Generally, it would seem failures have been more numerous than successes in the extended, intensive high-quality uses and performances of the media. There is currently an urgent need for examples and model operations that are conspicuously successful and which do not require rationalizations and apologetic justifications. Accordingly, the search persisted for these factors, contingencies, and conditions which closely related to the termination or failure of projects which were launched with hope but ended with despair. Growing maturity and sophistication of research, development, and application methods and perspectives have led to the possibility of defining misconceptions, false expectancies, and misinterpretations which have related to less than desirably successful instructional media operations.

The early stages of media research proceeded with the expectation and hypothesis that it was productive to define limited sets of variables of communication processes or conditions and to experimentally determine their relative contributions to learning. It was believed that the contributory variables and characteristics could be included in the production and use of films, television, and radio and that thereby their effectiveness as instructional units could be improved. The factoring out of such variables as rate of development, the subjective camera view, form of address, and immediate knowledge of results did not easily summate in production procedures nor were conditions of use easily built into the designs of learning strategies.

The transfer and generalization problems have shadowed and disturbed research and experiment-oriented media men. The achievement of control has been very elusive over transfer from one stimulus condition to others, one set of response conditions to others, and from learning conditions to realistic on-the-job performance conditions.

The sampling problem has been most difficult to solve. Given several versions of a film or television program used in experiments with adequate numbers of learners, generalizations about the variables built into the programs depend on that number of versions or variables of experimental films or television programs and not on the number of learners, when the generalizations are about these media.

Many experiments with media have been done with groups, even large groups, and classes of learners. Earlier more often than currently, radio, films, and television were called *mass* media. Group exposures and group testing apparently eclipsed many individual differences related to learning contingencies. Intensive, individualized case-by-case research like that of programed instruction with teaching machines and computers was required to reveal critical *matched interactions* between learning program characteristics and individual learner characteristics.

Frequently, relatively limited amounts of content have been selected or produced—often not very well produced—for experimental purposes. Even when parts of courses and whole courses have been the experimenters' stimulus materials, rarely have they been sensitive enough about the interaction effects of the "experimental" course with other course demands being made on the experimental subjects or learners. Compensation processes often have led to "improved" courses with learning made easier merely by permitting learners to put more effort on the difficult courses and to reduce efforts expended on the course that was *"improved."* There exists the need to consider in such experimentation the entire workload or total learning demand made on each individual student and to assess the patterns of distributing effort over the whole range of studies.

There has been neglect in media research of the requirements for active response to instructional materials. The misconception is that significant amounts and relevant kinds of learning can occur without personal involvement, active responses, and repeated practices. These must all be included for appropriate, reinforcing kinds of learner materials. Uses of instructional media without *requiring* response, practice, and participation have led to many programs being of low quality and lesser effectiveness for learning than was possible and desirable.

The tug-of-war continues today as it has in the past between the *professional* media producers and learning psychologists, programmers of learning materials, and communication theorists. Effective communications, including shared value systems, remain to be established between these groups in order that the quality of instructional materials may benefit from the application of helpful principles from the areas of perception, cognitive processes, and learning as well as from the appropriate skills and arts of professional producers. The elaboration of production techniques and formats does not necessarily increase the instructional performance quality of radio, film, and television programs. Indeed, some but not all elaborations and dramatizations may interfere with certain kinds of targeted learning.

Finally, an expectation that has affected quality is that desired learning can occur without the instruc-

tional processes being targeted to clearly defined learner characteristics and conditions, without clearly specified learner objectives, and without "feedback" of cues and information that tell the learner the degrees to which he is approximating his expected levels and objectives.

Having reviewed negative cases from seminar discussions, I shall now summarize briefly the general points of consensus expressed during the seminars.

SEMINARS CONSENSUS

Throughout the seminars and for more than 117 hours of intensive group discussions, participants agreed that the quality and effectiveness of instructional materials are determined by a very large number of resources, decisions, actions and interactions, and people–thing contingencies. When quality is defined as the production of defined changes or improvements in behavioral performances, then all contingencies to effectiveness must be controlled throughout the life history of the instructional materials or programs of instruction. The life history contingencies include the social context, conceptualization of the learning tasks, designs of instructional procedures and materials, production or procurement, library functions and distribution of materials, conditions of use, and

Table 1
Sequential Operations of an Instructional System

Phase 1	Planning and designing	Defining social needs and justifications
		Statement of general purposes and goals
		Defining specific requirements and specifications
Phase 2	Procuring and producing	Searching, finding and transforming, or creating and producing
Phase 3	Librarying	Classifying, storing, and retrieving
Phase 4	Distributing	Distributing, disseminating, diffusing
Phase 5	Using and assessing	Conditions of use, displays
		Learner interactions and reinforcement
		Assessing and evaluating
Phase 6	Cycling effects	Providing cybernetic feedback to all decision points

complex sequences of evaluations and the reporting of results to those who need them, especially the learners.

Progressively during the 12 seminars in which discussions were so focused as to yield information and best judgments about the factors and contingencies of quality, 10 sets of factors or conditions were defined and elaborated. Generally following the chart outline used to provoke and guide discussions, the 10 panels of contingencies were debated and elaborated. A general sequential order was given the panels of contingencies, but it was agreed that there would be many variations of the order of events and actions over time. Table 1 shows one possible ordering arrangement in six phases of the sequential operations.

There have been so many different schematic systems proposed that it is futile to propose another in detail. Nevertheless, the scheme as visualized conforms to the definition used by Thornton and Brown:

> The materials, equipment, and other interrelated elements (including human components) of an assemblage that operates in an organized manner in handling appropriate encoding of instructional messages and the distribution, use, and reinforcement of information. To be effective such a system must be sensitive to various stimuli and include elements of appropriate response, feedback, and adjustments.[7]

My alternative definition is the following:

> A bounded open or closed system that includes all those components, elements, factors, operations, and conditions which are interactive and significantly related to the attainment of results or objectives of a defined educational effort.

The following are brief abstracts of important concepts about each of the 10 panels of events which describe a model of the life history of a unit of instruction using media.

Consistent with systematic learning and communication theory is the requirement that the relevant characteristics of the target population be known thoroughly and used if effective learning and communications are to occur. Furthermore, the relevance and validity of an instructional activity depends on definitions and justifications in terms of the social needs of target populations. Clearly the social wants and needs are many, and therefore the ordering of priorities is a requirement of the design phase of the planning of learning strategies. Considerations of available resources and costs relative to estimated results are necessary. And finally, criteria need to be formulated that will serve as the basis of judgments about the social values of the media-based instructional effort.

General purposes and goals need to be stated at several levels of abstraction in order to reflect social values and responsibilities as well as to prepare the conceptual context for the next stages of designing learning strategies. Hierarchies need to be constructed of instructional–learning purposes, goals, and objectives expressing common meaning of themes but which vary in levels of semantic abstractions and language.

Within the hierarchy of goals, the knowledge of target population, and defined "entrance competencies performance" and abilities, as well as a knowledge of the potentials of media, *specific* operational objectives can be defined. The critical task is to estimate for future determination the changes which are anticipated in the cognitive, attitudinal, and behavioral domains of the target population. Difficult judgments must be made on the means required to produce the estimated, deserved, and expected changes. Selections must be made from among a wide range of alternatives of the best or most effective mediated learning strategies and styles, the communication *modes*. These should also be congruent with the kind of content and messages. Media selection will relate, also, to the practical question of where the target population is located, when it can best be reached, and at what costs. Generally, when the learning strategy design phase has been completed, the information and specifications will be a full blueprint which can be followed and will guide the remaining sequential operations.

The procurement phase may follow one of two courses: If the appropriate materials exist for implementing the designed learning strategy, then the performance *quality* depends on the care and skills exercised in the search, selection, modification and transformation, and testing activities. If the materials do not exist, then quality depends on the adequacy of production. Often the search-and-find operations for extant media are so difficult, time consuming, and expensive that the alternative of production is selected.

When production is indicated, then the vast repertoire of production requirements, skills, principles, and creative potentials needs to be brought to bear on the problems. The seminar discussions repeatedly reflected the need to apply the patterns of programming instructional materials using the audiovisual and print media. It became evident to many seminar members, including those with media production experience, that new formats, styles, and patterns of media productions are not only possible but are urgently required. Repeatedly the suggestion was emphasized that intensive testing of the performances of instructional materials on small samples of the target audience should be a simultaneous part of the production methods. Single-medium productions are giving way to the production of learning units in multimedia, multimode packets. Among other functions, these coordinated packets could put into effect a strongly positive production variable, *repetition with variations* with consequences for learning and stimulus–response generalizations. During the seminars it was proposed repeatedly that media like films and television, live or recorded, are multimode media. Whole programs of complex and varied instructional programs can be produced within the broad channels, formats, and communication modes carried by these media. The sharp lines are fading, furthermore, between the print and nonprint modes when viewed from the vantage point of programming instruction.

Extended discussions occurred about the resistance of educational institutions to using, as they might be used, the "new" electronic media for instructional purposes, and sometimes it was recognized that the management and pattern of productions, along with many other conditions, relate to the acceptance or rejection of instructional media. Regardless of the *inherent quality* of productions, unless the materials are used, they do not have *real quality*.

The following suggestions weigh positively on the problem of professional acceptance: technical qualities are demanded. Users are most likely to accept media-based instruction if they share in its planning. Teachers want and need materials that are flexible and can be ordered or reordered and adapted to the requirements of conditions of use. Fully produced and closed courses tend to be rejected while core-of-units and limited-concept units tend to be accepted. Instructional roles of teachers are changed by media uses. The better the media are and the higher quality, the more the roles of teachers may be changed. Productions should be left open and flexible, therefore, and the new roles and duties of teachers need to be specified. This practice would help avoid the "teacher displacement effect."

For many more learning purposes, materials are needed for the uses of individual learners working independently of teachers. In these areas, learners' roles need to be specified.

Some seminar members proposed that the widespread practice of using media materials to supplement other instructional functions should be changed. The media should carry the *basic essentials of content*. That content which is agreed to be most fundamental and the least likely to antiquate should be produced in core units and core courses of curriculums.

Generally, the seminar discussions and consensus confirmed that equipment and apparatus or the "hardware" of instructional technology greatly exceed the development and availability of instructional units, courses, programs, or the "software."

The research and development centers, the regional educational laboratories, universities, and business and industry are the agencies which presently have "software" production capabilities. There may be a need, however, for additional and uniquely designed instructional media production centers like the one at Newton, Massachusetts, part of that area's Regional Educational Laboratory.

The next phase of the sequential operations is a set of functions which includes for the media all the library operations. Generally, the classification, storage, retrieval, and circulation of nonprint media materials have not been accepted by the traditional libraries. Whether or not this service will ever become a part of book libraries is questionable. Therefore, it seems necessary for the present to develop special libraries for the media. These may more and more become switching or originating centers for instruction where recordings on films, tape, or other information carriers are delivered to users electronically over cable networks or point-to-point transmission, and with displays provided by means of electronic tubes. Properly conducted media libraries, wherever administered, are essential and feed into distribution.

Distribution strategies should be selected and used in the service of the target audience. With increasing populations, crowding, and traffic congestion, seminar members judged that it will become progressively more desirable to transmit instructional programs to learners instead of having them travel to points of concentration. Thus, independent work and home study are likely to become more frequently used than formerly. New means of distribution that may become increasingly feasible are cable networks, satellite relays, and extended use of telephone lines, even for slow-scan picture distribution and laser beam transmission.

Some hopes were expressed that radio may even yet become an important distributive medium of instruction. It was observed that seemingly a more complex and expensive medium in America tends to drive out a less complex and less expensive medium. The effect of television on radio was the example cited, but also the use of computers instead of other media may be an example of the same nonadaptive tendency.

Whatever distribution system is selected, the purpose is to reach the learner at the place where and time when there are possibilities of effective learning. This involves another design problem, this time the design of the *conditions of use* of instructional materials.

By linkages of television receivers as in closed-circuit systems, instructional units and programs can be distributed and displayed in small spaces to small intimate groups or even to individuals. Study carrels, learning cubicles, computer terminals, home study centers, dormitory rooms, and quiet places in libraries can be optimized by electronic tube displays and earphones for individualizing reception.

Many general principles which theoretically should govern the specifics of instructing and learning can be put into effect in situations of use. Interferences can be reduced or avoided. Repetition and practice can be arranged. Clear and organized content in picture and sound can be provided. Study schedules and rates of progression from unit to unit of work can be regulated. It is becoming feasible, also, to provide reinforcement and knowledge of results through terminals of many kinds and by reciprocal lines of communication back to the program sources.

The management of the programs in relation to the targeted audiences is a function of the conditions of use. Both arranged and controlled or individually selected programs of study can be provided. Where packets of materials are made available on film, paper, or tape, the ordering and sequencing of units may be done at the use points. Selections of varied cassette-carried units can be made in terms of ability and achievement levels of students as well as in terms of their levels of interest and motivation. As exemplified by interactions with computer terminals, the modern learning conditions are becoming active and not passive. Even with televised instruction using printed response schedules, learners are compelled to be alert and active.

It is in situations of use where learning and behavioral changes are assessed. The seminars repeatedly touched on the standard testing problems. Two trends in thinking seemed to emerge. First and most importantly, assessment of learning and performance is being viewed as an essential and integral aspect of learning, and the assessments are most useful when given to or made available quickly and directly to the learner. The timing may be critical for the assessments and feedback to be most effective as reinforcement. Second, standard tests with norms are being rejected increasingly, first by activist students, then by some thoughtful teachers. Explorations were suggested of individualized assessment procedures provided for as integral parts of the programs themselves. It seems probable that, like much learning responsibility, that of assessment of progress and levels of achievement may best be accepted responsibly by students themselves.

The cybernetics of instruction and learning has been seriously neglected whether it involves short or long feedback loops, whether to the learner or to the educational designer or administrator. The seminar discussions led to concurrence that appropriate, condensed, and reliable information about a wide range of general and specific learning effects and the results of the use of media-based instructional programs should be communicated to all the people responsible for every one of the panels of events (see Fig. 1) which have been reviewed. The backward line of sequencing should begin with the learner, include the managers of situations of use, inform those responsible for procurement of programs, and involve the designers of learning strategies and formulators of objectives and purposes.

CONCLUSIONS

One of many important conclusions that came from the seminars is that there are many large, macroscopic educational management problems, such as planning, setting priorities, providing finances, approving methodologies, and other administrative decisions, which must be solved before the fine microscopic variables of the media can be controlled and applied for increasing the effectiveness and quality of instructional materials. Generally, throughout education the macroscopic override the microscopic factors that are contingent to the quality of instructional media.

Study of transcripts of the seminar discussions showed that five themes were developed and often reiterated.

1. The "systems approach" and systematic planning strategies were approved, and these frames of reference were used in defining many subordinate contingencies of the quality of instructional materials.

2. There was agreement and affirmation that the results of controlled and quantitative research on learning processes are most valuable guides in achieving instructional quality, but research results and learning principles require translation, transformation, interpretation, and synthesis before they can be usefully employed for regulating learning.

3. Educators, teachers, and students must learn to master modern instructional technologies and avoid letting those technologies control them.

4. Complex instruction generally will require more than one medium and mode of discourse. An important part of the design of learning strategies is the selection of appropriate combinations of modes and media to most effectively communicate defined content to target audiences of learners.

5. The greatest needs and challenges in the area of instructional technology are the procurement and effective use of units and programs to match existing equipment, and the production of materials for learning that have been proved and validated in terms of their performance effectiveness.

REFERENCES

1. A Study of the Impact of Research on Utilization of Media for Educational Purposes. Sponsored by NDEA Title VII, 1958–1968. Robert T. Filep, *Final Report,* 1970, and Robert T. Filep and Wilbur Schramm, *Final Report: Overview,* 1970. Study conducted by Institute for Educational Development, El Segundo, Calif. U.S. Office of Education Contract No. OEC–0–9–420246–3462 (010).

2. Selected Bibliography of Summarizing and Capstone Reports No. 1. Pennsylvania State University, University Park, Pa. 16801. U.S. Office of Education Project No. OEC–1–7–071142–4372.

3. Carpenter, C. R., and Carpenter, Ruth J. *Abstracts of Seminar Discussions on Quality Factors in Instructional Materials.* Pennsylvania State University, University Park, Pa. 16802. U.S. Office of Education Project No. OEC–1–7–0771142–4372. ERIC Media Center, Stanford University, Calif., 1968.

4. Carpenter, C. R., and Froke, Marlowe. *Description of a Practical Procedure for Assessing Instructional Film and Television Programs.* Pennsylvania State University, University Park, Pa. 16802. U.S. Office of Education Project No. OEC–1–7–071142–4372. ERIC Media Center, Stanford University, Calif., 1968.

5. Carpenter, C. R., and Carpenter, Lane E. *Educational and Instructional Facilities Evaluation: Preliminary Practical Procedures.* Pennsylvania State University, University Park, Pa. 16802. U.S. Office of Education Project No. OEC–1–7–071142–4372. ERIC at Stanford University, Calif., 1968.

6. Carpenter, C. R., and Reilly, Susan S. *Quality Factors in Instructional Materials: Significant Statements by Authorities.* Pennsylvania State University, University Park, Pa. 16802. U.S. Office of Education, Project No. OEC–1–7–071142–4372, ERIC at Stanford University, Calif., 1968.

7. Thornton, James W., Jr., and Brown, James W., eds. *New Media and College Teaching.* Washington, D.C.: National Education Association, 1968.

PART VI: MEDIA CHARACTERISTICS

Mobile Learning Laboratory: Educational Research and Development on the Move

Thomas C. Potter

A large white truck rolls up to the gate of a crowded elementary school playground. Several primary-grade children run to the fence to get a closer look. "Is it my turn again today?" they ask with hopeful smiles. Marilyn Mayo, a young teacher from Los Angeles County, steps from the cab and assures them that they will all have a turn again soon.

In a few minutes Miss Mayo will be ready to help the children learn to read using a new set of programed materials developed by the Southwest Regional Laboratory for Educational Research and Development (SWRL). One of the 20 regional laboratories funded under Title IV of the Elementary and Secondary Education Act of 1965, the Los Angeles-based organization is working on many projects. Among these is the development of reading-readiness materials for children of kindergarten age. Invaluable in this effort is the cooperation of the school districts of the far-flung region which includes Southern California; Clark County, Nevada; and Arizona. Teachers such as Miss Mayo, who is on a year's assignment from the Long Beach

Thomas C. Potter is on the staff of the Southwest Regional Laboratory for Educational Research and Development, Inglewood, California.

school system, are helping to gather data on programs being developed and tested in the schools.

One of the tools used by Miss Mayo and other researchers at SWRL is their new Mobile Learning Laboratory. This self-contained unit is designed as a safe, flexible, and durable classroom on wheels.

All equipment and personnel spaces are housed in an enclosed truck. No special training or licenses are required to drive the unit. Somewhat larger than a passenger car, the unit has automatic transmission and power brakes to reduce driving effort. Included are a 110-volt power plant with capacity for concurrent operation of video tape equipment, projectors, recorders, and lights as well as the air conditioner.

The floor plan, furniture arrangement, wiring, and lighting are as flexible as possible while maintaining highest safety standards. The interior may be arranged for use as a single classroom, or it may be divided into two separate rooms, each with direct access to the outside. A reversible one-way glass is provided in the sliding door partition between rooms so that either section may be used for observation purposes. Overhead lighting may be adjusted independently for each room.

The individual student desks were designed with side dividers, interchangeable glass or solid front dividers, and folding wall shelf. The desks are attached to the wall of the van for safety in transit, and as free-standing units they may be rearranged or completely removed. The wiring for each student station is contained in a plug strip on the walls.

Safety considerations have been a prime concern in the design of the unit. All electric equipment is grounded, carpeted steps and handrails are provided for children at both exits, and fireproof materials are used throughout. Both the interior and exterior of the van are designed to be as durable as possible. Inside walls of vinyl-covered masonite add a light and spacious feeling to the interior and are easy to maintain. General room lighting is controlled separately for front and rear compart-

ment from the teacher's console. Students have individual lights which may be dimmed with a single control at the teacher's console or turned off at the student stations.

Temperature and humidity are regulated through an 8,800 Btu air conditioner, and the walls and the roof of the van are insulated. The exterior is painted a light color for maximum heat reflection. During normal use direct openings to the outside of the van are closed.

Group video presentations may be provided either through the use of 8mm or 16mm motion pictures or a 35mm slide or filmstrip. A 20- by 25-inch rear projector may be remotely controlled from the teacher's console. The 35mm presentation media may be advanced manually, set on a timed advance, or programed to advance on signal from a tape. One stereo tape deck is equipped with a tone reading device for advancing the slide projector while simultaneously presenting the audio portion of a program.

Films may be viewed individually with an 8mm cartridge projector under the control of the student. The folding shelf beside each desk is designed for the projector; the solid divider provides a viewing surface. A Carousel projector with a 45-degree mirror and rear-screen attachment may also be used at the individual student stations.

Group audio presentations may be provided either through a 7-inch speaker mounted in the front of the van or through earphones at each student station. Individual audio presentation may be made through the student's earphones. The teacher's console is equipped with a switch panel enabling the instructor to provide each student individually with a variety of audio sources. For example, while some students may be listening to presentations from several different tapes, others may simultaneously be listening to instructions from the teacher or to the sound track of a film. At any time the teacher may override an audio presentation to an individual student or any group and speak to students directly.

Each student headset is equipped with a volume control and has an individual microphone attached. The teacher may talk and listen, listen and record, or record the verbal responses of any child or group of children. Storage space is provided in the van for printed materials and manipulanda as well as films and tapes.

When Miss Mayo brings her eight kindergartners into "their room" the children won't realize that three other groups of children from schools 10 miles distant have already worked in their traveling classroom today. Reading with their teacher about the adventures of Sam the Lion, the children will be unaware that they are stars of a video tape recording to be analyzed when the Mobile Learning Laboratory returns to the SWRL office that afternoon. While the children enthusiastically tackle a new concept in reading in their classroom on wheels, they are providing the data necessary for soundly based decisions on curriculum development.

It is anticipated that the classroom's wheels will log 10,000 miles during the current school year as it becomes a familiar sight at schools in the Southwest. Through the research capability of the Mobile Laboratory hundreds of children will have their "turn again today" to learn new ideas in new ways while helping to develop better materials and techniques for our schools.

Broadcasting and Education: ERIC/EBR Annual Review Paper

Consideration of educational broadcasting and of those who strive to apply broadcasting's technologies to educational purposes revives memories of Roman-style horseback riders, the last of whom we saw perhaps 35 years ago at a fair. For those too young to know and those schooled more in daredevils with machines than in daredevils with beasts, Roman-style riding consisted usually of two fairly large horses running parallel, a standing rider, and a minimum of reins and bits. The rider's feet were wide apart, one on the port and one on the starboard horse, and as near each horse's steady backbone as could be managed. Then, with little but these precarious footholds, four light reins for guidance and balance, a prayer for equine cooperation and momentum, the rider made a dash for glory.

It was thrilling to witness, more so because Roman-style riders shouted a lot. Well they should have, for any slip of feet, reins, rhythm, or cooperation and they became something in the range from contusion cases to countertenors.

By analogy, one horse is broadcasting technology. It is not only lively and well proportioned; it is

Warren F. Seibert is professor of engineering and education at Purdue University, Lafayette, Indiana.

Copyright © 1972 by the National Association of Educational Broadcasters. Used with permission from *Educational Broadcasting Review*, 139–150 (June 1972).

also replaced and refreshed often, as a Pony Express horse would be. So, just as the rider grows almost accustomed to a mount, one of different disposition is substituted. The horse under the other foot is the institution called education. It is always the older horse and notable more for longevity than for power, grace, or speed. It evidences also little thrill at the prospect of external guidance and team participation—or at most other prospects, for that matter.

The rider is any practitioner of educational broadcasting. For obscure reasons he volunteers to climb aboard this mismatched team more than once, while still thinking often of choosing one horse or the other, as his more conventional friends do. He could go comfortably and farther, as they seem to.

There are many things he tries not to think about: why he should expect cooperation now, when there has been so little before; why no one has prepared a manual to instruct him; how many people are watching—and what they expect to see; and whether the eventual honor of succeeding justifies the risk.

The question of audiences troubles him. He is fairly sure attendants are few and sure too that some of them come only to admire the young horse, others to venerate the relic. He suspects still others are there by default: if no motorcycle races are available, they settle for lesser disasters. It is hard to satisfy so many diverse expectations all at once. But friends attend too, and some family, and those persons remain characteristically hopeful that present imperfections will recede, as they often do, under the cumulative weight of experience, ingenuity, and dedication.

How is our uncertain rider on his mismatched team performing in the arena called state of the art of educational broadcasting? What follows is a sampling and a highlighting of broadcasting in education. It is not a claim to being an exhaustive treatment of the subject for several reasons: (1) thorough coverage is impossible in a field so broad and changeable; (2) some of the pertinent information is evanescent, ephemeral, and assorted other Buckley-isms (fans of Bob and Ray may know these as Susskind-isms), and hence uncatalogued and inaccessible for review; (3) several recent and major reviews have been prepared by others, most notably at the request of the Commission on Instructional Technology[1] (see papers by Breitenfeld,[2] Forsythe,[3] Hudson,[4] the NAEB,[5,6] and Rainsberry[7]), in the EBU's report of its 1967 Paris Conference,[8] and cumulatively in *Educational Broadcasting Review, Educational Broadcasting, and Educational Television*[9]; (4) there is a good possibility that what is before us is several fields, not just one named "educational broadcasting" and that any attempt to homogenize this mass for smooth sequential treatment would do violence and reveal insoluble lumps; and (5) although the implication of "state of the art" is that the time is ripe to report progress in planning–production and use of programs, that is hardly the case.

With only a few exceptions, the state of the art marches on the old road, while significant changes, technological and political, take place in the surrounding fields. As Schramm reported to the Commission on Instructional Technology, "The hardware has outrun the software. The tools are so fascinating that we have tended to watch them develop and marvel at them and to neglect the more mundane and messier questions of how to use them."[9] This has been typically true of technology in education, a low point having been reached in the early 1960s, when the number of designs for "teaching machines" at least equalled, if in fact did not greatly exceed, the number of available teaching programs for those machines to present.

The history of educational broadcasting is marked by a succession of new battles launched before old fields are conquered. This interpretation can be applied to a succession of events that, for example, saw radio almost deserted in favor of television, but before thorough development of the first; that saw color take broad precedence over monochrome but frequently without rationale for the change; that saw stations begun with few plans for service; and that sees interconnected networks and satellites considered where lower technologies may serve as well. The problem is very much the same as elsewhere in education: so long as objectives are not well developed and clear, the criteria applied in evaluation and choice are similarly diluted or lacking, and, in the place of meticulous choices, almost any enthusiasm can have its moment.

To expand slightly on the earlier hypothesis that educational broadcasting is too heterogeneous to qualify as an entity, it may be helpful to recall the many different labels that are worn by individual practitioners. They include, or in the past have included, nonprofit broadcasting, noncommercial broadcasting, cultural-informational broadcasting, alternative service broadcasting, instructional broadcasting, public broadcasting, and broadcasting technologies in instruction. And as if this were not heterogeneity enough, cable and other new forms of program distribution are rapidly decreasing the role of broadcast transmission and may in time provide at least one twin for each of the above varieties. As Mark Twain said after landing for the second time in the saddle of a bucking horse "almost on the high pommel; [this is] too much variety."

The uses of both radio and television continue primarily to be the uses known and practiced for years. With the advent of the Corporation for Public Broadcasting and its offshoots, The Public Broadcasting Service and National Public Radio, a few changes have appeared, most notably in the public affairs–news broadcasts (a continuing highly controversial activity),[10] in "The Great American Dream Machine" series, and in several imported series which have proved unusually successful. Increasingly, also, educational broadcasting not only seeks, as formerly, to reach many minority audiences, but also now to provide access by minorities to audiences of their choosing.

If significant changes develop in educational broadcasting during the next few years (and the past gives only a mixed basis for predicting them), they will in part be extensions of the trends just mentioned, but will likely be influenced more by developments we have hardly alluded to: micro-teaching, community antenna television (CATV), instructional television fixed service (ITFS), radio, and video cassettes.

MICRO-TEACHING

Micro-teaching is a special case and seems to reflect well the kind of accommodation which educational broadcasters should be able to lead and to make. Micro-teaching has developed at Stanford[11,12] as a technique in teacher education and in research on teaching which relies on technology from broadcasting. Using a single camera and a helical-scan recorder, teachers or teachers-to-be practice the several component or technical skills of teaching (e.g., establishing set, redundancy and repetition, use of higher-order questions), both to teach a small "class" and usually to record the performance for later review. The effectiveness of the methods has been well demonstrated, and the methods have spread widely in the field, to the point where perhaps half of the teacher training institutions now use them or some variants.[13] The importance of micro-teaching would seem to be not only that it has developed as an effective way to simulate and train for teaching, but as an effective educational use of broadcasting technology. As such, one might expect that educational broadcasters would have been the architects of the method, but they weren't. Educators of teachers were.

The future seems likely to hold a succession of similar challenges to the expertise of educational broadcasting. It will require development of methods and solutions which will not often be limited to the production of materials and their delivery through broadcasting, as now, but will require instead the analysis of educational problems or areas for service into components and the reassembly of those components, a sensitivity to audiences, their abilities and predispositions, and the inventiveness to visualize new solutions to fit the problem at hand. Both CATV and ITFS are elements to be considered or soon to be added and both are likely to influence many designs and solutions of the future. The pattern, as with channel access problems heretofore, is first a battle for recognition, then a struggle to occupy and protect the resource, then finally an instrument in the delivery of service. Education has long needed multiple-channel capability like that which ITFS and CATV represent. Neither the right nor the wherewithal to develop such services are yet assured, but it seems essential and likely that they will be.

RADIO

Radio is proving itself a most resilient weed. It was to have died about a decade ago but neither in nor out of education has that happened. Lately, it even enjoys a resurgence and its prospects now appear good. With the advent of television, educational radio was abandoned by many and written off as a clearly inferior medium, compounded by a poor record of past performance. Now it appears somewhat differently. It is economical at a time when economy draws attention, it continues to demonstrate the power to hold loyal and sometimes large audiences, its station numbers now exceed 500 (admittedly including many small FM stations, perhaps half with annual budgets of less than $10,000); and although it missed the Carnegie Report it made it into the Public Broadcasting Act and through to the founding of National Public Radio. Its health improves. Even its weakest relation, instructional radio, was the subject of a "Wingspread" conference[14] in the spring of 1970, arousing interest and suspicion that it also is reviving.

Domestically, educational radio has had difficult times all its life, including the recent years, although it continues in favor elsewhere and gives a good account of itself. Much will continue to be possible with sounds and spoken words, as can be seen in the growth of audio-tutorial teaching,[15] the impressive demonstrations of "binaural" sound which have come recently from Karl Schmidt and his coworkers at the University of Wisconsin, and the curious confirmations that even though normal speech proceeds at a rate of about 165–175 words per minute, people easily acquire the ability to comprehend speech at rates near 400 words per minute.[16] We have perhaps been undervaluing radio and its sense, hearing, together.

VIDEO CASSETTES

Video cassettes are important because of what they represent in the individualization of instruction. Educators have often spoken favorably of individualized learning and have known both from observation and from harder evidence that people learn individually. Yet somewhere between the favorable consideration of this principle and its implementation, with or without help from technology, interest has been diluted or lost. However, among the strongest trends now developing in education is that of individualization. The validity of the principle and the means or the media to do something about it are increasingly evident. Even television, which appeared originally as a medium suited to and sometimes only justifiable as one for mass teaching, can find a place among the instruments of individualized education. With the video cassette systems which are now beginning to appear in the market, it becomes possible to allow students ad lib access to instruction, much as with the other forms of individualization; in addition, it becomes possible to extend the usefulness of materials prepared originally for mass or group education, but accessible now to the individual learner as well.

MORE "SESAME STREET"?

With little doubt, the most important development in educational broadcasting in recent times has not been color, or satellites, or CATV prospects, or even the Public Broadcasting Act and the Corporation for Public Broadcasting combined, but "Sesame Street." It demonstrates powers that educational broadcasters have ascribed to the media and to their services from the beginning, except that now these things seem credible. It has, in the words of one writer, revived a demoralized field. In the midst of abundant superlatives and favorable comment, it seems especially important to pause and consider both the unfavorable reactions to "Sesame Street" and the evidence, if any, which might maintain belief in the series' importance and success. Detractors are by no means absent. First, there are those who offer the mild reminder that one series does not a network make—nor an educational system. Others, including unmistakable legislative friends, have heard the series' virtues repeated so often they are satiated. They must wonder whether nothing else is happening in educational broadcasting. In addition, the BBC has rejected the series as inappropriate for their purposes.

The list of skeptics and detractors is a long one and includes those with special interests in education of the disadvantaged, in the black community, and in television. Frank Garfunkel, a member of the former group, objects to memorization and recommends more spontaneous and "real" situations in the programs. Herbert Sprigle, with interests similar to Garfunkel's, has in addition conducted a small evaluative study[17] of the "Sesame Street" programs. He concedes that his is not a definitive study; nevertheless he offers anecdotes to challenge the series' value and his study's statistical results, which rely primarily on the Metropolitan Readiness Test. His results would be more useful, in our view, if the number of students were larger ($n = 24$ pairs), if the methods of assigning students to experimental and control conditions were clear, if the nature of

his control treatment were described in better detail, and if the sensitivity of his criterion measures were also better supported. His reporting is weak on each count, and some skepticism is thus warranted, especially since his results seem at variance with those of the methodologically more careful studies of Ball and Bogatz.[18,19] These latter evaluators offer evidence, now widely cited, which show that

1. Children who viewed the most tended to learn most.
2. In most cases the skills which received the most emphasis in programming were best learned.
3. Formal supervision of learners was not essential.
4. More viewing was attended by more learning in all studied subgroups (including the finding that ". . . disadvantaged children . . . who watched a great deal surpassed the middle class children who watched only a little."[20]
5. Very tentatively, the programs seemed uniquely effective for children whose first language was not English.

Others have criticized "Sesame Street": Robert Lewis Shayon, for borrowing too much from the high-pressure features of commercial television; the National Association of Black Media Producers, for increasing the gap between "haves" and "have-nots" and for failing, despite intention, to understand the motivation of black people; and a number of inventive educators, for channeling children in ways that do not serve their best interests.

But the demonstrated effectiveness of "Sesame Street," its wide appeal, and the acclaim granted it have not appeared to spoil its creators, and they acknowledge a number of failures in efforts thus far. But where, one asks, does a second example exist, created by either the critics or others, which combines a clear vision of a select set of educational goals, a marshaling of resources to serve those goals, plus a careful and repeated reference to evidence to improve the achievement of those goals? And where else in educational broadcasting are the examples of commitment and service to a population that is disadvantaged? It seems, then, from here that "Sesame Street" is not just acclaimed and certainly not perfect, but that it comes closer by far to the best in the field than whatever runs second.

EFFECTIVENESS AND EVIDENCE

It is impossible to write about the state of educational broadcasting without also judging, diagnosing, and recommending. Since Osgood's early research on meaning,[21] if not long before that, it has been clear that connotations are everywhere and by far the greatest of these are evaluative. The author therefore confesses to a bias that favors the instructional uses of broadcasting over most alternatives; that favors demonstrations of effectiveness and of impact over claims of ingenuity, conferred honors, or other good things which can momentarily distinguish an effort; and that favors evidence over all the rest. It seems that educational broadcasters have accepted, through some years of negotiation and precedent, a large commitment to serve education, and that now, when education's need for solutions has reached crisis proportions, a tilting of the balance to favor instruction is in order, if not overdue. It has been customary in educational broadcasting to evaluate work in a number of ways, only a few of which bear demonstrated relationship to effectiveness for stated purposes. Efforts in communication are addressed to purposes which may be more or less well stated, yet statements and evaluations in terms of them are still relatively rare. It seems a pity.

Finally, there is the broader matter of attitude toward evidence. Interest in evidence, especially the evidence that bears on one's work, would seem to say important things about curiosity, intellectual honesty, eagerness for progress, security and self-esteem, and professionalism. Educational broadcasting can achieve a highly significant place in the service of important human needs, but its speed in achieving this is importantly influenced by respect for and sensitivity to evidence.

Enough of those biases.

MEN AND FORCES

There are still questions concerning how the present state and the past progress in applying broadcasting to education have come about, whether they result from or occur independently of educational broadcasters. A case exists on both sides. On the reserved and less complimentary side, one sees the obvious match between the most prevalent methods of educators—largely verbal, inexorable, one-way communication directed at groups—and paralleling this, the clearest capability of the broadcast media, which can be described well in exactly the same terms. No special aptitude is needed to recognize this match or to create applications from it, and much educational broadcasting has been and still is in this category, unembellished. Neither can it be denied that broadcasting technology has continued to elaborate and refine, since its inception. From the beginning, the capabilities of broadcasting have overlapped the procedures of education, as indicated. Later refinements have continued to enlarge this overlap. This same growth and refinement has had major social consequences, since they have led to creation of audiences who now respond readily, almost instinctively, to the electronic media. To an increasing extent within education, but especially in the larger society, a broad electronic wave is running and is providing special momentum and advantage to educational broadcasting. From the viewpoint of educational broadcasting, the word which encompasses this correspondence of educational method and of broadcasting capability, this growth in refinement and versatility, and this acquired predisposition of audiences is "windfall."

The other side of the argument is more complimentary to first and second generation educational broadcasters, it is consistent with the lore of the field (not necessarily as a separate or independent point), and it may also be correct. In any case, it stresses the pioneering activities of a determined band who have had both the foresight and the skill to establish important landmarks in essentially hostile territory. Members of that band established stations against sometimes frightful odds, they achieved the reservation of broadcasting channels, they joined together to share programming and other limited resources, they repeatedly pieced together funds sufficient to continue impoverished operations, and they have worked ceaselessly to improve the climate for legislation and support. Considering the extent to which politics are involved in these accomplishments, and the abundance of adversaries (to say nothing of the apathy which greets any similar succession of changes, even from those disposed to be sympathetic) determined leadership becomes a plausible factor.

But it remains less important to make a choice between the forces of the times and those of great men than to consider and proceed to meet needs that press for attention. Grouped loosely into four sets, and put in an approximate ascending order of importance, they might be named intraeducational relations, creative accommodation to change, professionalism, and learning.

INTRAEDUCATIONAL RELATIONS

It is difficult to review developments in educational broadcasting without suspecting that it maintains better relations with its benefactors and means more to them than is the case with its presumed beneficiaries, although this situation seems to be changing. The mistake or the dilemma, whichever one chooses, seems very much the same as that of the politician who can serve no constituency except by being elected and reelected. Since struggles for survival are as common in educational broadcast-ing as they are in politics, there is some basis for these otherwise strange relationships. Nevertheless, an enlarged commitment to service and a more prominent concern for the educational interests of audiences are needed. Pessimistically, Carlson[22] is among those who see the continuing struggle for permanent, insulated funding of CPB as one that already affects fundamentally the role of public television and its services. He contends that PTV's role as a questioning gadfly in society is lost and that a choice has been made between the funds to survive and the privilege to question freely. He is similarly pessimistic about the freedom to develop substantial audiences, which would then threaten commerical broadcasting and would as a consequence be squelched. And he not only doubts that an open university, dependent upon broadcasting, as is now developing in Britain and to an extent in Germany, is attainable in these parts, but he questions its wisdom. (Readers interested in a positive consideration of these questions and of others concerned with the "open school" should see Wedemeyer's recent article.[23]) Carlson's apparent concern is for academic freedom, its vigor, and society's readiness to have advanced thought and iconoclasms broadcast, literally and figuratively. These concerns are not to be oversimplified or discounted, but there is a more hopeful view. First, data confirm that past restrictions on the themes and language of broadcasts have undergone unprecedented change within very recent years, and this change is continuing. Anyone listening to Public Radio's recent airing of sessions from the convention of the American Association for the Advancement of Science must have heard dialogue that was unusual, to say the least, both in its attitude and its language. Although stations undoubtedly received complaints and felt some pressures, nothing indicates that a legal or political crisis ensued. So, very practically and demonstrably, formerly sensitive subjects and formerly offensive language are no longer so sensitive or offensive. But more importantly, education always entails the risk of offending, and educational broadcasting continues to hold unique potential for enlarging access to education. To make either education or its broadcast programming intentionally innocuous would be very much like withholding the corpse from burial.

Although not always noticed and less often acknowledged, educational broadcasting has become a central member in the family of instructional technologies. Few could have predicted this a few years ago, since the family itself has only coalesced to be recognized within perhaps the last dozen years. But it is now unmistakable that an age of instructional technology has begun and that it encompasses the technologies of broadcasting. One would hope that educational broadcasters would welcome this development and would welcome the new opportunities to provide service that matters greatly to individuals and to major public institutions, many of them in desperate circumstances; but whether welcomed or not, the trends are clear. We would suggest that, as a consequence, some freedoms which in the past accompanied broadcasting's role as incidental, peripheral, and supplemental to education's main purposes will become serious derelictions, if continued. Educational broadcasting can be a major instrument in education and in the educational changes which are begun with technology. Educational broadcasting, more than the available alternatives, can deal simultaneously with problems of broadened educational opportunity and of educational quality. But to realize these, it must take more seriously its membership in the family of instructional technologies and volunteer more readily to assist in the solution of serious, central, contemporary educational problems.

CREATIVE ACCOMMODATION TO CHANGE

Most of us have learned to speak glibly about the rapid pace of social and technological change and we recognize also that these things impinge especially on educational broadcasting. But how deeply do these realizations go? What consideration have we given to the possibility of a future which is not simply an extension of the present? Even the most recent history can be instructive in this and will perhaps provide incentives to consider these prospects further. Consider, for example, that most present practitioners have been eyewitnesses to a succession of profound changes in the field. In less than 20 years, educational broadcasting has cycled through numerous phases and eras, creating and sometimes retaining variants and mutations. From the simple and fairly homogeneous days of educational AM radio have emerged social and technical inventions that can be quickly reviewed by citing just a few terms: tape, WOI-TV, Sixth Report and Order, Ford Foundation, closed-circuit, NET (RC), quadratures, Title VII, helical scan, Facilities Act, SCA, Samoa, ITFS, color, cassettes, porta-paks, Carnegie, CTW, CIT, and CPB. What are the comparable terms for the next decade? What will become of urban education, public telecommunication centers, satellites, individualized instruction, community colleges, compensatory education, CATV, the open university, and accountability? There are imaginative roles and relationships for educational broadcasting in each of these, or their opposite, but since educational broadcasting traditionally has not been the safest haven for traditionalists, there is at least a basis for hope that it will not now become one.

The challenge of expected change is of course not original. Most recently, it is the theme of the National Association of Educational Broadcasters' (and President Harley's) call for the establishment of public telecommunication centers.[24] An earlier precursor of that call exists, among other places, in Harley's 1962 address to the Philadelphia NAEB convention,[25] one part of which says

> *Despite the tremendous developments in electronic communications and the marvels still to come, the core of the methodology is and always will be people. Electronic technology will not apply itself. It must be applied by people who intimately understand its nature and use it to its ultimate potential. This means that we must develop*

new resources of first-rate personnel, who are not only skilled in the techniques of broadcasting and know educational methods but have understanding of the learning process and a good grounding in the social sciences. Much of the hope for excellence in educational broadcasting and in the use of the electronic media depends on the broad competence and dedication of people attracted to it as a career. We must attract to this newly emerging profession the very best imaginative minds of the land. And we must continually upgrade the quality of those already in the field so they are adequate to the requirements and demands of using the new media to its fullest potential.

This challenge is one which places a special premium on creativity and a special meaning on that much-used term. Additional changes, both in education and in broadcasting, seem as sure as the many changes recently witnessed, and for educational broadcasting to be effective, if not to survive, creative and strategic new patterns are necessary.

PROFESSIONALISM

The main theme of the Philadelphia address, and one to be stressed here as well, is professionalism. President Harley's consideration of the subject, a decade ago, relied on James Finn's analysis and definition of professionalism. Five criteria were to be satisfied. First, a profession must employ an intellectual technique and must apply it, second, to the practical affairs of man. Third, there must be a long period of training required for entry into the profession. Fourth, there must be a professional association closely knit, with a high quality of communication among members. Fifth, enforced standards and ethical requirements are needed. And finally, any group which would be called a profession must have an organized body of theory constantly expanded by research.

A similar but more complete consideration of professionalism and of the professionalization process is given by Wilensky.[26] His basis is the sociological study of occupations, from which he draws two primary and broad criteria: "the job of the professional is technical—based on systematic knowledge or doctrine acquired only through long prescribed training"; and the professional "... adheres to a set of professional norms." With respect to the first of these, he says further that "Any occupation wishing to exercise professional authority must find a technical basis for it, assert an exclusive jurisdiction, link both skill and jurisdiction to standards of training, and convince the public that its services are uniquely trustworthy." With respect to the second, also referred to as the "service ideal," he says "... professional status is governed also by the degree to which practitioners conform to a set of moral norms that characterize the established professions. These norms dictate not only that the practitioner do technically competent, high-quality work, but that he adhere to a service ideal—devotion to the client's interests more than personal or commercial profit should guide decisions when the two are in conflict."

In educational broadcasting, as in all aspiring occupational groups, there is much discussion of professionalism, but as Finn–Harley or Wilensky indicate, with little attention to strict definitions and to the responsibilities of professionalism. Most would agree that educational broadcasting is somewhere in transition, moving toward professional status, yet they would agree also that it is still some distance from the goal. To date, the full distance has been covered by few occupational groups, but to those who have made it, it presents a similar sequence: its practitioners begin by practicing full-time whatever it is that the occupation requires; they establish training schools within universities in order to develop a knowledge base and link it to practice; they form a professional association; they agitate politically to win legal protection of their chosen territory and of their sustaining ethical code; and they adopt a formal code of ethics to control the unqualified, unscrupulous, and overly competitive.

From these analyses it may be heartening to note that educational broadcasting satisfies several of the requirements of authentic professionalism, but disappointing to note also the number of requirements remaining and their stringency.

Professionalism was identified by President Harley in 1962 as the single string and note that he was satisfied to play on an imaginary and otherwise inferior cello. He and others among the leadership express this commitment not simply because professionalism carries elevation of social position for educational broadcasters—although it does that—but because it represents the principal avenue for realizing technical potentials they envision and for providing the improved, socially significant services for which there are such evident needs.

LEARNING

Last and most important of all are concerns that come under the heading of "learning." In educational broadcasting, as in most education, attention seems still directed, almost autistically, at program, stimulus, and origination elements, but rarely concerns itself directly with learning, effectiveness, or impact except anecdotally. Some see this situation as changing, and we are inclined to agree, but as with professionalism, there is a great distance to go. It is understandable that practitioners find it easier and more conclusive to manipulate the elements of broadcasting hardware, of program content, of production method, or even of the politics that influence support than to anticipate and manipulate ultimate impact on audience. Learning is admittedly a collection of processes which are complex, largely concealed, and by no means well understood, even by their experts. Nevertheless, learning and the closely related responses of human audiences will remain central to all that the educator, broadcaster, and educational broadcaster hope to accomplish. Although the full realization of this can be delayed, it must eventually arrive. Surely, then, the sooner the better.

Some of the reluctance to address the subject of learning derives also from questions of freedom and control that lurk in all technologies of learning. For this we recommend the counsel of the late E. G. Boring,[27] Harvard professor and dean of modern psychology, as well as a pioneer (kine era) television teacher, on WGBH. He responds to questions raised by "motivation research," a controversial subject from the late 1950s, but what he wrote applies much more broadly. In part, his view is the following:

> Persuasion and shaping the behavior of others is the chief social activity of the gregarious human race, and most of it is hidden! The Zeitgeist that prevents men from having original thoughts before the culture is ready to receive and reinforce them is the most hidden and persuading of all these forces and even the neonate is not free of it. It's education if you want it, propaganda if you don't. Religion if it's good, superstition if it's bad. Statesmanship if it's big, politics if it's small. Devotion if it's right, prejudice if it's wrong. Why are people so worried because forces of the kind they always depend on are influencing them on the sly? If Freud ever did anything for human civilization, it was to show that man's motivation is ordinarily inscrutable to himself. The good teacher has got as many hidden persuaders up his sleeve as has Madison Avenue.

The implications of the recommended, heightened, and early concern with learning are several. A renewal of commitment to research is required, not simply to advance professionalism, although it will do that, but to add to the small store of evidence and understanding which now exists. What is known currently is that the broadcast media can instruct, and can draw and hold attention, but little more is known. In addition, though, a quantity of informed opinion says that these media possess greater and largely unexploited powers. If this informed opinion is ever to be tested, refined, and sharpened, research must do it, and to do it, must acquire a standing beyond the best it has yet attained.

The most likely result to expect from research not as yet done is the more selective and discriminating use of broadcasting in education. Presently, the choice of medium and of format is made usually on the basis of intuition or of simple availability, and the validity of these decisions is rarely known or questioned. It stands to reason, some say, that the intuitions are basically sound and at best they could be improved only slightly, whatever the additional research might show. Perhaps so, but several things suggest otherwise. For example, one of the older studies from May and Lumsdaine[28] fails to reveal any difference *in student learning* between a crude pencil-sketch science film and a parallel, fully produced color film counterpart. Can contemporary specialists accept or explain such results? In addition, the world of commercial broadcasting and of film abounds with examples of production judgments which audiences would not validate. The responses of audiences outside of education, as well as in it, remain largely unpredictable a priori.

Perhaps the most provocative evidence comes from a small and little-known study by Rothkopf,[29] who asked a dozen educators to rank seven brief segments of instructional text material. They were to estimate the instructional effectiveness of each segment, all of them addressed to the same known objectives. From earlier work, he had a second ranking of these same segments, this ranking based on students' demonstrated success in learning from each one. The correlation between the two sets of ranks was $-.75$, in other words, extremely *high* and *negative*.

Several questions developed in the wake of the study. Were the educators sufficiently "expert"? Markle thought not, so she used the same study procedures with her own "experts."[30] Her correlation was $-.56$, which she interprets as a kind of vindication, since it failed (by the narrowest margin) to achieve statistical significance and, hence, could be regarded as if it were a zero correlation. However, additional unpublished work by Martin E. Smith, of Bell Telephone Laboratories (incidentally, Rothkopf's base also), continues to make the negative correlation of ranks seem more likely than the zero correlation which Markle suspects, or the moderate-to-high positive correlation which is preferred and implicit in the work of most communications specialists.

Markle questions the "expertness" of the educational judges and perhaps she should. We don't yet know. Broadcasters may take comfort also from the apparent differences between their media and their formats and those of Rothkopf, Markle, and Smith. We don't yet know about that either. Furthermore, there is the possibility that the materials judged and studied thus far were atypical and of poor quality—as Markle also intimates—and that otherwise sound judgments suffered. Again, we don't know. Or, possibly, some judges have the almost mystic powers required, while many do not, or judges have good days and bad days, or judges can empathize with some audiences but not with others, or.... We don't know. But before we proceed much further on the assumption that these judgments and their counterparts throughout education and communications are sound and reliable, we need some investigations to question or to validate them.

All who make production and programming judgments hold some conception, some model of the audiences they seek to serve. They are understandably prejudiced in favor of their conceptions, yet modest enough usually to acknowledge that they sometimes err. So, in the interest of audiences, practitioners, advancing professionalism, the curious, and even of society, it seems wise now to get on with the many pending inquiries, among which the suggestions above are only a few convenient examples.

Neither education nor broadcasting occur in a vacuum and most practitioners in educational broadcasting are acutely aware of the financial context in which they operate. Even though this is so and even though questions of financial support for educational broadcasting are especially of interest now, while solutions like those envisioned in the Carnegie Report[31] and the Public Broadcasting Act of 1967[32] are being both pressed and resisted, it seems inappropriate in this paper to dwell on these large and important matters. They are hereby acknowledged, however, with this closing from Santayana: "All things real have ideal possibilities and all ideals their material base."

REFERENCES

1. Commission on Instructional Technology, *To Improve Learning*. (Washington, D.C.: Government Printing Office, 1970).
2. Frederick Breitenfeld, Jr., *Instructional Television: The State of the Art*. (Prepared at the request of the Commission on Instructional Technology. Washington, D.C.: Government Printing Office, 1970).
3. Richard O. Forsythe, *Instructional Radio: Its Broad Capabilities as an Educational Delivery System*. (Prepared at the request of the Commission on Instructional Technology. Washington, D.C.: Government Printing Office, 1970).
4. Robert B. Hudson, *The School Broadcasting System in Japan*. (Prepared at the request of the Commission on Instructional Technology. Washington, D.C.: Government Printing Office, 1970).
5. National Association of Educational Broadcasters, *Television in Instruction: What Is Possible*. (Washington, D.C.: 1970).
6. National Association of Educational Broadcasters, *Observations on Instructional Television and Instructional Technology*. (Prepared at the request of the Commission on Instructional Technology. Washington, D.C.: Government Printing Office, 1970).
7. F. B. Rainsberry, *Educational TV in Canada*. (Prepared at the request of the Commission on Instructional Technology. Washington, D.C.: Government Printing Office, 1970).
8. Office de Radiodiffusion-Television Francaise, *Third E.B.U. International Conference on Educational Radio and Television*. (Paris: Mar. 8–22, 1967).
9. Wilbur Schramm, *To Improve Learning*. (Prepared at the request of the Commission on Instructional Technology. Washington, D.C.: Government Printing Office, 1970), p. 21.
10. "Public TV Salaries Raise Eyebrows on Hill," *Broadcasting* (Dec. 1971), 33–34.
11. Dwight Allen and Kevin Ryan, *Micro-teaching*. (Reading, Mass.: Addison-Wesley Publishing Company, Inc., 1969).
12. Dwight Allen and R. J. Clark, Jr., "Micro-teaching: Its Rationale," *High School Journal*, 51 (1967), 75–79.
13. Blaine E. Ward, *A Survey of Microteaching in NCATE-Accredited Secondary Education Programs. Research and Development Memorandum No. 70*. (Stanford, Calif.: Stanford Center for Research and Development in Teaching, Dec. 1970).
14. National Association of Educational Broadcasters, *Wingspread Report*. (Washington, D.C.: July 1970). (Typewritten)
15. S. N. Postlethwait, J. Novak, and H. T. Murray, Jr., *The Audio-Tutorial Approach to Learning*. Second ed. (Minneapolis, Minn.: Burgess Publishing Company, 1969).
16. Emerson Foulke and Thomas G. Sticht, "Review of Research on the Intelligibility and Comprehension of Accelerated Speech," *Psychological Bulletin*, 72 (1969), 50–62.
17. Herbert A. Sprigle, "Can Poverty Children Live on 'Sesame Street?'" *Young Children*, (Mar. 1971), 202–217.
18. Samuel Ball and Gerry Ann Bogatz, *The First Year of Sesame Street: An Evaluation*. A summary of the major findings. (Princeton, N.J.: Educational Testing Service, Oct. 1970.)
19. Samuel Ball and Gerry Ann Bogatz, *The First Year of Sesame Street: An Evaluation*. (Princeton, N.J.: Educational Testing Service, Oct. 1970.)
20. Samuel Ball and Gerry Ann Bogatz, *The First Year of Sesame Street: An Evaluation*. A summary of the major findings. (Princeton, N.J.: Educational Testing Service, Oct. 1970), p. 4.
21. C. E. Osgood, G. J. Suci, and P. H. Tannenbaum, *The Measurement of Meaning*. (Urbana, Ill.: University of Illinois Press, 1967).
22. Robert A. Carlson, "Public Television: Retrospect & Prospect," *Educational Broadcasting*, 131 (Jan./Feb. 1972), 14–24.
23. Charles A. Wedemeyer, "The Open School: Education's Runnymeade?" *Educational Technology* (Jan. 1972), 65–68.
24. William G. Harley, *A Statement on Educational Broadcasting and New Communication Technology*. (Presented to the Executive Board of Directors of the NAEB, May 1971). (Typewritten)
25. William G. Harley, *Educational Broadcasting: A Profession Within a Profession*. (Presented to NAEB Convention, Oct. 1962). (Typewritten)
26. Harold L. Wilensky, "The Professionalization of Everyone?" *The American Journal of Sociology*, 70 (1964), 137–158.
27. E. G. Boring, "M. R. (Motivation Research)," *Contemporary Psychology* (Feb. 1959), 46.
28. M. A. May and A. A. Lumsdaine, *Learning from Films*. Chapter 2: "Pictorial Quality and Color." (New Haven, Conn.: Yale University Press, 1958).
29. Ernst Z. Rothkopf, "Some Observations on Predicting Instructional Effectiveness by Simple Inspection," *The Journal of Programmed Instruction*, II, 2 (1963), 19–20.
30. Susan Markle, "It Figgers," *NSPI Journal*, IV, 2 (Mar. 1965), 4–5.
31. Carnegie Commission on Educational Television, *Public Television: A Program for Action*. (New York: Bantam Books, Inc., Jan. 1967).
32. The Public Broadcasting Act of 1967, *Educational Broadcasting Review*, I, 2 (Dec. 1967), 11–20.

Individualization of Instruction Through Reorganization

James S. Miles

Many lofty statements are published in university catalogs and annual reports expounding the philosophy, mission or goal of an institution of higher learning. In reality, however, the primary purpose of the university is to provide an environment in which any qualified student can develop individual expression, initiative, and intelligence through self-direction and self-evaluation in a program of specialization which will equip him for a vocation of his choice. I should state that in my interpretation the term vocation is expanded beyond the traditional idea of occupation to include training for life, in a more general sense. In any event, this goal must be met in an atmosphere which makes the most effective and efficient use of staff and facilities, allowing faculty the time to engage in stimulating and innovative teaching practices, professional growth, research, and public service.

The key to this educational pattern is the individual, the student as well as the professor. Individualization of instruction is not a new concept, but perhaps it is only now in the 1970s that we really have the capability of achieving it. Now it can be reached by combining educational methodology, psychology, and learning theory with telecom-

James S. Miles is director of educational television at Purdue University, Lafayette, Indiana.

munications and other forms of technology. This paper will attempt to illustrate this concept by describing a system in which the individual student is allowed to dominate the administrative system in which he pursues his education, thus tailor-making a course of study to his needs.

BACKGROUND

For some time I have felt that too great a percentage of the student's time at the university is spent in the "hunting and seeking" processes of securing information or in duplicating efforts in several courses, some of which are not relevant to his ultimate educational goals. Instead it seems that the student should be directing his energies toward the application of information which will have carry-over once he leaves the university. Therefore, the information transfer process must necessarily be made more efficient and expedient and must take place on a one-to-one ratio in the best possible learning atmosphere. This concept of individualization of instruction is lauded by all but practiced by few owing to sheer numbers of students in the university coupled with constraints of traditional teaching and administrative patterns.

With each increment in the student population at Purdue, more and more faculty members have become concerned about teaching methods. This has meant reorganizing the age-old structure of instruction consisting of lectures, laboratories, and recitations. Lectures have grown larger and have been given by television. Laboratories have grown alternately longer and shorter, and a few heretics today even suggest that we could do away with them altogether. Recitation groups have changed in all sorts of ways including size, regularity of meetings, and purposes. Not only have courses changed, the entire curricula of schools have been similarly modified, changed, and rechanged. Still in all, if a student wants 3 hours of credit at Purdue, he must have a certain number of contact hours with an instructor to earn that credit.

The most innovative of our staff have been able to work within this sort of restriction and still allow a great deal of flexibility. The audio-tutorial system utilized by Purdue's Department of Biology, designed by Sam Postlethwait, is perhaps the prime example of this sort of development. In turn, the audio-tutorial system recently led to the development of minicourses when Postlethwait decided that a total course, of one or two semesters, was not a suitable increment for a learning situation. Therefore, a total course was broken down into small conceptual units called minicourses to be mastered one at a time at the student's individual rate according to a tailor-made plan of study.

The unique idea of the minicourse is that students need not spend time in subsequent courses relearning the same material they have mastered simply because the material is required by a different department under a different course number. For instance, the student who plans to take two semesters of biology, one in botany and one in zoology, could conceivably take a number of minicourses which are common to both, thus avoiding repetition of material. Therefore, the concept of developing courses which fill multiple needs has developed.

Postlethwait and his colleagues readily recognize that they have gone about as far as they can go under the present constraints of the direct relationship of student–teacher contact hours to credit hours earned by a student. Something must be done to take advantage of the unique capabilities of technology to transfer information and move the responsibility for such information transfer away from the professor, who, although he must maintain responsibility for content, is perhaps at his worst in attempting via lectures and recitations to effectuate such information transfer.

MANDATE FOR INNOVATION

In last year's "Message on Education Reform," President Nixon called upon the nation's educators to take a new look at their current blackboard and textbook stage of communication. He said,

> There comes a time in any learning process that calls for reassessment and reinforcement. It calls for new directions in our methods of teaching, new understanding of our ways of learning, for a fresh emphasis on our basic research so as to bring behavioral sciences and advanced technology to bear on problems that only appear to be insuperable.[1]

For some time I, too, have been convinced that some drastic changes needed to be made, but not just in isolated instances as is so often the case in education. Rather, the total concept must be changed so that the potential of technology can be realized to the fullest extent. Technology operates best when incorporated into the systems approach, as evidenced in its adaptation to industry. The belief that the systems approach is also applicable to education underlies the philosophy behind the establishment of a degree program in instructional system technology at Chapman College in California in which the "techniques of systems analysis, learning theory and educational technology are combined and utilized to be maximally efficient and effective."[2]

There are always those who argue that technology must, by its very nature, dehumanize education. However, at a 1970 conference on "Humanizing Education Through Technology" at Vanderbilt University where I was a participant quite the contrary was concluded. In one summary of the conference, it was stated that "Technology neither humanizes nor dehumanizes education, however, the way it is used determines whether its impact is humanizing or dehumanizing."[3] Consensus further indicated that,

> At present, intelligent application of the computer seems the best way to cope with the vast differences among individuals and their various environments in today's society, for it offers learners and teachers alike a broad range of options for learning methods and learning itself and provides opportunities for choices in terms of various needs and occasions.[4]

I have taken these pleas for innovation to heart and have attempted to apply what is known about higher education and technology in a somewhat radically new approach which employs the systems concept. In preface to the description of this plan, it should be noted that it has been designed with my immediate concern, Purdue University, in mind. Even on the local level, implementation of this idea will take time—time for research, development, pilot testing, and eventual application of findings. In addition, it must be remembered that, as with any systems approach, continuing study, evaluation, and modification play an integral part. With this introduction, the following plan is offered as a possible course of action for individualizing instruction in higher education.

THE PROPOSAL

A student, in order to learn, needs many things. Among them are help in identifying his academic interests and goals and a course of study aimed at reaching these goals. The course of study should include three elements: (1) the transfer of information, (2) the opportunity and tools for individual study, and (3) the opportunity to apply what has been learned through synthesis, extrapolation, and so on. The Individual Dominated Educational Administrative System (IDEAS) is aimed at optimizing those opportunities for each individual student within a viable administrative framework.

In capsule form, IDEAS is a plan in which the student plays a greater role in the selection, sequencing, and pacing of his educational activities. Initially he would plan his curriculum to meet his individual needs, selecting subjects from a multitude of possible minicourses. Having selected certain content areas, he would acquire information at his own rate using the most efficient and effective channels for this "information transfer" element. In most cases the "opportunity to apply" element would involve direct face-to-face instruction with the professor in tutorial and seminar-type situations. However, where possible, advantage would be taken of technology for this process too. The "individual study" element which is the most visible of the unique features of IDEAS is described in further detail later.

At the fruition of this plan it is altogether feasible that each student, whether he lived in a dormitory, fraternity house, private rooming house, at home, or in an apartment, would have a *student study position*. Each such position would be outfitted with a console consisting of an 11-inch television monitor and augmented touch-tone pad, a cartridge audio tape recorder and player, and an electrostatic copying device. Each student console would be connected with a switching terminal by two pairs of wires similar to telephone wires. One of the two pairs would be capable of operating up to 10 megaherz and would carry the audio and video signals. The other pair would carry the control signals. Each switching terminal would be interconnected with the central storage and retrieval location which in turn would be capable of interconnecting with satellite storage and retrieval locations wherever these might exist, on or off campus.

It would also be possible for each student through his touch-tone pad to be able to access (1) the computer which stores his program of action and his record of accomplishments, (2) the computer which can provide direct assistance in finding the materials the student currently needs and information as to where and when integral lectures, seminars, or tutorial meetings are available, and (3) a computer which can assist with problem solving. Regardless of its origin, computer, printed page, microform or videotape, all material would appear on the student's television screen. All audio material would be heard on the accompanying speaker and if desired could be recorded on the cassette recorder. Material displayed on the television picture tube could, by means of the electrostatic copier, provide a hard copy for the student's later reference and use.

For this concept to become operable, as described, a systems approach must be incorporated into the educational pattern. Therefore, IDEAS is subdivided into eight operational units which would function in an interdependent manner to ensure compatability among all units in the system. The operational units are as follows:

Instructional program This group, which would numerically be the largest, would include faculty and media specialists who would be responsible for instructional units of work similar to "minicourses" numbering in the thousands which, when properly put together, would make an individually tailored course of study for each student. It should be reemphasized that the "minicourse" concept would include not only the recapture of information through the use of technology, but computer testing, tutorial meetings, seminars, and lectures as needed for each unique learning sequence. By making much of the content of these minicourses replicable, portable, and retrievable for use at the student's individual pace, the professor would be released from routine large-group instruction for more individual contact with students.

Curriculum counseling This group would provide the means by which each student could determine his goals and choose those units which would allow him to reach these goals from the thousands developed by the instructional program group.

Space utilization Plans for the utilization of physical space on campus to optimize the availability of space suitable for the individual small-group and large-group activities prescribed by the instructional program section would be handled by this unit. They would manage the physical resources of the university in a way which was compatible with the human resources.

Storage and retrieval This unit would optimize the use of all forms of technology (audio tape, videotape, color slides, photography, microform, etc.) to store and retrieve the materials developed or acquired by the Instructional Program section.

Computer program This group would be responsible for the programs which would enable storage and recording of (1) the units of work selected by the counselors, (2) the amount and quality of work done by each student, (3) information which would permit validation of programs and tests, and (4) a directory and citation service so that each student could access the materials he needs when he needs them and determine where and when nonstorable related activities are available.

Electronics system This group would be responsible for the switched network which would serve as an interface between the students and the computer and the stored material. This group would also be responsible for the student console described above.

Quality control This group would assume the responsibility for maintaining and improving the quality of this educational system. Through research and evaluation they would seek to develop new teaching techniques and methodology as well as new and more effective uses of technology. Their work would be based on the needs of the other groups, and communication would be carried out by the "educational generalist" who would be among the key personnel of this group.

Administrative system This group would be comprised of a body of administrators at all levels of the university. They would review the philosophy of higher education administration in light of the new concepts presented in IDEAS and then would set criteria for making the administration of this system viable.

RATIONALE

The preceding proposal for applying the systems approach to higher education has been built on several premises which need to be tested. First, it is my belief that such a system would not only be educationally viable, but economically viable as well. In my work as a member of the board of education of a local school district, I have always felt that we must change the currently accepted way of thinking on the part of educators who, when faced with 200 more students, automatically conclude that they need seven or eight more teachers

and rooms and at least three more school buses. However, the only possible alternative involves new administrative structures and the use of technology.

Second, the system can be designed in such a way that it would be replicable on any level and/or scale of educational endeavor. Such a program might well begin in a specific academic department as a testing ground and then be expanded to an entire school within the university and ultimately to the total university. It could also be adapted to junior colleges, elementary and secondary education, and continuing education.

CONCLUSION

For total efficiency, the overall concept of such a system must be accepted before any of the individual components can be implemented. The fact that this may call for reorganization of the basic blueprints of existing administrative structural patterns contributes to the uniqueness of IDEAS. However, it also contributes additional resistance to its adoption.

Just as in the case of the NASA program which depends on the support of the nation for its vitality, the technological know-how is available for IDEAS, but without the human element of the system, the total commitment of faculty and administration, such a plan can never get off the ground. This phenomenon often presents a much more insurmountable problem than even the design of the sophisticated technology required. As C. P. Snow once said,

> In a society like ours, academic patterns change more slowly than any others. In my lifetime, in England, they have crystalised rather than loosened. I used to think that it would be about as hard to change, say, the Oxford and Cambridge scholarship examination as to conduct a major revolution. I now believe that I was over-optimistic.[5]

REFERENCES

1. Richard M. Nixon, "Message on Education Reform," Mar. 3, 1970.

2. *Chapman College Catalog,* Orange, Calif., 1969–1970.
3. Walter A. Standbury (ed.), "Experts Point Way to Better Education Through Technology," *Product Engineering,* 26, Mar. 2, 1970.

4. *Ibid.*
5. C. P. Snow, "Miasma, Darkness and Torpidity," *New Statesman,* 42: 1587, 1961.

Video Tape and the Adult Learning Process

Ted Carpenter

No three fields are coming more rapidly or unexpectedly together than the fields of video tape, cable television, and adult education. In so doing, the traditional world of instructional television with its lifeless studios, dreary monologues, and lectures that tended to drag the worst of education out into the media, is rapidly being replaced by community-based and constituency-based education, bringing the energy of communities and the adult problem-solving process into the classrooms and television tubes of the country.

Adult education has always been plagued by two mistaken notions—first, that the main thing is to get undereducated adults high school GED or college equivalency diplomas, a commitment that leads to the degrading spectacle of adults being led by the hand by suffocating Dick and Jane teaching tactics or other carbon copies of curriculum designed for young children. The resentment and aversion adults have to such isolated and out-of-place techniques are related to a second common fallacy about adult education: the "You can't teach an old dog new tricks" school. Such a school of thought tends to assume that adults are rigid, set in their ways, over

Ted Carpenter is President, Broadside Video, Johnson City, Tennessee.

the hill, and that it is not worth the trouble to bring new programs, ideas, or information to them. Such a school of thought confuses the knowledge of the master (or teacher) with the savvy of the dog. It is the old dog who knows better than to waste his time and energy learning tricks that only serve to amuse or occupy his master (teacher) without significantly improving what is otherwise a satisfactory dog's life. Only adolescent pups or adolescent students are willing to consume large amounts of energy and time on generalized instructional material with no assurance at all that any of it will prove useful.

Thus, those who think adults are the most rigid or stubborn learners are failing to realize that adults are simply the most discriminating learners, with a clear perspective of what they need to learn and why they need to learn it. Most adults have life styles, career positions, family obligations, and social ties that clearly obligate their time and energy and motivate their learning process. Didactic, teacher–student, I–Thou educational programs are senseless and out of place for adult continuing education.

I recall someone telling me recently that there was a town in Minnesota that was essentially a company town for one large manufacturer who, being a wealthy man, was a patron of the arts who wished to raise the cultural level of the community. He provided large subsidies to anyone who built in the town using the designs of renowned architects, and commissioned several sculptures by Henry Moore that were prominently displayed in what has grown to be a lovely community. However, it shocked and grieved Henry Moore to learn that, after years of such exposure, the community voted in overwhelming majority for George Wallace in the last election—a preference in profound antipathy to the purpose of Moore's art. Apparently, Moore still grieves at this and fails to understand how this is possible. What he failed to realize is that young people in an isolated learning environment can perhaps respond directly to such enlighten-

ment, for they have little awareness or frame of reference to interfere with such an open learning process.

Adults, however, have long been accustomed to a pattern of work and thought that has more to do with a manufacturer's paycheck than his patronage. The patronage they cannot control, but the ballot they can and do. At least they are aware of the difference, which is rarely true of the adolescent, however lovely his perceptions. The essential difference for adult learning is not what you are exposed to, but where and how you work. The point is that the average adult has a distinct learning process that is highly keyed to his own perception of just what his problems and concerns are, and his proven ability to control the solution or learning process connected with those problems.

VIDEO AND PROBLEM SOLVING

Where does an adult go if he has a problem? Suppose that he receives a notice from his city officials that his home may be taken and his family moved because he is living in what has been declared an urban-renewal area. With all the public and private educational institutions in the average community, where does the adult go to solve such a problem? The public school says he is too old for anything but GED remedial work, which does not help his housing problem. The college says he can register for courses in real estate or urban planning, but he cannot leave his job and family for two semesters for general courses that still do not address his problem. Where does he go?

The fact is that there is almost no investment in problem-solving learning processes for adults in the average community. At the time when a person is motivated to learn—in the pursuit of solving a direct personal problem—is precisely when the least education is available to him, because to try to develop an institution or educational community for such a process would be prohibitively expensive. How can you maintain a faculty with skills equal to the myriad problems of adults? How can you meet in classes when adults have to work and maintain families? How can a facility accommodate a small group problem on the one hand and suddenly deal with, say, 3,000 residents of an urban-renewal area?

Video, cable, and closed-circuit television resources offer some exciting new solutions to the preceding dilemmas, solutions that are as economical as they are flexible. In the case of the urban-renewal area, we were confronted with that problem in a Tennessee community. We used portable video-tape equipment to bring together the experiences, ideas, and information of city officials, area residents, city planners, senior citizens, and housing officials. Housing officials carefully detailed financial payments for confiscated land and moving costs, information which residents had not clearly understood. Residents also clearly communicated their concerns, especially senior citizens with fixed incomes who did not want to risk new debts even for a better home, a concern housing officials had not been aware of.

Since video tape can be used the moment it has been recorded, we kept playing back the half-inch tapes so that neighbors heard neighbors, and officials heard and could evaluate their own presentations. The tapes were also edited into a 1-hour document about the urban-renewal project. That tape was played at a public meeting on urban renewal and at a city council meeting. It was also played back to the entire community through cable television, and was sent to the offices of the Department of Housing and Urban Development to educate them to the situation. In addition, the tape has been circulated to area public schools and colleges so that students could have direct exposure to the workings of contemporary community problems. The tape, by the way, was played at several different times on the cable—day, evenings, and weekends—to coincide with the times adults in the community could watch it.

The urban-renewal experience is only one of many in which video, cable, and closed-circuit television are able to meet needs in adult education that were previously considered impossible or unrealistic. Consider the case of an affluent professional surgeon whose profession demands that he keep up with constant and complex advances in the field. However, his demanding schedule and life style prohibit continual travel to the best educational centers in his field. One medical university is now video taping top surgeons performing new techniques. These video cassette tapes are then distributed to surgeons who can use and absorb the tapes as their time, schedule, and interest permit.

REVOLUTIONARY TECHNOLOGICAL COMMUNITY

Why haven't such things been done before? The answer is simply that there has not been an economy and a technology that could do the same thing without prohibitive expense. Film or broadcast television would cost tremendous amounts of money to start with, not to mention that the kind of equipment for such professional outlets is too complex and difficult to use without professional crews and, again, prohibitive expense. Also, film and broadcast, even PBS educational network, are oriented to the mass audience. To get a mass audience, you have to be slick, entertaining, and superficial enough to relate to most people. However, the more you try to do something for everybody, the less you do for any particular group or individual.

The potential of video, cable, and closed-circuit television is that it is not a broadcaster, but a narrow-caster—zeroing in on particular problems, communities, and constituencies. Portable ½-inch and ¾-inch video formats are now simple and economical enough to use so that the machinery is easily available to schools, public institutions, cable television, and community groups. Moreover, that same equipment is often tied to closed-circuit systems serving entire school systems or public institutions. That same video equipment can also be used to transmit video programming on cable television systems that serve entire communities. Most cable systems, as a matter of course, provide a channel to local school systems and a channel for public use at no charge. In turn, by sending tapes among schools, closed-circuit systems, video groups, and cable systems, extensive networks of video information, experience, and ideas can be created to serve constituencies and groups in large regions.

This is a revolutionary technology because it can make knowledge cheap and abundant in a decentralized, community-based, and consumer-controlled network. Most educational and broadcast media have been keyed to highly centralized, rigidly professional, commercially sponsored or subsidized, and large audience oriented programming. The ability to custom design and deliver educational services to a wide variety of adults in diverse communities and constituencies at a cost that makes large audiences irrelevant means that those of us who are involved with instructional media have to rethink our relationships to media and the technological community.

SIMPLICITY—USING TELEVISION
LIKE A TELEPHONE

One of the most important points to be rethought is that video technology should not be thought of like "television," and not as an extension of the traditional classroom. Both images conjure up a kind of centralized thinking, with a small group of skilled people developing curriculum or programs for a general audience. Rather, we should think of the technology of portable video and cable as we think of the telephone.

The telephone is our most sophisticated and highly developed communications tool. The billions spent on its development far outweigh the investment in any other media. Yet the striking feature of the phone is its personalized simplicity. We take for granted the immense amount of information, ideas, personal contacts, and other material that is custom tailored to our particular needs through the telephone. No one is hiring professional entertainers and staffs to write a series of excellent phone calls so that you can consult a telephone guide to find out which calls you want to listen to. A phone call is not something that needs an audience, subsidy, or advertiser to justify. If you "turn on" the phone, it does not suddenly come alive with a whole series of calls, but is only active when there is a need to communicate.

The telephone is a beautifully designed, economical, personalized, custom-tailored instrument for adult community education, decision making, and extensions of a community culture and life style. This is precisely what television can now offer, with the added visual dimension, now that video, closed-circuit television, and cable are breaking the psychology and economy of mass audience programming. People can begin to use television as a way to selectively connect with particular information, ideas, groups, cultures, and life styles. We can toss McCluhan back to the broadcasters with his notion that media is bigger than its audience and that the audience is "massaged" or shaped at the will of the media. The consumer can now be back in charge, selecting his own resources, controlling and shaping the technology of media for his own self-education or growth.

NO MORE TEACHER'S
DIRTY LOOKS

Where does this new technology leave the teacher in the classroom? Pretty far behind, especially when it comes to adult continuing education. "Teachers" are a product of centralized thinking, too, assuming that if you can only afford to bring a large "class" together at certain set times, you also cannot afford to bring all the people or experiences relating to a particular problem to that classroom.

So you develop a teacher whose business it is to know both the problem and the resources relating to the problem. The teacher is an economical halfway house or medium between students, problems, and learning resources.

However, when television and video come together, do you need the teacher? When instructional television first came into being, the equipment was expensive, immobile, and adapted to little more than stationary studios. The barren studio was little more than an empty classroom, and people in instructional television predictably filled the space with the "best" teachers, who simply lectured over the tube without the presence or interaction of students. Often dramatizations or clever uses of media made for more interesting programming, but, essentially, instructional media was still being used by traditional educators to talk about experiences and ideas from some place else, and now being delivered to students or audiences who were some place else. The technology of studio-based instructional television had not seriously changed or expanded traditional educational services.

Video is changing all this with its revolutionary economical and portable formats. If you can move the equipment economically, you go to the problem, experience, or resource directly, rather than working through teachers. In the case of our urban-renewal resident or busy surgeon, you take your equipment to the urban-renewal area or to the operating room where the housing official, homeowner, nurse, and surgeon become the real learning resources. In turn, cable and closed-circuit television systems make it possible to distribute these learning resources when appropriate to particular individuals or groups, regardless of teacher or classroom schedules. Such versatility, economy, and flexibility lead us, as media educators, to develop learning resources according to five principles that are common to both adult community education and the new media technology. These principles are discussed next.

Problem-level education   The ability to move our new media technology, and to adapt to a wide variety of learning resources and conditions, makes for our most important asset—the ability to relate to problems at the problem level. Again, adults are never more alive and open to community experience or knowledge or to receiving it than when confronting problems of import to their lives and futures. Whether the problem is urban-renewal activity, keeping up with career information, or understanding community services, we, as media educators, need to be where the actual experiences and problems are in order to develop sound material. Adults continually react to generalized instructional materials with comments like "That's all well and good, but in my community," or "In my job," and so on. When our region first confronted the energy crisis, we did not seek out teachers to talk of problems of energy use; we took our equipment to local power companies, coal dealers, service station operators, and even had the staff of the Tennessee Valley Authority do a video tape concerning how our particular region stood in relation to TVA power.

Peer-based, experience-based learning   It is important to relate to people who *actually experience* what is being discussed or probed. Adults, being discriminating learners, learned long ago to ask not just what is being said but "Who's talking?". If adults sense for a minute that someone is talking authoritatively about something they have never actually experienced, they shut their ears, which is why traditional educators, who are specialists in secondhand information, reach only passive, uncritical, and unselective adolescent audiences.

It is important to remember that administrators rarely experience anything. It is their job to see that others do. Unfortunately, one of the most common mistakes media educators make is to go to administrators who drone endlessly on about "projects, proposals, and priorities," without ever getting to the substance of the experience at hand. Always seek out farmers to talk about agriculture, as well as active staff agents of the county agricultural office, for example. The director of the medical school has far less to tell practicing surgeons than a good practicing surgeon does.

People naturally listen to and respect their peers if they feel that they have genuine experience or knowledge to offer. This is the basic *learning resource constituency of the media educator,* and not to realize it is to ignore your medium's greatest potential. Since you always end up having to get the views of administrators and public officials, it is often amusing to watch audiences react to them together with their peers. We recently prepared a tape of senior citizen's programs in our area. When the administrators (mostly young or middle-aged) talked, audiences were passive and distant, but when senior citizens came on the tube talking of actual program experiences, the audiences became animated and involved, absorbing every word.

Video is a very candid and informal medium. Its candor should not be underestimated either, and media educators should be aware that the more they rely on secondhand or distant learning resources, the more clearly that will come across on the video screen. A teacher-in-service tape for teacher training that does not rely heavily on the practicing teacher in the classroom or a job-training tape that talks to the supervisor instead of the man on the job is doomed to failure as a valid educational communicator.

As a final point, we should all remember that announcers or narrators have the least credibility of anyone. Better to have a farmer, homeowner, city planner, or surgeon who is actively experiencing the issue at hand be the spokesman on tape, no matter how halting or "unprofessional" their speech, as long as the basic content is correct and relevant. Announcers and narrators should be at best minimally used, if at all.

Education for decision making There are so many issues and problems facing contemporary communities and so little investment in keeping adults as informed participants in the decision-making processes that affect them. Whether the issues are land use, zoning, solid waste management, or urban renewal, the adult media educator now has the flexible technology to be a genuine resource to citizen education. We have involved public officials, planners, and citizens in many video documents of outstanding community issues that served as a resource for both public officials and planners.

We recently did a tape on land use and zoning that showed a traditional, isolated mountain community being seized to expand a national park, and another tape of county residents facing zoning for the first time. Both documents gave public officials a way to hear and relate to the citizen side of professional planning. The tapes are now used to educate other citizens on problems and issues in professional planning, and are also being used by public schools and universities to give students concrete insight into actual community problems. We are also using video with public officials to bring information to the public through cable television on housing, urban development, public schools, and the like, which was heretofore only available to public officials themselves.

Narrow casting—constituency-based education Many of the preceding suggestions for video materials would have been considered wasteful or irrelevant to most media people in the past because "only a few people" could use or receive any benefit from it. However, "only a few people" do anything, a fact of life that our mass media have neglected to serve. From that handful of people who are crazy about chess in any given community, to the handful of people most concerned about the role of women in a given community, to the small group of medical doctors keeping up with their profession, most sound educational services have to be delivered to the particular group or constituency most motivated to understand and use the services.

Video, cable, and closed-circuit television make such orientation possible. It is simply irrelevant to a cable and closed-circuit system how many people are watching a given tape. The production costs are minimal, program sources economical and abundant, and playback costs negligible. Ten people watching or 10,000 people watching is the same thing to a video–cable system. We therefore have the luxury of doing particular programs for particular groups, where they can really have impact and be appreciated.

Curiously, too, the video world has far greater freedom when it comes to the old mass media problem of objectivity and fairness. When time and resources are costly and scarce, as in broadcast television, a subject must be treated comprehensively, balancing all sides in one program, for if someone objects, they cannot be cavalierly invited to "do another program" for CBS, ABC, NBC, or PBS. Even local broadcasters have precious little open program time to allocate to diverse points of view on one subject.

Again, video, closed-circuit, and cable can fall back on the economy of abundance. Whereas the network and local broadcasters were lucky to present our region with three particular programs for senior citizens in all of this past year, we have had as many as three in one week for senior citizens in our particular area. Any questions of fairness or opposing points of view are met with hearty invitations to come on in and "do your program or video tape" and it will be aired and circulated obligingly.

Freedom, economy, and versatility are the catchwords of the video environment; rather than encouraging instructional media to turn in on itself to broadcast a generalized curriculum for the many, it should encourage media educators to narrowcast learning resources and educational services to highly motivated groups and constituencies where they can have the most impact.

Learning with a culture around it I recently made a tape of the director of the Regional State Planning Office concerning regional development. He said he hated to see himself on television; when I asked him why he said he sounded like a hick with his Tennessee accent. His reaction was typical of most areas of the country who have been imprinted with the assumption of national media broadcasters that regional inflections, speech patterns, accents, idioms, or mannerisms do not belong on television. Actually, the man from the Tennessee planning office has more reason to talk as he does on our local television than does Walter Cronkite to invade our living rooms with his clipped northeastern speech style and national news. It is one thing to train television personalities to talk clearly, but quite another to say they should not talk like they come from any place special. Such a point of view is a backhanded insult to all of us who do come from some place special.

Video media should not only accept but encourage local and regional cultural patterns and speech in their material. This should be encouraged not only as an honest confirmation of community diversity, but also because it is a sound educational environment. Peer education means not only bringing the experiences of similar people together, but also their language and life style. We developed a career education series for high school students in our area by going to area industries and taping workmen, laborers, and professionals at their place of work. To see people from their own community speaking their own language and talking about jobs that are actually available in the area had far more impact educationally on the students who viewed them than the "canned" career education series typically available from national media distributors. Learning with a culture around it is of even greater importance to gaining the trust and confidence of adults in any learning experience.

TECHNOLOGY AND COMMUNITY— BRINGING IT ALL BACK HOME

As part of our regional video project in Tennessee and Virginia, we have linked 17 public school systems and their educational television resources with 14 cable television communities and several universities. This is a highly sophisticated and advanced technological community. Working with many cooperating schools and cable systems, we are large enough to have a sound regional perspective and to command attention and resources. However, we are also small enough to hear and respond to our basic constituencies for the delivery of custom-designed educational and public media services.

Since our area is the heart of central Appalachia, our video outlets are wrapped in an Appalachian regional culture. High school students use portable video to explore the experiences of midwives, mountain musicians, and craftsmen in our region—an informal, consistent video document of the folkways, traditions, and life styles of our southern mountains. At the same time, the Tennessee Valley Authority, regional development districts, and other institutions provide information and materials on contemporary development in Appalachia. Citizens use video to talk of urban-renewal and traffic problems in urban areas, while city officials report on urban services by cable television. The University of Tennessee is starting a cable television college—courses for credit at home for adults unable to attend campus courses; and the University Center for Continuing Education is considering specialized programming for teacher in-service training and adult community education.

All these services are being delivered economically and abundantly through our video, cable, closed-circuit network. The same technology of television that, in its first state of development, took us away from ourselves to mass audience programming for generalized audiences that rarely reflected our individual or community needs now takes us one step further to a more highly sophisticated, flexible, and therefore simple visual technology, which like the telephone, brings communication back home as a concrete, personal, and selective learning tool.

PART VII: FIELD TESTING AND EVALUATION

Do We Field-Test the Media or Do We Mediate the Field Test?

George M. Higginson and Reeve Love

One difficulty in field testing educational products is that almost everyone in this realm has his own definition of just what field testing is. Educational vendors and publishers of textbooks and educational materials in particular have their own interpretations of field testing, whether or not they do any; and, in their case, one of the great anomalies is that they feign that their products have been thoroughly field tested, when in fact they really know little about field testing, its purposes, or its procedures. This discourse is intended to clarify the meanings of field testing to present its role in the development of instructional media and technology, and, conversely, to present the role of media and technology as part of the field-testing process.

What Is Field Testing?

Field testing is designed to ascertain whether an educational product or process, when placed in a natural environment, will bring about the behavioral changes it was designed to produce in students. If these changes occur, the data indicating such success will facilitate diffusion of the finished product after the testing. If, however, the product

George M. Higginson is an educational consultant affiliated with the Educational Development Corporation. Reeve Love is a free-lance writer, and an educational and media consultant.

effects only some of the changes or causes changes only under certain circumstances, the testing should pinpoint such limitations so that they may be overcome by refinement of the product or explained to its users.

It is possible that, in the field testing of any product, instructional media or some form of technology could be the principal method of presentation of the information. The media could also be used in the field testing, but not as an actual part of the product that is being tested.

Field testing is an expensive process, and it cannot be decided upon today and started tomorrow. It is a process that requires very extensive planning, which must be done beforehand or the entire process may fail. In effect, field testing is the last opportunity to guarantee the outcomes before the product is marketed, to pinpoint the limitations and identify and stipulate any specific procedures or needs in the instructions accompanying the product.

Why Do Field Testing?

Normally, field testing is part of the educational development process. Most educational development starts with ideas that are gradually selected, expanded, and repeatedly tried out with students close at hand. As information is obtained about the outcomes of these ideas, the product is refined and the development process continues with yet another test.

In some educational development there may be uncertainty as to which method of presentation is most successful for a particular sequence. Thus, part of the development process may necessarily be a determination as to whether some form of instructional media is preferable to another. In such case, the material and scenarios for several methods of presentation may be necessary and may require comparison as development progresses. Some of these will be eliminated in the course of develop-

ment, but it may not be until the final field testing that a judgment can be made on the final selection.

Another reason for field testing is that portions of the curriculum may be presented better in one medium than in another, so that when the work is finished the entire course may involve several methods of presentation in various combinations. These, then, have to be field tested to be sure that they fit together well, that the methods of presentation are optimal, and that the course is properly sequential.

Still another reason for testing is to obtain information that can be used during the marketing of the product. That is, information obtained during earlier pilot testing, when the product is undergoing frequent and severe revision, may turn out to be invalid and therefore useless for marketing the product. To market the product successfully, the most up-to-date and accurate information must be obtained.

Another reason for conducting a field test is to compare a product with other products that may be on the market to determine the relative viability and utility of these products. Several products with the same objectives may be on the market at the same time, and a comparison will thus be necessary to determine their relative worth.

Other things being equal, a developer or vendor who can refer to the field testing of his products, and have valid statistics to show, will probably be more successful than one who has not bothered with a field test.

In summary, field testing is an evaluation process with the ultimate purpose of validation of product objectives. Other purposes, which may be by-products, are the following:

1. To identify specialized conditions of success or failure.
2. To compile information about the product's installation and operation, including cost, manpower, training, time and timing, and any special facilities needed.

3. To accumulate market survey data so that the product developer can determine if or how to proceed.
4. On occasion, to initiate a method of widespread diffusion, in which hangups and areas of resistance are identified.

Who Does the Field Testing?

The obvious answer in most cases is that the developers of the product perform the field testing before they market it. In those cases, the rationale and the methodology for the field testing seem quite obvious. However, field testing may occur on other occasions. For example, a districtwide or statewide adoption process may suggest the possibility of several alternatives of materials for a given course. It would be useful for those in charge of adoption to buy samples of the two or three most promising, and to run a field test on them in different locales to determine which best serves their purpose. In such cases, the schools involved probably will not want to acquire special media equipment on a permanent basis, and should be able to rent the equipment for the field test. They may also want to rent additional media for evaluation of the materials to be field tested.

How Does Field Testing Get Done?

Without a doubt, the most difficult part of the field testing occurs right at the beginning: the first stage of work under the general heading of "planning." Every last detail of the field test must be planned in advance. All the equipment that will be required, method and cost of procurement, identification of people and their salaries, purposes of the test, places where the product will be tested, length of time required, number of reports, report forms, forms for all the tests—these and a thousand more details must be determined prior to beginning the test; otherwise it cannot be carried out properly.

The planning work thus includes detailing in advance all the steps that will come after the planning:

Site selection
Negotiations with schools
Logistics
Staff training for evaluators
Staff training for school personnel
Community relations
Monitoring
Development of instruments
Psychometric testing
Data collection
Data processing
Data analysis
Report writing
Report publication and distribution
Marketing and dissemination

Thus, there is a tremendous amount of detail to be scheduled and computed, a great deal of meshing and interplay that occurs among these steps during the planning, and an extensive amount of interaction during the execution and evaluation work of the field testing.

If there is a phase of field testing that is the second most important after planning, it is the evaluation work done throughout the process, which is really the primary purpose of field testing. The evaluation design for a field test has to be part of the plan. The variables that will be involved must be identified; the sites must be tentatively planned in accordance with those variables that specifically need to be tested. Information requirements about the variables and the methods of collecting, processing, and analyzing data also are part of the evaluation, but need to be designed during the planning phase. Evaluation work itself continues throughout the field testing, and conclusions can be reached only after the testing is complete and all the data have been collected, analyzed, and subjected to comprehensive examination. Evaluation is measured against the criteria that have been previously determined, and the conclusions derived from the evaluation are the result of these comparisons.

If, for any reason, the field test falters during its execution phase, immediate determination should be made as to whether the situation can be remedied in time, or whether too much valuable time and too many data have already been lost. If the latter is the case, it may be less expensive to call off the field test, make the necessary corrections, and start over again at a suitable time and place. If the test is not stopped and the failure can be corrected in time, remedial action must be taken immediately to make up the lost time and to prevent further loss of time, money, and effort.

Can a Medium or Audiovisual Other Than the Printed Word Be the Primary Mode of Presentation in Education?

This is a fundamental question with a simple answer. Not too long ago the answer would have been "no," that any audiovisual merely provides support for the primary method of instruction, which was either teacher or textbook. However, that is no longer true, and today many complete courses exist in television, computer-assisted instruction, language laboratory, or other forms of media. Some may be components of a larger course; but in many cases they are the only method of delivery of a portion of the course and not just support.

The questions then arise, how can they be field tested, and how can one be sure through field testing that they are sufficiently effective? These forms of media and educational technology are tested just like any other product. Evaluations are made at appropriate points, comparisons are made with other forms, and results are weighed against the objectives. (Of course, the instructional objectives should be properly written in terms of behavioral change and in measurable steps, so that it

may be determined whether or not the requirements are being met.)

Media may be used in ways other than as the primary means in classroom instruction. They may be primary for some form of individualized instruction or primary for some portion of staff development. In all these cases, however, the need for field testing remains the same as if they were a printed product.

Can Media or Audiovisuals Play a Secondary Part?

In many cases audiovisuals or media are presented as a device for enrichment and not as a primary means of instruction. In such cases, the field testing is somewhat more difficult; the basic information may have been delivered by some means other than the enrichment process, and testing for its acquisition through this process is not possible. However, the enrichment information should cause some change in the scope of knowledge, and testing to determine this change can be designed, but very carefully.

Can Media or Audiovisuals Have Other Educational Roles?

One of the best known uses of television in education (other than for classroom learning) is in the process of staff development. Here a teacher's performance is recorded on video tape during live instruction; afterward, classroom teachers and counselors are given the opportunity of reviewing the tapes together. At this point, a teacher sees any mistakes that he has made, learns a great deal about his own performance, and, in addition, obtains comments from his supervisors.

Another possible use for media and instructional technology is sales demonstrations during the marketing process. Here the materials or samples of materials are put together and then taken on the road to schools, districts, and boards where they are demonstrated. This demonstration may depict portions of the course, portions of a class in progress, and portions of the staff development process. Those viewing these samples get a realistic idea of the entire course. Still another use for the special medium is during the evaluation process of field testing. Although the product being field tested may not utilize media, media can be used to collect information for the evaluative stage. This form of evaluation information requires analysis by trained viewers after it is taken to the field-test headquarters and is fed into the evaluation process along with other psychometric data taken from the students.

What Are the "Down-to-Earth" Factors?

Probably the most crucial aspect of field testing is the total cost. Good planning work, properly done at the right time, will begin to reflect how astronomical some of the costs will be. But even these indications may prove insufficient. There will be expenses that are difficult to calculate in advance and (according to Love's law) these are always larger than anticipated, so the cost of testing can become prohibitive. Even worse, the investment may be entirely wasted if the right data are not collected from the right subjects and at the right time.

A second consideration in field testing of media and instructional technology is the possible entry of the "Hawthorne effect" into the field test. That is, the novelty of the media or technology being used may cause greater interest and subsequently greater success than would actually accrue if a lot of material were presented in the same medium. This effect, or its possibility, can be discounted to some extent; possibly it can be counteracted by the alternative presentations made for the sake of comparison.

Still another consideration on the practical side is that most media and instructional technology involve the purchase of equipment to be used in the classroom or as part of the instructional sequence. Such equipment may not be reusable at a later date if the format of the curriculum is changed, so the cash outlay must be a consideration for the eventual user. Consequently, those involved in the field test must find ways to make the product less expensive so that the user will not be taxed unnecessarily.

New instructional technology, new audiovisual techniques, and new media, like any other curriculum material or method of presentation, have to be field tested, evaluated, and weighed by persons who are experienced in this work. They have to be evaluated critically because of the possibility of the Hawthorne effect. However, if they are designed with creativity and are evaluated with the appropriate criteria and care, all media and instructional technology, no matter how attractive or how expensive, have vital contributions to make to today's education and to tomorrow's.

BIBLIOGRAPHY

Armsey, James W., and Norman C. Dahl. *An Inquiry into the Uses of Instructional Technology.* New York: The Ford Foundation, 1973.

Boyd, William J. (ed.). *Estimating Illustration Costs: A Guide.* Washington, D.C.: Society for Technical Communication, Inc., 1973.

Bretz, Rudy. *A Taxonomy of Communication Media.* Santa Monica, Calif.: The Rand Corporation, Jan. 1971.

Carpenter, Polly. *A New Kit of Tools for Designing Instructional Systems* (P-4611). Santa Monica, Calif.: The Rand Corporation, Apr. 1971.

Carter, Yvonne, et al. *Aids to Media Selection for Students and Teachers.* Washington, D.C.: U.S. Office of Education, DHEW Publication (OE) 74-21002, 1971 (an annotated bibliography).

———, et al. *Supplement to Aids to Media Selection for Students and Teachers.* Washington, D.C.: U.S. Office of Education, DHEW Publication (OE) 74-21001, 1973.

Forsythe, Richard O. *Instructional Radio: A Position Paper.* Stanford, Calif.: ERIC Clearinghouse on Media and Technology, Dec. 1970.

Gabor, Stanley G. "The Video Cassette as an Educational Reality." *Educational Technology,* Apr. 1972, pp. 35–36.

Higginson, George M., Carl S. Swanson, and Reeve Love. *CALIPERS: Planning the Systems Approach to Field Testing*

Educational Products. Austin, Texas: Southwest Educational Development Laboratory, 1969.

_____, and Reeve Love. "The Role of Media in Field Testing, or Whatever Happened to the Simple Life?" *Audiovisual Instruction,* Vol. 15, No. 5 (May 1970), pp. 35–37.

Hoban, Charles F. *The State of the Art of Instructional Films.* Stanford, Calif.: ERIC Clearinghouse on Media and Technology, Sept. 1971.

Klempner, Irving M. *Audiovisual Materials in Support of Information Science Curricula: An Annotated Listing with Subject Index.* Stanford, Calif.: ERIC Clearinghouse on Media and Technology, June 1971.

Love, Reeve. "McGuffey in McLuhan-Land: The Value of a Systems Approach to Education." Austin, Texas: Southwest Educational Development Laboratory. *Intercomm,* Jan. 1969.

Molenda, Michael H. "The Educational Implications of Cable Television and Video Cassettes: An Annotated Bibliography." *Audiovisual Instruction,* Vol. 17, No. 4 (Apr. 1972), 11 pages.

National Instructional Television Center. *Guidebook* and *Newsletters.* Bloomington, Ind.: Agency for Instructional Television, NITC, 1973–1974.

Rawnsley, David E. *A Comparison of Guides to Non-Print Media.* Stanford, Calif.: ERIC Clearinghouse on Media and Technology, Nov. 1973 (an annotated bibliography).

Rhode, William E., et al. *Analysis and Approach to the Development of an Advanced Multi-Media Instructional System.* Volumes I and II. Prepared for the USAF Human Resources Laboratory by the Westinghouse Learning Corporation, May 1970.

Smith, Mortimer, Richard Peck, and George Weber. *A Consumer's Guide to Educational Innovations.* Washington, D.C.: Council for Basic Education, 1972.

Radio: An Experiment in Communication Skills

George Taylor

The education of deprived children is perhaps one of the largest single challenges facing our society and our learning establishment today.

Authorities in both education and psychology have long recognized the underlying importance of identifying effective means for better learning contacts with such children. General recognition of their special needs has led to exploration and innovation in a number of educational areas.[1]

As is true elsewhere in education, the traditional approach has been to build programs from some promising theoretical framework without careful assessment of the nature and extent of program productivity. This absence of program evaluation has certainly deterred progress, most particularly for these children.[2]

Much research has been focused on the special needs of deprived children, particularly on the socioeconomic and cultural factors which appear to be closely related to academic achievement.[3] Effective remedial programs are absolutely essential for these children, yet there are very few effective methods identified, compared to the large numbers of innovative programs instituted.

George Taylor teaches at Coppin State College, Baltimore, Maryland.

This report describes one innovative and proven-effective program.

This unique program was made possible by a grant from the Ford Foundation to implement a special language arts program in Washington, D.C. During the 3-year life of the project a language arts program was conducted in 14 schools. At the end of the granting period the results were so encouraging that the program was continued and expanded by funds appropriated by the school system.

As a result of the success of this special language arts program, school officials began to explore other means of improving communication skills of deprived children. In search of appropriate methods, consideration was given to the utilization of radio facilities. Subsequently, a radio program was devised to assist regular classroom teachers, in four elementary, three junior high, and three senior high schools, to improve the communication skills of students.

The radio, as a means of communication, is but approximately 46-years-old; as an instructional tool it is even younger. Programming radio programs for schools are generally three types: direct instruction, appreciation, and enrichment. In most cases the content is directed toward a specific classroom use. A few of the school systems that have had success with experimental programs using the radio are St. Louis, Newark, New York, and Wisconsin.

Often a radio program only begins the enrichment cycle. Its purpose could be to introduce children to a variety of musical experiences that perhaps will lead to many related activities in art, social studies, and English.[4]

Henderson conducted a mathematics program through the use of radio in the Wisconsin public schools in grades 9 through 12. Based on the replies to the questionnaires administered, he concluded that proper use of the radio as a teaching media can enrich mathematics educational programs.[5]

Thus, this study was an attempt to evaluate the effectiveness of an educational radio program on communication skills. Specifically, this investigation attempted to determine the motivational capability of the radio when used as a reinforcement stimulus in the classroom, and to determine whether or not the utilization of the radio was an implement in improving communication skills.

The subjects were 274 pupils from four elementary schools, three junior high schools, and three senior high schools. All the subjects were attending schools in deprived neighborhoods in Washington, D.C. The 274 subjects were subdivided into two groups, an experimental group that consisted of 180 pupils and a control group that consisted of 94 pupils. The total population from which these samples were drawn consisted of 4,410 students.

The program consisted of broadcasting four different sound programs in relation to the four grade levels in 10 schools. They were (1) "Single Sound Complex"—primary level, (2) "Occupational Sounds"—intermediate levels, :3; "Sound Sequence"—junior high school, and (4) "Music Everywhere"—senior high school. The nature and intent of these broadcasts were designed to fit into the experiential background of the subjects. The complexity of the sounds were commensurate with the developmental stages of the subjects. Teachers' guides were distributed before the broadcasts with suggestions for stimulating class discussions, essays, dramatizations, art, and various language activities.

The research included the administration of questionnaires and interviews to subjects in both the experimental and control groups. Also, a classroom observation form was completed by an observer in the experimental schools. The experimental student group was administered a semantic differential and a Likert-type scale. The control group instruments varied to the degree that the respondents had not been exposed to the broadcasts.

Results from the semantic differential scale within the experimental groups of students on variables of attitude and judgment toward the

Table 1
Mean Scores of Experimental Group of Students on Attitudes and Judgment Toward the Radio Program by Grade Levels

	Mean Scores			
	Primary	Intermediate	Junior High	Senior High
Attitude	1.45	1.20	1.63	1.90
Judgment	2.06	1.76	2.43	4.01

overall radio broadcast and judgment of the sounds in the broadcast are summarized in Table 1.

The analysis of the data in Table 1 are based upon 7-point semantic differential scales for each grade level. Due to the positioning of the scales the lower the numerical value the more positive attitude indicated. Therefore, Table 1 shows that students of all four grade levels expressed a high positive attitude toward the program. Generally, all means fall within a 1.00–2.00 range on a 7-point scale. Specifically, the program was judged between extremely and moderately good, pleasant, interesting, and valuable. From the data it appears that students in all grade levels voiced favorable attitudes toward the broadcast. Mean scores are also reported for judgment of sounds. The sounds were judged between moderately and slightly smooth, beautiful, sharp, colorful, familiar, and interesting. The mean of 4.01, as reflected in Table 1, reveals

that the high school group judged the sounds neither smooth or rough, beautiful, or ugly, colorful or colorless. The results show that the primary and intermediate groups judged the sounds significantly more favorable than the junior or senior high school students.

The median test was employed to statistically analyze the data for significant differences between the four grade levels. The results are shown in Table 2.

Table 2 indicates that there was a significant difference between the senior high school and primary groups in attitude toward the broadcast. There were also significant differences between the high school and intermediate, and intermediate and junior high school groups. Significant differences were reported between the junior high school and primary group, the junior high and intermediate, and the senior high and intermediate group concerning judgment of the radio program.

Inspection of Table 1 suggests that the statistical differences contained in Table 2 could be interpreted to mean the elementary group generally judged the broadcast significantly more favorably than the junior high and senior high school students.

This finding with respect to the sounds is consistent with the group's relative attitude toward the overall broadcast. However, when the adjective

Table 2
Median Test Critical Values Between Four Experimental Grade Levels on Attitudes and Judgment Toward the Radio Program

Grade Levels	Primary		Intermediate		High	
	Attitude	Judgment	Attitude	Judgment	Attitude	Judgment
Primary						
Intermediate	1.55	1.37				
Junior high	.16	3.60[b]	11.35[a]	13.87[a]		
Senior high	4.33[b]	2.10	30.24[a]	10.77[a]	.53	.67

[a] $p < .01$.
[b] $p < .05$.

Table 3
Mean Values of Experimental and Control Groups by Grade Levels Concerning the Radio's Usefulness in the Classroom

	Mean Score	
Grade Levels	Experimental	Control
Primary	1.90	6.85
Intermediate	1.61	1.61
Junior high	2.00	2.32
Senior high	3.42	2.10

scale of interesting–uninteresting was isolated there were no significant differences found among the grade levels. The single rating of sounds on this scale, interesting and uninteresting, is perhaps more indicative of the broadcast sounds stimulating values than the other five scales employed.

Another important aspect of the research design was to determine how students judged the usefulness of the radio in the classroom. Comparisons were made within and between the four levels of experimental and control groups. Variations in judgment between the two groups reflected differences related to exposure and nonexposure to the classroom broadcast.

From the data in Table 3 the intermediate students in the experimental group rated the radio

most useful, followed by the primary, junior high, and senior high students.

Comparison of means for the experimental and control groups show several interesting variations. First, the primary children (control group), which had no experience with the radio in the project, had little respect for the potential of such aid. On the other hand, the experimental group very favorably suggested that if the radio is used students' low expectations dissipate. Second, there was essentially no change in the anticipated and actual value of the radio as viewed by the experimental and control group of intermediate and junior high school students. Third, the discrepancy between the senior high school students' expectations and actual value of the radio from exposure is opposite of the primary group. The senior high school (control group) anticipated the value of the radio as moderately good (2.10), as opposed to the experimental group's rating of slightly good (3.42), which is a statistical difference between the primary experimental and control groups.

The median test indicated that a significant difference existed between the high school and the intermediate students, concerning the usefulness of the radio in the classroom, at the .05 level of confidence. Results are reported in Table 4. The mean scores in Table 3 support the significant difference between the intermediate and secondary

Table 4
Median Test Critical Values Between Experimental (Group 1) and Control (Group 2) Groups by Grade Level on the Radio's Usefulness in the Classroom

	Primary		Intermediate		Junior High	
Grade Levels	Group 1	Group 2	Group 1	Group 2	Group 1	Group 2
Primary						
Intermediate	3.84[b]	7.43[a]				
Junior high	.18	9.39[a]	1.35	2.05		
Senior high	.06	8.66[a]	2.42	1.86	.13	.17

[a]$p < .01$.
[b]$p < .05$.

Table 5
Mean Scores from Likert-Type Scale Concerning Helpfulness in Course Work and Continuation of Broadcast by Grade Levels

	Primary	*Intermediate*	*Junior High*	*Senior High*
Helpfulness in course work	1.60	1.37	1.64	1.85
Continuation of broadcast	1.63	1.40	1.60	1.87

students in the experimental group concerning judgment of the radio's usefulness in the classroom. The control group of subjects also were asked to judge how beneficial they thought the radio would be in the classroom. With the exception of the primary group, all students thought the radio was moderately useful. There was a significant difference between the primary group and each of the other groups on this variable.

The experimental group of students felt that the broadcast provided them with a great degree of assistance in their course work; they voiced a concern that the broadcast be continued. Table 5 contains the means for the four grade levels.

The means of all grade levels fell between strongly agree (1.00) and agree (2.00) to the 5-point statement of "Such broadcast will be helpful in your course work." Generally all students thought the broadcast should continue. The analysis of this table related to the students' opinion of the broadcast's usefulness and interest in continuation are evidence that the radio in the classroom setting was very well received by the students.

The data suggest that the broadcast generated an enormous amount of interest among students. Teachers also voiced favorable comments toward the broadcast. Students were stimulated to voluntarily participate in discussions which not only enabled the teacher to give them immediate help in self-expressions, but also gave the teacher a chance to ascertain the nature and degree of basic language deficiencies. The broadcasts were highly successful in attracting and holding the attention of the students. There was an important variation among the groups characterized by a more intensive involvement of the senior high level and less involvement of the primary level as the program preceded. The radio as used in this project definitely stimulated the students and teachers and served as a powerful motivational force.

REFERENCES

1. Henry Clay Lindgren. Educational Psychology in the Classroom. Chapter 12. New York: Wiley, 1967.
2. Planning for the Evaluation of Special Education Programs. Washington, D.C.: U.S. Office of Education, No. OEG-0-9-372160-3553 (032), p. 1.
3. Martin Deutsh, Irwin Katz, and Arthur R. Jensen. "Introduction," Social Class, Race, and Psychological Development, pp. 1–6. New York: Holt, Rinehart and Winston, 1968.
4. Herbert E. Scuorzo. "Radio: Still an Important Educational Aid," Grade Teacher, 82 (May–June 1965), 126–129.
5. George L. Henderson. "Mathematics Via Radio in Wisconsin," The Mathematics Teacher, 59 (Jan. 1968), 56–62.

New Response to Educational Problems

Peggy Snyder

Utilizing the expert knowledge of leaders in both the academic and business communities over the past 2 years, the Educational Facilities Center (EFC) has been planning and developing a brand new concept for educational service: a permanent, year-round consultation and exposition center.

The idea became a reality earlier this year when temporary headquarters were opened at 223 North Michigan Avenue in the heart of Chicago.

Facilities first were opened to students and skilled instructors, engaged in actual demonstration learning operations in specially designed EFC "Learning Environment." Once operations were under way, the EFC activities were opened also to educators, school management personnel, and the general public, and an intensive visitation and summer workshop schedule has been taking place there since.

An expansion program is now under way for EFC operations, in preparation for late-1974 completion of the new, specially designed 34-floor Educational Facilities Center Building, which will rise at 444 North Michigan, just across from the famed *Chicago Tribune*.

Peggy Snyder is coordinator of communications, Educational Facilities Center, Chicago, Illinois.

The EFC concept was tested by a survey which reached many key educational leaders, immediately following the original proposal. Response to the survey made very clear the great need for a comprehensive educational program and centralized display center, where workable approaches to learning and educational problems could be realized, demonstrated, and exhibited.

Even the most experienced and dedicated teachers and administrators indicated difficulty in keeping abreast of developments in this $70 billion industry, many of which affect their current operations as well as their long-range planning.

With the increasingly rapid development of new learning information and theory, and the refinement and reexamination of existing information and theory, many new educational materials, programs, and products are now being developed.

The application of updated approaches and products demands a reliable, authoritative, and comprehensive central source for program and product information. Beyond that information need is the still more pressing demand for meaningful in-service programs to expedite and guide new applications.

Perhaps most significant is the great increase in demands for information and expert consultation for long-range educational facilities planning, involving the entire range of educational products and programs.

EFC has taken an enormous stride toward solving the many problems facing educators today by housing in one location educational consultants to advise on major issues ranging from individualizing instruction to facilities planning; by creating a center where innovative programs, materials, equipment, furnishings and systems can be examined, and by developing nontraditional, open-space learning environments where the practical application of new programs can be observed—*used by children as they were designed to be used.*

Scheduled visitation programs are offered daily at EFC for entire school staffs or for individual educators. An orientation program introduces the visitor to learning theories underlying the instructional approaches, materials, and equipment being utilized in the Learning Environment.

Educators then enter the environment where they observe, evaluate, and assess the instruction of language arts and mathematics. Small-group sessions of students and teachers provide useful ideas for the classroom, and the visiting teacher has an opportunity to discuss the use of materials in the environment so schools can select programs that can work supportively, rather than at cross purposes, as can happen so easily without examination and study.

After observing the class in session, the visitor then has the option of examining products and materials on view in the display center. He may select promotional literature to share later with a colleague, or by using EFC's educator—manufacturer liaison service he may receive specific price lists and further details about programs of interest to his district.

If a particular problem is especially significant, special arrangements are made by the EFC staff to offer the visitor a customized program on a particular issue. In either case—attending the daily visitation program or receiving a customized program—the educator has ready access to a previously unavailable resource designed to enhance his growth.

George D. Fischer, chairman of the board of EFC, is a past president of the National Education Association. He gained a reputation as an outspoken educator when under his "shirtsleeve" leadership NEA encountered, head on, education's social and economic problems. With the same determination for quality, he created an advisory committee when EFC was still a brainstorm of its parent company, Romanek & Golub, innovative Chicago area developers and builders. Since its inception, then, this committee has formulated the educational goals of EFC.

John Beck, executive director of the Chicago Consortium of Colleges and Universities, has played a double role in EFC's development. Instrumental as an advisor and consultant, Beck has also actively involved the consortium in the EFC program. Through his efforts, member colleges of the consortium assign student teachers to the center for 4 of their 8 weeks of preservice training.

Sound educational direction has also been provided by Evelyn Carlson, associate superintendent of schools, Chicago Board of Education, Robert Clark, superintendent of schools, Archdiocese of Chicago School Board, Austin Flynn, dean of the school of education, De Paul University, Ben E. Graves, consultant and project director of New Life for Old Schools Project, Educational Facilities Laboratory, Stanton Leggett, Stanton Leggett and Associates, Charles W. Fowler, superintendent, Community Unit School District 428, Wm. Brubaker, president, Perkins & Will Corporation, Raymond C. Ovresat, vice-president, Perkins & Will, Aaron Cohodes, president, Teach 'Em, Inc., and Dwayne E. Gardner, executive director, Council of Educational Facilities Planners.

Along with the consultative assistance of the National Reading Council, the advisory committee finalized the instructional goals for EFC.

Today EFC concentrates primarily on the elementary level of education. It was difficult, of course, to decide where to begin. The many areas of education, from preschool through the adult level, were considered. Given the fact that eventually every level would be represented in its permanent facilities, the logical first step was the core subject areas, reading and mathematics; the logical level—elementary.

Broadly speaking, the educational philosophy guiding all curriculum instruction at EFC is individualization of instruction. Preassessment tests are administered to each pupil enrolled in the Learning Environment to determine his ideal approach to learning: the British open-day philosophy, programmed instruction, or prescription—diagnosis.

Also taken into consideration when placing the student in a specific learning approach are his academic ability, social relationships, and favored learning style (e.g., one-to-one, small-group, or large-group settings).

Both the language arts and mathematics programs at EFC are formed around interest centers, comprised of educational materials, products, and supplementary teaching aids. The interest centers are utilized to review and reinforce desired objectives, but more importantly, they are instrumental in teaching children the intrinsic rewards of learning. Audiovisual materials and devices are considered of primary importance in every interest center.

Students are free to select the area they wish to explore at any given time. The addition of social studies and science interest centers further expands this exploration. As a safeguard, however, the teaching staff maintains a chart for each student which indicates the child's progress, direction, interest—and whereabouts. This allows the teacher to determine when a pupil requires added incentive to enter an area he may be neglecting, and to use intensely appealing materials, such as many modern audiovisual media, to help the student.

Of primary importance to the visitor is the knowledge that every activity and teaching approach applied in the center's program can be implemented in a traditional setting. The open-space concept, and indeed individualized instruction, can both be achieved if proper management systems are developed; meanwhile educational programs within traditional environments can be greatly strengthened and broadened.

Immediately after recognition was given to the need for an educational exposition center, a second need surfaced with force. It had many facets, but all focused on the same demand—a forum for encouraging continued professional growth. Thus, the multitude of requests from initial visitors to EFC literally molded its second concept—that of a service center for educators.

''Meaningful workshops and seminars scheduled

on a regular basis are lacking in the educational community," was the response of almost every teacher and administrator who visited the center during its first month of operation. Flexible physical facilities had been designed so it has been a simple task to create meaningful programs and house them at EFC.

Recognized workshop leaders representing a wide range of educational interests now share their knowledge and actively involve their audiences in problem solving weekly; crucial questions affecting literally every group involved in the educational process—students, teachers, administrators, parents—are examined periodically in a symposium format; insight into the more philosophical questions affecting American education is gained when speakers of national eminence are invited to address audiences at the center in a structured setting.

The practical question of how to constantly inspire children to learn is a universal problem. The teacher down the hall may have a creative idea, but seldom finds the opportunity to share it with her colleague. A teacher in Rhinelander, Wisconsin, can rarely share a successful approach to "set" theory with an elementary teacher in Des Moines, Iowa. Thus, the EFC *Newsletter for Teachers* was created, providing readers with a forum for publishing pretested classroom activities and opening the channels for sharing new and creative ideas.

Now when an administrator redesigns his school or plans a new faculty, he has equipment and furnishing needs in great variety. He pours through endless catalogues with entries numbering in the millions for every desk, partition, and chair he eventually selects, or his district budgets a sizable sum for consulting fees.

Within 6 months, however, he will have a third prerogative. By requesting a "dialogue instrument" from EFC and specifying his needs, the computerized Information DataBank will quickly scan its vast index, selecting company names and model numbers to fit his specifications—and his budget.

Far from being satisfied with its present programs, however, EFC will continue to rely on the demands of the educational public for direction in further developing services and resources. Every time a school meets at EFC for in-service training, or an association uses its facilities for special meetings, a new idea emerges from the many needs stated which can be implemented by the EFC staff.

In its temporary location, EFC represents today approximately one tenth of its future capability for providing programs, services, and facilities to the academic community. By 1974, when the new headquarters are complete, approximately 20 floors of comprehensive displays will serve to complement six floors of learning environments.

Each of the six floors will contain approximately three learning environments—at any given time. Then 18 separate subject areas will represent preschool through adult level education. Periodically, as new fields of study surface, the environments will be changed to maintain EFC's educational commitment and goals.

A nationwide search will be conducted when a new environment is created to identify those teachers with a reputation for excellence in their field. Leave-of-absence arrangements will then be made with the appropriate district so the teacher selected can develop and implement the curriculum for the new environment. In this way, EFC will offer the educational community truly outstanding microcosmic classrooms for examination and duplication.

If the center is to meet the ever-changing and complex needs of educators, an integral part of its future must be an extension of its present policy to provide ever-changing displays, exhibits, and customized programs. For this reason, one visit to the center cannot be considered final. In its present, scale-model proportions, one week offers a special U.S. Office of Education exhibit featuring library materials, products, and services; a second week features programs and materials in the area of speech.

By the same token, the instructional philosophies of the environments will constantly alter and improve, offering significant changes to be assimilated and assessed each time that an educator revisits EFC.

Finally, the remaining eight floors of the new headquarters will reflect an expanded version of today's conference rooms, auditorium, meeting rooms, and lounges. Educational conventions meeting in Chicago, associations requiring conference areas, and districts with in-service needs will find the physical resources they desire at EFC.

Today, for example, the Chicago Consortium is meeting at the center daily for a 6-week master's degree program in personalized learning; area B of the Chicago Board is utilizing conference rooms on weekdays for a 3-week course in basic art; and area C of the board will cosponsor a course in early childcare with Northeastern Illinois University which will meet at EFC on Thursday evenings from September through January—this will be the first course for credit to be broadcast over radio, incidentally. Similar uses of EFC's facilities will increase tenfold by 1974.

The EFC staff continually seeks new methods of serving its specialized public, but in the final analysis, only the reactions and requests of the educational community can dictate the center's direction and growth. Timidity and shortsightedness must be overcome, and the success of this major exposition and service center can help to achieve that goal for education. Every suggestion, every request, contains the kernel for policy which will benefit essentially every educator in America—and assure the success of EFC's primary commitment: *change.*

Can EFC be a catalyst for change? That's a formidable question. On the surface it infers not only that as an institution EFC must evaluate and select one philosophy over another, but that it set itself up as a utopian "goldfish bowl," subject to the scrutiny of its public. This inference is not totally accurate. Attempting to catalyze change does not preclude error, nor does it necessarily indicate that one philosophy is preferable to another. It can also mean, as it does in the EFC commitment, that *a nucleus for change must be provided,* that situations can be created and programs can be designed to stimulate the entire awareness process.

By offering model teaching situations for observation, quality products and materials for examination, and timely topics for review, EFC can help the educational public to create its own change, gradually but surely.

PART VIII: LEARNER CHARACTERISTICS

Effectiveness of Three Instructional Modes Employed to Transmit Content to Students with Different Aptitude Patterns

Wayne F. Virag

The individual in a learning situation is subjected to many and varied types of teaching materials, techniques, and phases of instruction, each of which presents a variety of content and information to be learned. The effectiveness of these learning situations is influenced by such factors as (1) the method of presentation and teaching materials employed, (2) the physical environment designed for learning, (3) the aptitude of the individual to learn the material presented, (4) the sociocultural background of the individual, (5) the quantity and quality of the individual's past experiences, and (6) the motivational climate or the needs and tensions present within the individual.

Much research has been conducted in evaluating the effects of these factors in an instructional situation. However, little research has been done that seeks to examine the relationships among the method of instruction, the materials, and the aptitude of an individual to learn. Consequently, there is a lack of reliable information relative to the nature of distinguishable aptitude characteristics and their relationship with various modes of instruction. The need for research related to media to consider

Wayne F. Virag is director of social studies education at the Virginia State College, Petersburg, Virginia.

individual student aptitudes was clearly expressed by Gagné (1965) when he noted that the key to effective learning is to match instructional methods and materials to the learning style of the individual (pp. 295–296); for in an instructional situation ". . . different individuals approach learning with different patterns of 'basic abilities' which may turn out to be those factors which appear consistently and dependably in factor studies" (Gagné and Paradise, 1961, p. 2).

Snow and Salomon (1968) defined *aptitude* as "individual difference variables which appear to facilitate or limit learning" (p. 7). For instance, a student who reads at the sixth grade level would probably have difficulty in reading and comprehending a college text in world history.

Communication and learning theory demand that the effect of a given stimulus or input on individual learning situations must be considered. The media are the means for providing stimuli, whether the stimuli are used to motivate, to direct attention, to set a goal, to evaluate, to guide thinking, to evoke a response, or to test for transfer (Briggs, 1967, p. 11). Consequently, the problem facing educational researchers is to establish the relationship of individual learning patterns to instructional media to determine which is the most effective method for a particular learning style.

The problem, however, is complicated by the fact that educational research which concentrates on the interaction of media with individual aptitude variables has resulted over the years in inconclusive evidence regarding observed differences that could be attributed to different instructional modes. Snow and Salomon (1968) suggest that the lack of conclusive findings might be due to the fact that data have been averaged and the results generalized to the total population (range of learning pattern).

RESEARCH INVESTIGATION

In the spring of 1970 research was conducted in an attempt to determine the effectiveness of learning content material presented through different instructional modes with distinctive characteristics to students with diverse aptitude patterns.

The content selected for study was the Bill of Rights. An overall teaching strategy was formulated for a 5-day unit and included (1) goals of instruction, stated in behavioral terms, (2) content summary of information to be presented, (3) planned tactics, sequentially arranged, and (4) specific materials to be employed.

Each of the five instructional lessons was presented by one of three instructional modes. The modes used were classified as conventional, low-verbal, and high-verbal.

The low-verbal instructional mode referred to a treatment consisting of a tape–slide presentation of the Bill of Rights (employed in the introductory lesson) and four films developed by Churchill Films Inc. The four films used in lessons 2 through 4 are entitled "Justice, Liberty, and the Law," "Speech and Protest," "Search and Privacy," and "Interrogation and Counsel." Each film is divided into four episodes. After each episode, a series of questions was posed relating to the constitutional issue involved, followed by a brief discussion.

The distinct feature of the low-verbal mode was that the stimuli or input information presented to the learner was in a fixed manner through two communicative channels—audio and visual. The fixed manner of presentation meant that the teachers and students involved in the experiment could not regulate the pace at which the information was presented.

The high-verbal instructional mode referred to a treatment consisting of a written account of the Bill of Rights (introductory lesson) as well as written descriptions and case studies of the constitutional issues (lessons 2 through 4). The written materials for lessons 2 through 4 were derived from the film dialogues. Each lesson was divided into four sequences. After each sequence, a series of questions was posed relating to the constitutional issue involved, followed by a brief discussion.

The distinct feature of the high-verbal mode was that the stimuli or input information presented to the learner was in a self-paced manner through one communication channel—written. Self-paced meant that the learner proceeded through the written material at his own pace, silently and without any verbal assistance from the instructor.

The conventional instructional mode referred to a treatment consisting of an oral account of the Bill of Rights (introductory lesson) as well as oral descriptions and case studies of constitutional issues (lessons 2 through 4). The oral content materials were presented in four sequences by the lecture method. Moreover, the content used was identical to that employed in the low- and high-verbal instructional modes. After each sequence, a series of questions relating to the constitutional issue presented was discussed.

The distinct feature of the conventional mode was that the stimuli or input information presented to the learner was in a fixed manner through one communicative channel—oral. Fixed manner in this case meant that the teacher, rather than the students, determined the rate at which information was presented and messages were received.

Essentially, the difference between instructional modes was in the channels employed (i.e., whether oral, written, or audio and visual means were employed in transmitting a message) and in the pace at which the stimuli were presented and received by the learner. Furthermore, the tactics employed following each sequence in each lesson were identical for all three instructional modes and were used only to clarify and reinforce the content.

Aptitude was defined as those abilities (i.e., intelligence quotient, reading level, and grade point achievement) that affect an individual's rate of learning. The assessment of aptitude ranges was accomplished according to the spread of scores on two different instruments (*Cattell Culture Fair I.Q. Test* and *Iowa Silent Reading Test CM & DM*) and to a measure of prior learning success, that is, fall semester grade point average in American history

classes. Three aptitude pattern groups (above average, average, and below average) were established in light of aptitude ranges so that performance on a particular aptitude variable (i.e., reading ability) could be compared with the three modes of instruction by statistical analysis.

A pretest–posttest evaluative instrument measuring three intellectual dimensions, knowledge, application, and opinion, was devised and administered prior to and after the treatment to ascertain the degree to which effective learning transpired. Effective learning referred to the significant difference of pretest–posttest scores on the evaluative instrument. Moreover, the pretest–posttest instrument was readministered 3 weeks after the treatment to measure the retention of information learned.

The evaluative instrument consisted of 57 test items and was administered in two parts. Part I of the examination assessed student performance on the knowledge and opinion dimensions in written form by a test booklet. Part II evaluated student gains on the application dimension presented by a tape–slide medium.

The knowledge and application items were used by the assignment of one point for each correct item completed. However, the opinion items, adopted from Allen (1965), were measured in terms of a 5-point Likert scale.

METHODS AND PROCEDURES

Amos P. Godby High School was selected from the three public high schools in Tallahassee, Florida (Leon County), to participate in the study. The sample, as originally designated, numbered approximately 250 eleventh grade students. Due to the effect of mortality at the onset of the study (i.e., student absenteeism due to a boycott of the schools), the sample size was considerably reduced. Mortality also accounted for the loss of students in the sample throughout the investigation. Consequently, the final sample in the study consisted of 165 students. This sample represented approximately 60 percent of the school's eleventh grade student population. They were enrolled in 12 American history classes taught by three instructors, each of whom taught four classes.

The general characteristics of the sample in terms of age, sex, race, IQ, reading level, and first-semester grade-point average in American history are presented in Table 1. The sample was representative of Godby's eleventh grade population in terms of race, age, and sex composition.

Three American history teachers were selected to participate in the research. Each teacher employed all three instructional modes, using a different mode in each of three treatment classes. A fourth class taught by each teacher served as a control group and received no treatment. The instructional mode was randomly assigned to each class by an ad hoc random procedure. This procedure was employed because the data collected from the *Cattell Culture Fair I.Q. Test* (Cattell and Cattell, 1960) revealed

Table 1
General Characteristics of the Sample

	Description		
Aptitude Variable	*Characteristic*	*Number*	*Percentage*
Race	White	92	66
	Black	73	44
Age in years	15	2	1
	16	95	58
	17	57	35
	18	9	5
	19	2	1
Sex	Male	91	66
	Female	74	44
IQ	Above average	62	37
	Average	54	33
	Below average	49	30
Reading level	Above average	61	37
	Average	44	27
	Below average	60	36
Semester grade-point	Above average	60	36
average	Average	56	34
	Below average	49	30

that the classes were unequal in terms of IQ composition. Instructional modes were randomly assigned to all classes. This ensured that each mode of instruction was received by students of each aptitude pattern. For statistical purposes, individual aptitude patterns within groups were analyzed rather than classes.

Students in one of three aptitude patterns who received one of the three instructional modes were evaluated in terms of their performance on the three sections of the evaluative instrument. This assessment was reported for each of the three aptitude variables—IQ, reading level, and semester grade-point average. A correlation of these three variables was conducted and it was found that a significant positive relationship existed. Therefore, students with a below-average IQ aptitude pattern were also likely to have a below-average reading level and semester grade-point average aptitude pattern. This was also true for students with an above-average or average aptitude pattern.

Two statistical procedures were applied to ascertain the amount and/or degree to which the content had been attained. Specifically, the *t* test and analysis of variance were employed. The *t* test assessed the significance of mean differences using a .05 level of significance for a one-tailed test. An analysis of variance was utilized to assess the magnitude of the variation in the dependent variable (i.e., test score) as a function of the mode of instruction and student aptitude pattern. Moreover, a *t* test comparison of the pretest–posttest means for the control group was conducted to ascertain whether or not significant mean gains on the three dimensions tested were present for any one of the three aptitude variables.

FINDINGS

The results of the research revealed that no single mode of instruction was consistently more effective than the other two for any particular aptitude pattern. However, on the knowledge dimension significant results were obtained and the following conclusions made:

1. Students who fall in the lowest of three aptitude patterns learn more effectively content related to the knowledge dimension from a conventional instructional mode.
2. Students who fall in the highest of three aptitude patterns learn more effectively content related to the knowledge dimension from a low-verbal instructional mode.
3. Students who fall in the middle aptitude pattern learn more effectively content related to the knowledge dimension from a high-verbal instructional mode.
4. Content is more effectively retained when initial gains were the result of the conventional instructional mode, whereas content initially learned as a result of the low-verbal mode is more readily forgotten.

IMPLICATIONS

Since different modes of instruction were found to be significant for students with various aptitudes, it appears that students effectively translate information presented in different ways. This implies that no one mode of instruction is more successful than another in transmitting information to be learned by all students. Therefore, the adoption of individualized instruction and/or the utilization of a variety of instructional modes would enhance learning for students of a wider range of aptitudes.

Students of below-average aptitudes performed better when the conventional instructional mode was used. This could be attributed to their familiarity with a lecture–textbook instructional pattern and their reluctance to modify existing learning patterns. Hence, a direct, personal approach that increases the chances for dialogue (i.e., questions and discussion) between the teacher and students would enhance learning for below-average students, producing a climate more conducive to comprehension.

Individualized instruction in the form of written materials would perhaps be the most effective way to convey information to average ability students.

Students with high aptitudes seem to translate information best through a multiple communicative channel (i.e., audio and visual) and thus would profit in learning by the enrichment of this form of communication.

Educators should be cognizant of the fact that the effectiveness of instructional modes does vary with respect to student aptitude patterns. Therefore, a sincere effort should be made to diversify techniques for transmitting knowledge.

REFERENCES

Allen, B. J. The construction of an instrument designed to measure student held attitudes toward certain American values as related to a jury of expert consensus. Unpublished Ph.D. dissertation, Florida State University, 1965.

Briggs, L. Instructional media: a procedure for the design of multimedia instruction, a critical review of research, and suggestions for future research. Pittsburgh: American Institute for Research, 1967.

Cattell, R. B., and Cattell, A. K. S. *Manual for the Cattell culture fair intelligence test, scale 2.* Indianapolis: Bobbs-Merrill, 1960.

Gagné, R. M. *The conditions of learning.* New York: Holt, Rinehart and Winston, 1965.

Gagné, R. M., and Paradise, N. E. Abilities and learning sets in knowledge acquisition. *Psychological Monographs: General and Applied,* 1961, *75,* 1–23 (Whole No. 14).

Snow, R. E., and Salomon, G. Aptitudes and instructional media. *Audiovisual Communication Review,* 1968, *16,* 341–357.

Improved Method for Instructional Development: Learner Types

Donald H. Britt

Literature today contains many articles lamenting the disenchanting results attained in education. One of the two basic causes is that courses developed and presented do not meet the precise needs of the students who take them. The use of learner types can cause substantial improvement by allowing the curricula to be precisely created and integrated for the separate, predetermined, specific needs of each individual's type.

Research conducted during the past 5 years at the University of Cambridge has demonstrated that individuals can be classified into learner types (LT) on the basis of their distinctive patterns of response in objective test batteries and instructional tasks. Further, the same response patterns which form a type are the instructional need statements of the type. Therefore, an instructional program and the entire curriculum can be scientifically designed to match the exact needs of each learner type.

When using computer-assisted instruction (CAI), or other audiovisual aids, it is not economical to create and manipulate an individual, separately designed program. This would require almost 1 billion programs in each course for the world's

Donald H. Britt conducts research at the Psychological Research Section, University of Cambridge, England.

school population. It is also very questionable practice to design only one program on each topic with the hope that it will fit the needs of all who take it. An economic alternative is the development of instructional programs which are scientifically designed to fit the needs of large groups of individuals classified by LT.

Isolation of LTs has been accomplished using the ICT Atlas 1 at Chilton and Atlas 2 (Titan) at Cambridge. Both machines are high-speed computers containing a large internal fast store. A multiple-agreement technique which matches every response for each individual with each response made by all other individuals was used. A type, when formed, contains only those individuals with identical response patterns—a procedure differing completely from the highly questionable use of "matched-groups." The univariate method, with its stress on a single process, was not used because it is possible that the total organism must be considered in the formation of valid learner types. The emphasis on the total individual during the formation of LTs is like the clinical method, except that the computer's memory and speed are used to extract from millions of comparisons the measurable regularities which exist in response patterns derived from specifically designed broad-spectrum tests and three instructional programs. Fifty-nine thousand data cards and 800 plus hours of computer time were used. The age range was from 9 to 19 years. Learner types were found to cross sex, age, time, and grades in their formation and found to replicate under a variety of conditions.

The unique response patterns which form a type are also the instructional need statements or programming specifications for the type. In order to provide a few examples, brief summary statements for three LTs—N.Q. and X—are included.

Learner Type N

If optimum results are desired, programs written for N must initially provide a considerable measure of security for the LT and no intimidation. If punitive corrections are programmed, there is evidence that they should be stronger than for Q. Quiet working conditions are not required, and more rapid pacing than for Q or X is desirable. Programs should anticipate that statements will be made by this type for the fun of the confusion the type can cause. The instructional program should be written to reduce its emotional impact. Incentives for N in the instructional program should include a strong sense of personal accomplishment and contribution to society, while gratifying the type's need for participation with companionable, social, and conversational groups that are not argumentative.

N requires material to be taught in several ways—deductively and inductively—with special programming procedures to prevent the LT from making errors when following instructions. (Q does not require this.) To expedite behavioral change, subjects of N should receive considerable explanatory justification for any statements, new procedures, or changes in course material. Evidence indicates that the overall behavioral change of N will be attenuated by drill in concept transfer, control of self, psychological and by providing programs designed to reduce confusion interference. N's lack of mental sensitivity, social sensitivity, and sensitivity for self requires special programming effort.

Learner Type Q

The instructional programs for Q need little motivational material and should use pressure (pacing, for instance). As long as Q is performing correctly, no feedback is required. While the programs should be paced, it is desirable to allow the type to work more slowly than learner type N. Programs for Q should inculcate a sense of group activity. Although noise level bothers this type, other general interferences do not. The CAI responses from these subjects will be straightforward. One of the rewards provided for the members of Q should be opportunity in the instructional program to debate the issues. It is desirable to include a remedial program to explain and provide examples on how achievement can be obtained in spite of age. Punitive measures need to be quite moderate, and some form of the concept of monetary reward should be programmed. With this type it is desirable to make use of the direct, practical, straightforward approach using Q's self-reliance. The type outlines the material that is being presented, and quickly learns terms. Because the LT has a large vocabulary, no attempt need be made to write down to a vocabulary level. Clarification of the writing of dates is required, because this type has difficulty in correctly learning them. As Q accurately follows instruction in branching and other directions with considerable precision, no special precaution need be taken in this matter, and direction can be kept minimal. Q is competent in generalizing, and a special, repetitive instructional program (required for N) is not required. Elaborate justification of a statement, a new procedure, or a change in course can be eliminated—thus speeding presentation.

The LTs were weighed on a series of characteristics, and a preferred weight range was established for programming purposes. Type Q has more characteristics in range than either N or X. It is useful to mention that an LT who is capable, and perhaps "top-of-the-class," still requires programs designed for his specific needs. From the casual point of view, it would seem that Q requires less programming effort and less specifically designed programs than N, because of the many assets Q possesses. This may account for the fact that usually only one program is created to teach a college course, and satisfaction in that program is expressed when all, or perhaps less than all, pass the course. LT theory indicates, however, that the time, effort, and strain required would be substantially lessened, and that comprehension, retention, and general understanding would be increased were the course designed to the specific needs of a learner type.

In a classroom, Q would be gratefully received by the teacher because the type is diplomatic, practi-

cal, sensitive to the needs of others, does understand others, makes logically valid statements, and has little feeling of persecution.

The motivational assets of Q from a programming point of view include generally assertive, desires change, has many interests, is motivated by money, and is sensitive to what others think of Q. As the type has good physiological control, less programming effort needs to be included to balance restlessness and to provide alternative methods for the operation of keyboards and other tools. Advantages also accrue because Q is dependable and intellectually exact. Logic capabilities include cross reference in spatial relationships, cross reference in vocabulary selection, validity in locating accurate statements, and alphabetic reasoning within the weight range.

Unfortunately, although Q has general sensitivity, the type lacks empathy and is not creative or perceptive. Further, the type may lack a realistic approach to life.

While Q ranks high in motivation, the type may lack self-direction and determination. Because of the frequency of measures of sensitivity, punitive correction must be very mild, or omitted and then built up.

Another specific programming problem is that Q has high-confusion interference when in noise, and has difficulty in perceiving correct artistic proportion or spatial construction. Therefore, in CAI and other forms of audiovisual instruction, the type will require special quiet console booths, earphones, or other procedures, and may not be able to perceive many of the programs presented in the cathode-ray tube. With the present level of information, a course in "aesthetic appreciation" for this type would be difficult to produce. However, further refinement will resolve this problem with detailed specifications.

Learner Type X

For X, although the instructional program becomes longer, it should be made interesting and stimulating while providing incentives, eliminating pressures or excesses, and avoiding arguments. Pacing is better left out. The LT should be asked about the fading of any cue before a reduction. X is insecure, and special programming precautions need to be provided to improve the type's self-concept. Yet, remedial programs on vocabulary building, educative role playing, and handling pressure are indicated. Programmed instruction should provide X with the sense of frequent individual activities and some social accomplishments. Directive course guidance should be scheduled, and aesthetic satisfaction can be used as reward.

Part of the difficulty being experienced by X may be that these people are creative, artistic, and sensitive, and this may not be in keeping with the wishes of the schools they attend. Because this type lacks general assertiveness, ego strength, and many interests, the programming effort should not start with course material as such, but rather with the attempt to create a valid attitude of readiness. Because the type has reasonably high capacity in perception and alphabetic reasoning, and can perceive visual relationships such as those which could be rotated on a cathode-ray tube or laser beam display, instructional programs for X should be designed to use these capacities, thereby reducing the negative effect of the lack of other attributes, such as concept transfer and dependability. This procedure could also be used to offset the effect of the possible differences in the proportions of LTs in the races.

Learner type X raises again the question of environment versus innate capacity. Audiovisual instruction can help X by providing programs designed to overcome the type's problems, yet there is always the question of how much time should be devoted to a given area. Perhaps a procedure could be included to drop the student from a given area if he learns so slowly that a continued effort in the particular field is unwarranted. The advanced CAI device, Autoteach, as suggested in an earlier work (1961), would need to have its programs set with some control of this kind until that day when so much was known of each learner type that all could be rapidly taught.

Position Paper to Further Individualization of Instruction in the Schools

Rita S. Dunn

The process of educating children has evolved from teacher-dominated instruction to child-centered environment to objectives-based learning. Recently, we have begun to recognize that each youngster learns in a manner which is uniquely his or her own, through perceptual strengths that either fortify or discourage the acquisition of knowledge and skills, and with a learning style that tends to dominate his or her every effort to achieve. Individualization is more than a philosophy, more than an instructional process, and more than a means whereby both the teacher and the student become responsible, cooperative human beings who are both dependent upon and accountable to each other and themselves; individualization is the recognition that for each student, whether child or adult, learning is a developmental construct which varies, often completely, from that of every other student.

Because not all educators realize that learning occurs under vastly differing conditions for each person, too many of our schools continue to operate daily instructional programs that are based on

Rita S. Dunn is associate professor of education, St. John's University, Jamaica, New York.

serious misconceptions about the learning process. Current teaching methods often *block* learning and promote a conformity that prevents the establishment of appropriate objectives for each student. Drastic instructional and organizational change is needed to revise and improve the teaching—learning process to permit students to strive for and reach self-fulfillment. This type of sweeping change for the better can best begin through a comparison of the common fallacies that now exist in our classrooms with the realities of how children learn, and by a consideration of the suggestions of the alternatives which an individualized program permits. (See Table 1.)

ALTERNATIVE TYPES OF INDIVIDUALIZATION

There are at least five basic ways to individualize instruction. These include varied emphases on prepackaged teacher- or student-determined diagnosis, prescription, materials, activities, assessment, and recycling.

Programmed Learning

Student skills and objectives are prearranged and packaged in short or longer sequences on a continuum ranging from the simple to the complex. In

Table 1

Fallacy	Reality	Individualization
1. Children learn by listening.	Some children learn by listening, others learn by seeing, and others must learn by touching or acting out. Children learn through different perceptions and, although repetition through varied perceptions tends to reinforce learning, information, skills, and values should be introduced through the child's major perceptual strength.	Children are given options to elect how they will learn selected material. Reinforcement through additional perceptual means is provided, but the youngsters determine how they will initially begin the learning process related to their instructional objectives. This process leads to student decision making, responsibility, and ultimate accountability.
2. A class of 25 students can learn identical content in the same specified amount of time.	Children (and adults) absorb varying amounts of content at different rates and at different times; they also vary in the amount and type of content they retain.	Children are given approximate time intervals during which they may complete their instructional objectives, but are permitted to pace themselves and to determine the amount of study and number of objectives with which they can cope. This process is guided by the teacher to encourage positive achievement.
3. All children can learn in depth if they will only concentrate.	All children can learn something about a given topic, but each child has a greater or lesser capacity to absorb details, concepts and nuances. Here, too, much depends on interest and the frame of reference of each youngster.	In conservative individualized programs, children are given some instructional requirements and then permitted some instructional options. In an open-ended individualized program, children are are permitted to study what most entices and absorbs them. A happy medium would lie somewhere between, based

Table 1 *(continued)*

Fallacy	Reality	Individualization
		on the recognition that most schools follow a definite (though flexible) curriculum, but that children learn most easily that which interests them.
4. A quiet school is a good school.	A consistently quiet school is a subdued school where children have been trained or coerced into patterns of behavior that are unnatural to healthy youth.	Some children require a quiet environment in which to learn, while others need verbal and sometimes social interaction; most youngsters require one or the other and combination of each at different times. An effective individualized program permits the youngsters to determine whether they will work alone, in pairs, or in small groups. Noise is as inconsistent with a well-functioning program as is silence. The sound of student and teacher interaction and activity is part of an effective learning environment.
5. Children should be admitted to school when they are five years of age.	Children should be admitted to school when they are "ready" to learn.	Children should be repeatedly diagnosed, prescribed for, and guided through the learning process. Some children should enter a formal and/or semiformal educational program earlier and/or later than other children, remain in school for varying amounts of time, be provided different kinds of experiences, and be encouraged to formulate programs, which vary extensively in terms of environment, objectives, resources, activities, focus, and self-direction.
6. Children should be in school for the same amount of time each day.	Children should be in school for the amount of time during which they are capable of being attentive, studious, positively active, or relaxed.	
7. Children should be maintained in school until they are 16 years of age.	Children should be maintained in school until they can no longer obtain positive learning experiences. Alternative programs, both in and out of school, should be provided for students who would benefit from them.	
8. It is better for children to remain on "grade level" with youngsters of the	It is better for children to be working at their maximum individual capacities with	Interage groupings which change with subject and interest areas are common. The

Table 1 *(continued)*

Fallacy	Reality	Individualization
same chronological age than to study with either much younger or much older children.	different age groups than to be either bored by the lack of intellectual challenge or frustrated by being unable to compare themselves favorably with their peers.	rhetoric about academic superiority frequently being inconsistent with emotional maturity holds little weight; there is virtually no evidence to substantiate that keeping the bright, immature child with his or her peers contributes to either maturity or adjustment.
9. There are special teaching methods that are panaceas for instructing children, e.g., "discovery" in social studies, "phonics" in reading, experimentation" in science.	Since children learn most easily through their strongest perceptual strength, the instructional method should relate directly to that modality. A cognitive, conceptual learner who enjoys reading may learn easily through discovery; the child who learns by talking and listening may not. A child who learns visually may experience difficulty with an essentially phonics approach. The youngster who learns tactually will delight in the experimentation, whereas the phonetically oriented learner may become bored or frustrated when required to go through an entire touching process.	Children are made aware of their instructional objectives, provided with alternative resources through which to learn, and then permitted to select the way(s) in which they will complete the learning process. Students are eventually trained to select goals and processes.
10. The teacher should be accountable for the child's learning.	The child should be equally as accountable for his or her learning.	Teachers are required to diagnose accurately, prescribe appropriately, and guide students through varied effective instructional techniques. Children are apprised of both their options and their responsibilities. Children who do not meet their responsibilities are cautioned and/or recycled into more structured programming.
11. A "great" teacher must be an excellent actor or actress.	A great teacher establishes rapport, respect, and a climate that creates an eased, personalized joy of learning and achieving for each of his or her students. Because many children do not learn unless they are actively involved in the process, the dramatic teacher may be amusing, but is not necessarily an effective instructor.	Children are permitted extensive and frequent opportunities to be involved directly with their teachers. The quiet, undramatic teacher may be as or more effective as his or her counterpart, depending on the personality ranges of the students.
12. Young children need a mother substitute and, therefore, the self-contained classroom, where one	Young and older children need a variety of challenging activities, many warm and responsive adults, other positive chil-	Children are exposed to a variety of adults and relate beautifully when the adults are responsive, caring, and effective in

Table 1 (continued)

Fallacy	Reality	Individualization
teacher is responsible for most of the instruction, is the best organizational pattern for primary grades.	dren, loving parents, and opportunities to become independent and responsible.	their assigned roles.
13. Each teacher knows what is "best" for the children in his or her class.	Every teacher is not like every other teacher; some are excellent diagnosticians, some are effective prescribers, some are outstanding guides in the learning process, and some are excellent at all or none of these functions.	Children are being granted on increasingly larger role in determining some, many, or all of their objectives in conjunction with their teachers. The more involvement the student gains, the more likely he or she is to be a motivated learner.
14. Children learn best through repeated, sequential periods that are spaced throughout the school day, week, or year, and are "articulated" with the same (or other) subject(s) in succeeding days and years.	Children learn in a variety of both structured and unstructured ways.	Children are repeatedly diagnosed to avoid unnecessary (and boring) repetition and are provided alternative schedules and patterns of learning.
15. Education occurs between 8:30 A.M. and 3:00 P.M. when children are in school.	Learning occurs whenever children are actively involved in stimulating experiences on their level of comprehension and interest.	Children are provided multiple options, multiple environments, and the freedom of scheduling themselves so that learning becomes self-selective to varying extents.

essence, the student is diagnosed by preestablished instruments and then programmed into the sequence at the point at which the materials are either developmental or partially repetitive for him. All students proceed through essentially the same sequence but may pace themselves and learn through materials appropriate to their level of comprehension and achievement. Programmed learning is individualized only in terms of rate and level. I.P.I. and Project Plan represent this type of individualization in a broad sense.

Instructional Packages

A variety of educational materials is made available to students who then determine the selection of materials with which they will work. Goals and activities may be either teacher- or student-determined, depending upon the amount of structure established by the individual teacher. Many of the British primary schools and the American open classroom and open corridor schools rely heavily on student use of materials to promote learning. When the materials are commercially produced (Elementary Science Study, Science A Process Approach, Science Curriculum Improvement Study, etc.), sequenced, and/or "packaged," they are called instructional packages. This method of individualization provides extensive opportunity for (1) student selection and exploration of materials based on interest, (2) the establishment of either teacher- or student-selected goals, (3) self-pacing, and (4) individual leveling. It is a much less structured method than programmed learning, and permits randomization of the learning process. Critics note that the teacher is not in control of what will be learned; many youngsters require structure and do not have the self-motivation and discipline to pursue learning by themselves over an extended period of time; and special skills of analysis, translation, and application are necessary to transfer a student's experiences with materials into knowledge.

Contracts

Teachers and/or students may determine educational objectives. Students then determine the resources through which they will learn, the activities through which they will apply and use what they have learned, and the small group techniques through which they will share what they have learned by interacting with others. Students assess themselves so that they are always aware of what they have learned and what still remains to be achieved. After this phase, teachers and students cooperatively participate in the terminal assessment. This method individualizes in terms of objectives, materials, activities, reporting, small group interactions, interest, learning style, perceptual strengths, and assessment.

Work–Study Experiences

Teachers and/or students cooperatively diagnose, prescribe, and assess. The student's learning environment is advanced into the community, industry, and business. The student's prescription encompasses academically oriented requirements which may be fulfilled while being employed. This is the method utilized by the Parkway School in Philadelphia, also called "The School Without Walls." It individualizes in terms of diagnosis, prescription, environment, materials, activities, and assessment. This form of individualization has been

used by high schools and higher education institutions.

Community Contributions

This method is essentially similar to the work–study experience but requires nonremunerative "giving" of self and time to community agencies and institutions such as orphanages, hospitals, social and welfare agencies, and citizens groups. It, too, individualizes in terms of diagnosis, prescription, environment, materials, activities, and assessment, and grants academic credit in relation to the completion of established objectives. Again, this method has been initiated with older students only.

Any individualized program is either directly related to or an outgrowth of one of these five forms. The degree to which a program utilizes teacher and/or student-determined goals, materials, activities, interests, and assessment devices determines whether it is called "individually diagnosed and prescribed," "personalized", "self-directed," "independent study," or "individualized".

OPERATIONAL DEFINITIONS OF SEMI-INDIVIDUALIZED AND TOTALLY INDIVIDUALIZED PROGRAMS

Many different types of programs have been introduced under the guise of "individualization." Some permit individual pacing and/or leveling, others encourage self-selection of objectives, others provide multiple learning options, and still others permit consideration of the child's learning style and perceptual strengths. Few programs are totally individualized and incorporate all these aspects into the overall instructional scheme.

The following are overviews of selected types of programs which meet *some* of the criteria for effective individualized instruction.

Individually Diagnosed and Prescribed Instruction

Student skills and objectives are prearranged and packaged in sequences on a continuum ranging from the simple to the complex. Students are diagnosed, programmed into the sequence at the level at which they are ready to learn, and then permitted to move through the prepared materials at their own pace.

Aspects of Individualization
Diagnosis
Self-pacing
Leveling

Personalized Instruction

The student establishes his or her own goals within the framework of the resources available. The student then follows the program and uses the resources established by the teacher, and is permitted to complete the program as quickly as he or she can or as slowly as is necessary.

Aspects of Individualization
Diagnosis
Self-selection of goals
Self-pacing
Leveling

Self-Directed Instruction

The materials and the procedures are determined by the student, but the school determines the objectives and the general structure of the environment.

Aspects of Individualization
Diagnosis
Self-selection of materials
Self-selection of learning activities
Self-pacing
Leveling

Independent Study

The student determines instructional objectives and activities, but the school usually selects a limited number of students or courses for this approach.

Aspects of Individualization
Diagnosis
Self-selection of goals
Self-selection of learning materials
Self-selection of activities
Self-pacing
Leveling

TOTAL INDIVIDUALIZATION

An operational approach to total individualization involves the *student* in the following:

Diagnosis

1. What does the student know (facts, concepts, and skills), to what degree of proficiency, and at what level in the several content areas for which the school and/or the student have established objectives?
2. What are the student's specific interests, skills, abilities, aptitudes, and degrees of maturity and motivation?
3. What are the student's perceptual strengths?
4. What are the student's best learning styles for various school or self-selected tasks? [Learning style is determined by analysis of the following items: the time of day when a student is most alert; whether he or she works best in quiet or with music or television, in company or alone, with food or without food, in leisure or under pressure, in a structured environment or in a relaxed one, by self-pacing or teacher-determined pacing, in need of accessories (food, gum, liquids) or not, sitting, lying down, or sprawling; the kind of lighting he or she needs; the time intervals during which he or she can

continue to study; the need for reward or incentive, type of clothing necessary, room temerature, etc.]

Prescription

1. What are the jointly determined objectives to be achieved by the student? Ultimately, the student may self-select objectives.
2. What are the alternative learning resources and activities available to reach those objectives?
3. What are the optional methods by which the student may demonstrate that he or she has attained the objectives?

Self-selection

1. How will the student plan his or her own progress?
2. What alternatives will the student be permitted to use, for example, additional media resources, learning activity alternatives, and/or human and/or environmental resources?
3. How may the student modify or apply objectives where and when appropriate?
4. How will the student interact with others in the learning process?

Teacher and cooperative assessment

1. How will the teacher and the student assess and redesign new objectives based on the individualized evaluation?
2. Which objectives and procedures may the student design in the interest of his or her own self-fulfillment?

3. How will the new, individualized experiences aid in additional diagnosis and prescriptions?

Aspects of Individualization

Teacher and student diagnosis
Teacher and student prescription
Student selection of goals, learning materials, activities, and instructional techniques
Self-pacing
Self-leveling
Self-assessment followed by cooperative assessment
Self-selection of *modus operandi*
Determined by learning styles
Objectives and prescription based on student interest(s)
Student creativity incorporated into self-selection aspects

ORGANIZING FOR INDIVIDUALIZATION

No stress-free, "perfect" guidelines for inducing change can be devised to facilitate the (individualization) process for all districts (Dunn and Blum, 1969).

REFERENCE

Dunn, Rita Stafford, and Hamilton S. Blum. *Individualizing Instruction*. New York: The Board of Cooperative Educational Services, 1969. (rev. 1970.)

Individual Learner Variables and the Prescribing of Instructional Methods and Media—Some Preliminary Findings

Roger W. Haskell

Increased demands from all segments of the population for educational accountability have placed educators in a rather precarious position. They are being called upon to find more efficient and more effective ways of educating students at a time when educational dollars are becoming increasingly scarce. Perhaps more than at any other time in history, demands are being placed on school personnel to make the educational system both more sensitive and more responsive to the needs of individual learners.

The educational response to such pressures may be seen in such educational innovations as differentiated staffing, open-entry open-exit systems, the ungraded school, the open school concept, and the like. Paralleling these innovations is a strong move to "individualize" and "personalize" the instructional process through the use of audio-tutorial instruction, programmed instruction, learning activity packages, and other individualized (and often times multimedia) instructional methods. An outgrowth of much of the foregoing is the fact that educators are increasingly involved in the prescribing of instructional materials for learners who are permitted to progress at their own rate of speed.

Roger W. Haskell is professor of vocational–technical education, University of Tennessee, Knoxville, Tennessee.

Much of what is being implemented in the classroom under the guise of educational innovation and educational individualization is being done without any substantial amount of research to support such changes. (This should not be interpreted to mean that I oppose such educational changes. My concern centers around the belief that educational decision makers have a long-range obligation to supply the missing data base upon which such educational innovations must ultimately rest. I see little evidence that this is being systematically done.) A notable exception is to be found in the research and experimentation that has been going on at the Learning Research and Development Center at the University of Pittsburgh. It represents a bold attempt to apply the concept of *prescribing instructional materials* for individual learners in a practical situation. (Bolvin and Glaser, 1968; Bolvin, 1968; Lindvall and Bolvin, 1967; Glaser et al., 1966; Lindvall and Bolvin, 1966). Additional research that focuses on the merits of such educational innovations is badly needed.

Although no systematic approach has been discernable in providing additional findings to our present research knowledge base, other studies have focused on related questions. For example, in the past several years numerous research studies have had as their central focus the attempted identification of instructional methods and/or media that will prove to be significantly more effective than some alternative instructional approach. The findings from such media comparison studies generally have presented a very confused picture regarding the efficacy of utilizing one instructional approach over the other. The most consistent finding has been that there is "no statistically significant difference" between the instructional methods and media under investigation (Saettler, 1968). When statistically significant differences have been found, they typically have not been consistent with other findings resulting from studies concerned with the same general problem area. Likewise, such findings have been difficult to

retain on those few occasions when it has been feasible and/or possible to replicate research studies that have previously reported such statistically significant results.

By way of illustration, research studies concerned with the relative effectiveness of programmed and "conventional" modes of instruction perhaps best exemplify the present state of such methodological research. Schramm's (1964) survey of some 36 studies dealing with the relative merits of programmed and conventional approaches indicated that, when achievement test scores were used as the criterion, 18 studies showed no significant difference between the two methods, 17 reported results significantly favoring the programmed approach, and 1 study reported a significant difference that favored the conventional method of instruction. Silberman's (1962) survey of research on the relative effectiveness of programmed and conventional instruction provides a similar picture of confusion.

Although the Schramm and Silberman surveys examined only two basic modes of instruction (programmed versus conventional), even a cursory review of the literature dealing with other media comparison research will yield an equally confusing picture. Yet such methodological studies continue to dominate much of the experimental research of recent years (particularly doctoral dissertation research), which suggests that researchers still believe (in spite of any consistent support from completed studies) that there is merit in pursuing this research area. Their persistence likewise forces one to examine other possible explanations for the multitude of inconsistent research findings resulting from such media comparison studies.

Instructional comparisons of the sort cited typically employ test measures and statistical procedures that tend to conceal the effects of individual differences. As Davis et al. suggest: ". . . some students may do better with one mode of instruction while other students do better with a second mode, but the use of the statistical mean would disguise this fact and on the average no differences between groups would be observed" (1970, p. 198).

Research undertakings that have been concerned with examining the effects of individual learner differences as they interact with various instructional methods provide some indication that the identification of such learner characteristics may be useful for *prescribing different instructional approaches* for different individuals. The findings reported by Eigen (1962) and Porter (1961), for example, suggested that the academic achievement of learners with equivalent ability levels was affected significantly by the type of presentation mode utilized.

The interaction between specific learner personality characteristics and classroom milieu similarly has been investigated by various researchers (Lublin, 1965; Snow et al., 1965; Doty and Doty, 1964; Traweek, 1964; Beach, 1960; McCurdy and Eber, 1953). The research findings from such studies suggest strongly that the academic achievement of learners who possess similar personality traits will be affected significantly depending on the instructional method selected. Thus, it may be that the best teaching method for *some* students may not be the best teaching method for *all* students. The most effective instructional milieu may thus be found in the *interaction* between various learner characteristics and instructional method rather than in the method per se. To be sure, such information is essential if we are to provide the research data base to support many of the educational innovations currently being contemplated. Likewise, such information ought to be extremely useful to educational practitioners who are intent upon making the school environment more responsive to the needs of individual learners.

The purpose of the present research undertaking, then, was to examine the possible relationship between selected learner personality characteristics and their academic achievement under instructional treatments that were basically traditional and

programmed. Of particular concern to the investigator was whether individual learners would be differentially and significantly affected by the method of instruction utilized and, if so, whether the characteristics of these learners could be specified in such a manner that one might significantly increase the academic achievement of learners by *prescribing the instructional method* to which they might be exposed.

METHOD

Subjects

Subjects for this study consisted of 163 students who were enrolled in one of nine industrial education drafting classes at two large senior high schools.

Instructional Content

The instructional content utilized during the course of this experiment consisted of a short unit on arc welding symbols. The unit included the basic symbols used on drawings and blueprints to designate various types of arc welds according to American Welding Society standards.

Treatments

The instructional content was presented to the experimental treatment group (four intact classes of students; $n = 78$) by means of a linear-type programmed instruction booklet (Bowman and Dixon, 1966). The same content was presented to the comparison treatment group (four intact classes of students; $n = 67$) by means of a lecture—discussion presentation mode. One group of students ($n = 18$) received no instruction relating to arc welding symbols and was used as a control group. Treatment conditions were assigned randomly to these intact groups of students.

Procedure

In the case of the experimental treatment, subjects studied the programmed material and were required to make written responses to the program as they proceeded. The teacher went over the first three or four frames of the linear program with subjects to ensure that they understood exactly how to proceed. Thus, with the exception of the first 3 or 4 minutes of the first class period, subjects studied the material at their own pace without any assistance from the teacher.

Subjects receiving the comparison treatment were exposed to a lecture presentation by teachers who utilized a series of 41 transparencies to help convey the content. These teachers also were provided with a content outline to help ensure that content coverage would be equivalent within the comparison treatment. Subjects, in turn, were requested to make either oral responses to questions or written responses on the chalkboard at the request of the teacher. They also were encouraged to ask questions of the teacher whenever they failed to understand any of the material being taught. Maximum treatment time was four 54-minute class periods (216 minutes). As was previously mentioned, the control group did not receive any instruction during the course of this experiment.

Instruments

The data for analysis were obtained from three sources. The Guilford–Zimmerman Temperament Survey (GZTS) was used to obtain measures for each subject on the following 10 personality factors: general activity (G), restraint (R), ascendance (A), sociability (S), emotional stability (E), objectivity (O), friendliness (F), thoughtfulness (T), personal relations (P), and masculinity (M). The Wonderlic Personnel Test (WPT) was used to measure the general mental ability of each subject. A researcher-developed, 72-item multiple-choice test (each item containing five possible alternatives)

was used to measure learner academic achievement. The Kuder–Richardson 20 estimate of reliability for this achievement test, which was initially established during an earlier pilot study, was found to be .95. The same reliability score was again obtained as a result of this experiment.

Data Analysis

Two analyses were made of the achievement test data. The first analysis (somewhat peripheral to the main research question) was designed to examine whether both treatment conditions worked equally well and whether students receiving treatments learned significantly more than those in the control group. A one-way analysis of variance (Downie and Heath, 1970) was used to test for significant differences among the mean achievement test scores of the treatment groups. In that the F ratio from this analysis was found to be significant, the Scheffé method for making all possible comparisons among treatment means was used to determine where the differences were (Winer, 1962). The Scheffé analysis indicated that there was no significant difference between the mean achievement test scores of the programmed and conventional instruction groups ($F_0 = .10$; nsd). As expected, however, both programmed instruction group ($F_0 = 25.0$; $p < .01$) and conventional instruction group ($F_0 = 23.7$; $p < .01$) achievement test means were found to be significantly higher than the mean of the control group.

The second and most important analysis was made to examine the possible interaction effects between selected personality characteristics of learners and their achievement test performance under each of the treatment conditions. Individual scores on each of the 10 personality traits measured by the GZTS were categorized into one of three groups: (1) scores that fell .5 standard deviations or more above the mean, (2) scores that were between .5 standard deviations above the mean and .5

standard deviations below the mean, and (3) scores that fell .5 standard deviations or more below the mean. Data were then analyzed using a 2 × 3 (treatments × levels of personality) analysis of covariance for each of the 10 personality variables. In each case, general mental ability scores as measured by the WPT served as the covariate, while scores on the achievement test served as the dependent or criterion variable. Where differences at the .05 level or less were found, Duncan's multiple-range test for ordered means was employed (Duncan, 1955).

Results

Results of the analysis of covariance statistical test indicated that, when adjustment was made for any existing differences in general mental ability (as measured by the WPT), two of the measured personality variables (general activity and friendliness) were still found to interact significantly with method of instruction. The analysis of covariance of scores on the achievement test for the personality variable general activity yielded the following F ratio ($F_0 = 3.35$; $p < .05$). The analysis of covariance of scores on the achievement test for the personality variable friendliness yielded the following F ratio ($F_0 = 3.14$; $p < .05$).

Analysis of Duncan's multiple-range test for ordered means indicated the following: the programmed learning environment tended to favor significantly those who scored low on the general activity personality variable and/or high on the friendliness variable. An examination of these two personality types, moreover, would tend to suggest the following: students who were inclined to be slow and methodical and who were able to focus their attention on accomplishing the task at hand (characteristic of those who scored low on general activity) were likely to perform significantly better in the self-paced programmed instruction setting. Likewise, students who could be characterized as agreeable and easy to get along with, who would

tend to be the more docile and nonthreatening type, and who would tend to shy away from competitive situations (high friendliness) also tended to perform significantly better with programmed instruction.

On the other hand, those who were more likely to be characterized as aggressive, more competitive, and more the questioning type of individual, as well as those wanting more variety from a learning situation (all characteristics of low scorers on the friendliness scale) appeared to perform better (and significantly so) under the more conventional type of instruction.

The analysis of covariance statistical test also permitted the identification of two other personality variables (restraint and emotional stability) as significant predictors of high academic achievement. The results of Duncan's multiple-range test for ordered means indicated that students who scored high on either the restraint or emotional stability scales performed significantly better ($p < .001$) when exposed to *either* programmed or conventional instruction than did their counterparts who scored in the low or middle range on these variables.

Thus, students who were found to be serious minded and persistent and who possessed an ability to stick with things (characteristics associated with those scoring high on the restraint personality variable) performed significantly better regardless of the instructional method to which they were exposed. The same thing could be said of those who could be characterized as cheerful and reasonably well composed (high emotional stability). They also performed better under either instructional setting.

Summary and Discussion

The purpose of this study was to investigate the relationship between selected personality variables of learners and their academic performance under two specific methods of instruction. The interaction between instructional method and levels of the personality variables of general activity and friendliness suggested that the effectiveness of the method of instruction utilized will vary as a function of certain student personality characteristics. Programmed learning, which occurred in an essentially solitary environment, allowing students to progress independently at their own pace, was constrasted with conventional instruction, which permitted a considerable amount of student–teacher interaction, required students to "perform" in front of classmates by making either oral responses or written responses on the chalkboard, and was teacher paced. The results of the present study indicated that these two learning environments differentially affected students' academic performance. This finding suggested that the characteristics of students could be specified in such a way that one could increase the effectiveness of learning by *prescribing* the instructional method to which the learner would be exposed. Moreover, this finding is generally consistent with the results of several earlier studies which indicated that individual difference measures may be useful for prescribing instructional treatment (Schoer, 1966; Lublin, 1965; Snow et al., 1965; Doty and Doty, 1964; Traweek, 1964; Eigen, 1962; Porter, 1961; Beach, 1960; McCurdy and Eber, 1953). At the moment, however, the research in this area has not focused sufficiently either on isolating the relevant predictor variables or on replicating promising studies that have been conducted to date.

The results from this present investigation, however, lead the investigator to speculate that the research question is even more complex than originally conceived. The general characteristics of learners who scored high on the emotional stability scale of the GZTS would tend to suggest that such persons are much more likely to be "thing" oriented as opposed to "people" oriented. Given the nature of the instructional content used in the present study, one cannot help but speculate that the interaction effect may be not only between particular personality characteristics of learners and the instructional method to which they are exposed,

but also may involve an interaction effect with the nature of the instructional content being utilized. Since the present study involved only one type of instructional content, however, it cannot provide any definitive answers regarding this speculation.

Likewise, one might speculate that to the extent that traditional (teacher-directed) instructional approaches are employed, various teacher personality types may tend to interact with various learner personality types in a manner that would significantly affect learner academic achievement also. Research that focuses on both these "speculations" ought to provide answers which will be useful to those interested in obtaining a clearer picture regarding the total dimensions of this general problem area. Obviously, to the extent that there is some validity to these speculations, it will indeed make the "prescription formula" a much more difficult one.

Granted, the relationships between individual learner characteristics and the educational milieu are highly complex. At the theoretical level, the idea of individualizing instruction by prescribing instructional methods for students who differ in important ways seems to be fairly sound. However, practical educational and/or administrative considerations may yet make the task of prescribing instructional methods quite impractical. There are many questions still unanswered and many problems still unresolved. As Briggs has pointed out: "One problem in applying the results of such research might be difficulty in incorporating all of the kinds of differences found into manageable media packages. In short, one may find unique sources of variance by intensive study of individuals, but one may not be able to vary media programs for each unique person characteristic" (1968, p. 173).

Indeed, the task of prescribing instruction may create more problems than it solves. However, the development of such instructional devices as the cassette tape recorder, the single-concept film projector, and programmed instruction, among others, should provide much encouragement to educators who are concerned with making the educational environment more responsive to individual needs and differences. The computer also may contribute in significant ways to this individualization by making specific instructional modifications feasible.

Whether the educational environment can or cannot be restructured to take into account the many and varied differences of individual learners seems to be a premature worry, however. The many implications of individualizing instruction to make learning maximally effective are indeed imperfectly understood. Moreover, researchers have only begun to identify the vast array of possible relationships between learner characteristics and the instructional environment. At the present time it seems more important to examine further the complexity of interrelationships between individuals and the learning milieu. Current research findings are sketchy, and much more information is needed.

Research evidence and/or practical considerations eventually may dictate abandonment of the idea that the individual prescription of instructional methods is possible or warranted. Yet, providing for such individual learner differences may be a first step toward making educational experiences more meaningful and rewarding to students.

REFERENCES

Beach, L. R. Sociability and academic achievement in various types of learning situations. *Journal of Educational Psychology*, 1960, 51, 208–212.

Bolvin, J. O. Implications of the individualization of instruction for curriculum and instructional design. *Audiovisual Instruction*, 1968, 13, 238–242.

———, and Glaser, R. Developmental aspects of individually prescribed instruction. *Audiovisual Instruction*, 1968, 13, 828–831.

Bowman, E. G., and Dixon, E. H. *Arc Welding Symbols—Programmed Instruction*. Troy, Ohio: Hobart Welding School, 1966.

Briggs, L. J. Learner variables and educational media. *Review of Educational Research*, 1968, 38, 160–176.

Campbell, D. T., and Stanley, J. C. Experimental and quasi-experimental designs for research on teaching. In N. L. Gage (ed.), *Handbook of Research on Teaching*. Chicago: Rand McNally & Company, 1963.

Davis, R. H., Marzocco, F. N., and Denny, M. R. Interaction of individual differences with modes of presenting programmed instruction. *Journal of Educational Psychology*, 1970, 61, 198–204.

Doty, B. A., and Doty, L. A. Programmed instructional effectiveness in relation to certain student characteristics. *Journal of Educational Psychology*, 1964, 55, 334–338.

Downie, N. M., and Heath, R. W. *Basic Statistical Methods*. New York: Harper & Row, 1970.

Duncan, D. B. Multiple range and multiple F tests. *Biometrics*, 1955, 11, 1–42.

Eigen, L. D. A comparison of three modes of presenting a programed instruction sequence. *Journal of Educational Research*, 1962, 55, 453–460.

Glaser, R., Reynolds, J., and Fullic, M. Studies of the use of programmed instruction in the intact classroom. *Psychology in the Schools*, 1966, 3, 318–333.

Haskell, R. W. Effect of certain individual learner personality differences on instructional methods. *AV Communication Review*, 1971, 19, 287–297.

———. *Effect of personality characteristics upon learning via selected modes of instruction—an experimental investigation*. Unpublished doctoral dissertation, Purdue University, Purdue, Ind., 1969.

———. The influence of instructional method on the teacher's ability to predict learner academic achievement—an observation. *Journal of Industrial Teacher Education*, 1972, 9, 50–55.

Lindvall, C. M., and Bolvin, J. O. Programed instruction in the schools: An application of programing principles in individually prescribed instruction. In *Programed Instruction*, Yearbook of the National Society for the Study of Education, 1967, 66 (Part II).

———, and Bolvin, J. O. *The Project for Individually Prescribed Instruction (The Oakleaf Project)*. Pittsburgh, Pa.: Learning Research and Development Center, University of Pittsburgh, 1966.

Lublin, S. C. Reinforcement schedules, scholastic aptitude, autonomy need and achievement in a programed course. *Journal of Educational Psychology*, 1965, 56, 295–302.

McCurdy, H. G., and Eber, H. W. Democratic versus authoritarian: A further investigation of group problem solving. *Journal of Personality*, 1953, 22, 258–269.

Porter, D. *An Application of Reinforcement Principles to Classroom Teaching*, Cambridge, Mass.: Harvard University Press, 1961.

Saettler, P. Design and selection factors. *Review of Educational Research*, 1968, 38, 115–128.

Schoer, L. Reactive inhibition as related to performance on programmed learning materials. *Journal of Educational Psychology*, 1966, 57, 86–88.

Schramm, W. *The Research on Programed Instruction: An*

Annotated Bibliography. Stanford, Calif.: Stanford University, 1964.

Silberman, H. F. Characteristics of some recent studies of instructional methods. In J. E. Coulson (ed.), *Programmed Learning and Computer-Based Instruction.* New York: John Wiley & Sons, 1962.

Snow, R. E., Tiffin, J., and Seibert, W. F. Individual differences and instructional film effects. *Journal of Educational Psychology,* 1965, 56, 315–326.

Traweek, M. W. The relationship between certain personality variables and achievement through programed instruction. *California Journal of Educational Research,* 1964, 15, 215–220.

Winer, B. J. *Statistical Principles in Experimental Design.* New York: McGraw-Hill Book Company, 1962.

PART IX: ASSESSMENT

Cost Effectiveness of Instructional Technology Alternatives

Frederick G. Knirk

Can a school district or a college afford to use "instructional technology?" Should they afford it? These are difficult questions to generalize about. Most generalized answers come from research involving the cost-effectiveness studies on the teaching–learning process. In these studies, we find a more relevant question: "How can one maximize learning and minimize the cost and time requirements?"

The instructional-technology-based teaching systems provide alternatives to the teacher-based teaching systems. We know that some teachers are "better" than others for particular students. Thus, we can generalize that some teacher-based systems are better than others. Behaviorally, this can be stated in the following manner: some teachers (1) help the students to like the course content and learning itself (output), (2) help the students to learn or reach the objectives (output), (3) require less time of the students to learn (input), and (4) require less money to help the students (input) than do other teachers. Some teacher-based systems are more cost effective than others in the sense that the "outputs" of the system are maximized and the "inputs" minimized. If a low-paid teacher does an

Frederick G. Knirk is an associate professor in the Department of Instructional Technology, University of Southern California, Los Angeles.

excellent job, then, according to our definition, a school board member can be fairly sure he has a cost-effective teacher or teaching system relative to other teacher-based systems. Unfortunately for this illustration, experience tends to improve a teacher so his or her output will increase with experience and thus the salary will increase. The real question still is, "What teaching system will be the most cost effective?"

To relate learning outputs to their required cost and time inputs, it is helpful to visualize the relationship of inputs to outputs in terms of efficiency. Learning efficiency would be in an ideal state if a student could take a "pill" and (1) know everything, (2) instantly, (3) at no cost. Although oversimplified, these are the three major components of a cost-effective formula for instruction. The efficiency of a teaching system is maximized by high objective attainment, minimum cost, and minimum student time, or

$$\text{efficiency} = \frac{\text{objective attainment}}{\text{cost} \times \text{time}}$$

It is important to restate here that cognitive, affective, and motor-skill objectives are all important. Most schools (thus teachers) want their students to like the learning process and the content as well as "knowing a lot." If these objectives are behaviorally stated, it is easier to know if the teaching system is doing its job. Behavioral measures of affective objectives may be reflected by attendance trends, tardiness to class, the number of books checked out of the library, and the like. Too seldom are affective objectives included in the determination of cost-effective instruction.

If the desired level of objective attainment is not obtained from a given teaching system, then that system should be eliminated from any further cost-effective analysis. A system that does not do its job is not worth anything and is certainly not cost effective. If the minimal level of acceptance for a set of objectives is that 80 percent of the students must get 85 percent on a test, then any teaching-system that cannot perform at that level must be rejected. The teacher, principal, curriculum coordinator, school board members, or other person(s) taking the responsibility for deciding to teach students reading (for example) by one method or system instead of another is the one who will make most of these objective attainment level decisions.

It has only been in the last two decades that instructional-technology-based systems have undergone the extensive evaluation and revision cycle required to generally ensure that the teaching materials could work almost independently of the teacher in the learning environment. These instructional-technology-based systems often require very little lesson preparation by the teacher, as the materials provide the structure, examples, reinforcement, and often motivation required for continuation of the subject area. These programmed instruction materials, computer-based materials, "teaching modules," "validated materials," or whatever they are called, provide the basis for teaching systems that sometimes allow students to learn a lot in a short period of time and at low relative costs to the taxpayers. These cost-effective materials should be used by curriculum planners in designing their programs.

Many cost decisions are made by individuals higher up the chain of command than the person who can take the responsibility for deciding on the acceptable level of objective attainment. The principal may have some discretionary funds but seldom can he make decisions to buy materials in a given year for amortization in future years. Seldom can he mix personnel and materials funds so that he could, for example, trade off a paraprofessional employee for some programmed materials. Cost-effective decisions are too frequently unobtainable when poor management exists.

The ex-mayor of New York, John Lindsay, was quoted on April 30, 1966, in the *New York Times*, while he was running for office, as saying "I am determined to analyze our educational expenditures and to insure that every dollar is spent with maximum effectiveness. . . . It is now almost impossible to make a meaningful analysis of the education budget in terms of specific goals, program elements, and program costs." When he left office, he still had not resolved this problem. On the West Coast, the California legislature attempted to mandate program planning budgeting systems (PPBS) procedures but it too became bogged down.

The tools that would help in making cost-effective curriculum decisions at the state or school level are available: flow charting, PERT, PPBS, dynamic analysis, min-max, and so on. Educators are infrequently trained in the use of these tools and techniques. This problem too must be overcome if cost-effective decisions are to become the rule rather than the exception.

Dialogues between instructional technologists and curriculum planners should be encouraged to resolve the real and imagined problems. One discussion, recently overheard, ran thus:

Question: How can we evaluate the cost effectiveness of instructional technology?

Answer: In general, educators should attempt to minimize the input and maximize the output of their systems just as other organizations do when they are concerned with their own effectiveness. Some experts recommend that student time be included in any analysis of instructional input requirements. They feel a student's time is valuable. In industry or the military, it is easy to determine the cost of the student's time—he is being paid; but in general education it is more difficult. We might say that one can evaluate the cost effectiveness of various instructional alternatives by determining those which require the least cost to the society and the minimum time requirement for the attainment of the desired instructional objectives. All these criterion will probably not be met by the same

alternative, so the decision process is not always simple.

Question: How will instructional output be determined?

Answer: By the same people who determine the instructional output today. Curriculum planners and the members of the society they serve will determine their objectives together. Instructional technologists would like to be considered a part of this group.

Question: What common denominator or unit can be used to measure these instructional input requirements?

Answer: The most common unit has been "cost per student per hour." The time expended by a teacher can be equated to dollar costs the same as the school plant and other services can. Although all educational economists do not concur that the cost unit should be based on a student-per-hour basis, this unit does allow comparability at a compact and usable time level.

Question: Will instructional-technology-based instruction be less expensive than conventional instruction?

Answer: If media are brought into an established and otherwise unchanged instructional system, the costs of using media will be additive; any media costs must be added to the existing instructional costs. A "savings" when using media is possible if (1) the teacher–pupil ratio is modified or if (2) the speed at which a student achieves his objective is measured and related to the cost for allowing a more efficient system. If the latter occurs, then more services may be offered to the student in the time he "saved."

Question: What are the actual costs of using instructional technology in cost-per-student-hour figures?

Answer: The answer to this question, unlike some of the other answers, which are merely difficult to provide, is impossible to provide at this time. Few research studies have specifically attacked the problem of costs, and the data that are available are inconsistent. Various instructional systems that make extensive use of television report from 2 to 20 cents per student per hour to use this medium. The basis for these costs is often extremely difficult to locate. In some cases the teacher costs and the amortized cost of the equipment is included and in others the administrative and overhead costs are also figured in. Other media cost data also fluctuate widely.

The rationale for technology in the home is evident. A washing machine is a time- and labor-saving device. Although you must initially spend some money to get the machine, most of us do it rather than take the clothes to the stream. The rationale for technology in the classroom is similar. Instructional technology can make learning more efficient.

BIBLIOGRAPHY

Bowman, Howard, and Douglass, Gordon, *Efficiency in Liberal Education.* New York: McGraw-Hill Book Company, 1971.

Jamison, Dean, Suppes, Patrick, and Wells, Stuart, "The Effectiveness of Alternative Instructional Media." *Review of Educational Research,* Winter 1974, Vol. 44, No. 1, pp. 1–68.

Machlup, Fritz, *The Production and Distribution of Knowledge in the United States.* Princeton, N.J.: Princeton University Press, 1962.

Umans, Shelley, *How to Cut the Cost of Education.* New York: McGraw-Hill Book Company, 1973.

Performance Accountability in Teacher Education

Simon J. Chavez

The winds of performance accountability sweeping the country, coupled with the growing desire of the teaching profession to achieve autonomy, seem destined to produce a dramatic change in teacher education. There seems to be little doubt that there will be a demand for accountability. Before accountability can occur, there is a need to determine who is accountable for the different components of preparation. The university cannot continue to consider itself the sole guardian of the preservice training of prospective teachers. Nor can the school system claim that in-service education is its exclusive domain. Education of teachers is a responsibility that must be shared in a school–university partnership.

The need for shared responsibility is clear. Yet it is not enough to agree that colleges use public facilities. The random assignment of student teachers to all schools, with teachers taking turns accepting student teachers is not conducive to accountability. What is needed are partnership schools.

Partnership schools would enable universities and school systems to share in the preparation and

Simon J. Chavez is chairman of elementary education, University of Dayton, Dayton, Ohio.

continuing education of teachers. The partnership school should not be limited to supplying experiences in student teaching, but should go much further. It should be a prototype of the newest and most efficient models—a laboratory in learning, providing quality education to its pupils while affording increasing involvement to prospective teachers from freshman to senior year. It should be staffed by experts in teaching who could demonstrate in practice the best theories of learning and instruction. In addition, it should include clinical professors from the university who would work in teams with teachers to seek and demonstrate promising innovations.

Establishment of partnership schools is only the first step toward accountability. In addition, there is need to define the processes required. This demands that the school–university partnership specify the benefits derived by those involved—teachers, pupils, student teachers, and university faculty. In essence, this need calls for a systems approach that not only identifies what we are doing, but collects the data that may give us insight into what we ought to do.

The first step in applying the scientific process to the problem of teacher preparation is the collection of data that can be analyzed. We need to know what information is likely to be useful. The following is an attempt to outline the types of information that we should begin to seek, although the topics will need greater amplification. Basically, this outline points to the following major topics: values accruing to those involved, entrance factors for newcomers in the program, data gathering instruments, data processing, and changes sought by partnership.

DESIGN OF PARTNERSHIP ACCOUNTABILITY

1. What values result from the partnership program of teacher education?
   A. To pupils:
      (1) Do pupils achieve more than if there were no teacher education program at this school? Specify gains shown on standardized tests.
      (2) Are there some desirable pupil outcomes in addition to those reflected in achievement scores? Specify changes in observable behavior of pupils and on community reaction.
   B. To cooperating teachers:
      (1) Do cooperating teachers perform differently because of the teacher education program? What specific changes have occurred since beginning the program?
      (2) What specific provisions for personal and professional growth have accompanied this program (planning, experimenting, sharing)?
      (3) What provisions have been made to help the teachers attain needed competencies?
      (4) What provisions exist for sharing, teamwork, and differentiated roles?
   C. To university students (prospective teachers):
      (1) What provision is made to combine theory and practice in courses and related field experiences? Specify.
      (2) What provisions have been made to involve students in their learning (planning, experimenting, analyzing, modifying)?
   D. To university faculty:
      (1) How are faculty selected (experience, specialization)?
      (2) What provision is made for continuing professional growth?
      (3) What provisions exist for participation in teams with classroom teachers?
2. What factors need to be assessed upon entrance into the program?
   A. Pupil factors:
      (1) Cultural background
      (2) Socioeconomic status

(3) Level of deprivation (enrichment experiences)
(4) Level of language development
  a. Auditory discrimination
  b. Visual discrimination
  c. Attentiveness
B. Teacher factors:
(1) Preservice teacher
  a. Initial perceptions and concerns related to self
    personal strengths
    personal weaknesses
    areas of needed development
  b. Initial perceptions and concerns toward teaching
    perception of what a teacher is
    reasons for wishing to be a teacher
    concerns about how to facilitate pupils' learning
  c. Attitudes
    enthusiasm toward learning and teaching
    sensitivity to children
    sensitivity to culturally different people
    attitude toward authority
    attitude toward work
  d. Personality
    concept of self
    reaction to frustration
    desire to risk and experiment
    feelings of adequacy affection
  e. Demographic background
    socioeconomic status
    cultural heritage
    experience with other cultures
    experience in leadership roles
    experience with creativity
(2) In-service teacher
  a. Present perceptions and concerns
    perception of role as a teacher
    perception of role as a supervisor
    perception of relationship to clinical professor

    perception of the value of teacher education
    commitment to teaching as a career
  b. Attitudes
    enthusiasm toward inquiry
    sensitivity to children
    sensitivity to culturally different people
  c. Personality
    concept of self
    feelings of adequacy (security)
    reaction to frustration
    desire to risk and experiment
    affection
  d. Demographic background
    socioeconomic status
    cultural heritage
    experience with other cultures
    experience in leadership roles
    experience with creativity
3. What instruments are needed to gather data?
  A. Biographical inventories
  B. Standardized tests
  C. Informal tests
  D. Opinionnaires
  E. Anecdotal accounts
  F. Self-reporting accounts
  G. Audio recordings
  H. Video recordings
4. How are data to be processed?
  A. Analysis of audio and video recordings
  B. Analysis of test scores
  C. Correlation of biographical data
  D. Utilization of computer system
5. What provisions does the program make to promote change in the partnership school?
  A. In-service education:
    (1) Involvement in development of program
      a. Provisions for planning
      b. In-service seminars
      c. Participation in teams
    (2) Refinement of teacher competencies
      a. Diagnosis of learning

b. Strategies of teaching
c. Analysis of instruction
d. Group dynamics
e. Action research
f. Individualized instruction

B. Preservice education:
(1) Personal–professional development
   a. Use of counseling to personalize learning
   b. Responsibility for learning
   c. Self-realization
   d. Communication skills
(2) Development of teaching skills
   a. Preactive planning and preparation
   b. Strategies of teaching
   c. Diagnosis
   d. Instructional categories
(3) Substantive background
   a. Anthropological basis
   b. Economic power
   c. Political involvement
   d. Cultural heritage
   e. Industrial culture
(4) Aesthetic experiences

C. Improvement of learning environment in partnership school:
(1) Community involvement
(2) Learning centers

D. Provision of instructional materials:
(1) Variety for individual needs and interests

E. Changes in curricular patterns:
(1) Interdisciplinary approach
(2) Inquiry processes
(3) Nongradedness
(4) Flexible scheduling
(5) Flexible grouping

F. Changes in administrative practices:
(1) Differentiated roles in staffing
(2) Ascending levels of specialization
(3) Use of instructional teams
(4) Provisions for staff planning, conceptualization, study, and evaluation

(5) Provisions for coordination with system, university, teacher organization, and community

ANTICIPATED OUTCOMES

The preparation of teachers has been a process of apprenticeship and transmission of folklore. Prospective teachers hear accounts of how their professors coped with situations in the past. They are encouraged to observe their supervising teachers before they practice doing the same things. Evaluation of performance in student teaching has leaned heavily toward following prescribed techniques. Little or no information is consistently collected to compare experiences at one time and one situation with other times and other situations.

Medley describes research in teaching as Baconian: "We do not know enough about the dimensions of the teaching act to be sure, when we plan an experiment, that we are not neglecting or controlling out the most important variable."

In a career that should be highly scientific, we have not yet collected raw data to be sifted for significant variables. We cannot be sure what variables are significant: What teacher behaviors produce what pupil behaviors? How do these behaviors vary with differing situations or differing backgrounds of pupils? How are these behaviors, or the recording and feedback, influenced by the perceptions of the one making the observation or analyzing the behavior? We do not know.

What seems obvious is a need to collect data that might lead to a hypothesis for identification of significant variables used in facilitating behavioral modification. We might even begin by leapfrogging into some hypothesis. One such hunch has been made that what a teacher is may be more important than what a teacher does. It is on the basis of such hunches that collection of data might be directed toward self-perceptions, personality factors, attitudes, and demographic background. In any case, let's begin to explore the dimensions with which we are dealing.

What Do You Contribute to Our Operation?

Henry C. Ruark

Not so many weeks ago, just before his school system opened with an intensive in-service week for all teachers, a friend of mine called me. He obviously had his foot on the panic button, hard.

His superintendent had just greeted him, on the day his vacation ended, with a very simple question: *What do you contribute to operation of our school system?* This superintendent was brutal enough to want facts and figures, not generalizations and slogans. This administrator's dilemma with the school board was real enough and practical enough, however; they *had* to cut *somewhere*.

What would you have told my friend, when he asked me what he should do *now* to justify a program that has been in operation for 10 years?

That's *just* what I told him, too. *He should have started 10 years ago* to get ready, to make sure he had the answers when the inevitable question came from management: What are we getting for all these dollars?

But he hadn't *been* there 10 years ago when his system first got started; his tenure goes back only 4 years, and he has been running like mad to stay ahead of demand and make the best use of every dollar and dime and minute, all that time.

So I made some suggestions, for what they were worth for him:

1. For 10 years of operation there had to be basic accounting for time and services, even if buried in school district office records. Much ammunition was available there, from capital outlay figures for each year, through numbers of learning situations serviced; types and kinds of materials circulated; teachers helped through in-service programs; publications, guides, catalogs produced.

2. A large part of his capital outlay during that decade had to come from federal- and state-granted funds, money the school district would probably never have spent otherwise. These funds were inevitably granted in large part because there was a basic learning support system to act as the medium of effective management for those dollars. It is hard to quarrel with specialized materials and equipment acquired with someone else's money; there *is a strength to be shown* when it can be proved that the district dollar often can bring in a state and a federal dollar to match or supplement its own impact.

3. His school district controller could give him specific cost-per-pupil figures he found, broken down by buildings serviced. On examination, he was able to show that those figures were economically better in schools where teachers were supported by effective media services; *more pupils* were handled in *more kinds* and *types* of activities, with better results, in those schools where strong and effective media operations were carried on.

4. His own institutional materials center operational records showed a steady and strong increase in teacher demand for materials over most of the 10-year history of the support system, with an accelerating rate during the past 5 years.

5. Another pertinent and relevant fact emerged from his study of all these statistics—there was much less teacher turnover (about 10 to 15 percent

difference) in those schools where materials and learning support equipment were strongest.

Furthermore, in some of the schools where teachers did seek to move on more rapidly, principals and the personnel manager were able to supply statements which linked their leaving to teaching conditions, *lack of materials and support, poor or little effective in-service work on new methods, materials, and techniques,* and other similar situations.

Would you believe that some teachers had even said they would prefer effective working conditions supported by modern teaching media and learning tools to a routine raise in pay? It is true; some realize that any practical-level raises are going to be heavily cut by inflation, and that their true rewards can come more effectively in better working conditions and increased satisfactions as they are able to do a better job.

All this took a number of weeks; and even with all this information, professionally presented with simple, clear graphics and a minimum of selling-pitch comment, my friend was unable to ward off some reduction in his budget.

But he did satisfy management that his operation was contributing in many ways to a more effective learning enterprise than could exist without its services; that in 10 years teachers had come to count on media and methods supportable only through such services; and that the damage and disillusionment and destruction of *teacher morale* and *instructional effectiveness,* due to deeper cuts, would be much more costly than could be covered by any dollar savings.

Perhaps the most important outcome will be that he has learned a lesson many more media administrators still must learn:

Someday, management is going to ask you to be accountable beyond what you now consider necessary—today's budgeting routines and reports.

Before too many more years, we are going to have to provide specific performance-proof of *media-in-action with learners and teachers,* as part of a general demand facing every element of the educational system.

Solving problems today can never do more than create the status quo *as it was before the problem*; management by crisis after crisis is no longer good enough, in the *economic* marketplace nor the *educational*.

And if you think you are *not* in the educational marketplace, just sit there complacent, comfortable, nonchalant—and ignorant. Your superintendent will teach you differently, any day now.

Standards for Educational Equipment: Evaluation and Validation Considerations

Philip W. Tiemann

Evaluation is a judgment-making process. Evaluation requires criteria, the variables of which are somehow measurable within a range from subjective to objective. The worth of judgments made depends upon the validity of criteria and the reliability of measurement. In this respect, evaluation is an iterative process. Successive attempts at evaluation permit refined measurement. Reliability increases as measures increase in objectivity (or as observers become more consistent when rating subjectively); and validity increases as more relevant criteria are identified and weighted accordingly, thus increasing the worth of judgments.

At any point during evaluation, a second process may take place—the setting of standards. A standard is an agreed-upon point or permissible range along a "score scale" of a criterion variable selected so as to accomplish some objective, for example, cost saving, administrative convenience, or minimum safety provision. The worth of any standard is a function of the validity of the criterion upon which it is based (which may depend upon how far the related iterative process of evaluation

Philip W. Tiemann is head of the course development division of the Office of Instructional Resources and associate professor of education at the University of Illinois, Chicago, Illinois.

Used with the permission of the author and publisher from *Educational Consumer,* H. Lundgaard, ed., Educational Media Council, Washington, D.C., 1973, pp. 51–60.

has proceeded) and of the degree of consensus with respect to the point or range which "defines" the standard. Once acted upon, the worth of standards may be investigated using the same regression techniques which are applied to express relationships between evaluation judgments and their consequences. In this respect, standards may be open to inspection and improvement, as may evaluation criteria.

Education equipment The term "educational equipment" refers to a variety of capital items across several categories, including school furniture and noninstructional equipment, and manipulanda in such forms as scientific apparatus, machine tools, gym gear, typewriters, Cuisenaire rods, or three-dimensional models. Another category is media. Educational media equipment is used to represent (to some degree) the real world— the tangible reality of field trips, manipulanda, and resource people, including teachers.

The term "educational equipment" is synonymous in one sense with "communication equipment"—a term which, although technically accurate, might best be avoided for two reasons. First, communication equipment too often connotes passive, one-way transmission of a stimulus. But the representation of reality to students (e.g., representation of a teacher or other resource person) may require some provision for active participation during the communication process to enable effective and efficient attainment of the educational goals by the student.

Second, "educational equipment" is employed not only to represent some slice of reality (i.e., to communicate some stimulus content) but also to enable students to attain some expanded capability, based on skills or appreciations acquired as a result of the educational experience. For this reason, determining the effect of the communication experience in terms of increased capability of the student must be a universal criterion, a primary concern in any evaluation of communication equipment used as educational equipment. The

effectiveness capability is treated here as one of the functional criteria of equipment.

CRITERIA LEADING TO STANDARDS

Equipment advantages Given some educational function to perform—that is, some reality to be represented—it seems logical to assume that to gain some advantage one or more components of educational equipment could be employed in preference to different equipment. This assumption suggests two important sets of criteria. First, advantages to be realized might be reflected in greater effectiveness (i.e., more educational goals attained by students, including affective considerations) as well as greater efficiency (i.e., reduced commitment of resources in terms of money, scarce materials, student time and effort, and staff time and effort). Second, items of educational equipment which are functionally equivalent may differ with respect to such factors as cost, reliability of operation (including maintenance), ease of operation, and availability.[1]

It thus appears that choosing a particular item of educational equipment requires a series of judgments to optimize the effect of several variables.

Effectiveness Instructional effectiveness—that is, provision for an increment of student capability—must be assured. The primary criterion is that the equipment must provide the representative function, the level of representation of the real world required by the educational situation. Such a determination is most properly made in the process of instructional planning. The media selection phase of instructional design has been a topic of analysis and comment by several writers (see Briggs et al., 1967; Gagné, 1970).

Tiemann (1968) has proposed a selection rationale based upon analysis of the objectives of instruction to identify the stimulus requirements of any communication. For example, terminal performance of students may require discrimination or generalization with respect to certain features of motion. The same objectives also may require the student to attend to and to generalize or discriminate certain sounds. An equipment item capable of representing both motion and sound would be indicated.

The rationale provides for stimulus properties identified as spatial (three-dimensional), color, motion, sound, tactile, taste, odor, and verbal description. Levels of representation from complete abstraction to "augmented" reality are postulated for each of these properties, guiding first-draft selection of equipment. Unsatisfactory attainment of students during developmental testing trials may suggest a shift to a "higher" representation level, usually at a greater production or distribution cost. Along the color continuum, for example, unsatisfactory student performance after viewing black and white television with "color-labels" might dictate a shift to color television or, if not available, simultaneous projection of color slides.

From the viewpoint of the stimulus requirements of the communication, as determined by design analysis, it can be seen that virtually no item of equipment provides unique capabilities for stimulus representation. A first task, however, is to identify those items of equipment that will provide the necessary representation appropriate to the intent of instruction as one factor of effectiveness.

Gagné (1970) has proposed additional functions of instruction that contribute to effectiveness and may occasionally influence the initial selection of a list of appropriate equipment. Among these are gaining and maintaining attention, ensuring recall of previously acquired knowledge, guidance in the form of verbal or visual "cues" or "hints," provision of feedback, establishing conditions for transfer, and assessment of outcomes.

Efficiency Consideration of these and possibly other effectiveness factors will limit the selection by function to certain equipment types. Next, it is appropriate to consider the relative advantages of these types with respect to the variables that influence efficiency within the parameters of the educational system where instruction will take place. As mentioned before, these variables would seem to include such criteria as cost, reliability of operation, ease of operation, and availability. Given adequate instructional effectiveness, these variables would seem to provide the criteria for establishing efficiency standards.

TYPES OF POSSIBLE STANDARDS

Standards which might be based upon the criteria mentioned are here identified in terms of general types.[2] (Procedures employed to set standards, and review of specific standards derived, are discussed elsewhere.) Thus, general types are set forth here in order to proceed to a discussion of evaluation and validation considerations with respect to these types.

Cost Understandably, educational administrators react to the cost factor. One of their effective instruments for establishing minimum cost is the referral for quotation procedure. The implementation of such procedures causes (or should cause) administrators to seek advice from their own or other equipment "experts" for adequate bidding specifications.

In this respect, the decentralization of educational purchasers—each dependent upon limited experience for evaluation of equipment quality—results in possible inconsistent specifications and attendant misuse of resources. The availability of standards would tend to improve the quality of specifications and also would conserve costs and the scarce resources of staff time devoted to evaluation that now occurs through personal contact, in-house data, biased information from sales representatives, and other limited sources presently depended upon for specification decisions. Standards with respect to cost per se would be of little use.

Functional capabilities It does not appear feasible to attempt to establish standards with respect to equipment capabilities that provide for those functions of educational communication exerting the most direct influence upon the paramount issue of effectiveness of instruction, for example, level of representation of reality, provision for active student response, or pacing capability. Once instructional intent has been matched with those items of equipment possessing functional capability to represent that intent (i.e., the media selection issue), then effectiveness is directly related to the quality of educational software employed.

In the earlier discussion of function, a media selection rationale was suggested as useful in identifying "situation-specific" standards during instructional design that could serve as guidelines for later developmental test trials with students, possibly leading to selection of different equipment. However, media effects are difficult to isolate from software effects. The ability to distinguish and associate effects with their appropriate causes also depends upon the experience of personnel conducting such formative evaluation both of materials and media. General standards just do not appear feasible.

Ease of operation The commitment of staff and student time will vary with the relative ease of equipment operation, whether operated by students individually, by instructional staff, or by support personnel on site, in a projection booth, from a central broadcast area, or other access facility. The criterion of greatest validity with respect to instructional effectiveness is that of the amount of time which, if committed by the instructional staff to set up or operate equipment, may cancel other activities and adversely affect the quality of instruction.

It is apparent that ease of operation interacts with cost. Relatively "operator proof" equipment (e.g., cartridge-loading projectors or recorders) can be purchased at added expense. With lesser equipment, teachers or students whose efforts might otherwise turn film projectors into film shredders (thus increasing materials costs) could be trained as operators; or operators could be provided. Any such provisions result in increased cost. Data available on the factor of comparative ease of operation would enable equipment users to make rational purchase decisions; optimum planning for operator training, if required; and equipment allocation according to existing operator capabilities.

Reliability of operation Reliability is used here to refer to equipment resistance to malfunction and casualty. Mean time before failure is a primary variable. Also included in reliability criteria might be routine maintenance intervals, and expense for maintenance and spare parts.

Obviously, reliability interacts with cost. Low-maintenance equipment usually implies increased initial cost. The availability and level of skill of maintenance personnel is a function of local resources committed. Training of maintenance and operating personnel increases cost. But local decisions with respect to such commitments depend upon the reliability of equipment.

If equipment reliability data were available, prospective purchasers could make informed trade-offs between initial acquisition costs and subsequent operating costs.

Emerging standards Emerging standards are those which exist in situations conventionall referred to as "compatibility problems," where the degree of consensus is not yet sufficient to result in standards of acceptable utility. Educational materials—that is, "software" items prepared to the "standard" appropriate for one or more items of equipment—are often incompatible for use with all other equipment.

The "hardware" compatibility problem arises only in respect to "software." Typically, some equipment has been acquired, often prematurely; and prospective users find that the materials planned for instruction are incompatible with the equipment available. The compatibility problem seldom arises if materials acquisition is able to precede equipment acquisition. And a teacher with effective "software" and one matching item of efficient equipment does not perceive any problem at all!

Equipment flexibility is one means typically employed to resolve the emerging standards issued. Phonographs having three or four turntable speeds are an example of flexibility afforded the user, obviously at some increase in equipment cost. However, for the user with no "software" problem—for example, possessing only 45-rpm records—the cost saving afforded by a single-purpose 45-rpm player may be realized.

If purchasers must acquire equipment in advance of materials, access to reliability and ease of operation standards would enable them to make decisions on the basis of the best available data, identifying the trade-off point between cost and level of quality and flexibility which they could afford.

Availability The necessity for having equipment available is the criterion followed to establish recommended inventory standards. A recent revision of such recommendations has been completed by the American Library Association and the National Education Association (1969).

EVALUATION AND VALIDATION OF STANDARDS

Efforts which result in quality evaluation and validation of standards for educational equipment require adequate commitment of resources in terms of time, capable personnel, data-processing expense, and distribution of results. Current limitations of funds suggest selection as to which types of standards require priority evaluation or validation. Cost and functional capability of equipment are not at issue here, because standards based upon these criteria do not appear to possess any predictive validity, as previously discussed.

Evaluation will be optimally costeffective if the bulk of efforts is directed to formative evaluation, that is, with considerable attention to evaluation during the process of standard setting. This would seem to require an interaction between information available from equipment manufacturers which specifies "what should be" (e.g., what should be the level of operator training) and from field observations of use which enable observers to determine "what is" (e.g., what is the median setup time in real classrooms).

Having thus established standards, the validation process—which could be viewed as analogous to summative evaluation—would be one of promulgating the established standards and of adequate field sampling to determine whether personnel are able to make use of the standards. Both questionnaire and interview processes would be appropriate, with emphasis upon the design objectives for creation of standards, to determine if the objectives are achieved by the use of standards in the field. For example, do equipment purchases based upon reliability standards require less commitment to specification writing and result in controlled maintenance costs?

Base of operation Standards with respect to ease of operation should be evaluated and validated as a first priority because of the relatively direct relationship between this criterion and instructional effectiveness. These standards are most likely to be expressed in terms of setup times, a fairly objective standard, or operator convenience, a fairly subjective standard, with respect to less complicated equipment. More complex equipment will most likely require standards which express level of competencies for operators—perhaps in terms of specific skills, the most valid measure, or in terms of training courses completed, a less valid measure.

In any event, the only appropriate data source for evaluation and validation is instructional personnel in the field, preferably teachers conducting or supervising instruction. It is important to make a distinction between service personnel, trained operators or audiovisual center people, and the constituents of their service—the teachers and possibly the students. A student who reports ease of operation of equipment in an audiotutorial laboratory will provide valid data, as will a teacher who must set up and use equipment. An inquiry of audiovisual personnel or of manufacturers' recommendations would be invalid and would not justify the cost involved in evaluation and validation.

Reliability of operation   Reliability would be an appropriate second priority. Reliability standards, most likely expressed in maintenance times and costs, must be evaluated and validated by investigation of on-site performance of equipment. To be valid, formative evaluation to establish standards must take into account the operational requirements placed upon equipment and the existing level of capability of maintenance personnel doing the work. While some form of centralized coordinating center might serve as a data-collection agent and, occasionally, a pretesting center, the primary data source should again be actual results in the field.

Eventually, standards might be refined with regard to such factors as level of training of operator and maintenance personnel, number of different operators using an item of equipment during a time period, and so forth.

Availability   Validation of the ALA/NEA (1969) recommended equipment inventory levels would appear to be a next priority. While availability seems to be at a level of concern equivalent to that of reliability, the use of recommended equipment levels must always be considered as open to interpretation in terms of local needs. A school, having identified a need for one particular item of equipment, is in more immediate need of validated reliability data than of information recommending two such items for that particular school.

Obviously, actual situations in the field are again the valid source for data. Investigation could profitably extend to interview of instructional staff to disclose what they might do if provided with additional capabilities.

Emerging standards   Resources committed to evaluation or validation of emerging standards which are, by definition, subject to less than useful consensus would result in the least-cost-effective expenditure of available funds. In addition, it should be recognized that the problems of compatibility which appear to be so severe to the service organizations, the audiovisual specialists, are of minor consequence to their constituents, the instructional staff.

Those few instructors who design and produce their own materials are usually working with equipment which has been available for some time. For them, the issue of compatibility would be irrelevant as they would prepare their materials for use with available equipment. However, the majority of educators seek and use commercially available materials, most of which have been prepared for use on standardized equipment. Since the compatibility issue is a secondary economic concern within the total educational system, the evaluation and validation of standards in this respect should be expected to rate a minor share of the available resources.

FURTHER OBSERVATIONS AND RECOMMENDATIONS

It would seem to be an exercise in futility to commit limited funds to establishment and validation of equipment standards when few materials available for presentation with the equipment are of demonstrated effectiveness (Komoski, 1971; Markle, 1970). One might ask what is to be gained by being optimally efficient in distributing instruction of undetermined effectiveness to students. However, indiscriminate acquisition of educational materials may be expected to continue—and there is a certain logic which argues for efficient distribution. One can hope that those educators purchasing materials will become more discriminating, and will be permitted the rights and resources necessary to adapt these usually copyrighted materials for optimally effective local use.

At any rate, the commitment of funds necessary to establish and validate standards should only commence when some reasonable assurance exists that the resulting standards will, in fact, have an effect upon our educational system and its suppliers.

Central coordination   A coordinating organization at the national level could assume most of the standard-setting tasks presently conducted, but seldom formalized, at the lowest levels of the system and now performed in a relatively inefficient and expensive manner. The centralized organization might take a form similar to that of the Underwriters Laboratory with the functions of developing, field testing, and revising techniques and procedures for continuous evaluation and validation of performance-based standards. The objectives of one member organization of the Educational Media Council, the Educational Products Information Exchange, have been similar in many respects to those projected for a coordinating standards organization.

To date, however, the effect upon the education system resulting from efforts to gain acceptance of availability standards and to approximate quality standards have been, indeed, meager (President's Commission on Instructional Technology, 1970). It is reasonable to question whether public funds should be committed either to development of equipment standards or to the creation of an adequately funded central standards facility (not to mention the purchase of the equipment itself) when no contingencies other than routine auditing operations exist to ensure a valid accountability for even an indirect effect of equipment upon the quality of instruction conducted by the public educational system.

Perhaps public funding of standards should be contingent upon establishment of some mechanisms of public control, designed to provide reasonable assurance that increments of quality will result. Since the issue is basically a matter of the allocation of limited resources, economists should be consulted.

Countervailing power   The concept of countervailing power as advocated by Galbraith (1952) would appear applicable. Briefly, when consumers are decentralized in relationship to produce sources, economic power rests with the producers. To retain their decentralized consumer market, producers find it necessary to respond at only a minimal level to consumer needs, that is, levels of reliability and ease of operation. Thus, the educational market, with its decentralized demand, has been "satisfied" in many cases with whatever level of quality of appropriateness was provided to the mass market.[3]

To deal with the problem, Galbraith proposes the concept of countervailing power, which is achieved through consumer cooperatives possessing one source of product demand capable of negotiating quality level and quantity cost as a precondition of purchase. A purchasing cooperative of such nature, while providing for cost-effective allocation of public funds, would not necessarily need to be established within a central government organization. Once established, however, the purchase functions of the cooperative would be guided indirectly by the validated standards available from the centralized educational equipment standards laboratory.

Cooperative purchasing   Administrative organizations at the lowest levels, even individual schools, would be free to consult available performance-based standards, make model and manufacturer decisions based upon local needs and funding, set cutoff delivery dates, and forward their purchase orders to the cooperative for final processing.

A cooperative might make purchases contingent upon manufacturer cooperation with the standards laboratory. New equipment under development could be forwarded by the laboratory to the field for on-site trial, with initial evaluation providing development and revision data to the manufacturer. Such trials could also provide "preliminary" standards data, providing for early discussion of emerging standards by all interested parties.

Federal agencies could benefit from the available validated standards to assure cost-effective expenditure of public funds. Such assurance could be gained simply by directing expenditure of federal funds only through the purchasing cooperative, thus ensuring that local needs and preferences at the point-of-use level would be reflected in all purchase decisions.

Need for valid standards It should be obvious that these recommendations should not be implemented unless validated standards are available to support the rational functioning of such a funding allocation system. Lacking such a system, that is, lacking some reasonable assurance that the existence of standards have an effect on the capabilities of our schools, it is questionable whether public funds should be allocated to the expensive process of developing, evaluating, and validating standards for educational equipment.

NOTES

1. Notice that the use of functionally equivalent equipment may be expected to result in instruction to a given level of effectiveness. As an example, two 16mm projectors used alternately with the same film would not be expected to account for variance in the effectiveness of instruction attributable to that film. However, equivalence in the representative function may vary across similar items of equipment. Two color television monitors of different quality might contribute to differential effectiveness of instruction if the reality being represented (i.e., the stimulus content of instruction) required color discrimination.

2. Panelists during the seminar recognized a concern for three types of equipment standards, as set forth in the summary, to include instructional quality standards, performance standards, and technical standards. As discussed here, quality standards influence the effectiveness of instruction; performance standards or, more precisely, performance specifications of equipment influence efficiency of instruction; and technical standards are related to the compatibility issue, discussed later in terms of emerging standards.

3. For example, one company's decision to limit its new 8mm film cartridge to a 4-minute running time was based on home use of 8mm cameras which generally accommodate 4 minutes of film in each load." John K. Hemphill, Director, Far West Laboratory for Educational Research and Development, quoted from letter to the Commission on Instructional Technology, July, 1968, in *To Improve Learning: An Evaluation of Instructional Technology*, Vol. I, Part 1, ed. by S. G. Tickton, New York: R. R. Bowker, 1970, p. 80.

REFERENCES

ALA/NEA. *Standards for School Media Programs*. Washington, D.C.: American Library Association and National Education Association, 1969.

Briggs, L. J., P. L. Campeau, R. M. Gagné, and M. A. May. *Instructional Media: A Procedure for the Design of Multimedia Instruction, A Critical Review of Research, and Suggestions for Future Research*. Pittsburgh, Pa.: American Institute for Research, 1967.

Gagné, R. M. "Learning Theory, Educational Media, and Individualized Instruction," in *To Improve Learning: An Evaluation of Instructional Technology*, Vol. I, Part 3, ed. by S. G. Tickton. New York: R. R. Bowker, 1970, pp. 61–74.

Galbraith, J. K. *American Capitalism: The Concept of Countervailing Power*. Boston: Houghton Mifflin, 1952.

Komoski, P. K. "$50,000,000 Educational Consumers Can't Be Wrong—But Who's Listening?" *Audiovisual Instruction* (Sept. 1971), pp. 13–15.

Markle, Susan M. "Programming and Programmed Instruction," in *To Improve Learning: An Evaluation of Instructional Technology*, Vol. I, Part 2, ed. by S. C. Tickton. New York: R. R. Bowker, 1970, pp. 293–297.

President's Commission on Instructional Technology. "To Improve Learning," in *To Improve Learning: An Evaluation of Instructional Technology*, Vol. I, Part 1, ed. by S. C. Tickton. New York: R. R. Bowker, 1970, pp. 7–104.

Tiemann, P. W. "Selecting Instructional Media," Presentation to the Advanced Institute, Annual Convention of the National Society for Programmed Instruction. San Antonio, April 1968.

Audiovisual In-Service Training

John J. Chalmers

In-service training can be used by a school system to fulfill its responsibility to keep teachers informed. Hence the audiovisual supervisor must recognize that a large and very important part of his work is involved with the in-service training of teachers in materials, equipment, technology, and methodology that did not exist when the teachers themselves were attending university.

While preservice training will tend to be generalized, audiovisual in-service work will tend to be specialized, and many times will take up where preservice training left off. In-service training should be designed to result in better job performance by teachers through instructing them in better utilization of media. Such instruction will require that teachers be taught some theory of media application, new skills such as those needed for preparation of instructional material, and even nitty-gritty things like how to change a projector bulb.

However, it should not be implied that the audiovisual supervisor merely shovels information to teachers and they soak it all in. Some responsibil-

John J. Chalmers is assistant audiovisual supervisor at the Instructional Materials Center, Edmonton Public School Board, Alberta, Canada.

ity surely rests with the teachers, but the audiovisual supervisor should offer the opportunity for teachers to profit from in-service sessions. "Even in classrooms where technology is employed widely and wisely, its success or failure depends on the extent to which the teacher perceives and applies new instructional models. It is for these reasons and others that there is a great and continuing concern for the extent to which pre- and in-service programs provide for the development of media competencies in teachers," says W. C. Meierhenry (in "Media Competencies for Teachers," *AV Instruction*, Jan. 1969).

In-service training can translate theory, research, and new technological developments into classroom practicality, but it does not have to be purely pragmatic; it can also keep teachers up to date on theory and research. However, the most important objective of media in-service training is to make teachers more competent through wise use of mediated instruction.

The in-service program should be consistent with the goals and objectives of teaching and educational trends, so that it does not become a spectator sport. A session on the operation of portable videotape equipment, even if well attended, would be of little use if the teachers didn't have a chance to use it.

In-service planning, like curriculum planning, should be planned in behavioral objectives to affect teachers and their methods. Also, like curriculum planning, in-service training requires progressional instruction in a continuous program which may move from general to specific, to immediate needs, or vice versa, depending on the situation.

Five of the many areas of audiovisual management which can be dealt with in in-service training are selection, utilization, production, evaluation and distribution. Each area may be considered briefly as to what implication it has for in-service training.

Selection of both materials and equipment requires that the teacher know what materials and

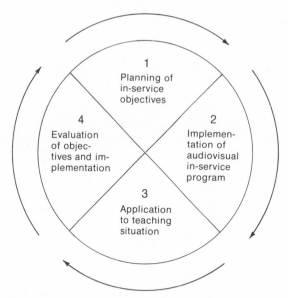

Figure 1
Four steps in continuous in-service development.

equipment are best suited to the instructional purpose, and know what is available. Critical analysis and an understanding of selection criteria will help a teacher make a wise choice.

Utilization of media for effective teaching requires that the teacher be given some instruction in the methodology of using media and in the actual operation of equipment. A knowledge of current trends in teaching, future possibilities, curriculum application and available facilities will help the teacher use media.

Production of instructional materials can fill a gap where no comercially produced materials are available. To do this, teachers will need some training in such techniques as mounting and laminating pictures, using graphics, making overhead projector transparencies, using the camera, recording tapes, and so on.

Evaluation of the use of media in the light of the objectives of teaching is one of the prime things that in-service teachers should learn to encourage effective use of media.

Distribution procedures of materials and equip-

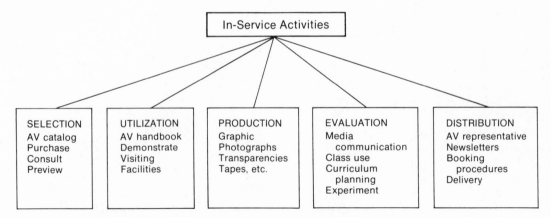

Figure 2
Representative sampling of the ways to realize the objectives of in-service activities.

ment both within a school and from a central system instructional materials center should be known to teachers. Working through in-service sessions, communication channels, and representatives in the schools, the audiovisual supervisor can ensure that the teachers know what resources are available to them and how they go about getting them.

In-service training should supplement and follow up preservice training, and be related to problems and facilities within a school system. For example, the Teachers' Workroom at the Instructional Mate-

rials Center (IMC) of the Edmonton Public School Board can be used as an in-service lab for instructions, and then be used later by teachers to prepare instructional materials on their own after they have learned how it's done.

In-service training can also be for students, who can be trained as equipment monitors, projectionists, and so on. In a large system this training likely will be a job to be done by the audiovisual representatives or teachers wtihin their own schools. Teachers, too, should know how to oper-

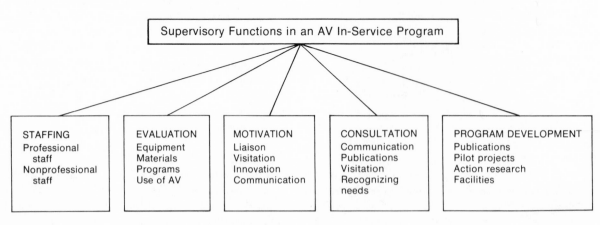

Figure 3

ate equipment, for they must be in a position to instruct students in audiovisual equipment operation, but still assume responsibility for it.

In working with intern teachers, the audiovisual supervisor can acquaint neophytes with his services while they are between college and full-time practice. In-service training for interns can include opportunities for observation, theory, lab work, practice, and presentation of lessons using audiovisual approaches.

Teacher aides and volunteer parent assistants can also be given in-service training appropriate to their duties. Because such persons often work closely with the teacher in the classroom, instruction in the preparation of materials can be particularly useful.

Audiovisual representatives (or building coordinators, as they may be called) in schools cannot be ignored. Because many such teachers already have university training or practical experience in audiovisual application, their in-service training may consist of coordinating central office services with schools or assisting the audiovisual representatives to operate their own programs within their own schools.

Building coordinators usually have little time, if any, for their duties and should be given some guidance as to what they are since they have taken on the additional responsibility or have had it thrust upon them. Contact with representatives through in-service sessions, newsletters, and personal visits can let the building coordinator know that his work is needed, necessary, and appreciated.

Central office personnel also need to know about the operation of the system's audiovisual services, although they may not need to learn the same skills as teachers. The program for them may take the form of public relations and information.

Thus it can be seen that the audiovisual supervisor of a school system will be called upon to plan a variety of in-service sessions appropriate to the objectives of the session and the persons who will be attending. To quote Meierhenry again (*ibid.*), "Many exciting developments are occurring in the

area of technology in education across the country from the teaching of how to thread a projector to subjecting the entire teacher education program to systems analysis and much of the content presented in individualized and mediated form." In-service education can certainly contribute to the excitement of modern teaching.

There are a number of ways of adapting to the particular in-service session. One method is face-to-face personal contact with an individual teacher or a group of teachers.

Using media to teach media can also be done. Owing to the large number of teachers, interns, teacher aides, and visitors who come to the IMC of the Edmonton Public School Board for an orientation tour, a synchronized slide–tape presentation is used to start the tour. Such use of media is appreciated for repeated use in saving man-hours and preventing monotony for both persons giving the tour and those taking it. During the course of a

Figure 4
Representative organization showing how various personnel contribute to the in-service program.

school year, the slide–tape set may be shown nearly 100 times, and it hasn't complained yet!

Likewise, video-tape presentations can be used. A series of video tapes was produced by the Edmonton Audio Visual Association and the Metropolitan Edmonton Educational Television Association for in-service work with teachers, including such topics as proper use of equipment, organizing resource centers, selection of media, and planning school media services. The tapes are primarily designed to be shown within a school at staff meetings as an item of professional development on the agenda.

In addition to regular school bulletins, special publications may be prepared to give information on a specific topic, such as how to use the overhead projector, producing tapes for use with listening centers, and using the camera as an instructional tool. General publications such as the *A-V Handbook* from the IMC of the Edmonton Public School Board might be used to give teachers an overall view of using audiovisuals and ways in which the IMC can serve them.

Tours of facilities, such as visits to the central IMC or exchange visits to other schools, can help teachers better understand school design and ways to use audiovisual media.

Demonstration lessons are also an effective way of showing teachers how audiovisual communication can be used in instruction. Rather than just telling teachers how to do something, the audiovisual supervisor and his staff should be prepared to show how it's done, and a well-planned lesson presented by a guest teacher is appreciated by students and teacher alike.

Some form of *follow-up* activity should be done whether in-service activities take the form of those outlined or other forms, such as convention programs, audiovisual institutes, short courses, or longer courses for promotional credit and salary purposes. It may take the form of a follow-up visit from someone on the audiovisual staff, a meeting with teachers to discuss how well the objectives of the program were achieved, or a survey questionnaire to get a critical examination from the participant.

Implications for Supervision

Improvement of staff is a function of supervision, particularly in specialized areas where in-service training is an effective means of reaching such an objective. Staff development, then, is a duty of supervisors, and one means of developing competencies is through supervisory functions applied to the audiovisual in-service program.

The audiovisual supervisor, however, should not consider himself alone in planning his in-service program. Contact with higher-level administrators, principals, building coordinators, teachers, and other resource personnel will ensure that the program is compatible with prevailing policies and philosophies. Such liaison will help determine needs for in-service sessions, and in turn open channels of communication.

In-service training, then, should be regarded as a professional activity which should become an individual obligation to accept, encouraged by good supervision in a continuous program of professional self-improvement. In-service training is not something static which is presented repetitiously several times during a school year. In-service training is a continuous dynamic process, flexing, changing, and adapting to best serve teachers and the entire educational system.

Nonprint Media and Mediaware Availability to Students at College and Universities

Devon Chandler

Mediated instruction in the classroom has become a reality at most institutions of higher education. Some institutions have extended the availability of nonprint instructional media and mediaware to both faculty and students. Unfortunately, at many institutions there exists a distinct difference between the availability to faculty and availability to students. "Ideally," availability of nonprint materials and related mediaware should be at the disposal of both teaching faculty and students on an equal basis (Pearson and Butler, 1970).

Educational media specialists have long observed that faculty acceptance and utilization of mediated instruction promotes ever-expanding demands for increased service. Student utilization is similarly stimulated when there is unencumbered availability of media and mediaware. Student awareness of the potential communication value of nonprint media is a result of both direction by faculty to the use of new information carriers and the spontaneous realization by the student that much informal instruction, information, and enjoyment can be realized from nonprint materials.

Devon Chandler is director of the instructional materials service, University of Montana, Missoula, Montana.

The key to increasing student use of media is convenient availability of nonprint media and mediaware. This availability should be similar to the general availability and circulation practices for print materials common to university and college libraries.

Wilcox, in a study to indicate dates for development levels pertaining to various instructional technologies reported that faculty surveyed predicted 1972 as a date for the availability of routine audiovisual technology, that is, use of classroom films, taped lectures shown on closed-circuit television or in listening laboratories, and the like. Education technologists predicted the availability of routine audiovisual techniques in 1974. The faculty-predicted date for routine audiovisual use in undergraduate instruction was given as 1975 and 1989 for graduate instruction. Student-initiated access to audiovisual communication tools, that is recorded lectures or demonstration materials, was given as 1975. Student-initiated use was predicted by faculty surveyed as 1979 for undergraduates and 1986 for graduates (Carnegie Commission, 1972).

The predicted dates may be valid for the limited definition stated in the Carnegie report for routine audiovisual techniques, but may be overestimated if the definition is given a broader scope of audiovisual applications such as filmstrips, slides, overhead transparencies, audio recordings, 8mm loop films, and the like, and the associated equipment necessary for their use.

To better understand what is practice concerning the availability of media, mediaware, and media service for student initiated use, 33 selected colleges and universities were surveyed. Institutions were selected to represent a wide geographic distribution within the United States and included both metropolitan and rural settings. All schools surveyed were state supported with a mean enrollment of 8,885 students. The enrollment range was approximately 4,500 to 15,500. Data from the survey are based on reports from 29 respondents.

Institutions reported an almost even division between primarily providing media services to faculty (52 percent), and the providing of equal service to both faculty and students (48 percent). Three institutions reported that graduate students had privileged loan and use of media superior to privileges extended to undergraduate students.

Thirty-one percent of the respondents indicated that media services were adequate to meet nonprint needs of faculty and students. Fifty-five percent felt that nonprint services were only moderate to adequate. Four percent reported nonprint services as being inadequate. Although there is no clear quantitative distinction between the meaning of adequate and moderately adequate, the opinion of each center's chief administrator is significant in broad terms. However, it may be concluded that there is a need to examine the individual center's needs in terms of what is typical practice in anticipation of service expansion.

AVAILABILITY OF NONPRINT MEDIA FOR STUDENT USE

A successful media program in terms of high purposeful media utilization is related not only to the availability of materials to both faculty and students, but also to the selection of the best content and format for the intended instructional purpose. It may be assumed that to provide even minimal service to the faculty, some consulting on media utilization must occur between media center staff and faculty. Equally important is the type and level of assistance available to students in finding and using nonprint media. Ideally, a media center should have personnel in a position similar to that of a full-time reference librarian, that is, a media reference librarian.

Surveyed institutions reported that weekly hours of media center operation ranged from 40 to 92 with an average of 54 hours. Table 1 presents a breakdown of responses concerning the type of personnel available to primarily assist students in the selection and location of nonprint materials. It was found that an average of 73 percent of the institutions reporting indicated a presence in the collection of the more commonly used nonprint media forms—films, slides, filmstrips, overhead transparencies, audio recordings, and study prints. The less common nonprint media forms—magnetic boards, program materials, realia, maps, and globes—were present on the average at 47 percent of the institutions.

These data are compiled in Table 2, which has been arranged to show the rank order of moderate to extensive student usage. The type of loan restrictions most commonly indicated are matched with each nonprint item.

Slightly more than one third of the respondents indicated moderate to extensive student use of the common nonprint media forms with an overall mean of 26 percent for all forms. An average of 22 percent for all institutions was indicated for minimal student use for all media forms listed. Student use of 16mm films and cassette tape recordings is the most popular. About one half the institutions reported extensive to moderate use for these items. Tape recordings, 8mm film loops, and disc recordings each were tallied at 38 percent of the institutions surveyed. A comparison of the availability (materials in the collection) to students of items 1 through 9 in Table 2 with student use (moderate to extensive) indicates that much less student use is made of the common nonprint media forms than should be expected at most institutions. Eighty percent of the institutions indicated a student availability for items 1 through 9; however, an average of only 35 percent was indicated for student usage of the same items.

AVAILABILITY OF AUDIOVISUAL EQUIPMENT FOR STUDENT USE

Most nonprint media requires some device that allows the user access to the contents stored on the carrier. Thus, the availability of suitable equipment

Table 1
Media Personnel to Assist Students with Selection and Location of Nonprint Materials

	Multiple Responses				Single Position Only			
	Parttime		Full time		Parttime		Full Time	
	N	%	N	%	N	%	N	%
Professional media reference librarian	2	7	4	14			1	3
Media specialist	4	14	10	34	1	3	3	10
Department secretary	2	7	11	38	2	7	3	10
Department clerk	2	7	9	31			1	3
Total respondents	10		34		3		8	

Other: One institution indicated student assistance and media specialist, but did not mark any category.

One institution indicated other in Instructional Resource Center, but did not mark any category.

Two institutions indicated that there was no such position in their operation.

Two institutions indicated no response.

Table 2
Nonprint Media Availability and Student Usage

Rank Order of Student Use	1		2		3		4		5		6		7		8		9		10		11		12		13		14		15		16		17	
	16mm films		Cassette recordings		8mm film loops		Tape recordings		Disc recordings		Film strips		Slide sets		Individual slides		Overhead transparencies		Maps		Program materials		Study kits/models		Study prints		8mm films		Magnetic boards		Realia		Globes	
Percentage and Number of Institutions Indicating:	N	%	N	%	N	%	N	%	N	%	N	%	N	%	N	%	N	%	N	%	N	%	N	%	N	%	N	%	N	%	N	%	N	%
Material in collection	24	84	21	72	20	69	24	84	20	69	22	76	24	84	20	69	25	87	15	52	15	52	20	69	19	66	15	52	15	52	12	41	12	41
Student use moderate to extensive	15	52	14	48	11	38	11	38	11	38	10	33	8	28	7	24	7	24	6	21	5	17	5	17	5	17	4	14	2	7	2	7	1	3
Student use minimal	4	14	4	14	6	21	5	17	6	21	8	28	9	31	10	34	5	17	4	14	6	21	6	21	4	14	7	24	8	28	5	17	11	36
Loan without faculty approval	10	34	15	52	12	41	19	66	16	55	16	55	14	48	13	45	20	69	12	41	12	41	17	59	18	62	8	28	9	31	12	41	10	34
Loan period 1 to 3 days	11	38	8	28	9	31	10	34	9	31	10	34	10	34	10	34	9	31	5	17	5	17	10	34	8	28	2	7	4	14	3	10	10	34
Use restricted to specific area only	9	31	4	14	6	21	5	17	4	14	4	14	5	17	4	14	2	7	4	14	3	10	2	7	1	3	4	14	2	7	4	14	3	10

Table 3
Audiovisual Equipment and Student Usage

Rank Order of Student Use	1		2		3		4		5		6		7		8		9		10		11		12		13		14		15		16		17	
	Tape recorder		16mm projector		8mm projector		Cassette tape recorder		Filmstrip viewer		Overhead projector		Opaque projector		Cassette playback only		Film strip/slide projector		Record player		Public address system		8mm motion picture camera		Microfilm reader		35mm still camera		Electronic patch cords		Portable VTR/camera/monitor		Bull horn	
Percentage and number of Institutions Indicating:	N	%	N	%	N	%	N	%	N	%	N	%	N	%	N	%	N	%	N	%	N	%	N	%	N	%	N	%	N	%	N	%	N	%
Equipment in collection	27	93	28	97	25	86	26	90	25	86	27	93	27	93	21	72	26	90	26	90	23	79	21	72	18	62	23	79	23	79	23	79	15	52
Student use moderate to extensive	18	62	16	55	15	52	15	52	13	45	13	45	13	45	13	45	11	38	11	38	10	34	6	21	6	21	5	17	5	17	4	14	3	10
Student use minimal	5	17	3	10	5	17	3	10	7	24	6	21	6	21	4	14	10	34	6	21	8	28	7	24	2	7	9	31	8	28	7	24	9	31
Loan with faculty approval	15	52	15	52	16	55	14	48	14	48	16	55	17	59	10	34	16	55	17	59	14	48	11	38	–	–	9	31	8	28	6	21	8	28
Unqualified loan to any student	3	10	3	10	2	7	4	14	3	10	3	10	3	10	4	14	4	14	2	7	–	–	–	–	–	–	–	–	1	3	–	–	–	–
Loan period 1 to 3 days	6	21	5	17	6	21	5	17	6	21	6	21	5	17	4	14	6	21	6	21	6	21	6	21	3	10	5	17	4	14	5	17	4	14
Use only in specified area	9	31	8	28	9	31	7	24	8	28	7	24	7	24	6	21	7	24	8	28	4	14	3	10	6	21	4	14	6	21	6	21	1	3

applicable to each nonprint format is important if the user is to have full advantage of the materials in the collection or for student-initiated activities. Data concerning mediaware availability to the student are shown in Table 3, which has equipment in rank order determined from data in the category of student use moderate to extensive. Student usage of audiovisual equipment appears slightly greater than student usage of media as shown in Table 2. For example, comparison between equipment and media usage in Tables 2 and 3 shows that audio tape recordings rank fourth (38 percent), whereas tape recorders rank first (62 percent). Such differences in usage between media and the equipment counterpart may be attributed to extra media availability; that is, students are likely to have either one component or the other and thus borrow the missing item.

Of note is the difference between the potential availability of overhead projectors and filmstrip or slide projectors and student usage of these items. It appears that the development of student usage is much less than would be expected or desirable in view of the reported availability of equipment.

SUMMARY

The appearance of new educational media during the past decade has stirred educators from traditional methods of instruction. The availability of this media to all potential users is the key to continuation of achievement in information transfer and instructional methodology. Much of the impetus gained by instructional technology at colleges and universities has been the direct result of efforts to improve information transfer in large group instruction. The reported near-even division among respondents having a primary media service re-

sponsibility to faculty and equal service to both faculty and students indicates that much work remains to be done if general student-initiated utilization is to become a reality by 1975.

In spite of the fact that half the institutions surveyed claimed equal service, with the exception of 16mm films, no type of media format reached 50 percent of student utilization. It must, therefore, be concluded that students are not generally aware of media availability or that loan restrictions inhibit student use. That students are not interested in using media or mediaware seems unlikely. Allen (1973), commenting on the lack of current research in media or mediaware utilization, states that data are lacking which support the defining of "educational objectives" and "instructional systems." These shortcomings can and must be corrected.

It is necessary to know the efficacy of different media programs, administrative procedures, and innovative practices. The leadership must come from within each organized media service unit in order to adapt to the needs of clientele served. This leadership must press against the framework of confinement, and strive to effect change and thwart the development of the ubiquitous status quo.

REFERENCES

Allen, William H. "What Do 50 Years of Media Research Tell Us?", *Audiovisual Instruction*, Vol. XVIII, No. 3, Mar. 1973, pp. 48–49.

Bennis, Warren. "The University Leader," *Saturday Review of Education*, Vol. IV, No. 50, Jan. 1973, pp. 42–44.

The Carnegie Commission on Higher Education. *The Fourth Revolution: Instructional Technology in Higher Education.* New York: McGraw-Hill Book Company, 1972, pp. 37–43.

Pearson, Neville P., and Lucius Butler (eds.). *Instructional Materials Centers—Selected Readings.* Minneapolis, Minn.: Burgess Publishing Co., 1970, pp. 194–202.

Silberman, Charles E. *Crisis in the Classroom (The Remaking of American Education).* New York: Random House, Inc., 1971.

Reducing Teacher Resistance to Innovation—An Updated Perspective

William F. VanWyck

Media professionals, more recently referred to as "instructional technologists," are responsible for implementing and fostering the adoption of a variety of innovative programs and devices to improve the teaching–learning process. Widespread adoption of costly and complex innovations has not been realized, as witnessed by the demise of many language laboratories, underutilized television studios, and defunct dial-access systems. Without doubt, instructional technology and its potential to improve instruction have progressed more rapidly than acceptance and utilization in the classroom.

With few exceptions, instructional technology has failed to live up to expectations. Although some can legitimately claim that lack of financial resources and inadequate administrative and technical support have hampered efforts to innovate, the largest single factor affecting adoption is teacher resistance. Because a climate of resistance and, in some cases, outright hostility still exist, we must reexamine our role as change agent and respond more realistically than we have in the past. We must assume a greater share of the responsibility for failing to significantly reduce teacher resistance.

William F. VanWyck is director of instructional resources, State University Agricultural and Technical College, Delhi, New York.

A professor recently asked if I was still disenchanted with many of my colleagues in the instructional technology profession for being overzealous about expectations, and for their criticism of teachers unwilling to accept new ideas. He was alluding to comments I made in an article, "Reducing Teacher Resistance to Innovation," published in the March 1971 issue of *Audiovisual Instruction.* With several years of additional experience on a wider variety of academic levels, it is even more apparent to me that to effectively reduce resistance we must be more practical in terms of objectives and expectations.

To develop an appropriate frame of reference, a brief examination of some of the characteristics of innovations is in order. An innovation can be perceived as having two basic characteristics: (1) an idea, method, object, or piece of equipment, which is novel to the individual or group, and (2) the anticipation that some desired change will result from the adoption of the novel idea, method, object, or equipment and related materials. According to Evans (1968), four major components influence the process whereby an individual or group becomes aware of, evaluates, and finally accepts, resists, or rejects an innovation: (1) the innovation itself; (2) the process, its introduction, promotion, and adoption; (3) the characteristics of the individual or group comprising the social system; and (4) the nature of the social system. Brickell (1964) suggests that major innovations require significant shifts in the normal operating procedures of six structural elements of a school or institution: teachers, students, subjects, methods, times, and places.

Miles (1964) lists 11 types of educational innovations; six of the more pertinent are the following:

1. *Boundary maintenance* innovation, which involves the introduction or extrusion of personnel through their boundaries.
2. *Size and territory* innovation, which involves changes in specified numbers of staff or groups within certain territories of the school system.
3. *Physical facilities,* which entails changes in the structural elements of the school, such as building modification, modules, flexible walls, and the inclusion of study carrels.
4. *Time use,* which concerns changes or reorganization of time such as yearly operated schools, modular scheduling, flexible scheduling, or the introduction of a trimester system.
5. *Goals,* which involves a change in specified goals such as those encountered in the inquiry or structured approach.
6. *Procedures,* which contain the majority of educational innovations. These would include the adoption of instructional equipment and materials, changes in instructional procedures, curriculum organization, and classroom composition.

Some innovations require acceptance or rejection by the entire school or institution with little freedom of choice for the individual. For example, the implementation of modular or flexible scheduling requires the commitment of the entire staff. Other innovations permit the individual to accept or reject independently of group action, such as in the development of a televised course or the implementation of a film-making unit.

Varied and complex forces, which we as individuals cannot control, tend to facilitate the desire for new patterns and procedures leading to improved instruction. Erickson (1968) suggests that special events of major importance such as threats of war, impending disaster, major discoveries, and massive legislative financial support tend to shock people into innovative action. The firing of Sputnik I in 1957 is an excellent example of this type of force.

Much of the literature on teacher resistance has been corroborated through many years of personal experience consulting with and assisting teachers on elementary, secondary, and higher education levels. Any sudden or formidable change in the traditional role of the teacher and any change affecting the communication process between teacher and student is likely to elicit some form of resistance. The current and historical role of the teacher is highly ritualized, and according to Hoban (1968) "any major change in ritual is likely to be resisted as an invasion of the sanctuary by the barbarians." This has become less noticeable in recent years as more enlightened, "media-oriented"teachers have been hired on all levels of instruction.

Many teachers and administrators feel that technological innovations tend to promote a mechanization of the instructional process, which thus becomes "dehumanized," resulting in a loss of feedback between student and teacher. Regardless of what many of my colleagues profess, technological change can and will be "dehumanizing" for certain students whose learning styles are not adaptive and/or implemented by insensitive or well-meaning but inadequately prepared teachers.

High per-pubil costs and prohibitive capital expenditures facilitate rejection. The degree of complexity of innovations, particularly those involving equipment, has a strong influence on acceptance, resistance, or rejection. If equipment is not technically reliable, simple to operate, and readily obtainable, resistance can be anticipated. Many have become "tuned out" because of disappointing prior experiences with innovative programs or devices, whose advantages have been exaggerated and limitations ignored.

Eichholz and Rogers (1964) formulated a list of rejection responses after analyzing teacher opinions about innovative failure. Some of the more relevant are rejection through ignorance, which existed when the innovation was unknown or its complexity led to a lack of understanding; rejection by maintaining the status quo, or the innovation was not accepted because it had not been used in the past; rejection through erroneous logic, or the use of rational but unfounded reasons for the rejection of worthy innovations; rejection through fulfillment, or the teachers are confident of the success of their own methods, making innovation unnecessary; rejection through interpersonal relationships, or if colleagues do not use it, why should I? The converse of this response, however, is in my opinion, the most significant factor in encouraging others to innovate. The demonstrated success of a colleague is more effective in facilitating desired change on the part of a reticent teacher than any other factor.

The literature also reveals a variety of techniques that tend to encourage acceptance and adoption. Less resistance can be anticipated if the innovation can be utilized in a variety of educational tasks rather than in one specific area. According to Rossi and Biddle (1966), an innovation is less likely to elicit resistance if it supports or slightly modifies current educational practice rather than changing or replacing the practice. Miles (1964) concurs by stating, "innovations which are perceived as threats to existing practice, rather than mere additions to it, are less likely of acceptance; more generally, innovations which can be added to an existing program without seriously disturbing other parts of it are more likely to be adopted."

Although some educators disagree regarding the role of the administrator as change agent, it is necessary for teachers and administrators to work cooperatively in a spirit of common professional concern to initiate desired change in instructional programs. Influential groups and individual teachers within an educational system play significant roles in implementing and fostering the growth of an innovation. Conversely, if not properly approached or prepared, these same influential groups or individuals may seriously hamper or completely block efforts to innovate.

Persellin (1968) contends that certain conditions must be present before innovations have a chance to succeed. They are (1) the educational community must perceive and emphatically express a specific need for change; (2) the need must be recognized by the community at large; (3) a state of the art in both methodology and media must exist for meeting the need in a cost-effective manner; and (4) sufficient funds must be available for paying the cost. I would add a fifth condition, adequately preparing teachers for change.

Significant change, complexity, inadequate communication, high costs, lack of understanding and teacher involvement, the innate conservatism of the educational establishment, and ineffective leadership appear to be the major obstacles in the path of adoption of innovation. Through greater understanding of the factors that tend to facilitate resistance, hostility, and rejection, we are in a better position to develop strategies for more effective implementation in the future.

We are quick to fault the educational establishment for failing to keep up with the progress of business, industry, the field of medicine, and the military. Educational institutions, however, are more susceptible to cultural restraints and the traditions and limitations of society. To be effective in our role as change agent we must remain sensitive to the belief, attitudes, ideologies, and traditions of local educational establishments and communities.

We should take advantage of the experience and wisdom of teachers in the planning process, particularly in the establishment of transitional programs to bridge the gap between the old and the new. Enlisting the support of influential groups and individuals is essential to the implementation and enduring success of an innovation. Teachers must be allowed, and should be encouraged, to participate in the evaluation and selection of equipment, materials, and policies related to their use. Clear-cut channels of communication must be established that provide for positive and negative feedback to avoid misunderstandings about objectives and potential changes required with implementation. Goodlad (1967) states that "the failure

of people to find success in innovation often results from their failure to understand the rationale."

We must prepare students and teachers for the demands on imagination that we as innovators thrust upon them. In-service programs and workshops must be carefully planned so that all involved are better able to handle the inevitable problems associated with change in an ongoing system. They should be designed to develop sequential growth toward confidence and competence. For example, a teacher should be familiar with the advantages and limitations and feel comfortable using a cassette tape recorder before being asked to utilize a speech compressor, which utilizes many of the same components, but is slightly more complex.

Ineffective leadership is the most important single factor in our inability to significantly reduce teacher resistance to innovation. We are far too often guilty of failing to practice what we preach and, as communications experts, failing to communicate. How often have we listened to a media professional lecture, without utilizing the media, on the advantages of using technology, and how often are we expected to view visuals that ignore legibility standards?

Many in our profession are becoming obsessed with multiscreen, multiimages presentations. Most teachers fail to see practical classroom applications, particularly when they find out how much time and effort are required to produce them. Why use three or more screens when one is sufficient to communicate the message? A few years ago I attended a workshop in which a multiscreen (six screens on three walls) presentation was to be the highlight of the afternoon. While the presenters were patting themselves on the back for their creativity, most teachers in attendance left shaking their heads in bewilderment. Not only did the message become lost in the confusion; switching and focusing from one wall to the other was an uncomfortable experience. I do not mean to infer that there is no place for multiscreen presentations, but I do feel we ought to place more emphasis on meeting practical classroom needs and less on trying to out "multiimage" our colleagues.

Promoting the utilization of more complex, esoteric technological innovations while failing to provide for the basic daily needs of our teachers has resulted in a loss of credibility. Although my views may be perceived as "heretical" by many colleagues, others are taking a more realistic view. Wyman (1974), in reference to the failure of media professionals to consider and capitalize on teacher preferences, states, "the unmet promise may be the fault of promoters of telecommunications who failed to realize an essential characteristic of the great army of classroom teachers who are primarily responsible for the day to day teaching and learning activities of all our students." We must regain the respect and confidence of our teaching staffs if we expect to have significant impact on increasing and encouraging greater acceptance and utilization of instructional technology in the future. The following are practical suggestions that I have found to reduce teacher resistance:

1. *Set realistic goals:* Select short-term goals and objectives that are achievable within short-term time limits. Seek to develop competency gradually, and encourage small successes as a framework on which to build. Teachers employ those processes and skills that in their training and background have made them feel secure and with which they have reasonable expectations of success.
2. *Demonstrate by example:* As experts in communications, we must make every effort to use the effective communications techniques that we promote. In correspondence with staff, utilize unique logos, attractive colors, redundancy, and the like, for reinforcement to ensure that our communication is received. This is particularly important in view of the proliferation of papers crossing teachers desks each day.
3. *Develop orderly and sequential growth:* Plan and implement demonstrations, programs, and

workshops based on teacher-expressed needs and interests, not on what you think they should know. These in-service-type programs should be flexible and diverse enough to accommodate the inexperienced at basic levels and the experienced on levels commensurate with their experience and backgrounds.

4. *Be more candid:* Emphasize to staff that effective utilization of media and technology will require considerable additional effort on their part. To avoid frustration and disenchantment, be certain staff is fully aware of limitations of equipment and related media, in addition to advantages and potential. Do not stress cost effectiveness. This term connotes to many educators an ability to accommodate higher student–teacher ratios. In an era of declining enrollments and staff retrenchment, linking instructional technology with cost effectiveness will surely create negative attitudes. In addition, I believe it inane to continue to sell instructional technology as a cost-effective mode of instruction. Anyone charged with the responsibility to repair and replace expensive equipment owing to rapid obsolescence, and required to keep pace with the proliferation and increasing cost of equipment, projection lamps, and parts (if they can be obtained), is quick to realize the fallacy. It is no longer feasible to justify instructional technology as the cost-effective panacea for accommodating hundreds of additional students in a classroom, a condition precipitated by teacher shortages. We must be realistic and promote technology on its ability to improve instruction and learning, rather than its cost effectiveness. Instructional technology should not be looked upon as a threat but as a valuable supportive service.
5. *Emphasize quality and selectivity:* Too much emphasis on quantity has resulted in many instances in "media overkill." The emphasis should be on a blend of media integration and personal interaction, which meets the diverse

needs of students and with which teachers feel secure and comfortable. Teachers should not be considered inferior because they fail to utilize technology. A dynamic lecturer is still far more effective than an inadequately planned and hastily implemented mediated presentation.

6. *Reward staff:* Wherever possible, build incentives into the system such as released or reassigned time or extra compensation. Give credit publicly, as often as possible, to those involved in effective utilization.

7. *Teach when possible:* Far too often we begin to lose sight of the problems and constraints faced daily by classroom teachers. An occasional stint in the classroom soon brings us back to reality and reinforces, in more practical terms, what assistance and service we should be providing for our teachers. It will bring back the frustrations of trying to use inoperative equipment in rooms with inadequate darkening facilities, of screens that are torn, too small, or cannot be adjusted to compensate for keystoning, and of searching for electrical outlets, extension cords, and adapter plugs.

Factors that tend to reduce resistance are teacher understanding and involvement, transitional programs to bridge the gap between the old and new, initial success, efficient and dependable support services, effective communications, and confidence in the media professional responsible for implementing desired change. By greater concentration on these factors, and less on the criticism of the educational establishment and on promoting change that exceed the needs and desires of most teachers, we should be able to further our cause more effectively.

We must not lose sight of the fact that continued growth and utilization of instructional technology is primarily dependent upon "grass-roots" acceptance of the need for improvement. We provide basically a support service for both teachers and students, and our greatest contribution should be in meeting their needs in the most efficient manner to improve the teaching–learning environment. This is not likely to occur without the respect, confidence, support, and cooperation of our teachers.

REFERENCES

Brickell, Henry M. "State Organization for Educational Change: A Case Study and a Proposal," in *Innovation in Education,* Matthew B. Miles (ed.) (New York: Bureau of Publications, Teachers College, Columbia University, 1964), p. 494.

Eichholz, Gerhard, and Everett M. Rogers. "Resistance to the Adoption of Visual Aids by Elementary School Teachers," in *Innovation in Education,* Matthew B. Miles (ed.) (New York: Bureau of Publications, Teachers College, Columbia University, 1964), p. 494.

Erickson, Carlton W. H. *Administering Instructional Media Programs* (New York: Macmillan Publishing Co., Inc., 1968), pp. 44–45.

Evans, Richard I. *Resistance to Innovation in Higher Education* (San Francisco: Jossey-Bass, Inc., 1968), p. 15.

Goodlad, John I. "Every Teacher Has the Opportunity to Innovate," *The Instructor* (Oct. 1967), p. 31.

Hoban, Charles F. "Man, Ritual, the Establishment and Educational Technology," *Educational Technology* (Oct. 30, 1968), p. 6.

Miles, Matthew B. (ed.). *Innovation in Education* (New York: Bureau of Publications, Teachers College, Columbia University, 1964), pp. 15–18.

Persellin, Leo. "Conditions for Innovation in Educational Technology," *Educational Technology* (Dec. 30, 1968), p. 5.

Rossi, Peter H., and Bruce J. Biddle. *The New Media and Education* (Chicago: Aldine-Atherton, Inc., 1966), pp. 21, 22.

Wyman, "The Unmet Promise of Telecommunications," *Audiovisual Instruction* (Apr. 1974), p. 70.

PART X: MANAGEMENT

Planning a Media Services Program— Initial Considerations

Richard D. Lennox

The following is a brief attempt to focus attention on some of the basic considerations necessary for initial planning of a comprehensive media services program. Such a program would have as its primary objective the provision of a maximum variety of instructional materials and strategies of use for the learners and learning managers it is designed to serve. These materials include all present and potential forms of information storage in addition to the traditional books, records, tapes, filmstrips, study prints, three-dimensional models, 8mm and 16mm films, videotapes, overhead transparencies, and so on, with the administrative capability and support for providing suitable tools and facilities for the use of these materials in a variety of learning environments, adapted to all basic strategies of learning methods including large- and small-group instruction and individual study. Out-of-school applications may also be dealt with in many instances.

Primary sources for the rationale and need for such facilities can be found in many places. Perhaps the most prestigious and forceful of these can be found in two recent publications: *Policies and*

Richard D. Lennox is director, Educational Media Center, Adams State College, Alamosa, Colorado.

Copyright © 1971 by the Association for Educational Communication and Technology. Used with permission from *Audiovisual Instruction, 1*(1), 71–73 (Dec. 1971).

Criteria for the Approval of Secondary Schools, North Central Association, 1968–1969, and *Standards for School Media Programs,* ALA and NEA, 1969.

Fundamental to the effective and efficient development of a media program is the need for very specific operational and/or performance objectives for the program. These are best stated in terms which will indicate observable and measurable results. Use of action verbs in specifying such objectives is most helpful. Some typical examples of the many specific operational objectives which may evolve from careful preplanning are given here to indicate the form of objective statement which can be readily translated into developmental actions and provide a basis for evaluating degrees of success in their achievement:

Example 1   The media program will provide capability for all students in intermediate social studies to be able to examine selected sound filmstrips, assigned by the learning manager. Such examination must be provided for either in the media center or as an out-of-school learning activity. No learner shall be required to wait more than two school days for access to such assigned materials and the facilities for examining them.

Example 2   The faculty or designated students shall be able to have thermal-type overhead transparencies, spirit masters, or mimeograph stencils prepared in the media production center from suitable original materials on not less than 1 hour's notice, when the request is accompanied by appropriate authorization for materials expenditures.

Example 3   The media center will provide centralized space and facilities for individual study of all types of resource materials housed in the center, for a minimum of 3 percent of the student body at any one time and for not less than 6 hours per school day. In addition, suitable spaces and facilities for not less than three simultaneous small groups of three to eight learners shall be available.

It should be noted that each of these examples indicates (1) the kind of function, service or performance needed; (2) conditions, location, times, and the like, under which the operation is expected; and (3) some clues as to the level, degree, or amount of service desired. These three elements should be as precisely stated as possible. Obviously, performance objectives which are established in the early planning stages may have to be revised, modified, or eliminated as the program is being developed and implemented.

To aid in the establishment of a set of initial operational or performance objectives, the following outline is offered. It is intended to be a guide in focusing attention on major and subordinate topics which are vital to any broadly based media services program in the contemporary educational mode. Any minimizing or elimination of certain aspects of any learning resource service is due to what is judged to be historically or traditionally "self-evident" elements of such a program. The data required on these analysis sheets will have to be determined on the basis of local needs and realities, then it can be translated into an action program for developing the initial media services and continually revised in terms of cost effectiveness and changing needs.

MEDIA SERVICES—ANALYSIS OF NEEDS

1.0 Performance objectives of media services
  1.1 Student–teacher direct communications functions
    1.11 Types–forms of information storage (videotape, filmstrip, 8mm film, audiotape in cassettes or reel-to-reel, 2- by 2-inch slides, 16mm film, microfiche, microfilm, bound books, pamphlets, study prints, charts, etc.)
    1.12 Modes of information presentation (in class, in media center, large groups, small groups, individual study, home study, etc.)
    1.13 Other
2.0 Local materials production capabilities

2.1 Duplication types (spirit, mimeograph, offset, thermal, photo)

2.2 Overhead transparencies (thermal, photocopy, diazo, etc.)

2.3 Photographic services (still, motion picture, copying, etc.)

2.4 Audio tape (reel-to-reel, cassette, studio recording, duplication)

2.5 Video tape (studio, classroom, remote)

2.6 Graphic arts design (types of original art work to be produced)

2.7 Flat picture mounting (posters, study prints, etc.)

2.8 Other

3.0 Support capabilities (actual and potential)

3.1 Full-time media professionals

3.2 Full-time paraprofessionals (indicate skills competencies)

3.3 Parttime media professionals

3.4 Parttime paraprofessionals

3.5 Volunteer adult aides

3.6 Student aides

3.7 Equipment resources

   3.71 Duplicating equipment

   3.72 Small-group and individual projection devices

   3.73 Large-group projection equipment

   3.74 Audio equipment (large group and individual)

   3.75 Video equipment (portable, studio, classroom)

   3.76 Photographic equipment (cameras and accessories, processing facilities)

   3.77 Graphic arts equipment

   3.78 Mounting, laminating, cutting tools

   3.79 Primary, bulletin, typewriters (specify lettering sizes and styles)

   3.79 Additional related equipment

3.8 Instructional materials resources (quantitative listing of software materials by types, films, records, tapes, flat pix, filmstrips, books, etc.)

3.9 Specialized furniture (storage cabinets/shelves, etc., for various types of materials, equipment, machines, card catalogs, vertical files, work tables, etc.)

3.91 Other

4.0 Financial commitment (normally expressed as annual dollars per average daily attendance

4.1 Initial remodeling and equipping of media services area

4.2 Annual capital investment (minimum recommendation $2/ADA plus federal and nonstate supports)

   4.21 Materials of instruction (all types include print and nonprint)

   4.22 Supplies for local conversion to instructional materials

4.3 Annual expendable supplies (basic estimate approximately 50 cents/ADA)

4.4 Salaries and wages

4.5 Other

Note: The above figures provide a basis for a total ADA cost estimate. When this figure is divided by total number of students who would benefit directly from the total media program, the ADA cost can then be compared to alternative applications of the same operating budget dollars for determining the priorities to be assigned to development of the program. These same figures can also be the basis of cost-effectiveness estimates. Annual evaluation of the program in operation in terms of instructional improvements observed and measured would, of course, be needed to determine a realistic cost-effectiveness index.

5.0 Environmental commitment

5.1 Total square feet area to be utilized for central administration

   5.11 Rough diagram of area to approximate scale showing all dimensions

   5.12 Availability of electricity and water in area (indicate potential locations on diagram)

5.2 Local production area(s)

5.21 Rough diagram of area to approximate scale showing all dimensions

5.22 Availability of electricity and water in area (indicate potential locations on diagram)

5.23 Materials storage
  (a) Raw supplies
  (b) In-process work
  (c) Completed work

5.3 Centralized resource use area(s)

  5.31 Rough diagram of area to approximate scale showing all dimensions

  5.32 Subdivide space to accommodate
    (a) Individual study
    (b) Small-group study
    (c) "Noisy" zones
    (d) "Quiet" zones
    (e) Totally controlled light areas
    (f) Supervision or monitoring stations
    (g) Traffic patterns
    (h) Open and closed storage of materials and equipment

5.4 Central audiovisual equipment storage and distribution area

5.5 Specialized additions, remodeling, etc., of selected teaching stations for use of specific media and methods

5.51 Light control
5.52 Wiring and plumbing
5.53 Audio–video wiring
5.54 Acoustic control
5.55 Other

BIBLIOGRAPHY

Additional data may be found in these sources:Erickson, Carlton W. H. *Administering Instructional Media Programs.* New York: Macmillan, 1968.

Haney, John B., and Ullmer, Eldon J. *Educational Media and the Teacher.* Dubuque, Iowa: W. C. Brown, 1970.

Pearson, Neville P., and Butler, Lucius. *Instructional Materials Centers: Selected Readings.* Minneapolis, Minn.: Burgess, 1969.

Banathy, Bela H. *Instructional Systems.* Belmont, Calif.: Fearon, 1968.

ALA/NEA. *Standards for School Media Programs.* Chicago: ALA, 1969.

McAshan, H. H. *Writing Behavioral Objectives.* New York: Harper & Row, 1970.

In addition, the following special issues of *Audiovisual Instruction* were devoted to articles directly related to planning and developing media centers and services:

October 1970—Facilities for Learning
September 1969—Instructional Materials Centers
May 1969—How One School System Uses Media
November 1965—AV Programs at the Building Level
May 1965—The Systems Approach
October 1963—Resources for Independent Learning
May 1963—Local Production

Push-Button Education
in University of Maryland's
Nonprint Media Lab

R. Ross Hempstead

Listening to a concert, ballet, symphony, or play while ensconced in an upholstered lounge chair and surrounded by a quadraphonic stereo system is one of the many experiences a student may have at the University of Maryland's Nonprint Media Laboratory.

As its first full year of academic service begins the media lab offers its patrons an extensive and varied repertoire of learning options. Its planning has involved a cautious but comprehensive venture into many distinct approaches to communications technology, with careful provisions for expansion as the overall system proves itself.

Basically, the lab is a matrix of audiovisual systems that capitalize on all nonprint media as they apply to self-directed instruction. It uses remote-access and direct-access information retrieval techniques, which are backed up by systems that can convert the systems into other formats.

When selecting a systems format like this it must be kept in mind that the student's concern is not with the ingenuity or resourcefulness of the electronics technician, but with the instructor's assignment for tomorrow's class. He needs to view a

---

R. Ross Hempstead is director of the Nonprint Media Laboratory, University of Maryland, College Park, Maryland.

biology dissection in high-resolution color video or to listen to the musicology selection in high-fidelity stereo without concern for program format or equipment operation.

To be truly brought into the instructional process, nonprint material must become as readily available and easily used as is print information. With the remote-access facilities of the laboratory, which include audio and video dial access, the process is simple. Choosing one of more than 100 carrels, rooms and other terminals equipped for dial access, the student dials a three-digit program number given to him by his instructor or by a librarian acquainted with the course requirements. Instantly, the program's visual materials appear on the color television monitor in front of him, while the audio is fed through his headset.

Complexity in the control room has achieved simplicity in the study carrel. Aside from audio volume, no adjustment of any kind is required of the student. If he needs assistance, an attendant in the immediate area is ready to help; again, challenges to the student are not with format, but with content.

If the program involves no viewing, the student may be more comfortable in one of the lounge or study areas served by transmitters broadcasting to wireless headsets, available from a desk attendant. This medium is particularly appropriate for listening to long lectures, plays, speeches, or other lengthy spoken material. Here, again, channel selection and audio volume adjustments are the only controls necessary; if the student leaves the transmission area, the headset turns itself off to conserve battery life.

Glass-enclosed rooms of various sizes, equipped with instructors' consoles and other control devices, provide opportunities for classes and other groups to hear/view/study/discuss nonprint materials. Of particular interest to students is a large quadraphonic concert room, furnished with 50 upholstered armchairs and sofas and equipped with four-channel sound; serious students of music may see here the potential for simulation of various orchestral effects. In addition to the specially scheduled concert or other featured presentation, these group study rooms receive all dial access and other remote inputs.

None of these remote-access facilities is inherently superior to the others, or to direct-access approaches, on any simply defined educational grounds. No facile generalization should be made as to their relative value; each is appropriate to a given instructional situation. A large, comprehensive campus, with literally hundreds of programs, departments, schools, colleges, and divisions, has need for a multidimensional approach. Other institutions may find fewer or more specialized systems better suited to unique needs. Each should be evaluated and exploited according to its demonstrated contribution to student learning by means of built-in research instruments.

In consideration of a second group of systems, those which provide direct access to nonprint media, this observation becomes increasingly significant. For certain course assignments, the student needs to exercise complete control over playback. He may need to start, stop, fast forward, or rewind that tape according to his own manner and rate of learning, often in conjunction with lecture notes, a printed text, or a diagram or marked musical score provided by the instructor to the lab.

Accordingly, all programs provided through dial access, wireless transmission, and other pre-scheduled formats, as well as thousands of catalogued titles, are also available on audio and/or video cassette tape. These are circulated in much the same manner as are the library's reserve print materials. Playback units for student use are installed in study carrels, tables, and glass-enclosed rooms. Simple to use, all units can operate in color and stereo, and produce a video quality equal to the best broadcast signals and audio fidelity comparable to conventional disc recordings.

The most important aspect of the laboratory is the nonprint collection itself. In the future the increasingly comprehensive and varied selection of

12,000 commercially prerecorded titles and campus-produced programs will be interfiled with print materials in the main catalog. In addition to curricular materials, a growing collection of titles for enrichment or recreational listening and viewing is provided. With the installation of playback units in classrooms, dormitories, and student centers, the audio and video cassette collection can be circulated in traditional library fashion beyond the lab area as freely as the book collection. The more easily used and readily secured dial access terminal can make prescheduled programs available at any time at any campus location.

Format conversion capabilities support all the systems in the media lab. Locally produced and other noncopyrighted recordings, films, and other materials are converted to audio and video cassettes for circulation. These same cassettes can be used for dial access purposes; for example, the U-Matic video cassette format has been interfaced with the dial access system, standardizing equipment and permitting free movement of software between the various facilities. The student who misses a prescheduled dial access program can check out the same material on cassette in subsequent weeks. Student review, course changes, and other important variables are readily accommodated.

Careful consideration must be given to copyright law; all format conversion must be performed in strict conformance to existing restrictions. Not unlike other contemporary situations, the technology of communications has progressed far beyond our legal means to cope with it, and restraint must be continually renewed, often at the expense of the educational potential of nonprint materials. Student needs can be placed above purely technical, but not above clearly legal, considerations in operating a distribution facility.

Resultant faculty exasperation and instructional limitations can generally be alleviated through careful system design and an efficient service operation. Perhaps this issue is among the most challenging in the process of developing the curriculum through nonprint media. Certainly, neither the law nor the technology shows signs of slowing the rate of change.

Once available, through direct purchase or through negotiation for copying privileges, the potential impact of nonprint material is becoming increasingly apparent. Shakespeare never intended that his plays be read as scripts, but rather that they be seen and heard as performances. The student of English literature, browsing the card catalog for such a work, finds these performances interfiled with the print versions. He may well choose both for his study purpose, locating each according to a corresponding Library of Congress call number.

Other equally significant examples suggest the potential extent to which this instructional process can be supported, enhanced, and developed. Original Pathé newsreel footage, dating from the turn of the century, provides a newly available wealth of primary source material for the historical disciplines. Physical education and dance have long relied upon film, as music and speech have used disc recordings. Through conversion to color video and stereo audio cassettes, these materials can now be circulated with the efficiency and security of books. The biological sciences, particularly medicine, find obvious applications in such facilities. The behavioral sciences are given new dimensions beyond the confines of the printed page. This list of potential curricular support continues endlessly, whenever sound and motion enhance the resources of the silent, static domain of the bound volume.

Even during the first few months of operation, students and staff as well as faculty and administrators have participated in this active instructional development. Not only in exploiting the initial installation but in expanding the planned system, services are projected for which the need was previously unknown. And so it goes, in circular fashion; instructional needs beget resource development, which in turn generates further perceived needs to stimulate the development of additional resources. Much of this seems altogether reasonable to the entering freshman, who has throughout his life viewed perhaps 15,000 hours of commercial and public broadcast television and seen hundreds of feature-length films. Although the great preponderance of his formal education is properly in the abstract, verbal world of print, he readily and naturally accepts its support by other media.

This student's-eye view of the initial system and its accelerating usage has subordinated its more technical aspects. However, a brief summary of a few technical details in each of its major functional areas might be helpful in understanding the system.

Remote-access facilities include audio and video dial access, quadraphonic playback, and wireless transmission. Most of the dial access stations are flush mounted in individual study carrels equipped with push-button dial pads, stereo headsets, and color television monitors.

Back-to-back student stations share equipment space, permitting a full work surface in each carrel. For example, monitors are mounted side-by-side facing in opposite directions, each protruding through the back panel which has been cut to the size and shape of the unit at that depth. Dial pads and headset jacks are mounted in the remaining space on the cover panel in each carrel; all other controls and adjustment devices are concealed, but readily available to the technical staff.

Regulation of internal air temperature and humidity is assured by intake and exhaust ventilation. Clear panels in each carrel are useful in posting program data, although an alphanumeric video character generator also serves this function.

The quadraphonic playback system is installed in a large, glass-enclosed concert room equipped with intercom to the control room, instructor control panel, ceiling-mounted speakers, acoustical draperies, and peripheral headset outlets. Wireless transmission antennas are mounted in zones delineated by the construction of the ceiling or the

configuration of study carrels; several areas are furnished with lounge chairs, sofas, and tables for comfortable listening to lengthy lectures and other assignments.

Sources include all open-reel and cassette audio and video tape; several dozen audio and video transports are vertically rack mounted in a control room bay, and a slide scanner permits immediate color transmission of slides with their synchronized tapes through the system. A speech reduction unit, and disc-to-reel, reel-to-reel, reel-to-cassette, cassette-to-reel, and cassette-to-cassette audio and/or video duplication equipment support the system. A color film chain provides a source for video cassette transmission and circulation of all projected formats, copyright restrictions permitting. These format conversion functions, as well as programing, maintenance, and faculty consultation activities, are conducted under the supervision of an electronics technician, his assistant, and the control room staff.

A central processing unit provides the timed, demand, and timed-on-demand playback options at each of hundreds of student stations throughout a 30,000-square-foot area. A student's selection of a program, and the duration of his listening to/ viewing of it, are recorded by the system and displayed upon demand in computer-printout format. Many other capabilities, including student-response operations, can be programed into this unit.

Student-controlled playback, through the direct-access facilities, operates under the supervision of an experienced librarian, who supervises the circulation of cassettes and administers a staff of several desk supervisors who direct the activities of 20 desk attendants throughout the 16-hour day, 7-day week. As to the equipment, carrel-mounted audio playback units accommodate chromium dioxide, as well as conventional ferrous oxide, Dolby-encoded recordings and other recently developed advances in cassette technology. These flush-mounted, playback-only decks are simple to

Table 1
Media Lab: Capabilities and Growth

Present	*Future (Increase)*
Audio–video transport of 10 control room sources to 96 carrels and 9 rooms	*Eight control room sources and 48 carrels and 9 rooms*
Audio transport of 22 control room sources to 15 table stations	*12 sources and 15 stations accommodating 150 headsets*
Audio transmission of 12 control room sources to 150 wireless headsets	*10 sources and 50 headsets*
Audio dubbing unit, disc-to-reel, reel-to-reel, reel-to-cassette and cassette-to-cassette, and cassette-to-reel, with speech compression and slide synchronization	*Additional speech compression and slide synchronization capabilities*
Audio–video dubbing unit, reel-to-cassette, cassette-to-cassette, and film chain system for conversion of 8mm, 16mm, and slide projections to audio–video tape	*Add to film chain system*
108 carrels equipped with audio cassette playback units	*48 units*
10 tables equipped with audio cassette playback units, providing 40 listening stations	*Increase the entire system*
4 rooms equipped with audio–video cassette playback units and dial access capability	*Additional dial access capability*
12 rooms equipped with audio–video cassette playback units	*6 rooms*
1 room equipped for quadraphonic audio playback by means of open speakers or 50 headsets	*50 headsets*
2 portable stations equipped for audio–video cassette playback	*1 station*
2 portable stations equipped for still and motion picture projection	*Increase of entire system*
12 carrels equipped for 8mm cartridge film projection	*Increase of entire system*
3 display cases wired for dial access of all control room sources	*1 display case*
22 carrels equipped for 35mm slide projection, including 12 with audio synchronization capability	*Expand entire system*

Note: System design provides for subsequent expansion to 500 student stations and other terminals elsewhere in the Nonprint Media Laboratory. With additional appropriate amplification, cable installation, and other interface provisions, the system design provides for subsequent expansion to terminals beyond the building.

operate and nearly impossible to jam. Video cassette playback units, stereo headsets, and color monitors are installed in small, glass-enclosed rooms for individual use.

Other rooms accommodate groups from a half dozen to several dozen students, and are equipped with instructors' consoles for control of audio and video cassette playback from ceiling-mounted monitors and speakers and table-mounted headsets. Similar, but portable, consoles provide playback control in other areas of the lab, and all rooms are equipped with dial access terminals. Many other student-controlled facilities are provided in carrels and rooms. For example, film projectors, including 8mm sound film cartridges and slide–tape devices, are provided for use when materials cannot be obtained in or transferred to video cassettes.

Through remote and direct access, closed-circuit transmission, and student-controlled playback, and many other approaches, an increasingly varied array of learning options becomes available to the university library. The entire system is carefully integrated for flexibility. Each of the several systems complements the others; control room capabilities support them all. Moreover, these distribution facilities are to be further enhanced by the development of planned production facilities on the campus (see Table 1). This whole is greater than the sum of its parts, as the university accelerates its progress in effecting curriculum development through communications technology.

The Development of Instruction: Focus on the Learning Resource Center

Richard S. Meyers

The learning resource center (LRC) now serves as the focal point for instructional development on most community college campuses and, to a lesser degree, in 4-year college–university situations and in K-to-12 education.

Historically, the concept has developed and gone through a process of refinement during several periods of time, with the basic philosophy changing somewhat during these periods:

a. 1941–1967: *Teacher's storehouse*—Teacher-oriented collections of all media materials, commercially acquired and stored centrally; central storage of equipment; media seen as "aids to instruction."

b. 1960: *Teacher's production storehouse*–Primarily teacher oriented collections of all media materials, commercially acquired and locally produced (primarily by teachers); stored centrally; central storage of equipment; growing importance of media as more than mere aids to instruction.

c. 1967: *Learning center production storehouse*—Learner-oriented collections of all media materials and equipment, commercially

Richard S. Meyers is instructional media coordinator, Grossmont College, El Cajon, California.

acquired and locally produced (by paraprofessionals); stored centrally only when unfeasible to decentralize into learning areas; media are indispensable to instruction based on their own attributes.

Of present concern, the four key points of the learning center production storehouse philosophy as they affect the LRC and instructional development place emphasis on the following:

The learner The days when "good teaching" (subjectively determined) was the objective of the educational profession as an end in itself are fast drawing to a close. The effect of teaching (in measurable learning or indications of learning) is becoming the crux of the educational system. An emphasis on the development of the individual to his maximum potential, by whatever means available, in a systematic approach using all available theory and research in learning, communications, and perception is "instructional technology."

2. Decentralization Decentralization means the placement of software and hardware wherever learning can best be served: in the classroom, in the learning centers, in small-group situations, for individual use, and so on.

3. Paraprofessionally operated production facilities for local production, maintenance, and inventory of media materials to meet learner needs This particular facet rapidly became crucial to successful LRC services. With the shift from teacher-oriented education to learner-oriented education, teaching materials took on new importance. In providing for individual differences, the importance of a variety of materials to serve a variety of students is obvious.

New methodology and new approaches to subject area and to time use of staff and students, and the ever-growing trend toward specific definition of learning outcomes, have also built great pressures for creation, development and refinement, and adaptation of a broad range of media. Commercially produced materials must be developed to gain a profit; the more students that can be served by an individual piece of software, the greater likelihood of profit. The goal in producing commercial media software is often to make it as specific as possible about a subject of wide interest. Commercial software concerning national interests is abundant, regional interests, scarce, and local interest, next to nonexistent. The importance of local production to meet unique local needs has become highly evident.

4. The inherent and integral worth of media in the instructional process Controlled research and continued practical use of media for over 50 years have continually demonstrated the effectiveness, in both cognitive and affective modes, of various mediated approaches to learning. Gradually the uses of media as aids *to* instruction have been replaced by media *in* instruction. Programmed instruction cannot be regarded as an "aid" to instruction for the program is the instruction.

Valid uses of media for their intrinsic values to the communicative process are here to stay. Media used at the whim of the instructor are certainly misused; media professionals must educate those who fail to see the intrinsic worth of the mediated experience if the field is to reach its potential to effect learning in measurable terms. Media must become an integral component of a systematic learning process.

Learning Resource Center as a Focal Point of Learning

An active program of LRC communications and involvement of others in LRC affairs may make the center a focal point of learning in its service role of design, production, and/or teaching of instructional systems on the entire campus. What services the LRC does not do in toto in becoming a focal point of learning it should do in inspiring and supporting faculty.

In a limited sense to be aware of or sensitive to any public is to be aware of its basic drives or needs. It is not implied

*that the most primitive wants of man must be exploited in
any vile sense to achieve success in public relations. In a
more kindly interpretation, to be sensitive to and solicit-
ous of these needs is an initial kind of respect to pay to the
individual or to a public (American Association of School
Administrators, 1959).*

The concept of public relations involves communication, and communication is the cornerstone
of all LRC functions. The LRC must communicate
about and for its survival. The finest LRC is without
value unless the teaching staff and administration
know what materials and services *are available* and
the ease with which they can be attained (Gehrke,
1968).

In-service training by various methods to increase teacher involvement in the LRC should be a
regular LRC service. Although the LRC must offer
in-service training to increase instructional media
utilization, it does not always succeed in developing an educational climate favorable for instruction
through a media support program. To achieve such
a climate, Margoles (1969) offered three broad
guidelines:

*1. There are a variety of strategies for conceptualizing the
formation of attitudes toward media; therefore, media
consultants should direct their attention to the effect of
their clients' personal and organizational goals, the
available mediated messages and equipment, those messages that offer minimum control over the professor's
presentation and those that offer maximum control.*
*2. The more a professor uses media, the more he wants to
locate messages that are compatible with his style of
presentation; therefore, media personnel should work
with department chairman in setting up policies for the
development of a comprehensive (Learning Resource)
Center.*
*3. Before a professor will make good use of media, his
attitudes toward media in general and in specific situations must be modified; before these attitudes can be
changed, the professor must see himself as distinct from
his beliefs about the barriers to using media. Different
message campaigns should be directed toward different
faculty members at different times; one type of message
should contain information that negate beliefs about the
barriers that exist in using media; another message would
inform professors about the worth of media and the
reasons for using it.*

The LRC director must actively seek administrative involvement in the LRC if it does not already
exist. It goes without saying that the involvement
the LRC director should seek is "total" involvement. Total involvement includes *administration,
faculty, students,* and *community.* Several colleges
in their quest for total involvement require media
professionals to teach in their respective media
technology programs (Faris, 1969; Wright and
Berry, 1963). By teaching, media professionals
themselves not only are actively involved in the
operation of the center but also in the use of the
center. Additionally, these media professionals by
teaching are involving the media center with students and thereby serving multiple functions.
Further, by teaching, they are in actuality evaluating
the effectiveness of media and the LRC.

From a knowledge of education one would
probably conclude that most "professional"
educators and school systems were reluctant to
change; unfortunately, this is correct.

*The reluctance on the part of educators and school
systems represents a paradoxical situation. Teaching and
learning consist of trying to bring about behavior
changes. The purpose of education is to develop individuals who are adaptive and creative. Therefore all the
efforts of the teacher and the major purpose of the
educational enterprise are to bring about planned change
in the individual. Why persons who are committed to this
kind of objective for all the pupils for whom they have
responsibility should reject or be neutral about planned
change in their practices as teachers is a gnawing and
perplexing question. (Meierhenry, 1964).*

Keuscher (1968) found several practices characteristic of innovative colleges. These practices are
applicable to planning for involvement in the LRC.

1. Well-defined goals.
2. Systematic gathering of data on the community.
*3. Close contact with lay committees, 4-year institutions,
and employees.*
4. Well-defined procedures for decision making.
*5. Open channels of communication within the college
and between the college and the community.*
6. Resistance to community pressure groups.

Innovation can be fostered by

1. Visits to centers of innovation.
2. Educational conferences.
3. Reading.

4. *Agents of change—administration, faculty, students.*
5. *Appropriate budgets.*
6. *Foundation and government grants.*
7. *Budget restriction (can work at times to compel college staff to innovate).*
8. Special facilities for teaching (learning resource centers). *(Johnson, 1969, pp. 262–279)* *(Emphasis added.)*

All the *facilities* in the world *cannot create a plan* for instructional development; faculty must be involved, administration must give active commitment, and media professionals must constantly strive for their goals.

Media professionals are most often the key to instructional development in the various LRC's. Three basic concepts for media professionals can be defined; they are intertwined and interconnected, and of utmost importance in all areas of LRC operation: professionalism, involvement and flexibility.

1. Professionalism   This is the cornerstone to successful enlightened leadership and relevancy. The professional instructional technologist should be totally informed on every aspect in the field, from research in learning, communications, and perception theory to the latest technological breakthrough which may affect educational processes and/or institutions. Being informed is the first step; the instructional technologist must also have the courage to stand up for his knowledge. Further, professionalism requires an active, searching, seeking, enthusiastic mind investigating and doing active research in finding "a better way." There is no easy way out; reading, traveling, courses, workshops may help, but *the spirit to know is the key.*

2. Involvement   There are two types of involvement which are critical to the LRC:

a. From within—the LRC director must be involved professionally, and in the affairs of the campus in general; it is inconceivable that responsible administrative leadership in affairs of the campus can be exercised without the input of the affairs of campus.

b. From without—a vital LRC service program is

infused by involvement with the college community; innovation and involvement are linked; a LRC director must actively search out and employ involvement in the affairs of the LRC. As with professionalism, involvement requires effort.

3. Flexibility   It has often been said that change is the only certainty; within the LRC, it is more than a certainty, it is an every-minute event. Flexibility must permeate all operations of the LRC, but, most importantly, must permeate the mental makeup of the director and staff. An inflexible LRC will not long exist when societies, governments, technology, education, life styles, and values are changing.

Within the processes of education leading to behavioral and attitudinal change, instructional technology is devoted to providing direction toward this change through behavioral science. The LRC is the administrative agency for directed change through instructional technology. Therefore, not only should the LRC be flexible to accommodate change, but should promote it, be a catalyst for it, welcome it. Whenever services, staff, or building are considered, plan for flexibility. Build flexibility in whenever possible. Flexibility, in the final analysis, is the ability to meet the future.

Future innovation in education is directly linked to the level of LRC staff participation in the design of instructional systems. In the words of B. Lamar Johnson:

> It is clear that (learning resource) centers can and do stimulate, encourage, and support innovations in teaching. This is particularly true when the staffs of such centers are highly qualified both in assembling, producing, and administering multimedia instructional facilities and in the practices and principles of learning and teaching. They work with teachers as members of teams planning educational experiences designed to achieve specific instructional objectives.

The LRC can provide for the organization and the application of resources in a systematic manner in order to solve instructional problems.

> We must devise a new structure for learning. . . . The new

(LRC) concept envisions not only a learning location, but also a teaching area and a center for media and technology in instruction. It is also . . . a collection of innovations and ideas for the future, and it is the key location for the interaction of different stimuli for learning (Masiko, 1966).

REFERENCES

American Association of School Administrators. Public relation for America's Schools. In *28th Yearbook of the American Association of School Administrators of the NEA*. 1959.

Faris, G. An AV center that practices what it preaches. *American School and University*, Mar. 1969, **41,** 47–48.

Gehrke, M. N. Starting a graphic service in an instructional materials center. *Audiovisual Instruction*, Apr. 1968, **13,** 360–363.

Johnson, B. L. *Islands of innovation expanding: changes in the community college*. Beverly Hills, Calif.: Glencoe Press, 1969.

Keuscher, R. K. "An appraisal of some dimensions of systems theory as indicators of the tendency to innovate in selected public junior colleges." Unpublished doctoral dissertation, University of California at Los Angeles, 1968.

Margoles, R. A. Guidelines for implementing media support services at the college level. *Audiovisual Instruction*, Nov. 1969, **14,** 69–71.

Masiko, P. Miami-Dade Junior College. In B. Lamar Johnson (ed.), *The Junior College Library*, UCLA Junior College Leadership Program, Occasional Report No. 8. Los Angeles: UCLA School of Education, 1966.

Meierhenry, W. C. *Media and educational innovation*. Lincoln, Neb.: University of Nebraska, 1964.

Wright, C. W., and Berry, K. R. At Central Washington State Colleges. *Audiovisual Instruction*, Apr. 1963, **8,** 222–225.

Starting an Audiovisual Department from Scratch

L. George Lawrence

Planning an effective operation of audiovisual (AV) facilities can be vexing. What kinds of considerations are vital for starting the department and for maintaining an adequate schedule of services? While the present article cannot be all-inclusive, it might provide a premise from which to start.

Let us consider the most basic and necessarily most complex situation: the new school. It's still under construction. There is no student body, no AV equipment of any kind. A skeleton staff of administrators has been assembled. Temporary quarters are provided in a rented, off-campus building. We enter the situation while the hard core of the new school's executive personnel determines and forecasts AV requirements.

During these early formative years, the school's overall character will be determined. In the case at hand, it will be a liberal arts college. Thus, the academic syllabus places emphasis upon the humanities, teacher education, natural and physical sciences, business administration, social sciences, and physical education. The college will deal with undergraduates, conferring the degree of

L. George Lawrence is director of audiovisual services, California State College, San Bernardino, California.

Bachelor of Arts. In addition, it will provide a 1-year supplementary course in education, leading up to a teaching credential for its student-teacher interns.

This overall profile may now be narrowed down to specific details in areas of AV support programs for the instructional staff. This is done by considering the syllabus. The humanities are to emerge as dominant; courses in foreign languages, art, music, theatre arts, English, and some related peripheral courses will be included. Thus, specific AV needs start to emerge. The language people will need a language lab, input materials, a dubbing station, tape erasers, various electronic auxiliaries, monitor stations for permitting students to use their own tape recorders, and the like. The music department will need sound systems of studio quality, reverberators, multitrack stereo mixing systems, slide projectors for showing materials, and so on.

However, as we assemble our equipment lists, certain educated guesses must be made. Most enthusiastic and highly talented teachers frequently elect to make their own AV source materials. A history teacher, for example, might desire a set of 35mm cameras and electronic slide duplicators for picking up information from *Life* or the *American Heritage* magazine, or special cutting equipment for transforming what he considers "biased" filmstrips into half-frame projection slides, to be shown with material obtained from other program sources. He mixes things to be complete.

The education department might have special needs as well. If, for example, the AV facility is obligated to train student-teacher interns in AV display practices, the AV coordinator must enter a request for not-so-modern (i.e., old and used) projectors in his equipment schedule. Students frequently encounter this old equipment in various school districts and are completely at a loss if their college-supplied training experiences revolved around new and modern equipment only. And how about television for teacher education? Or did Bloom's taxonomy emerge as a coding instrument for individual in-class teaching performances? If so,

what kind of a video tape recorder will be used? And how about electronic ancillaries—like putting a coding signal on video tape at 10-second intervals?

The preparation of a specific, highly detailed AV equipment inventory can be simplified by using published guidelines. A good, working reference is contained in *College and University Business*, 41:4, pages 70–71. Entitled "What You Need to Start an A-V Program," it elucidates basic requirements and equipment inventories, including what and how much to buy. It's fair to point out, however, that such and similar directives frequently cannot be adopted "as is." Budgetary and other considerations jump into view as well. But information such as this can be combined with operational data obtained from other, established institutions. Field trips are instrumental, but findings should be interpreted with caution. For a given model might be superficial and cannot be adapted directly to your own situation.

It goes without gainsaying, perhaps, that the overall profile of projected AV operations is subordinated to type and depth of actual services expected of the emerging AV facility. Here at California State College (San Bernardino), after 4 years of operation, our schedule of services includes the following:

Projection of films and slides; television operations for teacher observation studies; training student-teacher interns in AV practices; and ordering films for the academic staff. (*Note:* All our films are rented from universities, county school districts, foreign consulates, and industry. This practice results in exceptional, up-to-date materials and very large savings to the college. The only films purchased and permanently retained deal with our three principal foreign languages and Skinnerian teaching techniques.) Services also include photographic services, graphic arts, dubbing of audio and video tapes, faculty consultations, exhibits, facilities planning, equipment maintenance, engineering, manufacture of situation-tailored AV television apparatus, and custom design of scientific instruments.

Thus, equipment inventories have been geared to accommodate all these functions. However, our profile is unique in that we manufacture source materials and special equipment systems to accommodate many special teaching situations. Statewide queries, distributed to California's state colleges and universities, revealed that we are all-encompassing in AV operations. But such was demanded by our local situation, and similar inclusiveness may be neither defendable nor demanded at other schools. We also have a publications program and have started to make particulars of programs and electronic AV instruments available to professional journals. Manufacturers might pick up these new ideas as time goes on, leading to an overall improvement of contemporary instructional systems.

Generally speaking, it was found that traditional AV equipment items suffice for standard operations. It cannot be overemphasized, however, that AV coordinators must consult with individual faculty members directly in order to discern equipment needs. It is difficult to do this in a new school situation, since there is no faculty available, although many will be on hand a few weeks ahead of time. This is a dilemma, of course, but can be met by making the equipment pool somewhat larger than is immediately called for. Experience has shown that even a padded inventory will be utilized at its fullest in actual service operations, especially if instructors have easy access to equipment. Indeed, it promotes the schedule of services if certain courtesies are provided. Moving and running projectors for teachers is appreciated. Unfortunately, as the department's functions increase with the growth of the campus, this convenient practice will be next to impossible to defend. It's to that end, then, that considerations should be made when planning the schedule of services, since associated personnel problems—even if help is available in the form of student assistants—are not always easy to solve.

Personnel is a tricky subject. Indeed, what type of AV coordinator is suited best for a given school? It is largely a matter of temperament how well a coordinator defends his points and principles. The military (in whose service I, and many others, first developed an interest in AV) demanded "stand-by and readiness" at all times, making AV-based personnel training operations all-inclusive from a technical point of view. There is a great element of autonomy in this, if integrated with peripheral training programs. Simplified versions of it can be applied to the civilian situation. Specific questions are these: Should the AV coordinator be an engineer with a strong technical background but have no teaching experience in elementary schools, or, at the opposite end, be an Ed.D. with no technical experience but a profound teaching background?

It's a matter of choice, but here are a few defendable points. If there will be no AV staff other than the AV coordinator himself for several years to come, the engineer-type person is the logical choice. Almost always, these people can perform all AV operations, including design and construction of special equipment items, in addition to administrative, creative, and other duties. Later on, as specific instructional philosophies emerge, it is beneficial to have an Ed.D. at the helm of overall AV operations. However, to avoid creative talents opposing one another and defending conflicting policies, it is best if both the technical man and media director (the Ed.D.) have reasonably autonomous territory of their own. The choice of personnel is subordinated to the school's syllabus and the associated technical considerations. However, quite early in the personnel-hiring phase, the administration must decide what kind of supervision and administrative control the AV coordinator shall receive.

If the projected new school is small and has a limited growth potential, the *librarian* is the best man for supervising the AV coordinator and his needs. The library's secretarial staff can type orders, collect mandatory reference catalogs, and so on.

That's fine, as long as the school is small and AV services are minimal. Here, the AV coordinator functions primarily as a circulation clerk and little else.

A different pattern emerges if the school grows rapidly. A dramatic growth potential brings with it the need for a fairly talented and sophisticated staff. Special, dominating considerations are these: It must be fully realized that AV materials and services are intended to be used *during* instruction and are prepared *ahead* of actual target dates. By contrast, library services generally are provided as a *result* of instructional activities. Furthermore, by virtue of its very makeup and the ability to provide both professional and creative services, the AV department manufactures instructional materials. This holds true especially of those situations for which ready-made commercial items cannot be procured. To apply the same thing to the library simply means this: If an instructor wants a special textbook dealing with a certain subject, and assuming that the library has none in its holdings, the library staff would have to write, print, and bind one for him!

Robert Heinich, professor of education at Indiana University, gives an even more lucid description of these dramatic AV and library differences in his excellent treatise "Systems Engineering of Education II: Application of Systems Thinking to Instruc-tion" (Education and Training Consultants, No. 3.1.3.92, 1968). Indeed, as the author points out, given requirements and operational profiles stem from functional differences, and changing the *level* of operation changes the nature of performance. Audiovisual staff must be selected to cope with any and all aural and visual problems that might arise during departmental operations. A written test may be given to AV work applicants to ensure against shipwreck later on.

While AV operations must be viewed from as many aspects as possible, the schedule of services and personnel considerations are the substance of a formative undertaking. Once the department has been installed and operates as a faculty-support activity, it is most advisable that a permanent committee be formed to make recommendations for procurement of new equipment systems, delineate budgets and space, and be allowed to suggest an overall AV service profile. This committee or council, recruited from faculty members, frequently can be instrumental in many ways. The faculty as a whole will generally concede to new AV activities if it has a definite voice in final decisions. It is this type of internal cooperation which permits progressive AV departments to render the very best service possible.

Planning a
Learning Resource Center:
A Retrospective Look

Richard M. Winant

This paper is a retrospective discussion of the development of a learning resource center in a medical college. Both positive and negative ideas, plans and deletions took place in the conception and design of this building. One important point is that it matters little that this learning resource center is being utilized by a medical school, for the steps required in this development would be required by any setting.

The learning source center is an edifice. Nothing more. Before this kind of structure can be built it is necessary for a learning resource concept to be established. The concept is an exciting one because any instruction or instructional material that is utilized in the curriculum of an institution is a learning resource, and from the acceptance of this thought can explode an endless array of resources. These are limited only by imagination, applicability, and finances. Resources can include faculty members, administrative members, staff members, members of the community, textbooks, computer programs, instructional television, periodicals, slides, kits, and so on. The overriding problem is how to get maximum utilization out of materials required for a learning resource concept. In most

Richard M. Winant is director of biomedical communications, Meharry Medical College, Nashville, Tennessee.

cases this is a learning resource center where all materials can be centralized and made accessible to the departments throughout the institution for instructional purposes. Materials can be viewed as supplemental aids, review materials, self-instructional, or remedial. The more these materials are used after they have been evaluated positively, the greater the cost effectiveness. The learning resource concept becomes paramount to ensure that a future learning resource center will be used to the utmost and thus be worth the financial resources and human resources that must be dedicated to it.

A learning resource concept must be supported by every level of the institution to be successful. This includes the governing board, administration, departmental chairman, faculty, students, and in some cases members of the community. Since the support must come from so many levels, they must be exposed to the learning resource concept prior to any commitments. To accomplish this a plausibility study and pilot program must be established. The plausibility study would look at the entire curriculum, institutional facilities, and budget requirements to see if money can be allocated for a pilot program. Beyond this consideration, deliberation must take place to ascertain if monies could be allocated, if justified, for such a learning resource center and program, then a pilot program should be established.

The first step in this pilot program would be to hire a director of learning resources who would chair a committee consisting of faculty and administration members. The director would look to this committee for advice on institutional environment, school politics, and the support necessary in his endeavors to do a needs assessment. This needs assessment, if done prior to any establishment of a learning resource continuing education program concept, would be groundless. Therefore, a strong in-service education effort under the supervision of the director of the learning resources center would become a top priority. This effort would include faculty workshops on self-instructional packaging,

classroom presentation, course design utilizing learning resources, educational hardware operation, media selection and acquisition, and the like.

This continuing education program would require the recruitment of some personnel and the services of consultants in areas where personnel could not be funded during this period. Such skills as instructional technology, media production, educational technology, media librarianship, and evaluation would be represented to conduct and supplement the continuing education program. After a period of exposure to learning resource concept, the faculty would take part in a needs assessment. This needs assessment would cover such subjects as curriculum design, application, services required in the learning resource center by each department, projected faculty improvement with the learning resource concept, numbers of students planned in future years, and so on.

The director would also, if an established institution is to develop a learning resources center, coordinate all present capabilities toward establishing a learning resource concept. The director would be made a member of the curriculum committee to provide a learning resource concept presence at their meetings. One primary and most important step that must be taken by the institution after the first commitment to a learning resource concept possibility is the structuring of the curriculum. The curriculum must establish, if it has not already, specific objectives, for costs must be projected and then priorities finally placed on which departments should be developed first in relation to learning resources. Experience has shown that it is best to work with those faculty members who wish to become involved with the learning resource concept, the idea being to make them models of the best teaching possible.

No service can possibly serve all the faculty at the same time so it will be necessary to establish priorities over a number of years so that each department will know when its turn to take full benefit from the services will come. This must be done in the pilot program stage because it is a factor in gaining support for a learning resource concept from the very beginning. If the history department is not going to be helped for 6 years, this must be made clear.

Another consideration in this pilot project would be the need for the development of satellites. These satellites would make the possible learning resources center materials more accessible to the student. The size of the campus would dictate whether the satellite was necessary since accessibility is the key to the success of any learning resource program.

The learning resources committee chaired by the director will have to make a report to the faculty as a whole of the findings of the pilot program. I would suggest a faculty retreat be planned to accomplish this task. During the retreat, the basic building would be designed on the needs assessment and the overall view of the faculty and institution toward a learning resource concept.

The actual building, which will be the functioning center of the unique learning resource concept of that institution, will have several considerations to resolve. First, the teaching processes must be approached; the number of large lecture halls and size, the number of small group study areas and size, and the number of single concept study carrels all must be considered. Administrative offices, conference rooms, technical processing, reference area, circulation area, resource-research development area, maintenance area, educational technology area, lounge area, and exhibit area must be considered. A director's suite may be designed consisting of administrative offices, conference rooms, and planning rooms. The planning room would contain graphic illustrations of the present status of the programs, money, and organization, thus representing a total system design. The production area of the learning resources center might contain graphic arts and illustration area, sound studio and control rooms, photography–cinematography studios, copy room, editing room,

engineering area, workshops, and storage area. There may be a modeling area or a workshop area. Offset printing and general storage for the entire building needs to be viewed and decided upon. Here, again, the most important is the size of the institution and the commitment to the learning resources concept.

One area many institutions do not consider, but one of primary importance, is the development and the evaluation of materials locally produced or modified. This function would be supported by instructional research and development area. It would contain administrative offices, conference rooms, illustration room, offices, and secretarial space. Other functions of the learning resource center might be continuing education, which would need a location and possibly satellite development and coordination space. Again, on a large campus the satellite development program is as important as the total learning resource center development program, in that without accessibility the people who have learned about learning resources concept and accepted it in a developing curriculum will not find it flexible enough to support their needs. Further, the purchase of materials both in producing and acquisitions will not get full benefit simply because of the lack of accessibility. A satellite program in a large institution is just as important as a learning resource center and is an integral part of the total and not to be separated.

When the entire faculty at the retreat has had time to discuss the proposal submitted by the committee, all their recommendations and criticisms will be considered by the committee and the director. On the basis of this a formal proposal for learning resources center itself will be written. This proposal will need to be looked at by consultants outside of the institution and by the director to finalize the applicability and plausibility of actually accomplishing the plans. Then the estimated cost will be derived based on the size of the institution and size of the learning resource center and its service. A total cost projection will be made for the entire program, the building, equipping the building, and the personnel needed. This will be submitted to the administration of the institution and thus the governing board. It is at this point that the pilot program will cease. If the decision is to be made to cut back on certain areas, it is recommended that entire areas be cut out, not just sections of areas. It is better to have a complete nonprint and print media library than have half a print and nonprint media library and half a production area, or it is better to have a complete print and nonprint media library and production area than half a production area and half an instructional development area, and so on. Simply cut out the entire sections of concept and building instead of sections. The governing board again will have to look at the entire projected budget requirements, the curriculum structure, the building, the staff in the satellite development, total organization or structure, and interrelationships within the institution and make a judgment as to whether or not to proceed.

If the decision is to proceed, an architect and engineering firm must be hired to design the building. The director and the committee will work closely with this architect and engineering firm to ensure that the proposal designed by the faculty, students, and administration is carried out in a functional design rather than an aesthetic design. It will be the architect and engineering firms' primary responsibility to engineer a building that will reflect the learning resource concept as developed by the institution.

First drafts, revisions, and final drawings will be reviewed. When the final drawing is accepted by the director and the committee, administration, and governing board, bids will be let. At least 20 percent above the amount of money of the winning bid will be placed aside for change orders within the building during construction. Technology changes so very rapidly that from the time of the bid to the time of final construction it will probably be advantageous to change some structure. It will also be advantageous since through human error omis-

sions will be made, and the possibility of lower quality materials being used will be great.

The architect, engineer, director, and college should hire a construction clerk to keep up with the billing and oversee the construction of the building, thus providing the constant review necessary to ensure that the architect and engineering concepts based on the proposal drawn up by the faculty will be followed completely. Any structural changes that the general contractor desires must be okayed by the architect, engineer, director, and construction clerk before made.

One key element in design and implementing a learning resource center along lines of resource concepts is the actual equipping of the building. Office furniture, decor, and equipment should be selected by interior decorators to ensure pleasant working conditions. People who will work in this building will be highly motivated and feel more important in attractive rather than unattractive spaces; they will feel that the institution cares more about their attitude. However, the really important part of equipping the building is the library equipment, the educational hardware, computer equipment, production equipment, and the like. To do the very best in market research, one must hire consultants on all these aspects and develop proposals that reflect the most advanced and economic equipment possible. The expense committed to this equipment, especially television and computers, necessitates a strong budget for consultants to work with the director and those who have been hired to carry out the program. When the bid list has been designed, it should be submitted to the governing board to make sure they realize the expense that will be laid out. Even though they have seen the projection it will be necessary for them to see "the amount of money spent." I would also suggest that after the final bid has been let, and it should be a systems design bid list, 20 percent beyond the bid list should be set aside to allow for changes of the equipment and additions. Specific steps should be set up in installing and maintaining the equipment.

On completion of these steps money should be submitted to the vendor and bonding should be established. One ought only buy enough educational hardware to support your opening day requirements. Let the software dictate the hardware.

Staffing is a key area for the development of a learning resource concept and/or center. As I have noted, a director will have been hired first, and then individuals necessary for developing a continual education program for faculty, students, staff, and administration on learning resource concept. The size of the institution would again reflect the number of people that would be hired. By the time the building is ready, the head of each unit should have been hired and some assistants, that is, technicians to assist them in their duties. With the completion of the building the entire staff should be hired. Take time in hiring and make sure that your salaries are competitive nationwide. Try to draw the very best people possible. If you want high-quality material, do not expect to train people in house and obtain high quality at the same time. It is better to hire a very good person than two or three mediocre individuals.

The last category that must be considered in this retrospective view of development of a learning resource center is the budget. While in projections the budget should be made quite clear to the governing board, administration, faculty, and students, and a commitment made to it. A rule of thumb may be helpful. The budget should not be less than the cost of the most expensive unit of the institution. The reason behind this is that the learning resource center program and satellites will have to support the entire institution. In budget planning a management informations system that enables the director to present to the administration and thus to the governing board the progress of his unit and the exact cost of the separate services is paramount to continued funding, since cost effectiveness in education and cost accounting in education will be most important in the future. You will note that earlier, I stated a planning room was necessary in the director's office. If this is a very

small facility, I would still think a planning room necessary to enable the director, and those responsible to him for the function of the services, to graphically visualize and discuss the program by unit. The key to success in learning resource is in working your way into the curriculum to make the learning resource concept a part of the institution, and then to make delivery of services a necessity based on positive cost effectiveness.

To go further into staffing and financing, Fred L. Christen, in a position paper for the Health Sciences Communications Association in BIO '73, made the following three points on staffing:

1. It goes almost without saying that the first strategy regarding staff is to see that they are competent. Those doc's out there that have been conveying information to students for years are extremely bright, multitalented people. Their students are also real bell ringers. Any person who is going to work with them has to be good.

   There is an article in the November 1972 issue of Psychology Today that makes some very pertinent points concerning selecting staff for innovation. It is entitled "Who Sank the Yellow Submarine?" and is a post mortem on what went wrong in the great attempt to turn the Buffalo campus of SUNY into a great multivertsity between 1966 and early 1970. That was a massive attempt to cause innovation in an academic setting. Looking at the wreckage of that attempt, one of the prime movers cautioned

   A change oriented administrator should be damn sure about the persons he recruits.... An academic community can tolerate a great deal of eccentricity. But it will brutally reject an individual it suspects of masking mediocrity with a flashy commitment to innovation. (.116) Get competent staff.

2. Get staff that is compatible with the function you chose, that is, to be facilitators of information transfer. The staff of your LRC are not the providers of information, they are the facilitators of information transfer. Not everyone you might hire will be willing to take that role. That is no reflection on them as individuals, but the LRC is no place for what the elementary ed majors call a telling teacher.

3. Now my third strategy for staff may be mixing apples and oranges a bit, but it needs to be said anyway. It deals with how you manage to accomplish 1 and 2 above. I hope you believe in management by objectives, just as you believe in instruction by objectives. Everyone deserves to be managed well, and management by objectives is an excellent approach. But as

Douglas McGregor said in his helpful little book,
Leadership and Motivation, *the boss must still be boss.*

*My third strategy for staffing is to manage by
objectives but, when management by objectives fails,
manage by staffing. Don't reject entirely the need to
manage by changing staff once in a while. There are a
lot of good people in the world. Not all of them will fit
on your team; not all will fit on mine.*

Christen went on to describe four models of
funding a learning resource center. They are models
A, B, C, and D.

*The first, Model A, is heavily dependent on fee for service
with little stable institutional funds. That is a model that
has been common in the past and still is in use in a
number of schools. Its main disadvantage is that without a
stable funding base it is very difficult to plan for future
change or to lead in introducing innovation to institutional programs.*

*Model B solves that problem. It provides heavy institu-
tional funding with little dependence upon fee for service.*

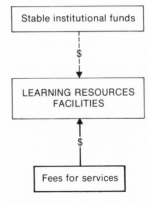

Model B

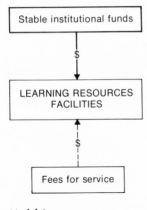

Model A

*This model solves the problem of Model A in that long
range innovation can be planned; the qualified professional, educational, and technical staff needed to produce changes can be hired. But it loses the strong link
back to faculty needs and interest of Model A. Most of us
would be willing to accept that loss if we could be so
fortunate as to live under Model B – but few of us are that
fortunate.*

*Model C depicts an LRC minimally from stable institu-
tional funds, moderately from fees for services, and
heavily from special educational grants and contracts. It's
a dependent funding base, probably every bit as dependent as Model A's. But where Model A was dependent*

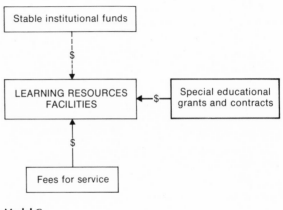

Model C

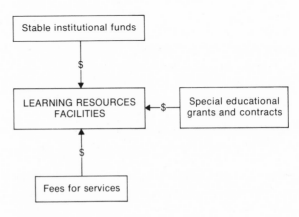

Model D

upon fee for service and thus under pressure away from innovation, Model C dependence upon getting grants establishes a countervailing pressure toward innovation.

Model D is obviously the preferred model. It has sufficient stable institutional funds to enable continuity and staffing for innovation. It has sufficient dependence on fees for service to encourage responsiveness to faculty needs and the tantilizing prospect of Grants and Contracts is there as the icing on the cake.

Although Christen is director of instructional communications for the University of Texas Health Sciences Center at Dallas, his thoughts are applicable to all competitive salaries. The funding must be by objectives if at all possible. A learning resource program is a viable one if the staff are seen as colleagues and facilitators to the faculty in transferring knowledge, skills, and experience to the students.

In ending, one must view the learning resource concept in terms of instructional development, production, and utilization that can provide design and support for any print and nonprint media within the budgetal and usage constraints of the institution. The learning resource center is only the physical plant required to implement the program.

BIBLIOGRAPHY

American Library Association and National Education Association. *Standards for School Media Programs.* Chicago: American Library Association, 1969.

Brown, James W., and Norbery, Kenneth D. *Administering Educational Media.* New York: McGraw-Hill Book Company, 1965.

Brown, James W., Lewis, Richard B., and Harcleroad, Fred F. *AV Instruction Media and Methods,* New York: McGraw-Hill Book Company, 1969.

Chapman, Edward A., St. Pierre, Paul L., and Lobans, John, Jr. *Library System Analysis Guidelines.* New York: John Wiley & Sons, Inc. (Interscience Division), 1969.

Erickson, Carlton W. H. *Administering Instructional Media Programs.* New York: Macmillan Publishing Co., Inc., 1968.

Green, Alan C. (ed.). *Educational Facilities with New Media.* Washington, D.C.: National Education Association, 1969.

Health Sciences Communication Association, BIO '73 HeSCA Position Papers. Richmond, Va., 1973.

Kaufman, Roger a. *Educational System Planning.* Englewood Cliffs, N. J.: Prentice-Hall, Inc., 1972.

Kemp, Jerrold E. *Planning and Producing Audiovisual Materials, 2nd Edition.* San Francisco: Chandler Publishing Company, 1968.

Lyle, Guy R. *The Administration of College Library, 3rd Edition.* New York: The H. W. Wilson Company, 1961.

National Audio-Visual Association, Inc. *The Audio-Visual Equipment Directory, 20th Edition.* Fairfax, Va., 1974.

Pula, Fred J. *Application and Operation of Audiovisual Equipment in Education.* New York: John Wiley & Sons, Inc., 1968.

Wilson, Louis R., and Tauber, Maurice F. *The University Library: The Organization, Administeration and Functions of Academic Libraries, 2nd Edition.* New York: Columbia University Press, 1964.

Winman, Raymond V., and Meierhenry, Wesley C. (ed.). *Educational Media: Theory and Practice.* Columbus, Ohio: Charles E. Merrill Publishing Company, 1969.

PART XI: FACILITIES

Designing Spaces and Facilities to Accommodate Instructional Technology

Ann Fallon and Phillip J. Sleeman

Of prime importance in the design process, unfortunately often overlooked, is the clear identification of the *philosophy* underlying the design of the learning–teaching center. From the writer's point of view, the *learner* is the central concern of all the professions, regardless of the means of communication and the learning environment. Second in line of importance is the professional educator whose role, in its most simplistic form, is that of transmitting information to the learner and providing him with the skills and materials necessary to ultimately affect an international culture, a culture of sophistication not yet realized in present-day societies. Third is the identification of and continued development of the curriculum and curriculum materials necessary to communicate effectively and efficiently with the learner. Learning–teaching facilities must be flexible enough to allow change with ease, as learning–teaching and curriculum needs constantly change. If nothing else is considered in designing facilities it is imperative that one provide adequate space

Ann Fallon is reference librarian, Mugar Library, Boston University, Boston, Massachusetts.

Phillip J. Sleeman is director of the instructional media center and professor of education, University of Connecticut, Storrs, Connecticut.

allotments for present and future expandable growth patterns. If these provisions are made, then significant and necessary changes can be immediately implemented.

Involvement of the learner, teacher, curriculum specialist, media specialist, administrator, and architect in the initial design process can minimize frustrations and dilemmas caused by ill planning. As the facility is primarily for the benefit of the learner, any combination of elements that make the design of the facility more effective and successful as a communication vehicle should be utilized.

The authors Glenys Unruh and William Alexander, in their book *Innovations in Secondary Education*, published by Holt, Rinehart and Winston, stated:

> *Innovations in School Building Designs provide tangible evidence of the changing nature of education. As attitudes of the educational world are undergoing a transformation, so are the architectural structures. Instead of beginning with courses, texts, and class periods in making decisions about school facilities, the modern educator begins with the individual student and the wide variety of options (media, materials, staff, time, space, community resources) that functional architecture can make possible. Furthermore, in planning the building, the educator also considers the economics, politics, geograpny, social needs and potential resources of the community. No one standard schoolhouse for all communities can possibly be designed to meet the complex mix of variables to be considered in various localities; but one fundamental principle does prevail. The shape and atmosphere of the new schoolhouse must serve a variety of approaches and practices, must be flexible and versatile, and must be capable of constant adaptation to new goals and new functions.*

Regardless of the type of facility being designed (i.e., learning center, library, television facility, data-processing center, language laboratory, campus within a city, college health center, school for urban renewal, school or college media centers, dormitories, and individual learning stations, to mention a few) some basic considerations of acoustics, lighting, space, flexibility, mobility, security (against theft and damage), cost, heat, and electronics are involved. More important, however, than these basic and necessary minimum require-

ments is the careful research and identification of the learner and teacher communication needs (objectives) combined in a package called learning or curriculum materials. Until the learner, teacher, and curriculum needs are accurately and specifically identified, one cannot realistically design effective learning and teaching objectives, which are the foundation for design and development of successful facilities.

The bibliography of educational facilities which begins on page 333 was prepared for the purpose of assisting innovative educators, boards of education, school building committees, school facility planners, architects, superintendents, media specialists, principals, librarians, and teachers in planning contemporary school facilities.

As an initial beginning, one might pay particular attention to the following publications:

1. *Designing for Educational Technology*, 1971.
2. *Multi-Media Classrooms Revisited*, 1971.
3. *New Spaces for Learning*, 1966.
4. *Educational Facilities with New Media*, 1966.
5. *Instructional Hardware, A Guide to Architectural Requirements*, 1970.

While these publications of the Educational Facilities Laboratories (447 Madison Avenue, New York 10022) appear dated, many of the ideas and combinations of ideas are still relevant and very timely in today's planning.

To conclude, the learner, teacher, and curriculum are of prime concern; not the "monument to architecture." Research and identification of learning–teaching and curriculum objectives *must* be the prime guide and foundation of design of the learning environment. It is imperative that educators realistically and honestly concern themselves with these prime objectives. Spending a significant portion of time on research and identification will ultimately expedite the architectural planning and final building, and more accurately solve current and future learning problems. With the present stringent economy and rising cost of education, accountability is the yardstick of measurement, and this is as it should be. If the above considerations are carefully followed, the writer is confident that those responsible for designing, planning, and implementation will be accountable.

More important, one will be significantly assisting today's youth in their preparation for an exciting and complex tomorrow; and that is the ultimate yardstick of measurement and success.

Thoughts for Facility Planners

Ann Fallon and Phillip J. Sleeman

In the Golden Age of government money for education, no one thought or surmised that within a few years, the old-time definition of the 3 R's would be radically changed by the President of the United States. In the April 1973 issue of *The Saturday Review of Education,* Ronald P. Kriss stated that "Nixon's Three R's are: reducin'—retrenchin'—'n' retrogressin'." Superintendents, principals, architects, teachers, and parents should think seriously about what this presidential statement is doing and will do to educational planning. All involved in facility planning should provide themselves with current information by reading articles relating to all areas to strengthen specifications. They should prepare themselves to be able to discuss and evaluate the ways in which educational facilities are being contemplated for the present and the future. The structures to be planned should reflect the goals and concepts toward which educators aim to improve education by providing facilities to accommodate the trends of the 1970s.

The major concern of all planners is the devaluation of the dollar, the lessening of government

Ann Fallon is reference librarian, Mugar Library, Boston University, Boston, Massachusetts.

Phillip J. Sleeman is director of the instructional media center and professor of education, University of Connecticut, Storrs, Connecticut.

support, the increasing participation of parents in the planning process, and the accountability required of all within the educational structure. These four elements alone should make all who will be responsible for the housing of students realize that they *must* be a well-informed group. This can only come about by a day-to-day awareness of the rapidly increasing printed material being made available by those who have been involved in facility planning. By reading this material, many problems can be averted before decisions are reached in the board room of the school system or later when the building is visible. How many educators ever spend some time reading about such topics as design, light, sound, space, heat, and maintenance? Not enough, we suspect. Little wonder that, in the past, educators have been lax in informing architects who are at times uninformed about the needs of the school and the learners. Educators, at times, have been taken in by building contractors who know little about the concerns for educational facility development.

The schools that receive awards are in the small minority when one considers the size of our country and the money which has been available during the past 10 years. It has been a poor record for the improvement of educational facilities on a larger scale in the United States. One rarely reads about the casualties involved from the planning stage to the actual completed building. Now that the economic squeeze is on, published reviews are citing the ways to remedy past errors and advice is being given to improve present conditions. Today's educators should read the accounts of the experienced facility planners, so as not to duplicate the misfortunes encountered by planners at the suggestions of architects and members of the building industry. Costly ventures may be averted if the facility planning group is thoroughly informed and has done some research of their own. Now that the 1970s have arrived and educators find themselves with very limited budgets, they must give serious study to obtaining the best results for the future school building and seriously consider renovations of older buildings.

New ideas and innovations are plentiful; systems and approaches to learning are being reviewed for their validity; existing school buildings are being closely examined for their usefulness and potential for remodeling. Economy is the word which has the school-minded person rethinking and reevaluating plans which only 2 years ago would be expected to be approved with positive financial backing. There is a growing need for physical plant revision to accompany current problems such as changing educational programs, family mobility, decentralization, urban–suburban problems, and training for vocational careers, to mention a few.

The compilers of this bibliography hope that this introduction to the literature of educational facilities will prove useful to all school building planners of the 1970s.

Selected Bibliography of Readings of Educational Facilities, 1965–1974

Ann Fallon and Phillip J. Sleeman

"AASA's Oscars for School Architecture Go to Parkway North, Palo Alto High," *Nation's Schools* 92:33–34, July 1973.

Abercrombie, E. A., "Beginning Maintenance Kit," *Audiovisual Instruction* 15:77–78, September 1970.

Abeson, Alan, and Berenson, Bert, "Facilities Must Support, Not Stifle," *Nation's Schools* 84:65–67, October 1969.

Abramson, Paul, "AS&U's Exclusive Maintenance and Operations Cost Study," *American School and University* 44:40–54, February 1972; 44:36+, June 1972.

———, "AS&U's Second Annual Maintenance and Operations Cost Study," *American School and University* 45:25–34, February 1973.

"Academic Building Designed for AV," *American School and University* 43:21+, May 1971.

Ackerman, James S., "Listening to Architecture," *Harvard Educational Review* 39:4–10, February 1969.

Adams, Hugh D., and others, "Administrator's Guide to Air Conditioning Basics," *Nation's Schools* 83:94+, June 1969.

———, "An Administrator's Guide to the Higher Education Act of 1965," *American School and University* 38:35+, March 1965.

Adams, J., "Planning: the Ultimate Method of Controlling Costs," *Community and Junior College Journal* 43:20–21, April 1973.

Adams, V. A., "What's Behind Rising Insurance Costs?" *School Management* 14:27–33, June 1970.

Allen, William H., "Instructional Media Research; Past, Present and Future," *AV Communications Review* 19:5–18, Spring 1971.

American Association of School Librarians, "Architectural Awards to Seven Libraries," *Library Journal* 93:1566+, April 15, 1968.

———, "Architecture Evokes Heritage—Without Traditional Problems," *College and University Business* 42:75–77, April 1967.

———, *Knapp School Libraries Project,* Advisory Committee Report, 1966.

———, *Schools for America.* Washington, D.C., National Education Association, 1967.

———, *Standards for School Media Programs,* American Association of School Librarians, Chicago, ALA, 1969.

"Americanizing the Open School," *Nation's Schools* 86:45–48, September 1972.

"An Addition Effects a Transportation," *School Management* 16:15–17, August 1972.

Anderson, B. R., "Mainstreaming Is the Name For a New Idea; Learning Resources Center for Special Education," *School Management* 17:28–30, August 1973.

Anderson, Gerald, "Let the Sun Shine In," *American School and University* 42:29–30, September 1970.

Anderson, J. W. "Generalist: Vanishing Instructional Developer," *Educational Technology* 12:21+, June 1972.

Anderson, Robert, "Educational Improvement Center: A Hotbed of Ideas," *School Management* 16:25–27, June 1972.

Anderson, R. A., "Open Learning Places: Matzke and Holbrook Schools," *Educational Technology* 10:13–15, June 1970.

Anderson, Scarvia B., "Accountability: What, Who and Whither?" *School Management* 17:28+, September 1973.

"Annotated Bibliography on the Cost of Education," *Audiovisual Instruction* 16:25–28, November 1971.

"Annual Blue Book of Audiovisual Materials," *AV Guide:* 46th Annual Guide, December 1971.

"Annual Cost of Education Index 1970–71," *School Management* 15: entire issue, January 1971.

Arnold, C., "Technology and School Building," *Educational Technology* 10:10–13, June 1970.

Arnold, Jim, and others, "Safety and Economy for University Facilities," *American School and University,* 44:18+, September 1972.

"Articulated Library; the New Yeshiva University Library," *Architectural Forum* 133:56–59, November 1970.

Ashley, Warren H., "At MacDonald, It's Anything But Middle of the Road," *American School Board Journal* 156:22–26.

"Audio-visual: 1970–1971: Report on Multimedia Technology in Higher Education," *College Management* 5:11–13, October 1970.

"Award-Winning School in Massachusetts Prepares for a Multiplicity of Teaching Situations," *School Management* 16:28–29, July 1972.

Bailey, Sherm, and Rowley, Lloyd, "A School for Today and Tomorrow: Mt. Stuart Elementary School, Ellensburg, Washington," *Journal of Health, Physical Education, and Recreation* 40:31–35, September 1969.

"Bard Awards Single Out Two University Projects," *Interiors* 130:10+, July 1971.

Bareither, Harlan D., and Schillinger, Jerry L., *University Space Planning: Translating the Educational Programs of a University into Physical Facility Requirements.* Urbana, Ill., University of Illinois Press, 1968. 153 p.

Barerdt, Jack, and Shoehr, Keith, "Plan for Flexibility and Growth," *American Vocational Journal* 44:25–30, January 1969.

Barkey, Patrick, "Office Landscape: A New Concept for Library Planners," *Library Journal* 94:4358–4359, December 1, 1969.

Barnes, Edward L., "Architect Edward L. Barnes on Basic Mistakes in Designs for Performing Arts Facilities," *American School and University* 44:18–23, November 1972.

Barr, Richard H., "Before Cost Control: A Posture for Public Work," *Architectural Record* 143:93–94, May 1968.

_____, *Bond Sales for Public School Purposes, 1967–68.* Washington, D.C., U.S. Government Printing Office, 1969. 8 p.

Barrett, J. A., "Design Looks Like a Shopping Plaza and Works Like a Library," *College and University Business* 55:34–35, July 1973.

Beauford, B., "Health and Safety Codes in Secondary Schools," *National Association of Secondary School Principals Bulletin* 55:75–79, October 1971.

Beckman, M., and Langmead, S., "Planning Library Buildings," *Canadian Library Journal* 28:114–120, March 1971.

Beckman, Ronald, "The Human Factor in Design—More Than Just A Pretty Chair," *American School and University* 43:20+, April 1971.

Bedell, R. K., "Heating Systems Provide Spark for School Environment," *Nation's Schools* 86:58–59, September 1970.

Beder, R. M., "Structural Requirements of Library Buildings," pages 13–17. (Mount, H. E., editor, *Planning the Special Library.* Special Libraries Association, 1972.)

Beilby, A., "Future: Some Implications for Educational Technology," *Audiovisual Instruction* 17:63–65, May 1972.

Berger, Ronald, "How Rule 288 Can Save Colleges Money on Urban Renewal Land," *College and University Business* 39:53–54, November 1965.

Berke, J. S., "Current Crisis in School Finance: Inadequacy and Inequity," *Phi Delta Kappan* 53:2–7, September 1971.

Berkeley, E. P., "Sculpture in Space; School Building in the New Jersey Countryside," *Architectural Forum* 134:46–51, April 1971.

Berlowitz, M., "Thermal Environment and Learning; Summary of Thermal Environment of Educational Facilities Booklet," *Audiovisual Instruction* 15:77+, October 1970.

Bern, H. S., "Wanted: Educational Engineers," *Phi Delta Kappan* 48:230–236, January 1967.

Bertrand, J., "Shasta College: Growing into an Individualized Learning Program," *AV Guide* 51:10–12, April 1972.

Bessey, G., "Community and School," *Royal Institute of British Architects Journal* 75:364–368, August 1968.

Beswick, N. W., "A Big City Neighborhood Plans a School," *American School Board Journal* 157:25–28, April 1970.

_____, "Bibliography: New Library Buildings, 1960–1967," *Special Libraries* 59:36–38, January 1968.

_____, "Big Air Grab: Use of Air Rights for Construction," *Time* 91:89–90, May 17, 1968.

_____, "Instructional Materials Centers: An American Experiment," *School Libraries* 15:133–141, July 1967.

"Better Buildings Faster for Less," *American School and University* 44:9–10, May 1972.

Betts, Wayne F., "Instant Space . . . Getting What You're Ready For," *American School and University* 43:26–29, June 1971.

Bezman, M., "RAS; Research in School Facilities," *Architectural Design* 401:350–351, July 1970.

Binning, Dennis W., "Survey Reveals Design Attitudes on Campus," *College and University Business* 42:62–63, February 1967.

Bisdorf, Donald, and Terwilliger, Gloria, "A Team Approach to Campus Planning," *American School and University* 43:38–42, November 1971.

Boardman, Thomas H., "Budget Preparation and Presentation," *Audiovisual Instruction* 12:238+, March 1967.

Bock, J., "Two-Year Academic Library Buildings; Five Years of Junior College and Community College Construction of Libraries, Learning Resource Centers, Instructional Media Centers and Learning Skills Centers," *Library Journal* 96:3986–3989, December 1, 1971.

"Bold Symmetrical Design Anticipates a Variety of New Teaching Options," *Architectural Record* 151:105–108, April 1972.

Boles, Harold W., *Step by Step to Better School Facilities*. New York, Holt, Rinehart and Winston, Inc., 1965.

Bowers, G. R., "A Board with Perseverance Put Oakwood over The Top," *American School Board Journal* 157:21+, July 1969.

Brady, Robert S., "Pseudopodial High School Can Shrink or Spread Its Learning Center," *Nation's Schools* 81:42–45, June 1968.

Branscombe, F., "I M C for Old and New Schools," *Audiovisual Instruction,* June 1968.

Brick, E. Michael, "Learning Centers: The Key to Personalized Instruction," *Audiovisual Instruction* 12:786–792, October 1967.

Bried, Raymond, "Design Your Plant to Avoid Maintenance Sore Spots," *Nation's Schools* 83:100–102, April 1969.

Brooks, Gene, "Free-Span Construction Stresses Low Cost," *College and University Business* 38:64–66, March 1965.

Brooks, Martin, and others, "Cues for a New School Committee," *Instructor* 78:73–74, February 1969.

Brooks, R. A., "Planning Better Schools: the Educator–Architect Thing," *National Elementary Principal* 52:68–75, September 1972.

Brotherton, F. Philip, and Brubaker, Charles W., "Analyzing Master Plan Influences," *Junior College Journal* 37:22–27, April 1967.

"Broward County Schools Work For Student Involvement in Their AV Learning," *School Management* 17:48+, May 1973.

Brown, James W., and Norberg, Kenneth D., Administering Educational Media. New York, McGraw-Hill Book Company, 1965. pp. 34–71.

———, Lewis, Richard B., and Harclerood, Fred F., *A-V Instruction: Media and Methods,* Third Edition. McGraw-Hill Book Company, 1969. 621 p.

Brown, Robert M., "The Learning Center," *AV Communications Review,* Fall 1968.

Brubaker, B., and H. Patterson, Jr., "New Directions in School Planning," *Architectural Record* 148:121–134, November 1970.

Brubaker, Charles W. *What's Happening to the Campus? A Brief Review of Many Individuals' Observation on How Physical Facilities for Higher Education Are Changing in Response to New Needs.* Chicago, Perkins and Will Partnership Co., 1968. 13pp.

———, and Leggett, Stanton, "How To Create Territory for Learning in the Secondary School: The Turf Concept for the Multischools," *Nation's Schools* 81:67+, March 1968.

Brubeck, Thomas, and Vanston, A. Rorke, "Designing an Early World," *American School and University* 44:28–30, November 1972.

Bruning, Walter F., "Build Mistakes out of Your Middle Schools," *American School Board Journal* 158:17–24, July 1970.

———, "Building Educational Facilities to Meet the Region's Needs," *Appalachia,* pp. 14–16, December 1968–January 1969.

———, "Building Types Study: Some Current Answers for Urban Schools," *Architectural Review* 142:177–192, October 1967.

———, "How to Design Campus for Lower Maintenance Costs," *College and University Business* 38:79–81, April 1965.

Bruno, E. W., "Building for the Seventies; a Selected List of Materials on the Various Aspects of Library Construction, News Notes," *California Librarian* 65:510–513, Spring 1970.

————, "Building Portfolio," *School Management* 17:53–55, January 1973.

"Building Problems: What Are They? How Can You Solve Them?" *College Management* 8:24–27, June 1973.

Burns, J., "Joint Standards: Media or Mediocrity?" *Educational Technology* 11:53–56, September 1971.

Bushnell, D. S., "Application of Technology in Vocational Education," *Educational Technology* 11:9–11, March 1971.

Butler, R. C., "New Manual on Space Planning and Management," *College and University* 46:775–781, Summer 1971.

Caigan, Robert A., "Designing for Use," *American School and University* 43:38–40, May 1971.

Caldwell, Harold, *Planning for New Media in Kansas Schools,* Topeka, Kansas, Kansas State Department of Public Instruction, 1968. 13 p.

California State Department of Education, "Campus of Many Spaces," *Architectural Forum,* pp. 24–30, May 1970.

————, *Fantasies and Facts About School Libraries.* Sacramento, Calif., Bureau of School Planning, California State Department of Education, 1968. 11 p.

Callan, L. B., and D. E. Rowe, "Role of School Sanitarian," *Journal of School Health* 42:360–362, June 1972.

Campbell, C. C., "From Classroom to Complex A-V Lab in Forty Days," *American School and University* 43:41–42, December 1971.

Campbell, E. A., "What Not To Do When You Build a School," *School Management* 17:34–36, June 1973.

"Campus Buildings Designed for Student Use," *American School and University* 43:34–39, April 1971.

Cannady, William, *New Schools for New Town.* Houston, Texas, School of Architecture, Rice University, 1968. 60 p.

Canty, Donald, *Your Building and Your Architect.* Washington, D.C., American Institute of Architects, 1968. 20 p.

Capson, A. M., *Model Four-Year High School Plant for Pittsburgh for 5,000 Students.* Salt Lake City, Utah, University of Utah, 1968. Doctoral Dissertation. 235 p.

Cardinelli, Charles F., "Carol Murdock Elementary Opens Its Walls to the Future," *American School and Universities* 42:46–47, March 1970.

————, "Effective Use of the Resources Center," *National Association Secondary School Principals Bulletin,* pp. 49–57, September 1966.

Carlson, J. E., "College Construction; the Emphasis Is on Classrooms," *Architectural Record* 150:75+, September 1971.

Carpenter, C. R., "Pennsylvania State University: The Instructional Learning Systems and Research Center," *A-V Instruction* 10:134–145, February 1965.

"Carpet Tiles: Plus and Minus," *Nation's Schools* 87:60–62, February 1973.

"Carpeted Interior Replaces Concrete Exterior: Dade Christian School, Hialeah, Florida," *American School and University* 44:40+, July 1972.

Carswell, E. M., and Dagne, F. A., "Physical Facilities for a Non-Graded School," *National Elementary Principal* 47:34–41, January 1968.

Carter, J. B., "Learning Labs Spur Back-to-School Movement," *American Vocational Journal,* 46:32–34, January 1971.

Castaldi, Basil, *Creative Planning of Educational Facilities.* Chicago, Rand McNally & Company, 1969. 363 p.

Caudill, W. W., and Brooks, R. A., "Open Space Schools: Report by American Association of School Administrators," *American Institute of Architects Journal* 57:52+, February 1972.

"Caves, Not Cages and Children Learn in Them; Avery Coonley School, Downers Grove, Ill.",

American School Board Journal 158:20–22, May 1971.

Charney, M., "New Schools for New Towns," *Architectural Forum* 131:70–71, September 1969.

Chase, William E., and others, *Basic Planning Guide for Vocational and Technical Educational Facilities.* Washington, D.C., U.S. Government Printing Office, 1965. 32 p.

Chase, William M., "Chicago Latin School (Box Full of School),"[23] *Architectural Forum,* May 1970.

_____, "Design for Regenerating a City," *American Education,* pp. 9–13, March 1970.

Chase, W. W., "Educational Facilities Charrette," *Educational Technology* 10:20–21, June 1970.

Christine, E. R., "Planning Your Resource Center," *American School and University* 43:24–28, September 1970.

Church, J. G., "Making a Wide Variety of Educational Resources Available," *Audiovisual Instruction* 18:40+, April 1973.

Churchman, C. West, "On the Design of Educational Systems," *Audiovisual Instruction* 10:364+, May 1965.

Clark, R. J., "Building for the Future: Upper Moreland Junior High School, Willow Grove, Pa.," *Audiovisual Instruction* 16:46–48, November 1971.

Clay, Rena, "Hub of the Instructional Program. A Casebook of Library Services," *American Libraries* 1:170–172, February 1970.

Close, Winston A., "Plan for Planning," *College and University Business* 40:41+, June 1966.

Coakwell, Richard G., "Renovate or Demolish: Ohio State Decides to Demolish," *American School and University* 44:30–34, June 1972.

Cockshaw, Peter A., "President Enters Construction Fray," *American School and University* 43:12–15, May 1971.

_____, "President's Wage Stabilization Plan Won't Curb Soaring Construction Costs," *American School and University* 43:6+, June 1971.

_____, "Skyrocketing Construction Costs Force Curtailing of Building Expansion Plans," *American School and University* 43:16–17, March 1971.

Coffey, S. J., "Planning Facilities for an Educational Program," *Clearing House* 45:169–173, November 1970.

Coles, Robert, "College Building: What's Forcing the Price Up?" *College Management* 4:22–33, July 1969.

_____, "Those Places They Call Schools," *Harvard Educational Review* 39:46–57, February 1969.

Coll, J. Patrick, "TREND—To Get the Most from Federal Dollars," *School Management* 16:32–34, July 1972.

Collier, Art, *The Village Concept of Campus Planning.* Minneapolis, Minn., Bible College, 1968. 20 p.

Collins, George J., "Coming on Strong: Systems Building," *American Institute of Architects Journal* 52:67–68, November 1969.

_____, *Current Trends in School Construction.* Boston, State Department of Education, 1968. 14 p.

Colton, F. V., "Basic Approach to the Design –Specialist–Teacher Relationship," *Audiovisual Instruction* 17:24–25, October 1972.

Committee on Educational Finance, "Construction Material, Personnel Trends and Projections in American Educational Institutions," *American School Board Journal* 154:17–32, January 1967.

_____, *Local, State, Federal Partnership in School Finance.* Washington, D.C., National Educational Association, 1966.

_____, *The Challenge of Change in School Finance.* Washington, D.C., National Educational Association, 1967.

"Compare and Choose an Emergency Lighting

System," *Nation's Schools* 86:108+, October 1970.

Conrad, M. J., and others. *School Plant Planning: An Annotated Bibliography.* Columbus, Ohio, Ohio State University, School of Education, 1968. 70 p.

"Consumerism; Symposium," *Audiovisual Instruction* 16:9–11, September 1971.

Coody, Ben E., and Sandefur, Walter S., "Designing Schools for Variability," *Educational Leadership,* March 1967.

Coombs, D. H., "Information Sources in Educational Technology," *Audiovisual Instruction* 16:32+, June 1971.

Cooper, L. G., "Making the Most of an Educational Consultant," *School Management* 15:16–17, September 1971.

Corgan, C. Jack, "Overhead Planning for Open-Plan Schools," *American School and University* 44:48–50, November 1972.

Corrigan, D. D., and Galvin, H. P., "Cost of Audio-Visual Instruction," *School Management* 10:111+, June 1966.

———, "Library Building, Consulting, Problems, and Ethics," *ALA Bulletin* 62:505–510, May 1968.

Corvetti, Gordon, and Howell, Bruce, "Help for the Man in the Middle," *School Management* 15:22–23, March 1971.

"Cost of Audio-visual Instruction 1970–1971," *School Management* 14:25–29, October 1970.

"Cost of Education Index 1971–1972," *School Management* 16:21–57, January 1972.

"Cost of Education Index 1972–1973," *School Management* 17:24–43, January 1973.

Council of Educational Facility Planners, *Educational Facility Abstract Journal.* Columbus, Ohio, Council of Educational Facility Planners, 1968. 148 p.

———, *Facility Technology: Catalyst for Learning.* Columbus, Ohio, Council of Educational Facility Planners, 1968. 50 p.

———, "What Went Wrong? The I M Center," *American School and University,* p. 53, April 1968.

Crawford, Lura. *Criteria for School Site Selection.* Palo Alto, Calif., Stanford University, 1968. 12 p.

———, "Cross Keys Have a Firm Foothold on the Future," *American School Board Journal* 157:40–42, September 1969.

———, "Functional Staffing for the High School Library," *School Libraries,* March 1966.

———, "Media Resources Centers Development," *Illinois Journal of Education,* 59:25–32, September 1968.

Crouch, C. L., "Veiling Reflection Studies and Their Effect on School and Office Lighting Systems," *Illuminating Engineering* 62:36–34, June 6, 1968.

Cummings, William G., "The Design Process... Do Community Colleges Have Anything in Common?" *American School and University* 44:38–41, December 1972.

Cutler, Marilyn H., "Lincoln High Was Worth Waiting For," *American School Board Journal* 157:28–30, October 1969.

———, "Templeton Did More Than Retread a District," *American School Board Journal* 157:32–34, May 1970.

———, "This One-Room School Is Anything But Antiquated," *American School Board Journal* 156:17–20, June 1969.

———, "What's New and Bright in Schools?" *American School Board Journal* 156:9–20, January 1969.

Cyr, H. W., "Why Not the Instant Media Center?" *School Libraries* 20:21–23, Spring 1971.

Darling, Richard L., "Changing Concepts in Library Design," *American School and University,* pp. 255–258, May 1965.

———, "DAVI Commission on School Plant

Design—Report," *Audiovisual Instruction,* p. 158 February 1967.

———, "The School Library Quarters," *Bulletin of the National Association of Secondary School Principals* 306:37–44, January 1966.

David, Louis, "Planning Built-in Equipment for New School," *School Management* 15:20–21, March 1971.

Davis, Donald L., and Shaver, John A., "New Ideas in Urban Education," *Nation's Schools* 83:67–82, March 1969.

Davis, Gerald, "Building Programmers Act as Translators," *College and University Business* 41:84–86, October 1966.

Davis, Harold S., *Instructional Materials Center: An Annotated Bibliography.* Cleveland, Ohio, Educational Research Council of Greater Cleveland, Staff Utilization Project, 1967.

Davis, H. S., and Crotta, D. J., *Instructional Media Center: An Annotated Bibliography.* Cleveland, Ohio, Educational Research Council of America, 1971, 32 p.

Davis, James T., "Curriculum Expanding Facilities," *Science Teacher* 36:26–27, February 1969.

Deal, John V., "The Automated High School," *Nation's Schools* 87:36–40, October 1972.

Deasy, C. M., "When Architects Consult People," *Psychology Today,* pp. 54–57, 78–79, March 1970.

———, "When a Sociologist Gets into the Act," *American Institute of Architects Journal* 49:72–76, January 1968.

DeBernadis, Amo, "To Carrel or Not to Carrel? That Is the Question," *Audiovisual Instruction* 12:439–440, May 1967.

———, and others, "Media, Technology and IMC Space Requirements," *Audiovisual Instruction,* pp. 108–117, February 1965.

DeCarlo, Giamcarlo. "Decision Maker 1985: An Account of Efforts at National and Local Levels to Raise the Visual Literacy of America," *American Institute of Architects Journal,* 49:34–44, February 1968.

———, "Why and How to Build School Buildings," *Harvard Educational Review* 39:12–34, February 1969.

DeCecco, J. P., "New Instructional Formats; the Media and Media Research in a Crisis Age," *Viewpoints* 46:165–181, September 1970.

Deever, R. M., and Moore, H. E., *Design for Lifetime Learning in a Dynamic Social Structure: Education 1980 A.D.* Temple, Ariz., Arizona State University, Bureau of Educational Research and Services, 1968. 148 p.

Dembinski, Frank J., "Design Awards: Outstanding Examples of College Academic Architecture," *ALA Bulletin* 61:29–30, January 1967.

———, "Design in the Environment: Sculpture, Churches, Buildings, Automobiles," *School Arts* 69:27–34, April 1970.

———, "Functional Plan Fits Physical Plant Building," *College and University Business* 38:77–78, April 1965.

Denholm, D. H., and T. E. Morgan, "Architect's Aid: a Computer," *American School and University* 43:43–46, November 1971.

DeVriese, R. H., and others, "A.S. and U.'s 1968 Specifying Guide," *American School and University* 41:30–31, November 1968.

Diamond, R. M., "Flexible Approach to an Independent Study Facility," *Educational Technology* 10:29–31, December 1970.

———, "Students Do Their Educational Thing at Fredonia's Independent Learning Lab," *College and University Business* 49:52–53, July 1970.

Dingham, C. Wesley, "The Cost of a School," *American School and University* 44:45+, September 1971.

Dixon, B. D., and others, "Project Uplift," *Illinois School Journal,* p. 195, Fall 1968.

Doak, Dick, "Iowa Media Center," *Educational*

Screen and AV Guide 49:10–11, February 1970.

Dobson, C. R., and Leatherman, D. G., "Educational Technology: A Selected Bibliography," *Educational Technology* 12:25–28, May 1972.

Doerken, E. W., Jr., "Media Center Orientation; Look, Listen and Do," *Audiovisual Instruction* 17:62+, December 1972.

Doi, James I. "Don't Be So Casual About Colors in Your Classroom," *American School and University* 42:32–33, April 1970.

———, "Organization and Administration, Finance and Facilities," *Review of Educational Research* 35:347–360, October 1965.

Douglas, H. L., "Designing Facilities for Learning: an Experiment at Burlington County College," *Audiovisual Instruction* 15: 57–58, October 1970.

Douglas, Paul M., "Where to Find the Funds for Auxiliary Facilities," *College and University Business* 42:59–63, March 1967.

Drassel, Margaret Ralston, "Library Invites Use—and Makes It Easy," *College and University Business* 42:39–41, June 1967.

Dudley, G. A., "Billion Dollar Client: Progress Report on New York's Unique State University Construction Fund," *Architectural Forum* 129:74–85, July 1968.

Dukiet, Kenneth H., "Furniture and Furnishings Survey," *School Management* 17:16–18, March 1973.

"East Orange School to Be Designed by Community," *Progressive Architecture* 52:35+, March 1971.

"Easy Way To Expand Facilities," *American School and University* 46:26–27, December 1973.

Eatough, Clair L., "What Tomorrow's Library Will Look Like," *Nation's Schools,* March 1966.

Eberle, Robert F., *The Educational Edifice in a Time of Change.* New York, Communications Seminar, Inc., 1968. 96 p.

———, "The Open Space School" *Clearinghouse* 44:23–28, September 1969.

"EDP Without EDP Equipment," *School Management* 15:24–25, April 1971.

Educational Facilities Laboratories. *Educational Change and Architectural Consequences.* New York, EFL, 1963.

———, *Instructional Hardware—A Guide to Architectural Requirements.* New York, EFL, April 1970.

———, *The Impact of Technology on the Library Building.* New York, EFL, 1967.

———, "Modern Energy Systems for Existing Schools," *American School and Universities* 46:38–46, November 1973.

———, "New Ways to Beat the High Cost of School Construction," *Urban Review* 6:20–24, May 1973.

———, *The School Library: Facilities for Independent Study in the Secondary School.* New York, EFL, n.d.

Educational Specifications: School Planning Series 3. Palo Alto, Calif., Stanford University, School Planning Laboratory, 1968. 25 p.

Egan, Mary Joan, "The Library—An Environmental Learning Center," *Audiovisual Instruction* 14:24–25, September 1969.

Ehrenkrantz, Ezra, "Electronics: New Hope for Vandalism Control," *Nation's Schools* 81:62–65, April 1968.

———, *Engineering Systems for Education and Training.* Washington, D.C., National Security Industrial Association. Proceedings of the Conference, June 14–15, 1966. This series of articles concerns the design of instructional systems primarily for the armed forces. The article by Launor Carter of Systems Development Corporation "Adaptation of Technology to Education" on pages 101–104 will be of particular interest to public school educators.

———, "What's Happening in SCSD and Why," *Nation's Schools* 83:55–57, April 1969.

"Eight All-Electric School Buildings," *American School and University* 45:25–27, January 1972.

Einhaus, J., and Gregory, J., "Getting the Community into School Design: Interview," *American School and University* 44:28+, April 1972.

Ekstrom, Rurik, "This May Be Your Next Bag," *American School and University* 43:30–35, June 1971.

"Elementary Classrooms Cluster Around Material Center," *American School and University* 43:29+, October 1971.

"Eleventh Annual Cost of Building Index," *School Management* 16: Entire issue. September 1972.

Elstein, H., and Hartz, F. R., "Standards, Selection and the Media Center: Where Are We Now?" *Audiovisual Instruction* 15:35–39, December 1970.

Ely, D. P., "Defining the Field of Educational Technology," *Audiovisual Instruction* 18:52–53, March 1973.

English, F., and others, "Educational Success Planning: Reducing Chance as an Aspect of School Innovation," *Audiovisual Instruction* 16:20–22, May 1971.

Ensign, William L., *Renovate and Modernize or Abandon and Build.* Chicago, Research Council of the Greater Cities Program for School Improvement, 1968. 4 p.

Envick, D. D., *A Comparison of Equipment Materials and Processes of the Plastics Industry with That of Selected Secondary Schools.* College Station, Texas, A. and M. University, 1968. 150 p.

————, "Environment for Learning: Dykes H.S., Atlanta, Georgia. *Interiors* 129:136–141, November 1969.

Environmental Design Center, *Bibliography of Environmental Design References.* Madison, Wisc., University of Wisconsin, ERIC Clearinghouse on Educational Facilities, 1968. 62 p.

Equipment Guide Committee, American Industrial Arts Association, *A Guide for Equipping Industrial Arts Education Facilities.* Washington, D.C., 1967.

Eriksen, A., "Space for Learning," *National Association of Secondary School Principals Bulletin* 57:12–126, September 1973.

Ernst, Leonard, "New Building Cost Formula: Bidding Equals Budgets," *Nation's Schools* 83:73–75, May 1969.

————, "Will Design/Build Bidding Fulfil Its Promise?" *Nation's Schools* 93:33–36, April 1974.

Evers, W. C., "Media Seminar on Media Cost-Effectiveness," *Audiovisual Instruction* 15:77+, June 1970.

Exton, Elaine, "Will Profit-Orientated Industries and Uncle Sam Determine What's Taught in American Schools?" *American School Board Journal,* p. 15, March 1966.

Eye, Glen G., and others, "Facility Sharing Works for Washburne and Skokie Schools," *American School and University* 42:38–40, April 1970.

————, "Factors You Must Consider When Designing TV Studios," *College and University Business* 44:3+, May 1968.

————, "Instructional Technology and Administrative Decisions," *Educational Technology* 9:24–27, December 1969.

"Facts About Cooling It: Two Similar Schools with Different Air Conditioning Systems Provide Facts for Comparison," *School Management* 15:33+, May 1971.

Falk, Norman, "New Standards for Classroom Lighting," *American School and University* 44:21–28, March 1972.

Faris, G., "AV Center That Practices What It Preaches," *American School and University,* p. 47, March 1969.

————, "Federal Money for Education: Programs by the United States Office of Education for

Construction," *American Education* 3:13–17, February 1967.

———, "Feedback on Three Schools," *Progressive Architecture* 50:134–145, March 1969.

Farrell, R. "Selecting Heating and Cooling Systems," *American School and University* 44:18–20, January 1972.

"Fast-Track: How It Slices Costs and Speeds up Construction," *American School Board Journal* 159:14–19, August 1971.

Feldman, E. B., "Cut Costs and Win Friends By Planning or Remodeling Schools for Easy Maintenance," *Nation's Schools* 92:36–38, July 1973.

———, "Twelve Ways to Save on Maintenance Costs," *American School and University* 44:11–12, June 1972.

Ferendino, A. J., "High Honors for the Education Park," *American Institute of Architects Journal* 48:52–54, December 1967.

"Field of Educational Technology: A Statement of Definition," *Audiovisual Instruction* 17:36+, October 1972.

"Fifty-Seven of the Best A-V Offerings You'll Find Anywhere," *American School Board Journal* 160:25–28, September 1972.

Fergusson, J., and Fleischman, R., "What Should a Schoolhouse Look Like?" *American School and University* 46:22+, November 1973.

Finchum, R. N., *Extended Use of School Facilities.* Washington, D.C., U.S. Government Printing Office, 1967. This study is a review of the experiences of nine school districts in the use of public school facilities more extensively by nonschool and community organizations. It is one of a series of related studies on school buildings known as the *School Plant Management Series.*

Fink, N. W., and Pansino, L. P., "Renovating the Old School," *School Management* 16:30+, March 1972.

Finley, O. E., Jr., "Help for Boards and Superintendents: How To Get the Most from Your A-V Dollar," *American School Board Journal,* 160:29–30, September 1972.

Finley, R. M., "Stop Stumbling over Technology; A Superintendent's View," *Nation's Schools* 86:78–80, October 1970.

Finn, J. T., "Labor Requirements for School Construction," *Monthly Labor Review* 9:40–43, August 1968.

Fischer, G. D., "Whole Thing: A Service for Administrators," *School Management* 16:34–36, August 1972.

Fischer, J. H., "School Park," *Education Digest* 33:8–11, June 1968.

Fischer, R. E., "Building Process in the 1970's: the Trouble with Systems," *Architectural Record* 148:148–153, October 1970.

Fitch, J. M., "Flexible Design Matches Curriculum: A Feeder Junior High That Complements the High School," *American School Board Journal* 155:8–9, January 1968.

———, "Fourth Library Building Awards," *American Library Association Bulletin* 62:497–504, May 1968.

———, "Future of Architecture," *Journal of Aesthetic Education* 4:85–103, January 1970.

Fitzroy, D., "What You Should Know About Acoustics," *School Management* 14:20–27, August 1970.

"Five Contemporary Schools," *Architectural Record* 149:125–138, May 1971.

"Flexible Design of Elementary School Provides for What Is and What Is to Be," *School Management* 17:41+, March 1973.

"For Efficient Maintenance Create a System," *Nation's Schools* 87:80+, January 1971.

Ford, Harry J., "The Instructional Resources Center, an Enabling Facility." Minneapolis, Minn., Burgess Publishing Company, *Instructional Materials Centers—Selected Readings,* pp. 136–140. (Pearson and Butler, 1969.)

"Forty-Two Bright Things Boards Will Buy This Year for Their Schools," *American School Board Journal* 158:23–30, September 1970.

"Four A-V Wonders Boards Will Buy in the Seventies," *American School Board Journal* 158:45–47, November 1970.

Fowler, C. W., "Fill Those Loopholes in Your Architect's Agreement," *Nation's Schools* 90:55–57, September 1972.

Fredrickson, J. H., "Analysis of Conventional and Experimental Approaches to School Design and Construction," *Educational Technology* 12:60–63, July 1972.

———, "Before You Call an Architect; a Checklist for Planning New Facilities," *American School and University* 44:72+, May 1972.

———, "So You Want to Compare School Construction Costs?" *American School and University* 44:16–20, December 1972.

"Freedom, Partitions and Native Stone: School of the Month," *Nation's Schools* 87:92–93, October 1971.

Friedman, Arnold, "Well-Designed Environment Can Pay for Itself," *College and University Business* 42:56–58, February 1967.

Fry, G. A., "Discomfort Glare Produced by Continuous Luminous Ceiling," *Illuminating Engineering* 63:411–414, August 1968.

Fuller, William S., "How the Space Factor Can Provide Flexible Planning of Facilities Use," *College and University Business* 38:62+, May 1965.

Furgusson, Jeremy, "Science Facilities: Ten Ideas Upgrade School Labs," *American School and University* 44:15+, September 1972.

"Furnishings for Educational Facilities," *Interiors* 131:117–121, December 1971.

"Furnishings for Educational Facilities," *Interiors* 132:112–119, December 1972.

"Furniture and Furnishings for the Open Plan," *School Management* 15:16–19, March 1971.

Furno, O. F., and Doherty, J. E., "Cost of Building Index: 1970," *School Management* 14:15–17, July 1970.

———, "Specialized Facilities in Today's New Schools," *School Management* 14:15–19, August 1970.

Fusaro, J. F., "FY 1966, An Exclusive Report on Federal Aid Programs," *American School and University* 39:27–53, December 1966.

———, "Toward Library-College Media Centers: Proposal for the Nation's Community Colleges," *Junior College Journal* 40:40–44, April 1970.

Gaines, Edythe J., "Accountability—Getting Out of the Tangled Web," *Nation's Schools* 87:55–58, October 1971.

Ganigan, Richard, "You Can Accurately Predict Land Acquisitions Costs," *College and University Business* 43:35–36, August 1967.

Gans, Herbert J., "Report of the Center for Urban Archaeology," *National Elementary Principal* 49:14–16, January 1970.

Gardner, J. C., "Building Workable Buildings," *American School and University* 44:8+, August 1972.

———, "Component System for Mass-Produced Schools," *American School and University* 42:18+, April 1970.

———, "Contract Cleaning—Is It Practical?" *American School and University* 43:62–63, February 1971.

———, "How Much Light Is Enough?" *American School and University* 44:14–16, January 1971.

———, "Safety and Maintenance," *American School and University* 43:8+, March 1971.

Garlock, J. C., "Gateway School: The Richard C. Lee High School, New Haven, Connecticut," *Progressive Architecture* 48:146–151, November 1967.

———, "PERT: A Technique for Education," *Educational Leadership* 25:345+, January 1968.

Gauerke, Warren E., and Childress, Jack R., *The Theory and Practice of School Finance.* Chicago, Rand McNally & Company, 1967.

Gerlett, Robert C., "Making Room for Your Media," *Educational Screen and AV Guide* 48:16+, June 1969.

Gibson, C. D., "How to Shed Light on Flexible Learning Space," *Nation's Schools* 81:68–73, May 1968.

Giesy, John P., "A Working Relationship—How the Central IMC Relates to IMC's at the Building Level," *Audiovisual Instruction* 10:706–708, November 1965.

Gilbert, L. A., "Design for Learning," *Design* 242:26+, February 1969.

Giles, L., "Planning Community College Resource Centers," *American Libraries* 2:51–54, January 1971.

Gilkdy, R., "Designing Space for Use of Instructional Hardware," *Clearing House* 45:255–256, December 1970.

Gilliland, John W., "How to Guarantee Long Life for Your Carpeting," *American School and University* 41:51–52, September 1968.

Gilman, D. A., "Can Instructional Technology Survive the Joint Media Standards?" *Educational Leadership* 28:155–157, November 1970.

Glanz, Edward C., "How Three Financing Methods Compare," *College and University Business* 42:68+, March 1967.

Glasrud, G., "Multi-Unit School Depends on the IMC," *Wisconsin Library Bulletin* 67:17–19, January 1971.

Glass, Ronald, and Murphy, Judith, *Educational Change and Architectural Consequences: A Report on Facilities for Individualized Instruction*. New York, Educational Facilities Laboratories, Inc., 1968. 90 p.

Goldstein, B. M. *Audiovisual Instruction* 10: February 1965. Entire issue is devoted to media influence on school design.

———, "Automated Specification Processes Save Time, Reduce Error," *Architectural Record* 143:93–94, January 1968.

———, "Award Winning Elementary Schools: SCSD Approach Relaxes Classroom Arrangement," *Nation's Schools* 81:65+, January 1968.

———, "Award Winning High Schools: Systems Approach Puts Components Together," *Nation's Schools* 81:46+, January 1968.

———, *The Federal Financing of Higher Education*, Washington, D.C., Association of American Universities, 1968. 32 p.

———, "School Architecture: The Public Is Flunking Its Course," *American School and University,* 44:12–16, November 1972.

———, "Total Media Dreams Become a Reality at St. Cloud State College," *Audiovisual Instruction* 15:16–22, October 1970.

———, "When Your Board Decides to Build," *School Management* 13:74+, July 1969.

Goodwin, Georie J., "An Educational Tool for All: A Casebook of School Library Service," *American Libraries* 1:164–165, February 1970.

Gores, Harold B., "Buildings Will Be Shaped to Educational Concepts," *College and University Business* 40:52–54, June 1966.

———, "School Building Costs Are Really Chicken-Feed," *Nation's Schools* 81:68–75, February 1968. (Also *Education Digest* 33:12–15, May 1968.)

———, "Schoolhouse in Transition," *Educational Change: The Reality and the Promise,* Edited by Richard R. Gaulet. New York, Citation Press, 1968. Pp. 73–80.

———, "Schoolhouse of the Future," *National Elementary Principal* 52:10–13, September 1972.

———, "Schools in the 70's: The Case of the Relevant Schoolhouse," *National Association of Secondary School Principals Bulletin* 54:134–138, May 1970.

———, and Green, A. C., "Building Ideas That Save Money: Interviews," *American School and University* 43:12–16, February 1971.

Grady, W. F., "Technology: the International Scene," *Audiovisual Instruction* 15:76+, June 1970.

Graves, B. E., "Inspired Learning Space," *American Institute of Architects Journal* 57:16–18, February 1972.

———, "Modernization—A Multi-Billion Dollar Market," *American School and University* 42:2+, June 1970.

———, "Modernization: a Special Report," *Nation's Schools* 87:57–72, April 1971.

———, "R—for the Three R's: a Plea for Improved Design of Present Day Schools," *Interior Design* 40:220–221, April 1969.

———, "Repair or Replace: Here's How to Decide," *American School Board Journal* 159:25–30, April 1972.

———, "School Modernization," *Nation's Schools* 89:74–75, January 1973.

Grayson, L. P., "Costs, Benefits, Effectiveness: Challenge to Educational Technology," *Education Digest* 38:6–10, September 1972.

"Great Room: A Radical Departure in School Design," *School Management* 15:24–27, December 1971.

Greeley, Andrew M., "A Guide to Conferencemanship," *Nation's Schools* 88:36–38, December 1972.

Green, A. C., "Physical Setting for Self-Instruction," *AV Media* 4:32–39, Spring 1970.

———, "Places for Higher Learning: Some Ideas and Some Cautions," *Community and Junior College Journal* 43:7–9, April 1973.

Green, Alan C., and others, *Educational Facilities with New Media.* Interim Report of a project being conducted by the Architectural Research Staff, School of Architecture, Rensselaer Polytechnic Institute, Troy, New York, under the terms of Contract Number OE 3-16-031 between Rensselaer and the United States Office of Education, January 1965.

"Greenwich High School," *Architectural Record* 150:133–138, November 1971.

Gregory, Jules, "Getting the Community into School Design," *American School and University* 44:28–32, April 1972.

Grimes, G. H., and Meeder, T. L., "Establishing Regional Media Centers: The Personal Prerogative," *Audiovisual Instruction* 17:50–53, March 1972.

Grumman, D. L., "How to Select the Right Energy Sources," *School Management* 14:22–23, December 1970.

Guerin, David V., "Implications of the Communications Process for School Plant Design," *Audiovisual Instruction,* p. 815, October 1967.

———, "Media's Influence on Design," pp. 50–55, Pearson and Butler, *Instructional Materials Center—Selected Readings.* Minneapolis, Minn., Burgess Publishing Company, 1969.

Guernsey, John E., *A Guide for Planning and Construction of School Facilities in Georgia: Industrial Arts Facilities.* Atlanta, Ga., State Department of Education, 1968. 150 p.

———, *A Guide for Planning Industrial Arts Laboratory Facilities.* Salem, Ore., State Department of Education, 1968. 43 p.

———, *Guidelines for an Adequate Investment in Instructional Materials.* Washington, D.C., National Education Association, 1967.

———, "How Oregon School Keeps out Airport Noise," *Nation's Schools* 80:65, May 1967.

Haas, Warren J., "The Role of the Building Consultant," *College and Research Libraries* 30:365–368, July 1969.

Hamilton, C. H., "University Learning Resources and Instruction Management," *Educational Technology* 11:14–16, May 1971.

Hamrick, R. G., "Daring Approach Yields Comprehensive High School," *Education* 93:105–107, November 1972.

Hansen, D. E., "Systematic Approach to Learning Resource Center Design," *Educational Technology* 12:63–64, August 1972.

Hansen, Richard, "Preserving the Past and Building

for the Future," *School Management* 17:8–13, February 1973.

Harlow, N. R., "Planner to Architect," *Journal of Education for Librarianship* 9:5–12, Summer 1968.

Haro, John, "Flexibility: Can It Stave Off Building Obsolescence?" *College and University Business* 42:51–53, June 1967.

Harrison, C. B., *Factors Affecting the Cost Maintaining Floor Coverings in School Facilities.* Nashville, Tenn., University of Tennessee, 1968 (Dissertation Abstracts 29, p. 1393-A, 1968).

———, "Hartford Came Up with This Winning Combination for Helping Itself," *American School Board Journal* 157:36–39, September 1969.

Harrison, C. H., "Keep Staff Informed of Building Proposals," *Nation's Schools* 93:70+, March 1974.

Harrison, Charles H., "How Specialists Match Schools and Executives," *Nation's Schools* 88:58–60, September 1972.

———, "How to Keep the Public Aware of Building Needs," *Nation's Schools* 87:36+, June 1971.

Hartley, H. J., *Educational Planning–Programming–Budgeting: A Systems Approach.* New York, Prentice-Hall, Inc., 1968. 304 p.

Hartley, James W., "Designing a School for Audio-Visual System," *American School Board Journal,* 151:40+, April 1965.

Hartz, Frederic, "Planning School Libraries for Independent Study," *Clearinghouse,* November 1965.

Hartz, Frederic R., and Elstein, Herman, "Public Relations and Secondary School Media Center: The Director's Role," *Audiovisual Instruction* 15:61–63, January 1970.

Hatch, Don, "Students Unions: An Architect's Viewpoint," *American School and University* 38:30–31, September 1965.

Hatfield, F., "Media Center: Symposium, with

Introduction by W. A. Brown," *Instructor* 80:51–62, November 1970.

Hatfield, Frances, and Gullette, Irene, "Individualized Learning in the Flexible School. A Casebook of School Library Services." *American Libraries* 1:169–170, February 1970.

Hauf, Harold, and others, *New Spaces for Learning: Designing College Facilities to Utilize Instructional Aids and Media.* Troy, N.Y., Rensselaer Polytechnic Institute, 1966. Although this report is intended to guide college planning committees, there is much in it for the public school teacher and administrator. It will assist planners in arriving at appropriate large-group instructional facilities for effective, efficient use of instructional aids and media.

Haviland, D. S., "Temporary Facility Comes into Its Own," *American Institute of Architects Journal* 57:27–33, February 1972.

———, and Winslow, W. F., "Designing for Educational Technology," *American Institute of Architects Journal* 54:27–40, October 1970.

Heinich, R., "Technology and Teacher Productivity," *Audiovisual Instruction* 16:79–82, January 1971.

"Help for Boards and Superintendents: How to Get the Most from Your A-V Dollar," *American School Board Journal* 159:29–30, September 1972.

"Here Comes the 'New Furniture'," *Nation's Schools* 88:41–43, June 1972.

"Here Is a School That Turns Kids On," *Architectural Record* 152:127–130, July 1972.

Hess, Terry, and Mundt, Fred, "Please Mr. Architect. . ." *Audiovisual Instruction,* p. 835, October 1967.

Hickman, Warren L., "Campus Construction for Academic Survival; the Importance of the Curriculum in the College Building Program," *Journal of Higher Education* 36:322–330, June 1965.

Hill, F. W., "Economic Crunch Gives Reprieve to

Many School Buildings," *American School and University* 43:10+, July 1971.

———, "Intriguing Construction Concepts," *American School and University* 46:16+, March 1974.

———, "Less State Educational Aid Seen," *American School and University* 44:8+, June 1972.

———, "Long-Range Building: Do We Need New Yardsticks?" *American School and University* 44:79+, May 1972.

———, "New School Designs, New Center, Old Parochial Aid Problems," *American School and University* 42:14–16, April 1970.

"Hillsboro Went from Contract to Systems School in Eight Months," *American School Board Journal* 158:28–29, January 1971.

Hinst, K., "Educational Technology: Its Scope and Impact, Consequences for Educational Policies and the Organization of the Teaching–Learning Process," *Educational Technology* 11:39–44, July 1971.

Hoffer, William, "A Purchasing Co-Op: Help for Hard-Pressed Budgets," *School Management* 15:30–31, April 1971.

Hoffman, Jonathan, "Alternatives in a Public School System," *School Management* 16:14+, July 1972.

Hong, I., "Philosophy and Attitude of Educators Towards the Concept of the IMC," *Educational Screen and A-V Guide* 50:10–11, May 1971.

Hooker, T. A., and Ambrose, A. A., "Architects Can Help You Win the Inflation Game," *Community and Junior College Journal* 43:10–14, April 1973.

Hopkinson, R. G., "Environmental Research and Building Practice," *Light and Lighting* 61:210–213, July 1968.

Horn, Francis H., "Have a Look at Furniture to Fit the Schools of the Seventies," *American School Board Journal* 157:28–29, December 1969.

———, "How 18 Award Winning Schools Compare," *Nation's Schools,* 85:49–66, January 1970.

———, "How 1967 Award Winning Schools Compare," *Nation's Schools* 81:30+, January 1968.

———, "How to Build a Superb School: Mt. Anthony Union High School, Bennington, Vermont," *Fortune* 77:143+, April 1968.

———, "How to Design a Quiet School: Additions and New Structures," *American School Board Journal* 156:21–25, October 1968.

———, "How to Keep Building Cost Comparisons Honest," *School Management* 9:66–74, April 1969.

———, "Meeting Higher Education's Physical Plant Needs," *American School and University* 39:40–41, February 1967.

Horton, L., and Horton, P., "Learning Centers: A Working Bibliography," *Audiovisual Instruction* 15:60–62, December 1970.

Hostrap, R. W., "Using Media in the Library: Library-College Concept," *Educational Technology* 12:59–60, July 1972.

"How Do the New Ideas Sound After the First Year?" *School Management* 15:17–19, October 1971.

"How Sixteen Award-winning Schools Compare," *Nation's Schools* 87:41–59, January 1971.

"How to Help and Hinder Your Architect," *American School and University* 43:18–20, March 1971.

"How to Make Sure Great Schools Get Designed for Your District," *American School Board Journal* 160:25–27, August 1973.

"How to Style a 'Sesame Street' School," *Nation's Schools* 89:52–54, February 1973.

"How to Use the Cost of Education Index," *School Management* 17:22–23, January 1973.

Hughes, J. M., "In What Shape Is Your Community College?" *American School and University* 40:34–37, February 1968.

Hutchinson, George A., "Evolution of a Learning

Center," *College and University Business* 42:81–84, May 1967.

"Ideas from Award-Winning Schools," *Nation's Schools* 89:47–62, January 1973.

Ingham, George E., "Teacher Preparation Through Multimedia Facilities," *Audiovisual Instruction*, pp. 1054–1056, December 1967.

"Instant School Ready When You Are," *American School and University* 43:25–26, June 1971.

"Instructional Material Centers for Handicapped Children," *American Annals of the Deaf* 118:402–403, April 1973.

"The Instructional Materials Center—Philosophy, Facilities and Design," *Audiovisual Instruction*, October 1967 (entire issue).

"Instructional Technology: Symposium," *Today's Educator* 59:33–40, November 1970.

"Instructional TV System Gets Mixed Reviews," *American School and University* 44:31–33, July 1972.

"Insulation Material Helps Speed School Construction," *School Management* 15:38+, June 1971.

"Interior Design by Committee—Can It Work?" *American School and University* 43:28–32, April 1971.

"Interior Design: Portable Desk, New Theories and Practices in Education Are Making Traditional School Furniture Obsolete," *Progressive Architecture* 52:96–101, February 1971.

Iowa State Higher Education Facilities Commission, *Application Procedures for the Construction Grants Program of the Higher Education Facilities Act of 1963 and the Equipment Grants Program of the Higher Education Act of 1965.* Des Moines, Iowa, 1968.

Irwin, Michael D., "Modeled from Industry, This School Is Anything But a Factory," *American School Board Journal* p. 8, June 1970.

Isaacs, D. L., "Self-Instruction Laboratory Teaches Audio-Visual Equipment Usage," *Audiovisual Instruction* 16:70–71, March 1971.

Jackson, W. D., "Regional Media Centers for the Deaf," *Educational Technology* 10:45–48, August 1970.

Jacobs, James W., "Organizing Instructional Materials Services at the Systems Level," *ALA Bulletin,* p. 148, February 1968.

Jaeggli, R., "Systems Buildings," *Audiovisual Instruction* 15:73–74, October 1970.

Jaquith, L. C., "Accuracy of Estimates: Close But Never Perfect," *Architectural Record* 143:87–88, May 1968.

Jaworshi, Ferdinand, "Twelve Common Mistakes in Library Interior Planning," *American School and University* 45:16–20, January 1973.

Jellema, W. W., "Consultants Clearinghouse Could Be Colleges: One-Stop Answering Service for Problems," *College and University Business* 52:47–49, April 1972.

Johansen, J., "Litchfield Junior High: Bridges, Blocks, and Railroad Ties," *Progressive Architect* 50:72–77, August 1969.

Johns, R. L., "Coming Revolution in School Finance," *Phi Delta Kappan* 54:18–22, September 1972.

Johnson, John M., "So Why Snub the I M C?" *American Vocational Journal* 44:16+, October 1969.

Johnson, Kenneth E., "Ten Essential Human Factors in Office Planning and Design," *American School and University* 44:49–52, January 1972.

Johnson, Marvin, "Facilities and Standards," *Library Trends* 17:362–373, April 1969.

————, "How to Plan a Good Library from Scratch," *Nation's Schools,* March 1966.

Johnstone, J. W. C., "Age-Grade Consciousness," *Sociology of Education* 43:56–68, Winter 1970.

Jones, Richard A., "Eight Guidelines for Planning a Vocational Technical Education School," *American Vocational Journal* 44:36–40, January 1969.

Joseph, J. H., "Media Bureaucracy," *Audiovisual Instruction* 16:60–61, May 1971.

Joseph, S., "Leeds Grammar School," *Tabs* (Standard Electric Company, Ltd.), pp. 23–33, September 1965. Describes a multipurpose hall for a standing audience of 1,000 which can be converted to an auditorium for 350 seats, with flexible staging arrangements.

Joyce, W., "User-Orientated Resources Center Makes Format of Media Ireelevant," *College and University Business* 48:80+, May 1970.

Kaufman, J., *Lighting Handbook.* New York, Illuminating Engineering Society, 1968.

Kaul, D., "Ideal Way to Finance Schools," *Nation's Schools* 89:7+, March 1972.

Kelley, Gaylen B., "Technological Advances Affecting School Instructional Materials Centers," *Library Trends* 17:374–382, April, 1969; also in *Audiovisual Instruction* 14:42—48, September 1969.

———, Taylor, Rex, and Bedard, Ronald, "Educational Technology in Southeast Alaska," *Audiovisual Instruction,* p. 1094, December 1967.

Kelly, J., and Chaloff, C., "Architect–Student Collaboration Made Master Planning Possible," *College and University Business* 53:30–32, August 1973.

Kemp, J., "Future Ain't What It Used to Be," *Audiovisual Instruction* 17:12–14, June 1972.

Kent Public Schools, *Kent High School Library—Learning Center,* Kent, Washington, 1967.

Kenton, M., "Design-in with Unit Ventilation," *American School and University* 40:48, January 1968.

Kentucky State Department of Education, *Purchasing Manual.* Frankfort, Ky., Kentucky State Department of Education, 1968. 66 p.

Kessler, W., "Facilities Programing," *Audiovisual Instruction* 15:75–76, October 1970.

"Kids Love a Classroom All Their Own," *Interiors* 131:150+, April 1972.

Kiesling, Herbert J., *High School Size and Cost Factors, Final Report.* Bloomington, Ind., Indiana University, 1968. 153 p.

———, "King School Turns Its Back on Distraction," *American School Board Journal* 157:29–32, February 1970.

King, J., "New Ways to Build, or How to Get Your School Built Before You Retire," *National Elementary Principal* 52:17–22, Spring 1972.

Kingsbury, H. F., and Taylor, D. W., "Guidelines for Acoustical Design of Classrooms," *Sound and Vibration* 2:16–28, October 1968.

Kling, Vincent G., "Designing New Facilities for Continuing Education," *American School and University* 45:17–20, February 1973.

Knirk, F. G., "Acoustical and Visual Environments Affect Learning," *Audiovisual Instruction* 15:34–35, October 1970.

———, "Learning Space Specifications," *Educational Technology* 10:22–25, June 1970.

Koerner, T. F., and Parker, C., "Happiness Isn't Necessarily When a Board Gets the Kind of School It Deserves: Special Report," *American School Board Journal* 157:13–23, January 1970.

———, "Journal Special: The Kind of New School You Want," *American School Board Journal* 157:13–23, January 1970.

"Koffeklatsches: a Good Way to 'Get to' the People," *Nation's Schools* 87:100–102, October 1971.

Kohn, Sherwood D., "Three High Schools Revisited: Andrews, McPherson and Nova," *Profiles of Significant Schools Series.* New York, Educational Facilities Laboratories, p. 29, July 1967.

Kolflat, F., "What's Going on in On-Going Education; Continuing Education Centers," *American School and University* 46:65–69, October 1973.

Konnert, M. William, "The Missing Ingredient in Budgets," *School Management* 16:36–37, November 1972.

Korman, F., "Costing AV Materials: A Job Approach," *Audiovisual Instruction* 19:15–18, April 1974.

Kramenz, H. W., and Storkel, S. J., "Does Your Board Room Say Welcome?" *American School Board Journal* 159:20+, August 1971.

Krasnoff, Howard O., "Architects Are Con-Artists," *American School and University* 44:16+, January 1972.

Kreider, J. A., "Bibliography on Library Planning," in Mount, H. E., *Planning the Special Library*, Special Library Association, 1972, pp. 80–94.

Kurtzman, David H., "A City University's Multi-Million Dollar Plant Expansion Program," *American School and University* 39:41+, May 1967.

Kypress, Frank, "New Buildings for New Generations," *American School and University* 37:25–28, February 1965.

Lacy, W. D., and others, "Building for Education," *Royal Institute of British Architects Journal* 75:349–381, August 1968.

Lambert, S. M., "Financing a National Standard of Education," *Today's Educator* 61:42–43, April 1972.

Lanford, O. E., "New Kind of Facilities Planning," *College Management* 6:4+, September 1971.

Langmead, S., and M. Beckman, *New Library Design: Guidelines to Planning Academic Library Buildings*, New York, John Wiley & Sons, Inc., 1971. 117 p.

Lappin, C. P., "At Your Service: The Instructional Material Reference Center for the Visually Handicapped," *Teaching Exceptional Children* 5:74–76, Winter 1973.

Larson, Milton E., "A Checklist of Facilities-Planning 'Musts'," *School Shop* 28:98–99, April 1969.

Lavin, Richard J., "Layman's Use of 'Quality Lighting' Appraisal Systems," *Illuminating Engineering* 63:355–360, July 1968.

———, "Learning Center Focuses on Multi-Use Library: Eaglebrook School, Deerfield, Massachusetts," *Architectural Review* 139:164–167, February 1966.

———, *Learning Environment*. New York, American Electric Power System, 1968. 24 p.

———, "New Technique Improves School Facilities Planning," *Audiovisual Instruction* 14:58–59, October 1969.

———, "Simulation, Standards and the Seventies: Media Center Design," *School Library Journal* 16:50–51, November 1969.

"Layman's Guide to School Planning," *Nation's Schools*, 1971. Special Publication.

Le Grand, Y., *Light, Colour, Vision,* 2nd edition. London, Junt, Hunt, Chapman and Hall, 1968.

"Learning Can Be Fun: Challenge in Play and Education Builds a Child's Confidence," *Industrial Design* 17:28–29, November 1970.

"Learning Center Designed for Electronic Media," *American School and University* 43:30+, October 1971.

"Learning Centers Plus," *Architectural Forum* 135:32–35, December 1971.

"Learning Resources Center at Santa Barbara," *Architectural Record* 152:118–119, July 1972.

"Learning Resources Center: Easy on Eyes and Ears," *American School and University* 43:37–39, October 1971.

Lee, Todd, "The Systems Built Schoolhouse and Beyond," *American School and University* 45:22–26, January 1973.

Leonard, W. P., "Playing the Instructional Technologist Game," *Audiovisual Instruction* 17:46+, June 1972.

Leu, Donald J., and Candoli, I. Carl, "Educational Facilities Data," *Design for the Future* Volume II. Chicago, Board of Education, 1968. 123 p.

———, *Feasibility Study of the "Cultural-Educational Park" for Chicago*. East Lansing, Mich., Michigan State University, 1968. 83 p.

———, "Library and Media Center for Fisk's Future: Academic Libraries," *Library Journal* 94:4404–4405, December 1, 1969.

Lewis, E. A., "USOE Bureau of Libraries and Educational Technology," *Audiovisual Instruction* 16:57+, September 1971.

Lewis, P., and Deal, J. V., "Coming Attractions in Technology: Interview," *Nation's Schools* 86:70+, October 1970.

———, and Midjaas, C. L., "Educator–Architect Teams: Interview," *Audiovisual Instruction* 15:52–55, October 1970.

Lewis, Philip, "Hints from Huron About Circulating Cassetts," *Nation's Schools* 89:70–72, November 1972.

———, "How to Plan a Learning Lab," *Nation's Schools,* 90:54+, December 1972.

———, "Improved Security Devices Offer 24-Hour Protection," *Nation's Schools* 87:72+, January 1971.

———, "Need More Wall Outlets? Plug into Technology," *Nation's Schools* 90:42+, July 1972.

———, "New Dimensions in Educational Technology for Multi-Media Centers," *Library Trends,* April 1971.

———, "Simulators Go Places by Going Nowhere," *Nation's Schools* 89:70–72, February 1972.

Liberman, H., "Regional Media Centers: A Survey," *Audiovisual Instruction* 17:46–48, March 1972.

"Library Designed for Intensive Community Use," *Architectural Record* 149:109–114, April 1971.

Licklider, J. C. R., *Libraries for the Future.* Cambridge, Mass., MIT Press, 1965.

———, "Lighting That Does Much More Than Provide Illumination," *Architectural Review* 144:147–149, August 1968.

"Lightweight Structures for Education," *American School and Universities* 45:27–30, July 1973.

Lindeman, L. R., and Gillespie, J. E., "Multi-Media: Essential Component for Disseminating Education Excellence," *Audiovisual Guide* 52:18–20, January 1973.

Lindman, Erick, *The Federal Government and Public Schools.* Washington, D.C., American Association of School Administrators, NEA, 1965.

Lineberry, C. S., "Problems and Solutions in Developing In-House Educational Technology Capability," *Educational Technology* 10:34—39, December 1970.

Lins, L. J., *Administration of Certain Federal Higher Education Acts of Selected States.* Madison, Wisc., Wisconsin Coordinating Council for Higher Education, 1968. 34 p.

Locatis, C., "Regulating the Education Marketplace: Standards for Equipment and Materials" *Audiovisual Instruction* 17:33–37, December 1972.

Lorenz, Robert B., "Architecture and the College Library," *Audiovisual Instruction,* p. 836, October 1967.

Loughary, John W., "Future Developments of Man–Machine Systems in Education," pp. 223–234, in *Man–Machine Systems in Education.* New York, Harper & Row, Inc., 1966.

Love, John W., and McGee, James E., "Florida's Inventory of School Facilities," *School Management* 16:23–26, December 1972.

Ludwig, Merritt C., "Grinnell's College Forum Is Informal by Design," *College and University Business* 39:48–51, December 1965.

Lysaught, J. P., "Contingency Management and Educational Technology," *Educational Technology* 11:69–71, April 1971.

Macbeth, E. W., "When the Walls Come Tumbling Down," *School Management* 15:18–21, August 1971.

MacConnell, James D., and Schiller, Clark E., *A Basic Reference Shelf on Facilities for Instructional Media. Series I, Using Educational Media: Guide to the Literature.* Stanford, Calif., ERIC Clearinghouse on Educational Media and Technology, 1968. 15 p.

MacDonald, A. H., "Planning for the Second

Century: An Approach to Library Planning in Theory and in Practice," *Atlantic Provinces Library Association (APLA) Bulletin* 32:7–20, March 1968.

Mahal, J. Kenneth, and Olson, Ray E., "An Architect's Approach to Vocational School Planning," *American Vocational Journal* 44:31–35, January 1969.

_____, "Major Library Fulfills the Master Plan for Boston University's Central Campus," *Architectural Record* 143:125–128, January 1968.

"Make-Do Site Makes an Unusual School," *School Management* 15:15–17, July 1971.

Manning, Peter, "Manplan 4—Community School," *Architecture Review,* January 1970. Entire Issue: British School Architecture.

_____, ed., *Primary School: An Environment for Education. Design 230,* February, 1968. 60 p.

"The Many Ways of Tile," *School Management* 16:26+, July 1972.

Margolies, J. S., "New Projects by Victor Lundy," *Architectural Forum* 131:78–83, November 1969.

"Marland States Position on Key Issues," *Nation's Schools* 88:37–40, April 1971.

Marland, S. P., Jr., "Educational Technology; a Vote of Confidence," *Audiovisual Instruction* 17:48+, October 1972.

Marlowe, John W., "Media and Money," *Audiovisual Instruction* 141:57–60, May 1969.

Marshall, J., "Design Without Precedent," *Times Educational Supplement* 2747:92–93, January 12, 1968.

Martin, L., "Education Without Walls," *Royal Institute of British Architects Journal* 75:356–361, August 1968.

Martin, Sheila K., "The Cost of Audiovisual Instruction Survey, 1971–72," *School Management* 15:11–15, November 1971.

Masiko, Peter, Jr., and Bauwsma, Frank, "New Learning Centers Stimulate Media Innovation at Miami–Dade," *American School and University* 39:60–62, May 1967.

Mason, Ellsworth, "A Well Wrought Interior Design," *Library Journal,* pp. 743–747, February 15, 1967.

_____, "Non-Book Media: Libraries Take a Second Look," *American School and University* 43:12+, October 1971.

Massman, V., "Deficiencies in Modern Design," *Mountain Plains Library Quarterly* 12:21–23, Spring 1967.

Matthews, A. L., "Preparing Architectural Specifications on School Buildings," *Education Product Report* 4:46–48, October 1970.

Mattox, D. V., Jr., "Design Communications Facilities Cooperatively, Not Piecemeal," *Audiovisual Instruction* 15:74+, June 1970.

Maver, T. W., "Space–Time Interface; a Systematic Approach to the Problem of Flexibility in Educational Buildings," *Architectural Design* 43:44–46, January 1972.

McAdams, N. R., "Super-Librarian and Sub-Architect: The Anomoly of the Role of the Building Consultant," *Library Journal* 9:5827–5831, December 1, 1966.

McAlister, D. W., and Sisler, G., "Utilization of a College-Wide Independent Learning Center," *Journal of Home Economics* 63:119–120, February 1971.

McAnulty, Laura, "Media-Based Learning Resources Center," *Audiovisual Instruction* 15:50–54, February 1970.

McBride, O., "Library Media Center of Today," *Educational Leadership* 28:151–154, November 1970.

McConeghy, G. L., "School Building: A Plea for Logical Development," *Audiovisual Instruction* 15:45–46, October 1970.

McCorkle, J., "When Does a Library Become a Media Center?" *School and Community* 57:10+, May 1971.

McCutcheon, S. C., *A Conceptualization of the Nature and Principles of Institutional Planning.*

Bloomington, Ind., Indiana University, 1968. Doctoral Thesis. 187 p.

McDougal, Russell, and Thompson, James J., "The Multimedia Classroom: Planning and Operation," *Audiovisual Instruction* 121:827–829, October 1967.

McGrady, D. S., "Schools Without Walls: Selected Readings," *Audiovisual Instruction* 17:45+, September 1972.

McGuffey, C. W., *A Review of Selected References Relating to the Planning of Higher Education Facilities.* Tallahassee, Fla., Florida State University, 1968. 100 p.

_____, *An Evaluation Study of the College Facilities Program. Final Report.* Tallahassee, Fla., Florida State University, 1968. 152 p.

McHenry, Dean E., "Environmental Implication of the Concern for Community," *Liberal Education* 53:41–47, March 1967.

McPhee, Mary, "Building Manager Manages to Free Building Principal," *School Management* 16:36–37, October 1972.

McVey, G. F., "Equipping a Multi-Media Lab for Action," *American School and University,* p. 3, November 1968.

Mead, M., "Planning Media Centers: Prescription vs. Communication," *Educational Screen and Audiovisual Guide* 48:8+, October 1969.

Medd, D., "People in Schools: An Attitude to Design," *Royal Institute of British Architects Journal* 75:262–268, June 1968. Discussion, 75:285+, July 1968.

Melnyk, A., "Architecture of Academic Libraries in Europe: Bibliography 1960–1970," *College and Research Libraries* 33:228–235, May 1972.

Mercer, M. G., "College Planner, Architect Team Prevents Campus Building Jumble," *College and University Business* 48:70+, January 1970.

Merlo, Frank P., "Discarding an Old School Building," *School Management* 15:37–38, May 1971.

Mersky, R. M., and David, J., "Selected Annotated Bibliographies on Library Floor Covering and Library Security 1940–1967," *Law Libraries Journal* 61:108–114, May 1968.

"The Message Is You—Guidelines for Preparing Presentations, Parts 1, 2 and 3," *Audiovisual Instruction* 16, January, February, and March 1971.

Messick, John D., "Learning Resources Center Is Built Around Instruction," *College and University Business* 39:60–62, November 1965.

"Metal Buildings Offer Answers to Construction Problems: Pre-engineered Metal," *School Management* 16:26–29, August 1972.

Metropolitan Toronto School Board, *Educational Specifications and User Requirements for Elementary (K–6) Schools.* Toronto, Can., Metropolitan Toronto School Board, 1968. 208 p.

"Miami's Innovative Schools," *Architectural Record* 146:153–168, October 1969.

Michigan State Department of Education, *Facilities Planning Documents Available from the Division of Vocational Education, Michigan Department of Education.* Lansing, Mich., Michigan State Department of Education, 1968. 2 p.

_____, *State Plan for Higher Education in Michigan,* (Provisional). Based upon the work of Dr. Harold T. Smith, Lansing, Mich., Michigan State Department of Education, 1968. 94 p.

Miller, Joseph, "Designing Educational Environments," *Science Teacher* 36:24–25, February 1969.

Miller, Leon, "How to Prepare a Long Range School Facilities Plan," *American School and University* 44:18–28, February 1972.

Miller, L. P., "Materials for Multi-Ethnic Learners," *Educational Leadership* 28:129–132, November 1970.

Miller, N., "Learning Resources Center: Its Role in Education," *Audiovisual Instruction* 16:48+, May 1971.

Miller, Richard P., "How to Plan Science Facilities

for the 70's," *Nation's Schools* 89:49–58, March 1972.

Mitchell, Robert E., "Behind the Bushes: Landscaped Offices Take Root," *American School and University* 44:38–48, January 1972.

Miura, T., "On Optimum Room Temperature for Light Work," *The Journal of Science and Labor* 44:1–9, March 1968.

"Mobile School Furniture System Provides a Total, Flexible Classroom Environment," *Architectural Record* 149:153+, April 1971.

"Modular Furniture Meets Rigorous Demands for Flexible School Spaces," *Architectural Record* 151:135–136, February 1972.

Montgomery County Public Schools, *These Are Your Schools 1968*. Rockville, Md., Montgomery County Public Schools, 1968. 150 p.

Montgomery, Roger, "Pattern Language," *Architectural Forum*, pp. 53–58, January–February 1970.

Moriarty, John H., "New Media Facilities," *Library Trends* 16:251–258, October 1967.

Morisseau, James J., "Educational Facilities Laboratory: A Catalyst for Innovation," *Educational Screen and Audiovisual Guide* 48:16–27, October 1969.

Morphet, E. L., and Jesser, D. L., eds., *Emerging Design for Education*. Englewood Cliffs, N.J., Citation Press, 1968. 240 p.

_____, *Planning for Effective Utilization of Technology in Education*. Englewood Cliffs, N.J., Citation Press, 1968. 372 p.

Morrison, D. Grant, *A Guide to Planning for Community College Facilities*. Washington, D.C., American Association of Junior Colleges, 1968. 65 p.

Murtha, D. Michael, *Systematic Methods in School Planning and Design. A Selected and Annotated Bibliography*. Madison, Wisc., University of Wisconsin, ERIC Clearinghouse on Educational Facilities, 1968. 43 p.

Myers, D. C., "Common Sense Approach to Facilities Design," *Audiovisual Instruction* 16:66–67, June 1971.

Mylecraine, Walter E., and others, *Projections of Public School Facilities Needs, 1968–1969 Through 1972–1973*. Washington, D.C., U.S. Government Printing Office, 1968. 16 p.

Myller, Rolf, *The Design of the Small Public Library*. New York, R. R. Bowker Company, 1966.

Myrick, R., "Behavioral Factors in the Design of High School Buildings," *Educational Technology* 10:16–18, June 1970.

Myrick, Richard, and Marx, Barbara S., *An Exploratory Study of the Relationships Between High School Building Design and Student Learning. Final Report*. Washington, D.C. George Washington University, 1968. 103 p.

National Electrical Contractors Association, "Balancing Lighting and Thermal Designs," *American School and University* 42:29–40, April 1970.

Neagley, Ross L., and Evans, N. Dean, *Handbook for Effective Curriculum Development*. Englewood Cliffs, N.J., Prentice-Hall, Inc., 1967. Chapter 10.

_____, and others, *The School Administrator and Learning Resources*. Englewood Cliffs, N.J., Prentice-Hall, Inc., 1969. Pp. 83–119. "Planning the School Plant for Optimum Use of Learning Resources"; also pp. 135–155, "Guidelines for Financing Educational Media Programs."

Nelms, Walter L., "Standardization of Educational Specifications," *American School Board Journal* 151:44+, January 1965.

Neville, H. R., "How to Live with Bigness," *Phi Delta Kappan* 47:430–432, April 1966.

_____, "New Dimensions: How 1968 Award-Winning Schools Compare," *Nation's Schools* 83:41–66, January 1969.

_____, "New Evaluative Criteria Geared to Detailed Ratings," *Nation's Schools* 84:56–58, August 1969.

_____, "New Federal Aid for College Construction," *American School and University* 37:34–35, 63–63, February 1965.

_____, "New Lighting Schemes for Integrated Designs," *American School and University* 40:44–46, January 1968.

_____, "New Trends in School Building," *School Management* 13:51+, July 1969.

"New Architecture at Lesley College Creates a City in Microcosm," *College and University Business* 55:34+, August 1973.

"New Environment: How Sixteen Award-Winning Schools Compare," *Nation's Schools* 89:45–64, January 1972.

"New Facilities for Higher Education: A Preview of the 1971 CUCE Architectural Exhibit," *American School and University* 43:24–28, March 1971.

"New Life for Old Schools," *National ELementary Principal* 52:76–86, September 1972.

"New Schoolhouse: Symposium," *National Elementary Principal* 52:6–92, September 1972.

Newman, F. M., and Oliver, E. W., "Education and Community," *Harvard Educational Review* 37:61–106, Winter 1967.

_____, "New Schools—Editorial Coverage of a Number of New United States Schools," *Architectural Record* 144:151–166, November 1968.

_____, "1965 Tops All Records—$6.1 Billion for Educational Construction," *American School and University* 39:25–32, September 1966.

"Nine Ways to Conserve Gas Energy," *American School and University* 44:28–34, January 1972.

"1971 Community and Junior College Design Awards," *American Institute of Architects Journal* 55:26–29, February 1971.

"1971 Cost of Building Index," *School Management* 15:12–16, June 1971.

"1972 Cost of Building Index," *School Management* 16:19–20, September 1972.

"1972 Library Buildings Award Program," *American Institute of Architects Journal* 57:41–47, April 1972.

"1972 Plant Planning and Purchasing Directory," *American School and University* 44:28–34, May 1972.

"1973 Cost of Building Index," *School Management* 17:12–27, June 1973.

"1973 Cost of Building Statistics," *College Management* 8:12–33, June 1973.

"1974 Award-Winning Architecture," *American School and University* 46:19–23, March 1974.

"Non-Graded School Designed for Team Teaching," *Architectural Record* 151:110–111, April 1972.

North Carolina State Board of Education, *Educational Specifications: School Planning Series 3.* Raleigh, N.C., North Carolina State Board of Education, Division of School Planning, 1968. 4 p.

North Central Association of Colleges and Secondary Schools. Commission on Secondary Schools. *Policies and Criteria for Approval of Secondary Schools, 1968–1969.* 61 p.

North, R. S., "Design Follows Concept: A Case Study of Facilities Development," *Educational Technology* 9:69–71, December 1969.

North, S. D., ed., *Proceedings for the Conference on Environment for Learning,* Madison, Wisc., University of Wisconsin, 1968. 145 p.

_____, *Considerations in the Development and Use of Facilities for Independent Study. A State-of-the-Art Paper.* Madison, Wisc., University of Wisconsin, ERIC Clearinghouse on Educational Facilities, 1968. 26 p.

Nova University of Advanced Technology, *Education Parks, 2nd Annual Nova University Conference, April 17–19, 1968.* Fort Lauderdale, Fla., Nova University of Advanced Technology, 1968. 84 p.

O'Grince, S. H., "Baltimore Expands Its Portables," *American School and University* 42:24–25, May 1970.

O'Hare, Michael, "Designer's Dilemma," *Daedalus* 98:765–777, Summer 1969.

Ofresh, Gabriel D., "A National Center for Educational Media and Materials for the Handicapped," *Audiovisual Instruction* 14:28–29, November 1969.

Oglesby, W. B., "Basic Elements for an Instructional Resources Center," *American School and University* 40:59+, September 1968.

Ohanian, V., "Educational Technology: A Critique," *Elementary School Journal* 71:182–197, January 1971.

Olson, J. C., "Pittsburgh's Bid to Blend Programs and Facilities: Great High Schools Project," *School Shop,* pp. 31–34, May 1968.

"One Room Schoolhouse, 1972 Style: An Open Plan Middle School with Split-Level Classroom Areas," *School Management* 15:17–20, April 1971.

"Open Plan Furnishings Borrow from Builders and Hospitals," *American School and University* 44:30–36, March 1972.

"Open Plan: They Tried It, They Liked It," *American School and University* 44:18–20, March 1972.

"Open Planning in Columbus," *Progressive Architect* 52:72+, February 1971.

Orne, Jerrold, "Academic Library Building in 1969," *Library Journal* 94:4364–4368, December 1, 1969.

Orne, J., "Academic Library Building in 1972," *Library Journal* 97:3849–3855, December 1, 1972.

O'Tuel, M. B., and Duncan, L. W., "Does School Appearance Really Count?" *School Management* 16:10–11, December 1972.

Papadatos, Steven A., "Color in the Classroom," *School Management* 16:26+, February 1972.

Pasciolla, Frank, "Communication—A Very Real Maintenance Problem," *American School and University* 43:30–31, May 1971.

Pasnik, Marion, "Factory Building to Modern School in Six Months," *School Management* 15:12–14, July 1971.

———, "Furniture—the Great Divider," *School Management* 16:14–15, May 1972.

———, "Noninstitutional School Furniture," *National Elementary Principal* 52:50–54, September 1972.

Pasnik, M., "Place Where You Can See How Things Happen: Educational Facilities Center, New York City," *School Management* 18:18–19, March 1974.

Pearce, David W., "The Architect Translates Program Into Plans," *College and University Business* 38:41–42, February 1965.

Pearson, Neville P., and Butler, Lucius, "Heddie School, Hightstown, New Jersey," *Interiors* 129:146+, November 1969.

———, *Instructional Materials Centers: Selected Readings.* Minneapolis, Minn., Burgess Publishing Company, 1969. 345 p.

Peck, J. E., "Future Developments in School Finance," *School Management* 16:11–14, August 1972.

Pele, C. J., *Current Bidding Practices of School Districts in Ohio with an Annual Budget of from $5 to $15 Million.* Athens, Ohio, Ohio University, 1968.

———, "People in Schools: An Attitude to Design," *Royal Institute of British Architects Journal* 75:262–268, June 1968.

Pell, Carroll J., "How to Set Fees for Community Use of Schools," *School Management* 16:21–22, December 1972.

"Penn 'Magnet' High School," *Interiors* 130:128–131, November 1970.

Perkins, Bradford, "A New Building Program Can Run Smoothly," *School Management* 15:35–37, September 1971.

"Permanent Additions Minimize Cost and Construction Time," *School Management* 16:30–31, December 1972.

Persselin, L. E., "Humanizing Education Through Technology: the View from an Ivory Foxhole,"

Educational Technology 11:18–20, June 1971.

Peters, B. F., "Student Body Turns It On," *American Education* 5:20–21, April 1969.

Peterson, H. N., "Developments in the Planning of Main Library Buildings," *Library Trends* 20:693–741, April 1972.

Peterson, S., "Before You Build Your Library," *West Virginia Libraries* 21:6–10, September 1968.

Philipson, R. L., "The School Site, Asphalt Jungle or Open Space?" *Michigan School Board Journal* 14:7+, January 1968.

Phillips, Murray G., "Learning Materials and Their Implementation," *Review of Educational Research,* June 1966.

Phillips, P. J., *Reactions of Students and Teachers to Carpeted Teaching Spaces.* Knoxville, Tenn., University of Tennessee, 1968. Doctoral Thesis. 107 p.

Phipps, H. Harry, "New Schools Need New Energy Concepts," *American School and University* 45:34–36, January 1973.

"Picking the Right Flooring," *American School and University* 44:27–30, September 1972.

Piele, P. K., "School Property," *Yearbook of School Law* 1972, pp. 51–76.

Pilafian, Suren, "A-V Supermarket," *American School and University* 39:45+, April 1967.

Pilat, F., and Struska, J., "Scientific Trends of Construction of Cinemas in Czechoslovakia," *Journal of the Society of Motion Picture and Television Engineers* 75:172–175, March 1966.

Pinnell, Charles, and Wacholder, Michael, *Guidelines for Planning in Colleges and Universities.* Volume 1: Planning System (112 p.) Volume 2: Management and Financial Planning (128 p.). Volume 3: Physical Plant Planning, Land Uses and Traffic. Austin, Texas, Texas College and University System Coordinating Board, 1968.

Planning and Equipping Industrial Arts Facilities. Augusta, Maine, State Department of Education, 1966. 50 p.

"Planning for Relocatable Buildings," *American School and University* 44:58–62, September 1972.

Planning Functional Facilities for Home Economics Education. Special Publication Number 12. Washington, D.C., U.S. Government Printing Office, 1965. 48 p.

Planning Model for School Facilities. A Planning Model for a Secondary School Utilizing a Multi-Dimensional Approach for Optimum Flexibility. Chelmsford, Mass., Chelmsford Park High School, 1968. 172 p.

Planning Your Purchases of Educational Materials, 1966–1969. New York, American Textbook Publishing Institute, 1966.

Plath, Karl A., *Schools Within Schools: A Study of High School Organization,* Secondary School Administration Series (edited by David B. Austin). New York, Teachers College Press, Columbia University Bureau of Publications, 1965.

Pohl, J. G., "Artificial Sound Blankets in Modern School Planning," *Architectural Science Review* 11:61–66, June 1968.

Poole, Frazer, G., ed., *The Library Environment: Aspects of Interior Planning.* Proceedings of the Library Equipment Institute, Chicago, ALA, 1965.

Porter, D. S., "How to Design a Working IMC, Bridge School, Lexington, Massachusetts," *Educational Screen and AV Guide,* p. 23, November 1967.

"Portland Community College," *Architectural Record* 147:144–147, June 1970.

Powell, J., "From Library to Media Center: There Is a Difference," *National Association of Secondary School Principals Bulletin* 55:79–85, March 1971.

"Practice What You Teach," *Interior Design* 41:118–121, September 1970.

Prakken, Lawrence W., ed., *Modern School Shop Planning.* Ann Arbor, Mich., Prakken Publications, 1967. 255 p.

"Preview: Growing Campus," *Architectural Forum* 134:14+, May 1971.

Progner, Jean, "National Library Week: The New Libraries," *Saturday Review* 52:28–30, April 1969.

_____, "P/A Design Citation: Walton High School Addition, Walton, Connecticut," *Progressive Architect* 49:126–127, January 1968.

Pulver, R., "Media Center: Planning the Space," *Instructor* 80:52–53, November 1970.

Purvis, Carol, "The Bibb County IMC," *Audiovisual Instruction* 14:32–33, September 1969.

_____, *Quantitative Standards for Audiovisual Personnel, Equipment and Materials.* Washington, D.C., Department of AudioVisual Instruction, NEA, 1966.

"Putting Ears and Eyes to Work: High Technology Audio-Visual Systems," *American School and University* 44:23–26, July 1972.

Quann, L. W., "Twelve Steps to Simplify School Construction," *School Management* 16:27–29, December 1972.

Quinn, J., "Facility Design with Maintenance in Mind," *American School and University* 40:38+, March 1968.

Rackowski, Wayne, "Budget Provisions for Replacement of Property," *School Management* 15:24–26, November 1971.

Randall, J. P., "Obtaining the Successful Library Building," *Focus* 26:62–63, Summer 1972.

Randall, W., "School Facilities—AV Checklist," *Audiovisual Instruction* 18:16–17, December 1973.

Ravlerson, J. D., Jr., "Innovation in Education: Needed, a New Profession—Educational Engineers," *Educational Technology* 12:40–41, August 1972.

Rebhorn, E., "Procedures for Planning Educational Facilities," *Man/Society/Technology* 32:299–333, March $973.

"Reclaimed Space for Vocational Schools," *American School and University* 44:23–31, December 1972.

Reed, Bob H., and Harper, William A., *The College Facilities Thing: Impressions of an Airborne Seminar and a Guide for Junior College Planners.* Washington, D.C., American Association of Junior Colleges, 1968. 74 p.

Reed, Robert H., "People, Processes and Time Equals Facilities," *Junior College Journal,* 37:20–25, November 1966.

Reid, John Lyon, "AS&U Interviews John Lyon Reid on Interior Design: Discussion Revolves Around Factors That Go into Interior Design, Especially in Cases of Open Plans," *American School and University* 44:46–49, September 1971.

_____, and others, "A Special Kind of Middle School," *Nation's Schools* 83:76–79, May 1969.

Reisberg, Sidney, and Bynum, Terrell W., "Changing Instructional Patterns in the University: A Prototype," *AV Communications Review* 19:198–212, Summer 1971.

"Remodel, Convert, Expand," *American School and University* 43:35–39, July 1971.

"Remodelling on a Shoestring," *Nation's Schools* 89:50–53, October 1972.

Renfrow, O. W., and Best, J. K., "From the Twenties to the Future," *Educational Leadership* 29:179–181, November 1971.

Rennhackkamp, W. M. H., "Lighting of Buildings," *Certified Engineer* 41:179–183, June 1968.

"Report on Facilities in New Schools and Additions," *School Management* 15:19–23, July 1971.

Resnick, Henry S., "High School with No Walls," *Education Digest* 35:16–19, March 1970.

"Resource Center Equipment Roundup," *American School and University* 42:44–46, September 1970.

Responsive Environment Learning Centers "Feedback from the Field," Conference Report, February 1968. Englewood Cliffs, N.J., Environments Corporation, 1968. 119 p.

"Reviewing the McMurrin Report," *Nation's Schools* 86:79+, October 1970.

"Revolution in Environments for Early Education: Furnishings for Educational Facilities," *Interiors* 130:90–93, December 1970.

"Rhode Island School Remodeled and Addition Built in One Short Summer," *American School and University* 45:66+, April 1973.

Rice, A. H., "Max Rafferty Misses the Point Behind a Well-Designed School," *Nation's Schools* 81:4+, March 1968.

———, "Should You Let Your Teachers Design Their Own Schools?" *Nation's Schools* 85:18–19, June 1970.

Richards, D. A., "Specialty Coatings Add Life and Facilitate Maintenance," *Nation's Schools* 83:112+, March 1969.

Richardson, Joe A., "Winnetka,'s Learning Laboratory," *Educational Leadership,* March 1966.

Rittenhouse, Carl H., "Educational Uses and Users," *AV Communications Review* 19:76–86, Spring 1971.

Robbie, Roderick G., "Flexible Future of Architecture," *American Institute of Architects Journal* 52:63–66, November 1969.

———, "Turning Point? The Systems Approach to Building," *Royal Institute of British Architects Journal* 77:254–261, June 1970.

Rogers, A. R., "Library Buildings and Equipment: Sources of Information," *Library Journal* 97:3876–3877, December 1, 1972.

———, "Systems Building: A Solution to the Cost Squeeze?" *Library Journal* 94:4360–4363, December 1, 1969.

"Role of the Community in Planning and Designing a New School," *School Management* 17:40–42, April 1973.

Rosich, J. M., "Work Order Control Aids Maintenance Program," *American School and University* 44:41+, July 1972.

Rossi, P. H., and Biddle, B. J., *The New Media and Education*. Chicago, Aldine–Atherton, Inc., 1966.

Rossman, Wendell, "Auditoriums: A Turn for the Better," *American School and University* 43:27–30, December 1971.

Rudiger, Charles W., and Pollack, Rubin, "Wealth's Effect on Education," *School Management* 16:16–20, February 1972.

———, "What This Year's Cost of Education Shows," *School Management* 17:21+, January 1973.

Rutrough, James E., "Building a New School Plant? The First Important Step in Educational Planning," *Clearinghouse* 44:378–380, February 1970.

"Safety and Sound Control Combine in Ceiling of Second Largest High School in the United States," *School Management* 16:42+, March 1972.

Sarthory, J. A., and Wade, D.E., "Stimulating the Acquisition and Allocation of Education Resources," *Educational Technology* 11:58–61, December 1971.

Saunders, Luther W., ed., *Profile of a Significant School, Clarksville—Montgomery County High School.* Southeastern Regional Center for Educational Facilities Laboratories. No Date.

"Save . . . for a Change, Ideas to Cut Costs," *Nation's Schools* 89:25–40, August 1972.

Sawyer, William C., "Design Considerations," *American School and University* 43:44–47, April 1971.

Scebra, J. B., "Checklist for Construction Planners," *School Management* 16:20+, June 1972.

Schiller, Clarke E., and others, "Media Center Design," *School Library Journal,* November 1969 (entire issue).

———, "School Building Portfolio," *School Management* 12:16–19, February 1968.

———, "School Planners Agree on Need for Education Specifications," *Nation's Schools* 83:99+, May 1969.

_____, "The School Scene—Change and More Change," *Progressive Architecture* 49:130–214, April 1968.

_____, "Schools for Free," *Progressive Architecture* 50:36+, September 1969.

_____, "Schools Planned for Continuity and Change," *Architectural Record* 145:135–142, March 1969.

_____, "Sound and Student Behavior," *Audiovisual Instruction* 14:92+, March 1969.

Schmelzer, R. W., "Design for Learning: Using Technology to Meet Student Needs," *College and University Business* 53:28+, August 1972.

Schmertz, M. F., "Analysis of Excellence: The New York State University Construction Fund," *Architectural Record* 149:105–128, January 1971.

"School Buildings," *Architectural Forum* 135:30–47, December 1971.

"School of the Month: Apollo Elementary—Bossler City, La.," *Nation's Schools* 87:89–91, May 1971.

"School of the Month: Ardmore Elementary—Bellevue, Washington," *Nation's Schools* 87:58–60, February 1971.

"School of the Month: Big Sandy School, Simla, Colorado," *Nation's Schools* 86:76–77, September 1970.

"School Property," *Yearbook of School Law—1971*, pp. 119–158.

"School Renewal: Recycling Old Space: Discussion," *American School and University* 44:18–19, June 1972.

"The School That Looks Like an Indian Village," *School Management* 15:12–15, September 1971.

"School Turned Inside Out to Solve Problems of Security, Heat, and Money," *American School and University* 45:68+, April 1973.

"Schoolhouse: A Self-Revealing Facility," *Design Quarterly* 80:92+, September 1971.

"Schools," *Progressive Architecture* 52:68–109, February 1971.

"Schools in a Hurry: Technology and Systems Techniques," *Progressive Architecture* 52:78–91, February 1971.

"Schools—New Uses for Old Buildings," *Architectural Record* 151:317–323, May 1972.

Schutte, Frederick, "That Elusive Eclectic Thing Called Thermal Environment: What a Board Should Know About It," *American School Board Journal,* pp. 17–22, June 1970.

Schwelk, Gene L., "How Oak Park Revitalized Its Library Resources," *Nation's Schools,* March 1966.

_____, "Million Dollar Carrels," *School Library Journal,* January 1967.

_____, "Science Complex Planned for Adaptability," *College Management,* Vol. 4, Building Portfolio, pp. 24–30, August 1969.

"Sculpture in Space: School Building in the New Jersey Contryside," *Architectural Forum* 134:46–51, April 1971.

Seidel, R. J., "Future for Education and Educational Technology: What Is the Question?" *Educational Technology* 11:37–38, July 1971.

Seitz, C. H. A., *Classroom Performance on Three Intellectual Tasks Under Normal Fluctuations in Atmospheric Pressure.* Baltimore, Md., Johns Hopkins University, 1968. 79 p.

"Services Centers for Schools," *School Management* 16:17–21, July 1972.

"Seven Maintenance Ideas from Industry," *Nation's Schools* 88:42–44, November 1972.

Shapiro, A., and others, "Model Middle School," *Nation's Schools* 91:45–52, May 1973.

Sharp, J. S., "Architectural Steps in Facilities Planning," *Audiovisual Instruction* 10:103+, February 1965.

Shaway, D. E., "Critic in Residence," *Clearing House* 47:52–55, September 1972.

Shemitz, Sylvan, "Lighting an Open Plan School," *School Management* 16:22–24, February 1972.

Sheppard, J. J., *Human Color Perception*. New York, American Elsevier Publishing Company, Inc., 1968. 192 p.

Sidwell, L., "Planning of Library Buildings," *Library Association Record* 72:93–94, March 1970.

Siegel, M. E., "Random Dumping of Educational Technology: Call for Systematic Study of the Implications and Social Consequences of Educational Technology on American Society," *Educational Technology* 10:31–32, June 1970.

Simmons, R. B., and Keller, C., "New Resource Center at Mineral Area College," *School and Community* 57:27+, April 1971.

Simmons, William, "Indirect Costs of Federally Financed Projects," *American School and University* 43:26+, October 1970.

Sine, David F., "Educational Parks," *NEA Journal*, pp. 44–47, March 1968.

Sippel, William, and Minnerly, Leander, "Engineering System for Tomorrow's Urban University," *American School and University* 42:32–33, April 1970.

———, " '68 Preview: Education," *Architectural Review*, pp. 47–59, January 1968.

Skidmore, C. E., "Fistful of Building Ideas You Can Use," *School Management* 12:78–81, September 1968.

Skirvin, W. J., and Berman, M. L., "Architecture and Education: The Behavioral Psychological Approach," *Educational Technology* 13:29–37, December 1973.

"Skyline Gathers K–12 Together Under One Roof," *American School Board Journal*, July 1968.

Sleeman, Phillip J., and DeMartinis, Ernest J., "Rent or Buy Films? A Research Project Offers Answers," *School Management* 15:9–13, October 1971.

———, and Goff, Robert, "The Instructional Materials Center: Dialogue or Discord?" *AV Communication Review*, p. 160, Summer 1967.

Smith, D. L., *How to Find Out in Architecture and Building: A Guide to Sources of Information*. New York, Oxford University Press and Pergamon Press, 1967. 232 p.

Smith, George N., *A Coordinated School Facilities Program for the Litchfield Park Area*. Tempe, Ariz., Arizona State University, 1968. Doctoral Thesis.

Smith, Herbert A., "Review of an Encounter with Educational Technology," *Educational Screen and AV Guide* 50:6+, May 1971.

Smith, L. W., "Practicality Plus Pleasure Equals a Valuable Courtyard," *Nation's Schools* 87:68–69, May 1971.

Smith, Mason Philip, "Maine's Multifaceted High School Library," *Educational Screen and AV Guide,* 50:8+, June 1971.

Smith, T. B., "Understanding Carpet Testing," *American School and University* 44:40–43, April 1971.

Snyder, P., "Educational Facilities Center: New Response to Educational Problems," *Educational Screen and AV Guide* 51:4–8, August 1972.

Solnitt, Albert, "Town and Gown: One Community," *Teachers College Record* 68:289–294, January 1967.

Sommer, R., "Reading Areas in College Libraries," *Library Quarterly* 38:249–260, July 1968.

Spaulding, S., "Developments in Education for the Seventies," *Audiovisual Instruction* 16:10–14, January 1971.

"Special Report: Individualization Through Automation," *Nation's Schools* 88:35–49, October 1972.

"Special Report: Technology in a Tight Economy," *Nation's Schools* 87:67–86, October 1971.

Spencer, M., and Glockner, M., "Have Questions? Ask ERIC," *Instructor* 81:116+, October 1971.

Spurlock, P. L., and Blumeyer, R. L., "Iowa: Sixteen Centers and a Place to Grow," *Audiovisual Instruction* 17:60–62, March 1972.

Stade, Charles E., "Effective Architect Probes Before

He Pencils," *College and University Business* 41:44–46, November 1966.

"Steel-Framing Solves Architectural and Site Problems for Boston Elementary School," *American School and University* 43:38+, January 1971.

Steffen, D. C., "Multimedia Classroom: Project Spoke, Norton, Massachusetts," *American Education* 7:28–30, August 1971.

Stephan, Edward, "Would You Risk Changing Heating Systems in Mid-Winter?" *American School and University* 44:18–21, January 1971.

Stewart, Donald K., "The Cost Analysis of Dial Access Information Retrieval Systems," *Audiovisual Instruction* 12:433+, May 1967.

Stewart, G. K., "Learning Spaces: Activities and Specifications," *Audiovisual Instruction* 15:63–64, October 1970.

Stilwell, W. E., and Schulker, S., "Facilities Available to Disabled Higher Education Students," *Journal of College Student Personnel* 14:419–424, September 1973.

Stone, C. Walter, "Planning for Media Within University Library Buildings," *Library Trends* 18:235–345, October 1969.

Stotz, R. B., "Comparing School Air Conditioning Systems," *American School and University* 42:25–26, April 1970.

———, *Quality Education for Elementary Schools.* Syracuse, N.Y., Syracuse Board of Education, 1968. 81 p.

Stowe, R. A., "Critical Issue in Instructional Development," *Audiovisual Instruction* 16:8–10, December 1971.

Strong, L. E., and Stephenson, W. R., "Science Lab Design: Much Flexibility at Low Cost," *American School and University* 44:16–18, September 1971.

Strumpf, Manny, "Maximum Security at Minimum Cost," *School Management* 16:28–29, February 1972.

Surpin, S., "Fluid University, 1996: Home Terminals, Hologram Libraries, Global Transmitters, and a System Unlike Anything We Know Today," *College and University Business* 51:8+, September 1971.

Szabo, W., "Introduction to Audiovisual Engineering," *AudioVisual Communications*, p. 7, June 1968.

Talbot, J. E., "Looseleaf System Manages $80,000,000 School Projects," *American School and University* 45:35–38, January 1972.

———, "School Renewal: Recycling Old Space," *American School and University* 45:18–28, June 1972.

Tanzman, J., "Blueprint for a District Resource Center," *School Management* 15:40–41, May 1971.

———, "The Complete AV Center—What It Takes to Do the Job," pp. 168–170 in Pearson and Butler, *Instructional Materials Centers: Selected Readings,* Minneapolis, Minn., Burgess Publishing Company, 1969.

———, "Media Offers Various Approaches to Your Subject: Institute on Evaluation-Accountability for School Administrators," *School Management* 15:46+, April 1971.

———, "Open House—the Living Room School," *School Management* 16:22–23, August 1972.

———, "What You Need to Build an Instructional Materials Center," *School Management* 15:62+, January 1971.

Tauffner, G. E., "Furniture and Related Facilities to Accommodate Multi-Media Activities in Libraries," *Library Trends* 19:493–507, April 1971.

Taylor, J., "Learning Resources Centers," *Royal Institute of British Architects Journal* 77:348–352, August 1970.

Taylor, James L., ed., *Library Facilities for Elementary and Secondary Schools,* Washington, D.C., U.S. Department of Health, Education, and Welfare, U.S. Government Printing Office, 1965.

Taylor, Kenneth I., "Creative Inquiry and the School IMC," *Audiovisual Instruction* 14:52–57, September 1969.

———, "How to Plan and Equip an Instructional Materials Center," pp. 145–150 in Pearson and Butler, *Instructional Materials Centers: Selected Readings,* Minneapolis, Minn., Burgess Publishing Company, 1969.

———, "Library Facilities and Instructional Materials Centers," *Wilson Library Bulletin* 63:137–138, May 1967.

Taylor, Robert S., "Planning a College Library for the Seventies," *Educational Record* 50:426–431, Fall 1969.

———, *Temperature Control: Honeywell Planning Guide.* Minneapolis, Minn., Honeywell, Inc., 1968. 26 p.

———, "This Resource Center Is Hub of School," *Education Canada* 9:10–13, June 1969.

———, "This Schoolhouse Is for Children," *School Management* 13:64–72, October 1969.

"Teaching in the Street: Converting the Streets Literally into Classrooms," *Progressive Architecture* 52:90+, February 1971.

"Technology in a Tight Economy: Special Report," *Nation's Schools* 88:67–86, October 1971.

"Technology: Pre-engineered Metal Building Systems," *Architectural Forum* 134:52–53, April 1971.

"Technology: The Cost of Education: Symposium," *Audiovisual Instruction* 16:7–18, November 1971.

"Telling the Education Story," *School Management* 15:28+, August 1971.

"Tenth Annual Cost of Building Index and Directory of Product Information," *School Management* 15, June 1971 (entire issue).

"Think Big: Combined Districts Build Five Schools At Once," *American School and University* 44:23+, December 1971.

"This Board Saw, Swallowed, Bought and Won," *American School Board Journal* 158:27–28, January 1971.

Thompson, Donald E., "Form vs. Function: Architecture and the College Library," *Library Trends* 18:37–47, July 1969.

Thompson, James J., "Instructional Systems and Educational Facilities", pp. 169–192 in *Instructional Communication.* New York, American Book Company, 1969.

———, "Three New Campus Buildings, Shaped by Site and Function, Reinforce Master Plan," *Architectural Record* 144:97–1;4, August 1968.

———, "Three Schools Boldly Adapt to Different New Teaching Methods," *Architectural Record* 143:123–130, February 1968.

———, and Aiken, Linda B., "Individual Study Spaces for Children," *Audiovisual Instruction* 14:38–40, September 1969.

Thomsen, C. B., "What Construction Management Can Do for You," *American School and University* 45:12–14, May 1973.

"Three Kinds of Insurance Your Board Needs Right Now," *American School Board Journal* 159:25–27, October 1971.

Throop, Harold, "Budget Guidelines for Responsible Management," *School Management* 16:16–17, June 1972.

Tidwell, R., "Portland Community College: New Community College AV Pattern," *Educational Screen and AV Guide* 48:12+, February 1969.

Tierney, William T., "The 20-room, One-Story School: Best Bargain?" *School Management* 13:70–72, July 1969.

———, "Title 12345: An Administrator's Guide to the Elementary and Secondary School Education Act," *American School and University* 38:39, June 1966.

Toffler, Alvin, ed., *The Schoolhouse in the City.* New York, Praeger Publishers, Inc., 1968.

Tonigan, Richard F., "New Plant Programs Ad Infinitum," *American School and University,* 39:67–68, September 1966.

———, "New Products Aim at Saving Time, Money and Environment," *School Management* 15:6+, May 1971.

_____, "Organizing a Plant Planning Program," *American School and University* 38:39–40, July 1966.

_____, "Plant Management and Good Community Relations," *American School and University* 39:69–70, October 1966.

_____, "Should Students Help to Clean and Maintain Schools?" *School Management* 16:8+, May 1972.

_____, "That Contractor Is a Real Louse!" *School Management* 14:22+, November 1970.

_____, "Total Energy Systems Prove Their Worth," *American School and University* 40:25–28, January 1968.

_____, "Using Facilities Effectively," *American School and University* 38:55–56, October 1965.

_____, "What Are the Latest Project Management Techniques?" *School Management* 16:6–7, July 1972.

_____, "What Can You Do to Keep Your Plant Management Operation Humming and Your Staff Productive?" *School Management* 16:8+, August 1972.

_____, "Who Should Plan Your Major Maintenance Projects?" *School Management* 15:41+, September 1971.

Torkelson, G. M., "Education/Industry Cooperation: Instructional Technology in Teacher Education: Report of Task Force on Instructional Technology," *Audiovisual Instruction* 16:48–49, March 1971.

_____, "Technology in Quality Education: Symposium," *Educational Horizons* 49:65–95, Spring 1971.

Tourtelot, Ed M., Jr., "Few Windows Keep the Viewing Inside," *College and University Business* 41:88–91, October 1966.

Townley, John, "Low-Cost Media Center Goes Up Fast," *American School and University* 44:42–43, October 1971.

Tranzman, F., "Pupil Power Helps Build AV Center," *School Management*, p. 80, June 1968.

Truesdell, W. H., "New Importance of Renovation," *School Management* 17:12–15, August 1973.

Trumble, C. J., "Maintenance Program Starts at Drawing Board," *College and University Business* 38:81–84, March 1965.

Trump, J. Lloyd, "Independent School Centers—Their Relation to the Central Library," *Bulletin of National Association of Secondary School Principals* 50:45–51, January 1966.

"Tunnels Used in Community School Plan," *School Management* 16:21+, February 1972.

"Twenty-Eight Ways to Build Mistakes out of Your Middle School," *American School Board Journal* 158:17–24, July 1970.

"Two Schools Garner AIA Awards," *American School and University* 44:49+, October 1971.

"Unauthorized Copying: A Bubbling Issue," *Nation's Schools* 90:69–74, February 1973.

"Unit Budgeting: Prelude to PPBS," *Nation's Schools* 89:41–44, September 1972.

University College Environmental Research Group, *The Use of Space and Facilities in Universities*. London, Bartlett School of Architecture, Unit for Architectural Studies, University College, 1968. 78 p.

"University Library," *Architectural Record* 152:116+, July 1972.

"University Library Combines Beauty and Function," *American School and University* 44:25–28, October 1971.

Unruh, Glenys, and Alexander, William M., Chapter 7, "Focus on: The Building," pp. 190–214 in *Innovations in Secondary Education*. New York, Holt, Rinehart and Winston, Inc., 1970.

"Unusual High School Air Conditioner," *American School and University* 44:25–26, December 1971.

Unwin, Derick, "Spaces for Learning and Teaching," pp. 173–191 in *Media and Methods: Instructional Technology in Higher Education*. New York, McGraw-Hill Book Company, 1969.

"Urban School Turns Inward," *Progressive Architecture* 52:86–87, February 1971.

"Uses and Misuses of Consultants: Discussion," *College and University Business* 52:37–46, April 1972.

"Using Students as School Design Consultants," *School Management* 12:81–84, November 1968.

Vallery, H. J., "Planning Tomorrow's Schools," *Educational Technology* 10:8–9, June 1970.

Vander, May G., "When Is a Frill Not a Frill?" *School Management* 12:14+, November 1968.

VanDeventa, J., "Realizing Low Cost Building Technology," *Science News* 94:372–375, October 12, 1968.

VanWych, W. F., "Reducing Teacher Resistance to Innovation," *Audiovisual Instruction* 16:90–91, March 1971.

Vergis, J. P., and Twyford, L., "Open Forum: Together or Separate: Viewpoints Concerning the Joint Media Standards," *Audiovisual Instruction* 15:22–29, October 1970.

Vinson, Lu Ouida, "Outstanding Innovation: Joint AASL–DAVI Standards for School Media Programs. Educational Trends and Media Programs in School Libraries," *ALA Bulletin* 63:235–237, February 1969.

Volvado, Frank R., *School Heating—Gas vs. Electric, Phase 1A—Effect on Construction Costs.* Aurora, Ill., Northern Illinois Gas Company, 1968. 60 p.

Wadsworth, Raymond, "AV Communications Becomes a Building Trade," *American School and University* 46:30–33, January 1973.

————, "Built-in AV Facilities for the Classroom," *American School and University* 45:83–84, May 1972.

————, "How Ceiling Height Effects Visual Presentations," *American School and University* 44:37–38, December 1971.

————, "How to Determine Seating Area for Good Viewing," *American School and University* 44:6–9, July 1971.

————, "1W, 2W, 3W, 4W, 5W, 6W Law for A-V Presentations," *American School and University* 44:18–22, October 1971.

————, "The TV Studio: Don't Faint at Its Cost," *American School and University* 45:45–49, March 1972.

————, "Twelve No-No's in A-V Presentations," *American School and University* 45:30–33, August 1972.

Wagner, Willis H., *Planning Industrial Arts Shops for Secondary Schools,* Educational Service Publication No. 31. Cedar Falls, Iowa, Extension Service, State College of Iowa, 1966. 32 p.

Wakefield, Howard E., *The Design and Construction of Libraries and Study Facilities: An Annotated Reference List.* Madison, Wisc., University of Wisconsin, ERIC Clearing House on Educational Facilities, 1968. 30 p.

Walker, Robert, "Space and Scholarship—New Chicago Teachers College, North," pp. 216–221 in Pearson and Butler, *Instructional Materials Centers: Selected Readings,* Minneapolis, Minn., Burgess Publishing Company, 1969.

Ward, W. T., "Remodeling to Accommodate the Multimedia Library Concept," *Audiovisual Instruction,* p. 811, October 1967.

Watro, J. P., "Visualizing the School Budget," *Audiovisual Instruction* 16:20+, November 1971.

Weber, David C., "Design for a Microtext Reading Room," *UNESCO Bulletin for Libraries,* 20:303–308, November–December 1966.

————, *West Virginia Commission on Higher Education Institutional Research Manual.* Charleston, W. Va., West Virginia State Commission on Higher Education, 1968. 120 p.

————, *What Everyone Should Know About Financing Our Schools.* Washington, D.C., Committee on Educational Finance, National Education Association, 1966.

_____, "What if? A Furniture and Furnishings Survey," *School Management* 16:12-13, May 1972.

_____, "What to Probe Before You Build," *College and University Business* 40:43-47, January 1966.

_____, "Which Shape Is Best for a New School?" *School Management* 12:26–28, October 1968.

Wedgeworth, R., "Budgeting for School Media Centers," *School Librarian* 20:29–36, Spring 1971.

Weeks, R. S., and Fischer, G. D., "New Educational Facilities Center: Interview," *Educational Screen and AV Guide* 49:6–7, September 1970.

West, P. T., "Architecture, Society and the Schools," *Educational Technology* 10:7–8, June 1970.

White, W. T., Jr., *Contractual Relationships Between School Boards and Architects.* Nashville, Tenn., George Peabody College for Teachers, 1968. Doctoral Thesis. 190 p.

"Why and How Glass Blocks Were Used in School Construction: A Case History Verifies Their Functional and Esthetic Values," *School Management* 16:46–47, July 1972.

Wildberger, M. E. "Programs for Developing Resources in Media Centers," *Audiovisual Instruction* 17:38+, December 1972.

Wilentz, J. S., *The Senses of Man.* New York, Thomas Y. Crowell Company, 1968.

Wilfong, R. T., "Cheap Land Is Not Always Cheap," *School Management* 16:32–33, December 1972.

Wilke, Hubert, "Planning Communications Facilities," *Educational Technology* 9:49–50, April 1969.

Willetts, D. A., "Adding Air Conditioning to an Existing Building," *School Management* 16:18–19, June 1972.

Williams, B. J., ed., *The Audiovisual Equipment Directory.* Fairfax, Va., National AudioVisual Association, 1969. An Annual Comprehensive List of Equipment.

Wilson, Ira G., and Wilson, Marthann E., *Information, Computers, and System Design.* New York, John Wiley & Sons, Inc., 1965. Page 182.

Wilson, William O., "Solving Space Problems Via Maximum Plant Use," *American School and University* 38:42+, September 1965.

Wiman, Raymond V., and Meierhenry, Wesley C., eds., *Educational Media: Theory into Practice.* Columbus, Ohio, Charles E. Merrill Publishing Company, 1969. Chapter 10.

Wines, Donald B., "The Direction of School Design," *Compact* 3:34–37, February 1969.

Winning, Stuart A., "Six Steps for Trustees in Selecting the Right Campus Architect," *College and University Business* 45:26+, October 1968.

Winston, Sheldon, "Expect the Worst: A Primer on Disaster Planning," *School Management* 16:30+, August 1972.

Wiseman, Robert C., "How to 'Buy Down' Without Buying 'Junk'," *School Management* 16:28–29, May 1972.

Wolin, R. B., "Occupational Center Uses Open Plan Concept," *Industrial Education* 62:46—49, March 1973.

Wood, Frederic C., "Rehabilitating Campus Buildings—Is It Worth the Effort?" *American School and University* 44:30–34, July 1971.

Worth, E., "Big City Security Job: An Interview," *School Management* 16:12–13, December 1972.

Wurtman, Richard J., "Biological Implications of Artificial Illumination," *Illuminating Engineering* 63:523–529, October 1968.

Wyman, R., "Mediaware Specification Guidelines," *Audiovisual Instruction* 15:106–109, June 1970.

Yates, Donald P., *Flexibility in School Plant Development and Utilization.* Knoxville, Tenn., University of Tennessee, 1968. Doctoral Thesis. 167 p.

Young, J. F., and Taylor, K. I., "Helps for Library Planning: General, Public, and School Libraries," *Wilson Library Bulletin* 63:168–169, May 1967.

Zelip, F. F., *Guidelines for School Planning and Construction.* Chicago, Association of School Business Officials, 1968. Research Bulletin #8, 88 p.

Zifferblatt, S. M., "Architecture and Human Behavior: Toward Increased Understanding of a Functional Relationship," *Educational Technology* 12:54–57, August 1972.

EDUCATIONAL RESEARCH INFORMATION CENTER RESEARCH IN EDUCATION ABSTRACTS

January 1968

Ed 012 555   Grittner, Frank, and Pavlat, Russell
Field Check Manual for Language laboratories, a series of tests that a nontechnical person can conduct to verify specifications.

Ed 012 556   Grittner, Frank, and Pavlat, Russell
Language Laboratory Specifications, a procurement guide for the purchase of language laboratory installations in Wisconsin. NDEA—Title III.

Ed 012 600   Toy, Ernest W., Jr.
Recommendations for the Development of the Library Program at Fullerton Junior College and Associated Campuses.

Ed 012 606
The Junior College Library. Report of a Conference Sponsored by UCLA, AAJC, and the Accrediting Commission for Junior Colleges of the Western Association of Schools and Colleges.

Ed 012 655   Gividen, Noble J.
High School Education for Rural Youth.

February 1968

Ed 012 959   Bambarger, Chester, et al.
A Report to the Board of Directors of the Little Rock School District, Little Rock, Arkansas. An evaluation of the progress toward the achievement of a racially integrated educational system and a projection of a plan for further action.

Ed 013 061   Tanis, Norman E., et al.
Guidelines for Establishing Junior College Libraries.

Ed 013 063   McBride, Wilma
The James Madison Wood Quadrangle, Stephens College, Columbus, Missouri.

Ed 013 109
Selected Bibliography on Junior College Libraries, 1955–67.

Ed 013 117   Van Egmond, Elmer, et al.
Operation Head Start, an Evaluation. Final Report.

March 1968

Ed 013 492   Witmer, David R.
Unit Cost Studies.

Ed 013 500   O'Brien, Richard J.
School Submodel for Large Urban Schools

Ed 013 524
Schoolhouse in the City. EFL.

Ed 013 527   O'Brien, Richard J.
Cost Model for the Large Urban School.

Ed 013 531   Kinne, W. S., Jr.
Horizontal and Vertical Circulation in University Instructional and Research Buildings.

Ed 013 532
School Site Analysis and Development. California State Department of Education, Sacramento.

Ed 013 535   Stoke, Stuart M., et al.
Student Reactions to Study Facilities with Implications for Architects and College Administrators.

Ed 013 608   Merlo, Frank P., and Walling, W. Donald
Guide for Planning Community College Facilities.

Ed 013 639   Sondalle, Marvin P.
Planning, Programming, Designing the Community College. Proceedings of a conference sponsored by the College of Architecture and Urban Planning and the Center for the Development of Community College Education. University of Washington, 1967.

Ed 013 649   Keim, William A., et al.
Report and Recommendation for a Learning Materials Center.

April 1968

Ed 014 153   Dost, Jeanne
Determination of the Location for an Area School.

Ed 014 194   Reida, Goerge W., et al.
Artificial Lighting for Modern Schools. A Guide for Administrative Use.

Ed 014 198   Greer, John T.
Experimental Learning Center.

Ed 014 202   Jacques, Richard G.
Performance Criteria: A System of Communicators for Mobilizing Building Industry Resources.

Ed 014 205   Izumi, Kiyoshi
Psychosocial Phenomena and Building Design.

Ed 014 207   Green, Alan C., et al.
Components for School Construction in the Mid-Hudson Region. Progress Report No. 1.

Ed 014 209   Haviland, David S.
Components for School Construction in the Mid-Hudson Region. Progress Report No. 2.

Ed 014 210   Morris, Lyle L.
School Building Projects. A Guide to Administrative Procedures.

Ed 014 228   McIntyre, Charles, and Honey, John B.
A Study of the Implications and Feasibility of the Full Application of Technological Aids to the Solution of Staff, Space and Curriculum Problems Associated with a Rapidly Growing Urban University. Final Report.

Ed 014 231   Cobun, Ted, et al.
Quantitative Standards for Audiovisual Personnel, Equipment and Materials in Elementary, Secondary and Higher Education.

May 1968

Ed 014 844   Wood, Frederic D.
Efficient Operation and Economical Expansion of Undergraduate Teaching Facilities of Urban Universities. Findings, conclusions and recommendations based on a case study of Drexel Institute of Technology, Philadelphia, Pa.

Ed 014 847   Larson, Theodore, et al.
The Effect of Windowless Classrooms on Elementary School Children.

Ed 014 850
Environment for Learning, a Research Study in Secondary School Design.

Ed 014 855   Caudill, William M., and Bellomy, Cleon C.
Spatial Approach to Planning the Physical Environment.

Ed 014 856   Richardson, L. S., and Caudill, William M.
Towards an Economic Flexibility.

Ed 014 857   Rowlett, John M., and Bullock, Thomas A.
Relationship of Cost to the Geometry of a Building.

Ed 014 859   Caudill, William, and Bullock, Thomas A.
Barriers and Breakthroughs.

Ed 014 860   Krenitsky, Michael V.
Approach to a University Library Design.

Ed 014 865   Bergquist, Robert
A School for All Seasons.

Ed 014 868   Weinstick, Ruth
Space and Dollars—an Urban University Ex-

pands. Case Studies of Educational Facilities. Number 2.

Ed 014 869
Planning Guides for Construction of Facilities at the State-Supported Colleges and Universities of Colorado.

Ed 014 870   Dober, Richard P.
The New Campus in Britain—Ideas of Consequence for the United States.

Ed 014 946
The Administration of Library Instructional Services in the Community College, Highlights of a Conference at Wayne State University.

Ed 014 970   Haskell, Barry S.
Forum-type Rooms—an Innovation in Classroom Design and Utilization.

Ed 015 023   Deutsch, Martin
Memorandum—Facilities for Early Childhood Education.

Ed 015 036   Marlow, Frank M.
The Current Status of Citizen's Advisory Committee with Emphasis on Those for School Building Needs in the Central Schools of New York State.

Ed 015 122
More Effective Use of School Libraries.

June 1968

Ed 015 607
Standards of Library-Media Centers in Schools for the Deaf. A Handbook for the Development of Library-Media Programs.

Ed 015 616
Structural Considerations in School Building Economy, Hartford, Connecticut.

Ed 015 617   Hensarling, Paul R.
"Glass Walls" and the Instructional Program.

Ed 015 618   Crouch, C. L.
Better Lighting Through Research.

Ed 015 620   Jackson, R. Graham
Materials for Modernization.

Ed 015 621   Resnick, Jerome J., et al.
Guide for the Evaluation of School Facilities.

Ed 015 623   Christiansen, Kenneth A.
Implications of New Media for Space and Building Design.

Ed 015 624   Graves, Ben S.
Hyde Park High School, Chicago; Orput and Orput, Architects, Named Winner of $2,000,000 Competition. New Life for Old Schools.

Ed 015 681   Wheeler, Robert C.
Elements of an Effective Audiovisual Program, A Handbook for Wisconsin Educators.

July 1968

Ed 016 359   Artz, Delphine, et al.
The Instructional Materials Center.

Ed 016 363   Green, Alan D., et al.
Components for School Construction in the Mid-Hudson Region. Final Report No. 3.

Ed 016 366   Knight, George A.
Guidelines for a City School Building Program. 25 illustrative documents, Houston, Texas.

Ed 016 369   Koppes, Wayne F., and Green, Alan S.
Modular Coordination and School Design. A State-of-the-Art Report to Architectural and Educational Professions. Final Report.

Ed 016 370
How 1967 Award Winning Schools Compare.

Ed 016 383   Brown, James W., and Aubrey, Ruth H.
New Media and Changing Educational Patterns, A Summary of the Preparations for, Presentations and Group Reports of the New Media Workshop, Tahoe City, California, August 1–7, 1965.

Ed 016 397   Joyce, Bruce R.
Man, Media and Machine—The Teacher and His Staff.

Ed 016 409   Ely, Donald P.
The Changing Role of the Audiovisual Process

in Education. A Definition and a Glossary of Related Terms.

Ed 016 411

Audio-Visual Instruction, an Administrative Handbook. Missouri State Department of Education.

Ed 016 710   McCarthy, Joseph F. X.

The Education Park—What Should It Be. Educational Specifications for the Northeast Bronx Education Park.

August 1968

Ed 017 118

NCSC Guide for Planning School Plants. National Council Schoolhouse Construction.

Ed 017 120   Gausewitz, Carl H.

Space for Audio-Visual Large Group Instruction.

Ed 017 121   Haviland, David S.

The Computer and the Architectural Profession.

Ed 017 129   McKay, Ronald L.

How to Keep School Noise at the Right Level.

Ed 017 135   Pierce, J. L.

Minimum Check List for Mechanical Plans and Specifications.

Ed 017 153   Hutchinson, George A.

Evolution of a Learning Center.

Ed 017 158

The Nation's School of the Month: Hithergreen Middle School, Centerville, Ohio. August 1967.

Ed 017 159   Condon, John T.

Planning and Development Procedures Leading to the Construction of Educational Facilities.

Ed 017 188   Schramm, Wilbur

The Educational Media and National Development.

Ed 017 315   Luecke, Fritz, and Sproesser, Gerry

Comments and Opinions of Students at Abington High School, North Campus, Con-

cerning the Library. A Report on the Results of a Student Open Committee.

September 1968

Ed 018 064

Manual of Planning Standards for School Buildings.

Ed 018 069

The Wightman Elementary School, New Life for Old Schools. Pittsburgh Design Study.

Ed 018 079   Shabe, Earl J.

Criteria for Deciding to Remodel the Existing School.

Ed 018 083   Horowitz, Harold

The Program's the Thing. The New Architect—Practice.

Ed 018 097   Doelle, Leslie L.

Acoustics in Architectural Design, an Annotated Bibliography on Architectural Acoustics.

Ed 018 098   Earthman, Glen I.

A Report on Space Utilization.

Ed 018 107   Evans, Benjamin H.

Architectural Programming—State-of-the-Art.

Ed 018 147

The Impact of Technology on the Library Building.

Ed 018 151

Schools Without Walls, Profiles of Significant Schools.

Ed 018 191   Wyman, Raymond

The Instructional Materials Center—Whose Empire?

Ed 018 195

Eliminate Taboos, Outfit Your Library in Six Months.

October 1968

Ed 018 860   O'Brien, Richard J., and Lyle, Jerolyn R.

Outline of an Urban Educational Model.

Ed 018 921

Planning the Secondary School Plant. School Plant Planning Series.

Ed 018 927   Clasen, Robert E.
Forty Years of School Plant Dissertations. A Review with Suggestions for Future Research.

Ed 018 941   Schwartz, Clem
Elements of Good Building Practices.

Ed 018 948
Solar Effects on Building Design.

Ed 018 958
Contract Documents and Performance Specifications.

Ed 018 982   Schramm, Wilbur, et al.
The New Media—Memo to Educational Planners.

Ed 018 984
Ed 018 985
New Educational Media in Action.
Case Studies for Planners, I, II, III.

Ed 019 102   MacConnell, James D., and Schiller, Clarke E.
A Basic Reference Shelf on Facilities for Instructional Media. A Series One Paper from ERIC at Stanford.

November 1968

Ed 109 756   Dost, Jeane
Reassessment of the School Location Problem. A Multi-functional Role for the School in the Urban Environment.

Ed 109 814   Doherty, Leo D., and Wheatley, Artrelle
A Review of Studies of Economics in Schoolhouse Construction.

Ed 019 815
Minimum Areas for Elementary School Building Facilities.

Ed 109 816   Lane, W. R.
Thermal Environment and Learning.

Ed 109 829   Flanigan, Virginia, et al.
Educational Specifications for Secondary Schools.

Ed 109 834   Kohn, Sherwood D.
Three High Schools Revisited—Andrews, McPherson and Nova. Profiles of Significant Schools.

December 1968

Ed 020 619   North, Stewart D.
To Create a School, a Design for Working Relationships.

Ed 020 621   Harmon, Darell Boyd
The Co-ordinated Classroom.

Ed 020 624   Liebeskind, Morris
Design and Construction of School Buildings. Proceedings, Association of School Business Officials of the United States and Canada, October, 1964.

Ed 020 633   Widdall, Kenneth R.
Selected References for Planning Higher Educational Facilities.

Ed 020 635
A Comprehensive Study for the Master Development Plan. Polk Junior College, Winter Haven, Florida.

Ed 020 646
Procedure for Requesting Approval of School Building Projects.

Ed 020 649   Mylecraine, Walter E.
Projections of Public School Facilities Needs, 1968–1969. Through 1972–1973.

Ed 020 650
Five-Foot Shelf Bibliography of New Media and Instructional Technology.

Ed 020 661
Highlights of Schools Using Educational Media.

Ed 020 670   Wade, Warren L.
TV Equipment, Systems, Facilities and Personnel—A Guide for School Administrators. A Study prepared for the California Public Schools Instructional TV Committee.

Ed 020 762
Study to Develop a Research Program for the

Design Development of Modern College Libraries. Final Report.

January 1969

Ed 021 303   Gust, Tim, and Shaheen, Elaine
References Concerning Architectural Barriers in High Education.

Ed 021 392
EFL College Newsletter 6, Fine Arts Facilities: Past, Present and Future.

Ed 021 398   Jullcrat, Ernest E.
Fire Hazards of Windowless Buildings.

Ed 021 412   Brubaker, Charles William
What's New in Urban School Buildings.

Ed 021 414
The School Scene—Change and More Change.

Ed 021 421   Bell, T. H., et al.
Utah School Buildings, 1964–1967.

Ed 021 428
Materials for School Construction.

February 1969

Ed 022 255   Davis, Harold S.
Organizing a Learning Center.

Ed 022 257   Davis, Harold S.
Instructional Materials Center, Annotated Bibliography.

Ed 022 318
Planning Schools for Use of Audiovisual Materials. Number 1 Classrooms, third edition.

Ed 022 324   Sanders, Luther E., ed.
Clarksville, Montgomery County High School, Clarksville, Tennessee. Profile of a Significant School.

Ed 022 325   Schwehr, Frederick E.
Planning Educational Facilities.

Ed 022 333
Why Standard Plans Don't Work. AIA School Plant Studies.

Ed 022 336

Acoustics and Educational Facilities. A Guide for Planners and Administrators.

Ed 022 340   McLeod, John W., and Possontino, Richard J.
Urban Schools in Europe. A Study Tour of Five Cities.

Ed 022 343
Suggested Steps for Planning and Building a New School Building.

Ed 022 345   Handbook on Planning School Facilities. West Virginia Department of Education, Charlestown.

Ed 022 347   The Marbrook School. An Elementary School Pilot Project of the State of Delaware.

Ed 022 343
Suggested Steps for Planning and Building a New School Building.

Ed 022 345
Handbook on Planning School Facilities. West Virginia Department of Education, Charlestown.

Ed 022 347
The Marbrook School. An Elementary School Pilot Project of the State of Delaware.

Ed 022 349
Factors You Must Consider When Designing TV Studios.

Ed 022 350
Designing the School Plant for Economy. School Building Economy Series. Hartford, Connecticut.

Ed 022 357
Bibliography of Environmental Design References.

Ed 022 362   Saettler, Paul
A History of Instructional Technology.

Ed 022 376
Innovation in Education: New Directions for the American School. A Statement on National Policy.

Ed 022 444   Merlo, Frank P.
A Guide for Developing Comprehensive

Community College Facilities. Rutgers, New Brunswick, New Jersey.

March 1969

Ed 023 254   Van Hoose, Richard
Manual for New School Construction. Junior and Senior H.S.

Ed 023 260   Waropay, V. M.
Choosing the Right Environment. A Study in School Design.

Ed 023 266
The New Northview Elementary School. Public School Reporter, Vol. 3, No. 1.

Ed 023 269   Collins, George J.
School Costs Are Rising and Massachusetts Vitally Needs Long-Range Planning for School Construction.

Ed 023 273   Hale, Bill, and Pflug, Liffen
The Truth on the Back of an Envelope.

Ed 023 278
How Award Winning Schools Compare. A Special Report.

Ed 023 287   Romieniec, Edward J., and Patterson, James
Higher Educational Facilities: Library of Source Documents. Summary Report.

Ed 023 290   Kiesling, Herbert J.
High School Size and Cost Factors. Final Report. Indiana U.

April 1969

Ed 024 211   Grant, Alfred E., and Essex, Stewart R., comp.
School Plant Planning Guide. A Reference and Guide for School Plant Planners and School Building Committees. Rhode Island State Department of Education—Providence.

Ed 024 215
Building Better Schools for Vermont.

Ed 024 216   Boggs, Bruce J.
The Nation's School of the Year. Valley Winds Elementary School, St. Louis County, Missouri.

Ed 024 224   Davis, Gerald
How to Buy a Better Building. The Value of a "Program."

Ed 024 226
Manual for School Administrators on School Plant Planning. Tennessee State Department of Education.

Ed 024 228   Adams, Hugh D., et al.
Handbook on Architectural Services.

Ed 024 230
Educational Specifications. School Planning, Series 3. North Carolina State Board of Education.

Ed 024 231
The Learning Environment. American Electric Power System, New York.

Ed 024 237
Planning Model for School Facilities. A Planning Model for a Secondary School Utilizing a Multi-Dimensional Approach for Optimum Flexibility. Chelmsford Park H.S., Chelmsford, Mass.

Ed 024 241   Reed, Bob H.
People, Processes and Time Facilities. A "Primer" on Planning New Facilities for Junior Colleges.

Ed 024 246
Educational Specifications for the South Campus Seattle Community College.

Ed 024 251   Murtha, D. Michael
Systematic Methods in School Planning and Design. A Selected and Annotated Bibliography.

Ed 024 253   Wakefield, Howard E.
The Maintenance of Educational Facilities. An Annotated Reference List.

Ed 024 254   Wakefield, Howard E.
The Design and Construction of Libraries and Study Facilities. An Annotated Reference List.

Ed 024 256   Wakefield, Howard E.
Evaluating Educational Facilities. An Annotated Reference List.

Ed 024 257   Wakefield, Howard E.
Educational Specifications. An Annotated Reference List.
Ed 024 258   Wakefield, Howard E.
Construction Costs of Educational Facilities. An Annotated Reference List.
Ed 024 273
Cost Study of Educational Media Systems and Their Equipment Components. Volume I. Guidelines for Determining Costs of Media Systems. Final Report.
Ed 024 277
Quantitative Standards for School Media Programs, Personnel, Equipment and Materials for Elementary and Secondary Schools.
Ed 024 280
Criteria Relating to Educational Media Programs in Colleges and Universities. With Evaluation Check List.
Ed 024 286
Cost Study of Educational Media Systems and Their Equipment Components. Vol. II. Technical Report. Final Report.

May 1969

Ed 025 100
Your Building and Your Architect.
Ed 025 108
Long Range Facility Plans for Unified School District No. 373, Harvey County, Newton, Kansas.
Ed 025 113   Boice, John
A Systems Approach to School Construction. Nevada University. Reno, Department of School Administration.
Ed 025 134
How to Design a Quiet School.
Ed 025 135   Kramer, Roger M.
The Use of Carpeting in the School. A Selected and Annotated Bibliography.
Ed 025 138   Conrad, M. J., et al.
School Plant Planning. An Annotated Bibliography. Ohio State University, Columbus, School of Education.
Ed 025 143   Wakefield, Howard E.
Flexible Educational Facilities. An Annotated Reference List.

June 1969

Ed 025 889   Williams, Charles F., and Johnson, George H.
A Pilot Evaluation of Instructional Materials Centers. Final Report.
Ed 025 918
Challenge—A Report Suggesting How an Old School Can Continue to Serve Youth if the Educational Program is the Prime Consideration.
Ed 025 925   Chase, William W.
Facility Design Considerations.
Ed 025 930   Wakefield, Howard E.
Designing an Environment for Learning. Proceedings of a Conference of Educational Survey Directors of Member Universities of the Committee on Institutional Cooperation.
Ed 025 931   Koppes, Wayne F., et al.
Design Criteria for Learning Spaces, Seating, Lighting, Acoustics.
Ed 026 204   Holland, Aurora B.
Evaluative Criteria for Secondary School Libraries.

July 1969

Ed 026 801
Schools for America.
Ed 026 803   Roberts, Charles
Can the Computer Design a School Building?
Ed 026 817
Recommended Guidelines for Facilities, Equipment, Grounds and Maintenance.
Ed 026 824   Bloomfield, Byron C., and Wakefield, Howard E.
Basis for Design Development. Facilities Pro-

gramming for a New Senior High School in the City of Green Bay.

Ed 026 828   Gross, Ronald, and Murphy, Judith
Educational Change and Architectural Consequences. A Report on Facilities for Individualized Instruction.

Ed 026 844   Theodores, James L., et al.
Crisis in Planning. An Analysis of Some Factors That Influence the Kinds of Schools We Have, How They Got That Way and What We Must Do About Changing Them.

Ed 027 049
How Does the Secondary School Library Become an Instructional Materials Center? Personnel, Program, Materails, Housing.

Ed 027 052
Library Technology and Architecture: Report of a Conference Held at the Howard Graduate School of Education, Feb. 9, 1967.

Ed 027 100   Merrell, Russell G.
Guidelines for Designing, Equipping and Furnishing Small School Learning Laboratories.

Ed 027 135   Davis, J. Clark, and McQueen, Robert
Planning Requirements for Small School Facilities.

August 1969

Ed 027 702
Educational Facility Abstract Journal 1968.

Ed 027 712   Johnson, Homer M.
Spaces for Innovation.

Ed 027 719
Instructions to Academic and Planning Committees who Are Charged with the Responsibility of Preparing Building Program Requirements for Capitol Improvement Projects. Revised July, 1968.

Ed 027 720   Reida, George W.
Trends in Schoolhouse Construction.

Ed 027 726   Wheeler, Lawrence
Behavioral Research for Architectural Planning and Design.

September 1969

Ed 028 590   Johnson, Marvin, R. A.
The School Architect, Selection, Duties, and How to Work with Him.

Ed 028 596   Nelson, Charles R., et al.
Evaluation of Elementary School Plants.

Ed 028 606   Dwyer, Francis M.
Recent Developments and the Impact of the Newer Media.

Ed 028 624   Loeffler, Margaret Howard
The Prepared Environment and It's Relationship to Learning.

Ed 028 625
Planning the School Administration Center. Report of the AASA Commission on School Administration Buildings.

Ed 028 629   Johnson, Frences Kennon, and Bomar, Cora Paul
Planning School Library Quarters.

October 1969

Ed 029 460   Hetzel, Walter, et al.
Legal Aspects of Educational Facilities.

Ed 029 461   Green, Alan C.
Environment for Learning: The 1970's.

Ed 029 462   McIsaac, Donald N., et al.
Time-Management Planning for Educational Facilities.

Ed 029 463   Wakefield, Howard E., and North, Stewart D.
The Design, Development and Administration of Educational Facilities. A Conceptual Framework.

Ed 029 470   Facility Technology—Catalyst for Learning.

Ed 029 476
New Ideas for School Construction.

Ed 029 623   Wilson, R. E.
The Librarian as a Media Specialist.

Ed 029 648
Instructional Materials Selection Policy.

November 1969

Ed 030 272   Leu, Donald J.
Planning Educational Facilities.

Ed 030 275   Lasswell, Thomas E., et al.
Actions, Objectives and Concerns. Human Parameters for Architectural Design.

Ed 030 293
Playback—A Dialogue of School's Design.

Ed 030 294
The Flexible School. Reprint from AIA, 1734 New York Ave., N.Y. Why Standard Plants Don't Work. AIA School Plant Studies. (One copy free of charge on request)

December 1969

Ed 031 033
New Building on Campus. Six Designs for a College Communications Center.

Ed 031 036
New Schools for New Education. A Report from Ann Arbor.

Ed 031 037   Murphy, Judith
Middle Schools. Profiles of Significant Schools.

Ed 031 045
What Went Wrong? Maintenance and Operation Errors to Avoid in Educational Facility Planning.

Ed 031 051   Mason, Ellsworth
Some Advice to Librarians on Writing a Building Program.

Ed 031 061   Gross, Ronald, and Murphy, Judith
Educational Change and Architectural Consequences. A Report on Facilities for Individualized Instruction.

Ed 031 069   Olfson, Lewy, et al.
On the Way to Work. Profiles of Significant Schools.

Ed 031 074   Kohn, Sherwood D.
Three High Schools Revisited—Andrews, McPherson, and Nova. Profiles of Significant Schools.

Ed 031 086
Standards for School Media Programs.

Ed 031 196   Fusaro, Jan
The Library-College Concept: Toward a 21st Century Learning Center Today.

Ed 031 347
Final Report of the Activities and Recommendations Made Under Title II, ESEA P.L. 89-10 Planning Grant for Model Saturated School Library.

January 1970

Ed 031 873   Clinchy, Evans
Wayland Senior High School, Wayland, Massachusetts. Profiles of Significant Schools.

Ed 031 875   Clinchy, Evans
North Hagerstown High School, Hagerstown, Maryland. Profiles of Significant Schools.

Ed 031 885   Rounthwaite, C. F. T.
Ideal Relationships Between the Architect and Physical Plant Personnel.

Ed 031 916   Hauf, Harold D., et al.
New Spaces for Learning: Designing College Facilities to Utilize Instructional Aids and Media. Revised.

Ed 031 957
Emphasis on Excellence in School Media Programs; Descriptive Case Studies Special-Purpose Grant Programs.

February 1970

Ed 032 719   Katz, William A., ed., and Swartz, Roderick G.
Problems in Planning Library Facilities. Consultants and Architects, Plans and Critiques; Proceedings of the Library Buildings Institute, Chicago, July 12–13, 1963.

Ed 032 725
Educational Specifications: University City High School, Philadelphia, Pennsylvania.

Ed 032 742
Educational Facilities Literature 1968: A Bibliographic Review.

March 1970

Ed 033 545   Kleeman, Walter Jr., ed.
A Bibliography for Interior Design from the Environmental Sciences.

Ed 033 548
Evaluative Criteria for Elementary School Buildings.

Ed 033 555
Supervision and Inspection of School Construction.

Ed 033 565
Guide for Schoolhouse Planning and Construction, 1969.

Ed 033 568   Isler, Norman P.
Temporary School Facilities. An Annotated Bibliography.

Ed 033 588
Plan for Progress in the Media Center. Iowa State Department of Public Instruction: Des Moines.

Ed 033 597   Pearson, Neville P., and Butler, Lucius
Instructional Materials Centers: Selected Readings.

Ed 033 598   Erickson, Carlton H. W.
Administering Instructional Media Programs.

Ed 033 616
Standards for School Media Programs.

April 1970

Ed 034 374
Guide for Schoolhouse Planning and Construction, Comprising Suggestions, Recommendations and Mandatory Requirements Relating to the Construction of Public School Buildings in the State of New Jersey.

Ed 034 382
New Trends in the Design, Cost, Construction of the Modern School Building.

Ed 034 390
Facilities Planning Guide for the Community College System. Massachusetts Advisory Council on Education, Boston.

Ed 034 392   Bennett, Philip M., ed.
AIA Architect–Researcher's Conference. Proceedings, 5th, Wisconsin Dells, Wisconsin, Sept. 25–26, 1968.

Ed 034 438   Coombs, Don H., et al.
Instructional Materials Centers: A Series Three Collection from ERIC at Stanford (December 1969).

May 1970

Ed 035 163   Price, D. Dana
When and What to Modernize.

Ed 035 175   Erwin, Clyde A.
School Design.

Ed 035 177   Zastrow, W. E.
A Report of the School Facilities Planning Conference for Architects, Educators, Industry at Wisconsin State University, Whitewater, June 14, 1967.

Ed 035 180   Benet, James
SCSD: The Project and the Schools: A Report from EFL.

Ed 035 185   Graves, Ben S.
A Geometric Approach to School Modernization.

Ed 035 270   Graves, Richard D.
A Study of the Problems of a Media Center and Innovative Practices in the Junior College.

June 1970

Ed 036 053
How to Prepare Educational Specifications Outline. Austin, Texas.

Ed 036 054
Evaluating Factors. Austin, Texas.

Ed 036 072   Saunders, Harry B.
School Facilities Survey.

Ed 036 078

A Five-Year School Building and Future Sites Program, 1966–1970.

Ed 036 079   Brewster, Sam F.
The Written Program: An Effective Way of Communicating with the Architect.

Ed 036 081   Martin, Dikran J.
The Educator's "Action" Office.

Ed 036 089   Esposito, Nicholas A., ed.
Instructional Media Center. Educational Facility Series. A Guide to Planning.

Ed 036 092   Stackman, Carl E.
Planning the Technology Area: Its Inflexibility by Weight of Mechanical Servicing.

Ed 036 100
New Problems in School Design: Comprehensive Schools from Existing Buildings.

Ed 036 105   Hunt, William Dudley, Jr., ed.
Creative Control of Building Costs.

Ed 036 128   Phillips, Derek
Lighting in Architectural Design.

Ed 036 134
Remodeling Old Schools.

Ed 036 139
"Second Guess." A New Concept in School Planning.

Ed 036 201   Powell, John, and Heidbreder, M. Ann
The Organization and Operation of Educational Media Selection Centers: Identification and Analysis of Current Practices and Guidelines for Model Centers. Interim Report Phase I.

July 1970

Ed 036 956
Instructional Materials Development Center. Annual Evaluation, ESEA Title VI-A.

Ed 036 967   Fitch, James Marston
The Aesthetics of Function.

Ed 036 973
Planning Schools for Use of Audio-Visual Materials, No. 3: The Audio-Visual Materials Center.

Ed 036 974   Castaldi, Basil
The Castaldi Nomogram. An Aid for Translating the Curriculum of Junior and Senior High Schools into the Necessity Numbers of Instructional Spaces or Classrooms.

Ed 036 983
Designing the School Plant as a Community Center.

Ed 036 992
Guidelines for School Building Planning.

Ed 037 011   Babcock, Ruth E., et al.
Planning the School Library.

Ed 037 014   Justus, John E., ed.
Athens Junior High School, Athens, Tennessee. Profile of a Significant School.

Ed 037 026
Ideas for Planning Your Instructional Materials Center. Administration; Conference and Independent Study; Listening and Viewing; Materials Production; Reading, Research and Borrowing; Storage and Maintenance. Massachusetts School Building Assistance Commission, Boston.

Ed 037 047
Space Guidelines for Libraries. Wisconsin Coordinating Committee for Higher Education, Madison.

Ed 037 082
Descriptive Case Studies in Nine Elementary School Media Centers in Three Inner Cities. Title II Elementary and Secondary Education Act of 1965. School Library Resources, Textbooks, and Other Printed and Published Instructional Materials.

August 1970

Ed 037 884   Reason, Paul L., and Tankard, George O., Jr.
Property Accounting for Local and State

School Systems. State Educational Records and Reports. Handbook III.

Ed 037 885   Taylor, James L.
School Sites. Selection, Development and Utilization.

Ed 037 886   Collins, George J.
National Inventory of School Facilities and Personnel, Spring 1962.

Ed 037 889   Martin, E. Edgar
Selected References on Facilities and Equipment for Elementary Schools.

Ed 037 898
Guidelines for Planning Computer Centers in Universities and Colleges.

Ed 037 911
Procedures for Review and Approval of School Building Plans and for Inspection of Building Projects.

Ed 037 912
Cost Reduction in Primary School Buildings. (Use of Efficiency Method)

Ed 037 918
School Facilities Survey for Unified School District No. 353, Sumner County, Wellington, Kansas.

Ed 037 919   Lewis, Chester M., ed.
Special Libraries: How to Plan and Equip Them.

Ed 037 930   Pena, William M., and Focke, John W.
Problem Seeking. New Deductions in Architectural Programming.

Ed 037 933   Kohn, Sherwood
The Early Learning Center, Stanford, Connecticut. Profiles of Significant Schools.

Ed 037 941   Bell, T. H., et al.
Utah School Buildings, 1967–1969.

Ed 037 945   Resnick, Jerome J.
Educational Facilities Evaluation Guide.

Ed 037 946   Singel, Raymond J.
Planning the Learning Environment.

Ed 037 948
Architecture and Education.

Ed 037 951   Sanoff, Henry
A Systematic Approach to Design. Research Laboratory Working Paper.

Ed 037 952   Dietz, Albert G. H., et al.
Systems Analysis in Building Design. Revised October 1967.

Ed 037 954
Higher Education in New Jersey: A Facilities Plan.

Ed 037 964   Isler, Norman P.
Operating Costs of Educational Facilities.

Ed 037 973   Davis, Gerald
The Independent Building Program Consultant.

Ed 037 976
Building Costs and Quality. Proceedings of the CIB Congress, 4th, Ottawa, Ontario, and Washington, D.C., 1968.

Ed 037 986
Education and Architecture in the 20th Century. The Design Workshop, Colleges of Applied Arts and Technology, Ottawa, November 18–19, 1969.

Ed 038 150   Lohrer, Alice
The Identification and Role of School Libraries That Function as Instructional Materials Centers and Implications for Library Education in the United States.

September 1970

Ed 039 026
The Kindergarten, a Place for Learning. Bulletin One: Materials and Equipment for the Fours and Fives.

Ed 039 059   Mickolic, Larry, et al.
Outdoor Education: Criteria for Relationships Between Camp and School in Planning for an Outdoor Education Program.

October 1970

Ed 039 736   Bright, R. Louis

Should Educators Generate Specifications for the Purchase of Equipment?

Ed 039 775   Alter, Chester M.
Instructional Technology and the Less Affluent College.

Ed 039 859   Dahnke, Harold L., and Mertins, Paul F.
Inventory of Physical Facilities in Institutions of Higher Education: Fall 1968.

Ed 040 155   Lessinger, Leon
Engineering Accountability for Results into Public Education.

Ed 040 228   Wolff, Max
The Educational Park: A Guide to Its Implementation.

Ed 040 236   Wolff, Max, and Rudikoff, Benjamin
Educational Park Development in the United States, 1969: A Survey of Current Development Plans with a List of Reports and References on the Education Park.

Ed 040 293   Larson, Milton E., and Blake, Duane L.
Planning Facilities and Equipment for Comprehensive Vocational Education Programs for the Future. Final Report.

November 1970

Ed 040 511
Directional and Informational Signs for Educational Facilities. A Selected Bibliography.

Ed 040 562   Tomei, Mario Joseph
An Analysis of the Experience and Effects of Computer Assisted Scheduling in Selected Institutions of Higher Education.

Ed 040 643
Meeting the Enrollment Demand for Public Higher Education in California Through 1977; the Need for Additional College and University Campuses.

Ed 040 930   Ayers, Jerry B.
Specifications for New College of Education Facilities.

Ed 041 094   Thomas, Thomas C.
On Improving Urban School Facilities and Education.

Ed 041 107   Schwalm, George H.
Transportable Industrial Arts Learning Laboratories. Evaluation Report, 1968–1969. ESEA Title III Project.

December 1970

Ed 041 375
Student Housing. A Selected Bibliography.

Ed 041 376
Facilities for Early Childhood Education. A Selected Bibliography.

Ed 041 377
Libraries and Study Facilities. A Selected Bibliography.

Ed 041 378
Analysis and Programming Educational Facilities. A Selected Bibliography.

Ed 041 379
Effects of Facilities on Educational Achievement. A Selected Bibliography.

Ed 041 467
Instructional Hardware: A Guide to Architectural Requirements.

Ed 041 473
Building for Tomorrow's Educational Programs.

Ed 041 556   Anderson, Lawrence B.
California Education in Environmental Design and Urban Studies.

January 1971

Ed 042 108
Regional School Design Workshop.

Ed 042 787   Boase, Paul H., and Glancey, Donald.
And Gladly Will They Learn, and Gladly Teach.

Ed 042 875

Guidelines for Preparing Educational Specifications for Agricultural Education.

February 1971

Ed 043 102   Nerden, Joseph T.
Vocational–Technical Facilities for Secondary Schools. A Planning Guide.

Ed 043 107
Education and Architecture in the 20th Century: A School Design Workshop (4th, Peterborough, Ontario, March 25–26, 1969).

Ed 043 142
Directory of Services for Handicapping Conditions.

March 1971

Ed 043 951
A Place in Society . . . for Everyone. Brandywine Educational Park.

Ed 043 958   Steward, G. Kent, ed.
Guide for Planning Educational Facilities. An Authoritative and Comprehensive Guide to the Planning of Educational Facilities from the Conception of Need Through Utilization of the Facility.

Ed 043 959   Ely, Donald P., et al.
Instructional Hardware/A Guide to Architectural Requirements.

April 1971

Ed 044 778   Robb, George
Radical New Programs for University Living.

Ed 044 800   Wehle, Fred, Jr.
How to Evaluate Competitive Products.

Ed 044 810
The Campus Plan.

Ed 044 811   Perry, Ione L., comp.
Post-Conference Report; Extended School Year Conference.

Ed 044 813   Earthman, Glen I.
School Without Walls.

Ed 044 852
New Jersey State Plan for the Construction of Mental Retardation Facilities.

Ed 045 112
So This Is How You Run a Media Center. Organizing, Administering, and Developing a School Instructional Media Center and Annotated Bibliography.

Ed 045 249   Miller, Peggy L.
School Gardens and Farms . . . Aspects of Outdoor Education.

Ed 045 354
The Community School Site, A Laboratory for Learning.

Ed 045 397   Engelhardt, David
Planning the Teaching Environment: Secondary Science Facilities.

May 1971

Ed 045 069   Burr, Donald F.
The Schoolhouse of 1980.

Ed 045 073   Abramson, Paul
Schools for Early Childhood. Profiles of Significant Schools.

Ed 045 075   Boice, John R., ed.
K/M Associates: A Case Study in Systems Building.

Ed 045 094
Educational Specifications: Elementary Prototype.

Ed 045 103   Ashley, Robert E., and Romney, Leonard C.
Planning Standards, Inventory and Utilization Data for Higher Education Facilities in Twenty-Seven States, Facilities Comprehensive Planning Program.

Ed 045 106   Berriman, S. G., ed.
Library Buildings 1967–1968.

Ed 045 163   Rogerson, Robert W. K. C., and Spence, Philip H.
A Place at Work: The Working Environment of the Disabled.

Ed 045 177
Educational Specifications for Physical Plant Exceptional Child Center: Facility for the Trainable Mentally Retarded.

Ed 045 178
Educational Specifications for Special Education Facility.

Ed 045 179
Educational Specifications for Center for Trainable Mentally Retarded.

Ed 045 186   Dunwoody, Robert M.
Educational Specifications for a Facility for Trainable Mentally Retarded.

Ed 045 604   Humphreys, Edward H.
Schools in Change; A Comparative Survey of Elementary School Services, Facilities, and Personnel, 1965–69.

June 1971

Ed 047 171
Preliminary Educational Specifications for the First Facility Fort Lincoln New Town Education System.

Ed 047 386   Candoli, I. C., et al.
A Look to the Future: Progress Through Facility Evaluation and Planning, and Appendix: Educational Facilities Evaluation. Dayton City School District. A Report for the Superintendent and Board of Education.

Ed 047 426
Higher Education Facilities Comprehensive Planning Grants Program. Bibliography.

July 1971

Ed 048 524   Gove, James R., and Page, J. Patrick
Feasibility Study of Full Year Public School Operation (Valley View 45–15 Continuous School Year Plan) by Detailed Analysis of Required Scheduling Plans and Accompanying Consequences. Final Report.

Ed 048 630   Nattall, Ronald, and Doyle, Richard J.
Toward a Model of School Operations: Relating Budgetary and Personnel Inputs to Indices of School Functioning. Working Paper.

Ed 048 639   Mann, Stuart H.
Least-Cost Decision Rules for Dynamic Management. Working Paper.

Ed 048 644
New York State Higher Education Facilities Comprehensive Planning Survey.

Ed 048 650
Technical Papers of the Association of Physical Plant Administrators of Universities and Colleges.

Ed 048 928   Utzinger, Robert C.
Some European Nursery Schools and Playgrounds.

August 1971

Ed 049 527
An Empirical Study of the Evaluation of Grant Applications Under the Higher Education Facilities Act of 1963. A Rating Technique for Decisionmaking.

Ed 049 543   Triechler, Walter W.
Thermal Environment for Classrooms. Central System Approach to Air Conditioning.

Ed 049 544   McMahon, Charles H., Jr.
Management of Time, Cost and Quality in Public Construction Today. (An Idea Whose Time Has Come.)

Ed 049 546
Educational Facilities Abstract Journal. Volume II, 1969.

Ed 049 547   Campbell, James R.
Developing Ways and Means for Minority

Group Inclusion in Construction Management.

Ed 049 549

Fathom One: Marine Science Training Center. Fathom Two: Lodgings for Commuting Students. Investigations of the Requirements for Two Types of Specialized Community College Facilities.

Ed 049 721

Architectural Determinants of Student Satisfaction in College Residence Halls. Final Report.

September 1971

Ed 050 432   Chick, Charles E.
Problems in School Planning.

Ed 050 434
Practical Applications of Data Processing to School Purchasing.

Ed 050 440   Nunnery, Michael Y.
Project Ideals: Special Services of the School District (Area I).

Ed 050 471
School Building Survey: Homer Central School District, Homer, N.Y.

Ed 050 472
School Building Needs: School District of the City of Benton Harbor, Michigan.

Ed 050 494
Implications of Instituting a Split-Trimester Calendar Plan in the Ann Arbor Public Schools. A Feasibility Study Report.

Ed 050 495   McKague, Terence R., and Penner, Glen H.
Rescheduling the School Year. The Report of a Feasibility Study for Saskatoon Public Schools.

Ed 050 503
Mental Retardation Construction Program.

October 1971

Ed 051 545
School Consolidation Survey: Iredell County: Mooresville, Statesville, North Carolina.

Ed 051 549
Open Plan. An Annotated Bibliography. Current Bibliography No. 2.

Ed 051 640   Witherspoon, John P., and Kessler, William J.
Instructional Television Facilities. A Planning Guide.

Ed 051 792   Newman, Loretta M.
Community College Reading Center Facilities.

November 1971

Ed 052 436   Lane, Cleve W., and Lewis, Robert B.
Guidelines for Establishing and Operating an Adult Learning Laboratory.

Ed 052 511   Hallak, J.
The Analysis of Educational Costs and Expenditures. Fundamentals of Educational Planning—10.

Ed 052 531   Nickerson, Kermit S.
Extended Educational Opportunities and the Extended School Year (Revised).

Ed 052 540
Year-Round School. Revised.

Ed 052 674
Title IV-A. Higher Education in New York State. Four Year Report.

Ed 052 784   Clark, Robert M.
Counseling Offices and Facilities: California Community Colleges.

December 1971

Ed 053 516
Physical Facilities: Exceptional Child Bibliography Series.

Ed 053 672   Kaiser, Bruce T.
Student Life Styles and Their Impact on College Union Planning. Final Revised Copy.

Ed 053 762   Metcalf, Keyes D.
Library Lighting.

January 1972

Ed 054 519   Edwards, L. F.
How to Reduce the Cost of Vandalism Losses.
Ed 054 563
Hawaii State Plan—Facilities for the Mentally Retarded.
Ed 054 728   Meek, Harry R., ed.
Ohio Higher Education Notebook 1971.
Ed 054 835   A Case for Change: A Function/ Facility Study, Dallas Public Library, Dallas, Texas.

February 1972

Ed 055 345
Short-Term Accommodation and Relocatable Facilities.
Ed 055 346
Relocatable Learning Facilities.
Ed 055 347
Schools for Intermediate Students.
Ed 055 357
Building Systems Planning Manual. Building Systems Information Clearinghouse Special Report Number Three.
Ed 055 366   Burr, Donald F.
Simu-School: A Tool and Process for Educational Planning. Final Report.
Ed 055 378   Boyes, Kenneth, and Francklin, Sandra, eds.
Designing for the Handicapped.
Ed 055 404   Abeson, Alan, and Blacklow, Julie, eds.
Environmental Design: New Relevance for Special Education.
Ed 055 417   Henderson, Diane D., et al.
What a Learning Resource Center (LRC) Could Mean for Georgetown University.
Ed 055 434   Humphrey, David A.
Getting It All Together; The Organization and Staffing of Educational Communications Centers for Higher Education.
Ed 055 443

The Report of the University Ad Hoc Committee on Instructional Media.

March 1972

Ed 056 383   Freese, William C.
Building and Contents Insurance.
Ed 056 384
Places for Environmental Education. A Report.
Ed 056 389
Colour in School Buildings. Fourth Edition.
Ed 056 395
Human Resources for United States School Boards. A Directory of Individuals with Various Professional Competencies for Assistance to School Boards.
Ed 056 422
Guide to Alternatives for Financing School Buildings. A Report.
Ed 056 423   Abeson, Alan, and Berenson, Bertram
Physical Environment and Special Education: An Interdiscipline Approach to Research. Final Report.
Ed 056 654
A Master Plan for Higher Education in Illinois; Phase III—an Integrated School System.
Ed 056 705   Markevick, Emily
A Librarian Plans a Library.
Ed 056 737
Annual Survey of Howard University: The Library System, Services and Facilities.
Ed 057 215
Planning for Safety on the Jobsite. Safety in Industry, Construction Industry Series.
Ed 057 244
A Guide for Planning, Drafting and Design Technology Programs. Section III, Data Collection and Analysis.

April 1972

Ed 057 446
A Study on Economics in School Construction.

Ed 057 447
Dramatic Arts Facilities.

Ed 057 448
CLASP/JDP: The Development of a Building System for Higher Education. University Building Notes.

Ed 057 452   VandenHazel, B. J.
The Windowless School: Some Biological and Economic Considerations.

Ed 057 456
Manufacturers' Compatibility Study. Third Edition.

Ed 057 463
Guide for Educational Planning of Public School Buildings and Sites in Minnesota.

Ed 057 484
Open-Space Schools Project.

Ed 057 485   Brunetti, Frank A.
Open Space: A Status Report.

Ed 057 751   Dahnke, Harold L.
Higher Education Facilities Planning and Management Manuals. Preliminary Field Review Edition.

Ed 057 938
New York State Appalachian Resource Studies; Community Facilities. Phase I: Inventory.

Ed 057 968   Bannon, Joseph J., and Storey, Edward H.
Guidelines for Recreation and Park Systems.

May 1972

Ed 058 469   Piele, Philip K., and Smith, Stuart C., eds.
Directory of Organization and Personnel in Educational Management. Third Edition: 1971–1972.

Ed 058 500
Economics in Education.

Ed 058 620   Piele, Philip K.
Educational Specifications. Educational Facilities Review Series Number 1.

Ed 058 621   Piele, Philip K.
Use of Computers in Planning Higher Educational Facilities. Educational Facilities Review Series Number 2.

Ed 058 623   Piele, Philip K.
Building Maintenance. Educational Facilities Review Series Number 3.

Ed 058 637   Oddie, G. B.
Development and Economy in Educational Building. The Fundamentals of Educational Planning: Lecture–Discussion Series No. 55.

Ed 058 659
School Board Policies on the Community Use of School Facilities. Educational Policies Development Kit.

Ed 058 672   Wells, Elmer
Vandalism and Violence: Innovative Strategies Reduce Cost to Schools. Education U.S.A. Special Report.

Ed 058 688
Special Education Facilities: Schools and Playgrounds for Trainable Mentally Handicapped Children.

Ed 058 878
Facilities Planning Conference for Community-Junior College State-Level Personnel.

Ed 058 906   Evans, G. Edward, et al.
Library Environmental Design: Physical Facilities and Equipment.

June 1972

Ed 059 435
University of Maine Adult Learning Center for the Model Neighborhood in Portland, Maine. Phase I. Final Report.

Ed 059 682   Acridge, Charles W., and Ford, Tim M.
Facilities Data System Manual.

July 1972

Ed 060 231
Child Care Centres.

Ed 060 246
Report of the Committee on Social Science Research.

Ed 060 444
Polyvalent Adult Education Centre: Concept and Description.

Ed 060 502   Clarke, Robin A.
The Feasibility of a System Building Programme for the Construction of British Columbia Schools, Studies and Reports.

Ed 060 508
Rosebery Count School for Girls, Epsom, Surrey: Sixth-Form Centre.

Ed 060 523
Open Space General Learning Facilities for Kindergarten, Primary and Junior Students.

Ed 060 526
Higher Education Facilities Systems Building Analysis. Summary Report.

Ed 060 527
Building Systems in the City. BSIC/EFL Newsletter.

Ed 060 529   Clinchy, Evans, et al.
Schools: More Space/Less Money. A Report.

Ed 060 530   Abramson, Paul, ed.
A Systems Approach for Massachusetts Schools. Study of School Building Costs. Summary Report.

Ed 060 531   Aldrich, Nelson W.
A Systems Approach for Massachusetts Schools. A Study of School Building Costs. Final Report.

Ed 060 536   Frost, F. J.
Higher Educational Facilities: Systems Building Analysis. Documentary Work Report.

Ed 060 547   Propst, Robert
High School: The Process and the Place. A Report.

Ed 060 559   Banghart, Frank W.
An Automated Inventory System for Educational Facilities. A Technical Report.

Ed 060 806   Taylor, Alton J.
Survey of Organizational Structures and Allocation Procedures for Instructional, Research and Faculty Office Space in Member Institutions of the National Association of State Universities and Land-Grant Colleges.

Ed 060 838   Hartzog, Arthur Butler
Guidelines for the Establishment of College Union Organization and Facilities on Certain Types of Two-Year Campuses.

Ed 060 857   Marples, D. L., and Knell, K. A.
Circulation and Library Design: The Influence of "Movement" on the Layout of Libraries.

August 1972

Ed 061 573   Baas, Alan M.
Building Renovation and Modernization. Educational Facilities Review Series No. 4.

Ed 061 574   Hershberger, Robert G.
Predicting the Meaning of Designed Environments.

Ed 061 575   Bartholomew, Robert, et al.
The Pre-School Child Near Environment: Variable Manipulation and Evaluation.

Ed 061 576
Thermal Environment in Schools.

Ed 061 577   Osman, Fred Linn
Patterns for Designing Children's Centers. A Report.

Ed 061 598
SEF—Academic Evaluation. An Interim Report.

Ed 061 599
The College Resource Centre. Colleges of Applied Arts and Technology.

Ed 061 600
Air-Supported Structures.

Ed 061 621   Dahnke, Harold L., et al.

Higher Educational Facilities Planning and Management Manuals, November 1–7, Revised.

Ed 061 622   Dahnke, Harold L., et al.
Higher Educational Facilities Planning and Management: An Overview. Higher Educational Facilities Planning and Management Manual One. Revised.

Ed 061 623   Dahnke, Harold L., et al.
Classroom and Class Laboratory Facilities. Higher Educational Facilities Planning and Management Manual Two. Revised.

Ed 061 624   Dahnke, Harold L. et al.
Office and Research Facilities. Higher Education Facilities Planning Manual Three. Revised.

Ed 061 625   Dahnke, Harold L., et al.
Academic Support. Facilities. Higher Education Facilities Planning Manual Four. Revised.

Ed 061 626   Dahnke, Harold L., et al.
General Support Facilities. Higher Education Facilities Planning Manual Five. Revised.

Ed 061 627   Dahnke, Harold L., et al.
Program Planning and Analysis: The Basis for Institutional and Systemlike Facilities Planning. Higher Education Facilities Planning Manual Six. Revised.

Ed 061 880   Eriksen, Aase
Scattered Schools.

Ed 061 892   Berlin, David M., et al.
Utilization of Instructional Space.

September 1972

Ed 062 589
Comprehensive Adult Learning and Counseling Center.

Ed 062 692   Walsh, David R.
Rating System for Evaluating the Acoustical Environment of Existing School Facilities.

October 1972

Ed 063 615   Baas, Alan M.
Modular Components. Educational Facilities Review Series Number 7.

Ed 063 616   Hutton, Jeoffrey, and Rostron, Michael
Comparative Study of Secondary School Building Costs. Educational Organization, Documents Number 4.

Ed 063 618   Johnson, Sharon Counts
Vocational Education Facilities. Educational Facilities Review Series Number 5.

Ed 063 630
Administration of Public Laws 81-874 and 81-815. Annual Report of the Commissioner of Education (20th, June 30, 1970).

Ed 063 652   Passantino, Richard J.
Found Space and Equipment for Children's Centers. A Report.

Ed 063 653
School Building—Why, What and How? Report of the Conference on School Building (Downsview, Ontario, May 18–21, 1971).

Ed 063 682   King, Irene A.
Bond Sales for Public School Purposes, 1970–1971.

Ed 063 868
1971 Annual Report: Coordinating Board, Texas College and University System.

November 1972

Ed 064 753   Baas, Alan M.
Open Plan Schools. Educational Facilities Review Series Number 6.

Ed 064 755
Lightweight Structures.

Ed 064 763   Ashton, Dudley, ed.
Dance Facilities.

Ed 064 764   Ragsdale, Lee, et al.
Dressing Rooms and Related Service Facilities

for Physical Education, Athletics, and Recreation.

Ed 064 901   Niehaus, Carl A.
Utilization of Telecommunications by Academic and School Libraries in the United States.

Ed 065 055   Evans, Jerome
An Exploratory Study. Facility Sharing Among Institutions of Higher Education in California.

Ed 065 062
Alliance for Greatness. A Comprehensive Study of Higher Education in the State of Delaware.

Ed 065 309
Outdoor Classrooms and School Sites.

Ed 065 643   Schoenheimer, Henry P.
Good Schools.

December 1972

Ed 065 897   Baas, Alan M.
Systems Building Techniques. Analysis and Bibliography Series No. 15.

Ed 065 899   Zucker, Charles B.
Results of an Initial Field Study of New Techniques for Citizen Participation in Educational Facilities Planning.

Ed 065 905
EA20: Education and Architecture in the 20th Century. The Design Workshop, Colleges of Applied Art and Technology (4th, Toronto, Ontario, November 16–17, 1971).

Ed 065 912   Maltby, Gregory P., et al.
Master Plan for School Facilities: North Clackamas School District Number 12—Milwaukie, Oregon.

Ed 065 913   Rosenman, Marvin Eli, et al.
Let's Have Inside–Outside Schools! Design Feasibility Study for the Renovation and Addition to the Burris Laboratory School, Muncie, Indiana.

Ed 065 934   Lieberman, Rachel Radlo
Urban Educational Facilities Options: If It Can Be Done in New York City, It Can Be Done Anywhere.

Ed 065 935   Sasserath, Simpson
From Hotel to High School: Converting a Residential Hotel into a New Type Senior High School. Report and Recommendations of the Concourse Plaza High School Planning Committee.

Ed 065 937
School Renewal. A Report Suggesting Ways That Any School System Might Approach a Total School Modernization Program.

January 1973

Ed 066 793   Baas, Alan M.
Environments for the Physically Handicapped. Educational Facilities Review Series Number 8.

Ed 066 846
Relocatable School Facilities. A Report. Educational Facilities Laboratories, New York.

Ed 067 123   Evans, G. George, et al.
Methods of Library Building Design . . . A Research Plan.

Ed 067 235   Bennett, Dean B.
Comprehensive Community Environmental Inventory, Yarmouth, Maine.

February 1973

Ed 067 850
Media Facilities, Equipment and Materials; Guidelines for the Development of an Instructional Media System. Part 2.

Ed 067 852
Media How Are We Doing? Guidelines for Development of an Instructional Media System. Part Four.

March 1973

Ed 069 293
    Student Library Resource Requirements in Philadelphia. Annual Report, Phase IV.
Ed 069 294
    Student Library Resource Requirements in Philadelphia. Evaluation Report, Phase IV.
Ed 069 295
    Student Library Resource Requirements in Philadelphia. Selected Materials Covering Joint Planning and Development of a Student Learning Center Demonstration. Supplement to the Annual Report, Phase IV.

April 1973

Ed 070 138   Baas, Alan M.
    Early Childhood Facilities. Education Facilities Review Series No. 9.
Ed 070 162   Hasenpflug, Thomas R.
    Planning Educational Facilities: The New Environment.
Ed 070 163
    Florida Schoolhouse Systems Project. Second Phase Report.
Ed 070 202
    Specifications for the First CSP Building System.
Ed 070 204
    Open Space Schools. Report of the AASA Commission on Open Space Schools.
Ed 070 205   Worrell, William K.
    School Custodial Services: Exemplary Standards and Practices.
Ed 070 626   Stover, Lloyd V.
    Environmental Impact Assessment: A Procedure.

May 1973

Ed 070 940   Dolff, Helmuth
    Can the Volkshochschulen of Today Answer the Requirements of Adult Education for Tomorrow?
Ed 071 144   Baas, Alan M.
    Science Facilities. Educational Facilities Review Series No. 11.
Ed 071 147   Piele, Philip K.
    Financing School Construction. Educational Facilities Review Series No. 12.
Ed 071 174
    Schoolhouse Systems Project: SSP 3rd Report.
Ed 071 198   Abbott, James F.
    Construction Management.
Ed 071 201   Featherstone, Richard L.
    An Assessment of the Detroit Public Schools Construction Systems Program.
Ed 071 203   Biedermann, Konrad, et al.
    Layout, Equipment and Work Methods for School Lunch Kitchens and Serving Lines.
Ed 071 205
    Listing of Schools Constructed with a Building System. Building Systems Information Clearinghouse Special Report Number Two.
Ed 071 642   Romney, Leonard C.
    Higher Education Facilities Inventory and Classification Manual.
Ed 071 869   Cate, Bill, ed.
    Directory of Environmental Consultants.

June 1973

Ed 072 504   Baas, Alan M.
    Libraries and Instructional Materials Centers. Educational Facilities Review Series No. 13.
Ed 072 513   Baas, Alan M.
    Luminous Environments. Educational Facilities Review Series No. 15.
Ed 072 544   McGrady, Donna S.
    Open School Elementary Schools: An Annotated Bibliography.
Ed 072 548
    Site Planning: Aurania Higher Education Center.
Ed 072 550

Twelve Small California Schools.

Ed 072 551   Gilliland, John W.
School Carpet: Guide to Selection and Care.

Ed 072 552
Profile Rating Wheel: An Instrument to Evaluate School Facilities. Revised Edition.

Ed 072 553
Portable School Buildings.

Ed 072 554
California State Board of Education Guide for Determining "Earthquake Unsafe" School Buildings.

Ed 072 566
Accessibility of Junior Colleges for Handicapped.

July 1973

Ed 073 531   Hughes, John R., ed.
The Community School and Its Concepts.

Ed 073 537   Picardi, E. Alfred
Closing the Credibility Gap in Construction Cost Estimating.

Ed 073 538   Lassiter, Frank
Equipment and Furniture Guidelines for Open-Plan Middle and High Schools.

Ed 073 539   Lassiter, Frank
Equiping the Open-School Plan, Equiping for Open Education.

Ed 073 550   King, Irene A.
Bond Sales for Public School Purposes.

Ed 073 742
Comparative Staffing and Operations Study for Physical Plant Functions of Universities and Colleges.

Ed 073 912   Jostad, Karen
Educational Lands Resource Assessment.

Ed 074 250
Building Materials Technology and Selling, A Distributive Education Manual and Answer Book.

August 1973

Ed 074 371   Seccatore, Luis A.
Course Scheduling to Find the Minimum Cost Set of Facilities Required.

Ed 074 586   Baas, Alan M.
Acoustical Environments. Educational Facilities Review Series No. 16.

Ed 074 587   Baas, Alan M.
Thermal Environments. Educational Facilities Review Series No. 17.

Ed 074 599   Haimsath, Clovis B.
Systems and the Changing Architectural Practice.

Ed 074 613   Gardner, John C., ed.
Programed Cleaning and Environmental Sanitation.

Ed 074 629   Turner, George E.
Architectural Building Programming: An Annotated Bibliography.

Ed 074 684
Directories of Services and Facilities: A Selective Bibliography. Exceptional Child Bibliography Series No. 638.

Ed 074 723   Stephens, Richard, and Hallock, Don
Suggestions Toward a Small Video Facility.

Ed 074 924
Utilization of Existing Facilities. Needs for New Facilities. A Discussion Paper for the Master Plan for Higher Education in Connecticut.

Ed 074 990   Dahnke, Harold L., and Mertins, Paul F.
Distribution of Physical Facilities Among Institutions of Higher Education Grouped by Level, Control, and Enrollment Size. Fall 1968.

Ed 075 001   Higgins, E. Eugene, et al.
Inventory of Physical Facilities in Institutions of Higher Education. Fall 1969.

Ed 075 008
Clackamas Community College Master Planning Program. Final Report.

September 1973

Ed 075 942   Bregar, William S.
Improvement of Elementary School Designs Through Simulation of Educational Activities. Final Report.

October 1973

Ed 077 078   Dell'Isola, A. J.
Project Management Controls With Systems.

Ed 077 089
Building Systems on the Campus, Part I, BSIC/EFL Newsletter.

Ed 077 090
Building Systems on the Campus, Part I, The University of Alaska, BSIC/EFL Newsletter.

Ed 077 099   Licht, Kenneth F.
The Occupational Safety and Health Act: Implications for School Administrators.

Ed 077 192   Buckingham, Betty Jo
Plan for Progress in the Media Center Facilities.

Ed 077 344   Holden, Richard R.
An Estimate of Construction Needs of Higher Education by 1980.

Ed 077 395   Deaton, Francesca A., comp.
A Bibliography of Higher Education Facilities Publications.

Ed 077 410
Higher Education in Maine: Its Facilities and Utilization.

Ed 077 432
Proceedings of 1st Annual Conference on Higher Education Institutional Research and Planning.

Ed 077 434
Comparative Unit Cost and Wage Rate Report on Maintenance and Operation of Physical Plants of Universities and Colleges.

Ed 077 656   Novak, Joseph D.
Facilities for Secondary School Science Teaching. Evolving Patterns in Facilities and Programs.

November 1973

Ed 078 285
1973–1974 Directory of Consultants for Planning Adult Learning Systems, Facilities and Environment.

Ed 078 508   Oswalt, Felix E.
Computer Profile of School Facilities Energy Consumption.

Ed 078 522   Baas, Alan M.
Site Development. Educational Facilities Review Series, No. 19.

Ed 078 804
Fact Book for the State University System of Florida, 1973.

Ed 078 875
The Myers Demonstration Library; An ESEA Title III Project.

Ed 079 509   Ristau, Robert A.
An Evaluation of the Educational Telephone Network (ETN) as an Instructional Delivery System for a Graduate Course in Career Education.

December 1973

Ed 079 806   Freund, Janet W.
The Development of a Suburban Junior High School Learning Center.

Ed 079 814
A Long-Range Development Program. McKeesport Area School District, Pa.

Ed 079 819
Physical Recreation Facilities, a Report. Educational Facilities Laboratories, Inc.

Ed 079 936   Enright, B. J.
New Media and the Library in Education.

Ed 080 083   Sanderson, Robert D.
The Expansion of University Facilities to Accommodate Increasing Enrollments.

Ed 080 677   Capson, A. Maurice
Eastern Utah Career Center at Price: Educational Specifications.

Ed 080 754
> Development of Cooperative Planning for Technical–Vocational Programs.

January 1974

Ed 080 857   Schantz, Harold J.
> Guidelines for Realistic Facility Planning for Schools of Vocational, Technical and Adult Education.

Ed 081 066
> Jefferson County Design/Build Program. BSIC/EFL Newsletter.

Ed 081 077   McGuffey, C. W., ed.
> Educational Facilities Survey: Atlanta Public Schools 1971–81.

Ed 081 212   Klitzke, Dwight Mark, and Starkey, John
> Resource Centers; Some Ideas.

Ed 081 324   Shaw, Paul C.
> Truth, Love and Campus Expansion. The University of Pittsburgh Experience.

Ed 081 335   Brunt, Judy, and Williamson, W. J.
> The Commuting Student Study Report II: Study Facilities.

February 1974

Ed 082 274   Baas, Alan M.
> Construction Management. Educational Facilities Review Series No. 20.

Ed 082 278
> New Academic Building: Newark State College. A Progress Report.

Ed 082 279
> Producers of Fast Incremental Space.

Ed 082 289   Cober, John G., and Reynolds, Robert N.
> Better School Buildings for Less Money: A Report of a Survey of 50 Pennsylvania School Buildings.

Ed 082 298   Thrasher, James W.
> Effective Planning for Better School Buildings.

Ed 082 299   Hawkins, Harold L.
> Appraisal Guide for School Facilities.

Ed 082 321
> The Economy of Energy Conservation in Educational Facilities. A Report.

Ed 082 352
> Facilities for Early Childhood Education. School Planning Guide Series Number 5.

Ed 082 358   Ensign, William L.
> Modernizing Educational Facilities—A Sketchbook Summary of Conferences.

Ed 082 372   Klepser, James E., ed.
> Protected Educational Facilities in Found Space. A Guide to Converting Noneducational Spaces into Safe, Healthful Environments for Education.

Ed 082 446
> Standards and the Education Consumer.

Ed 082 602   Morisseau, James J.
> Recycled Space and Found Space.

Ed 082 764   DuMond, Ernest G., and Meffert, Benjamin F.
> Facilities for School Library Media Programs.

Ed 082 900
> Educational Opportunities of Rural School Consolidation.

Ed 082 940   Mills, Edward D., and Kaylor, Harry
> The Design of Polytechnic Institute Buildings.

March 1974

Ed 083 665   Baas, Alan M.
> The Educator and the Architect. Educational Facilities Review Series Number 21.

Ed 083 666   Baas, Alan M.
> Joint Occupancy. Educational Facilities Review Series Number 22.

Ed 083 670   Ward, Dilbert B.
> Schools in Kansas with Tornado Protection—Shawnee Mission Public School.

Ed 083 671
> Career Cluster Facilities Guide.

Ed 083 672   Dibner, David R.
    You and Your Architect.
Ed 083 689
    Manual of Regulations and Recommendations
    for School Building Planning and Construc-
    tion.
Ed 083 692   Foster, Donald M., and Foster, Rick
    A Career Development Center: A Model for
    School Employee Development.
Ed 083 698
    Financial Implications of the Extended School
    Year.
Ed 083 700   Bird, Walter W.
    A New Generation of Air Structures.
Ed 083 718   Cheek, Becky
    Planning Playgrounds for Day Care.
Ed 083 720
    Reports of CEC Study Committee on Construc-
    tion Management.
Ed 083 721
    Designs for Science Facilities.
Ed 083 992   Leonard, Lawrence E., et al.
    Public Library Construction Under LSCA, Title
    II. An Evaluation.

April 1974

Ed 084 398   Fischer, Joseph, and Messier, Joseph
    Building Maintenance Syllabus. New York
    State Education Department, Albany, New
    York.
Ed 084 666   Tarapata, Peter
    Planning for Change. Spaces for Career Prep-
    aration, Document 4. Michigan State Universi-
    ty, East Lansing Continuing Education Service.
Ed 084 704   Cooper, Paul D.
    Full State Funding of School Construction in
    Maryland: An Appraisal After Two Years.
Ed 084 705   Chick, Charles E., et al.
    School Construction Programming in Florida,
    K–12.
Ed 084 775   Hostrop, Richard W.

Education Inside the Library-Media Center.
Ed 084 888   Bomar, Cora Paul, et al.
    Guide to the Development of Educational
    Media Selection Centers.

May 1974

Ed 085 527
    Guidelines for Planning Facilities Home
    Economics Education, Secondary Schools.
Ed 085 538
    Career Cluster Facilities Guide.
Ed 085 833   Cramer, Harold L.
    Orienting Users for New Facilities. A Report.
Ed 085 851   Hood, Diane M.
    Independent School Building Projects. State of
    the Art Recommendations.
Ed 085 875
    School Sites: Selection, Development and
    Utilization. Educational Facilities Laboratories
    Series: A Guide to Planning.
Ed 085 876
    Educational Specifications. Educational
    Facilities Series: A Guide to Planning.
Ed 085 902   Wolff, Max, and Stein, Annie
    A Plan for Middle Schools, Buffalo, New York.
    A Study of Sites, Organization and Program.
    Part III, Component 4. Final Report.
Ed 085 903
    Suggestions for Guidance Centres, Secondary
    Schools.
Ed 085 904
    Suggestions for School Boards Considering
    Rehabilitation of Old Building. Rehabilitation
    of Schools.
Ed 085 905
    Science Laboratories for Secondary Schools.
Ed 085 906
    Home Economics.
Ed 085 907
    Special Educational Facilities for Emotionally
    Disturbed Children.

Ed 085 908

Physical Education Facilities for Elementary Schools.

Ed 085 909

Suggestions for Industrial Arts Facilities for Elementary and Secondary Schools.

Ed 085 910

Music Facilities.

Ed 085 911

Technical and Occupational Shops. Volume I.

Ed 085 912

Technical and Occupational Shops. Volume II.

Ed 085 945

Florida's Educational Facilities for Exceptional Children, 1968–1973.

Ed 086 119

Planning a Consortium of Colleges and Universities for Equal Opportunity in College Construction.

Ed 086 120

Comparative Unit Cost and Wage Rate Reports on Maintenance and Operation of Physical Plants of Universities and Colleges.

Ed 086 342   Bartholomew, Robert, et al.

Child Care Centers: Indoor Lighting: Outdoor Playspace.

Ed 086 375

Children's Spaces: Design for the 70's; Planning Educational Facilities in the Elementary School for Very Young Children.

June 1974

Ed 087 085

A Systems Approach to the Practice of Architecture. BSIC/EFL Newsletter.

Ed 087 086

Proceedings. Association of Physical Plant Administrators of Universities and Colleges Annual Meeting (60th, Honolulu, Hawaii, April 7–12, 1973).

Ed 087 097

School Libraries: Their Planning and Equipment.

Ed 087 113   Zeisel, John

Planning Facilities to Discourage Vandalism.

Ed 087 115   Grealy, Joseph I.

How Can School Security Be Strengthened?

Ed 087 127   Saunders, Charles B., Jr.

Fewer Dollars, Shrinking Enrollments, Fixed Cost: New Financial Dilemma.

Educational Research Information Center (ERIC):

Research in Education—Résumés and Indexes (1968, 1969, 1970, and 1971).

Monthly abstract journal announcing recently completed research and research-related projects in the field of education.

Educational Media and Technology—ERIC, Stanford University, Stanford, California

Facilities for Education—ERIC Clearinghouse of Educational Facilities, University of Wisconsin, Madison, Wisconsin, Howard Wakefield, Director

Collection of ERIC microfiche (almost the entire collection) can be used at

Harvard: basement of Longfellow Hall, Graduate School of Education Library, Appian Way and Brattle Street, Cambridge, Mass.; telephone: 495-4225 or 495-3424. Hours: Monday–Friday, 9–11 P.M.; Saturday, 9–5 P.M.; Sunday, 2–10 P.M.

ERIC has also published the *Current Index to Journals of Education,* which abstracts research material.

In selecting the ERIC abstracts for this bibliography, we confined ourselves to the following descriptors and material found in the United States and Canada:

Building design
Educational environment * Educational facilities

Educational planning, evaluative criteria
Facility expansion
Facility requirements, property appraisal
School buildings, school construction
Consultants
Library facilities
Construction needs

PLACES CONTACTED FOR BIBLIOGRAPHIC RESEARCH

American Institute of Architects
1735 New York Avenue, N.W.
Washington, D.C. 20006

Architectural Forum
Whitney Publishing Co., Inc.
18 East 50th Street, New York, N.Y. 10022

Architectural Record
McGraw-Hill Publication
330 West 42nd Street, New York, N.Y. 10036

AudioVisual Instruction—DAVI Publication
1201 Sixteenth Street, N.W.
Washington, D.C. 20036

Building Science Directory
Building Research Institute
1424 Sixteenth Street, N.W.
Washington, D.C. 20036

Croft Educational Services
100 Garfield Avenue
New London, Connecticut 06320

Directory of Membership and Business Highlights
Council of Educational Facility Planners
29 W. Woodruf Avenue
Columbus, Ohio 43210

Educational Facilities Laboratories
477 Madison Avenue
New York, N.Y. 10022

ERIC Clearinghouse of Educational Facilities
University of Wisconsin
Madison, Wisconsin 53706

ERIC Clearinghouse of Educational Media and Technology
Stanford University
Stanford, California 94305

Illuminating Engineering Society
345 East 47th Street,
New York, N.Y. 10017

Massachusetts State Board of Education
School Facilities Director: George Collins
182 Tremont Street
Boston, Massachusetts 02111

National Council of Schoolhouse Construction
317 Manly Mills Building, 1405 Harrison Road
East Lansing, Michigan 48823

Research Council of the Great City Schools
1819 H Street, N.W.
Washington, D.C. 20006

United States Department of Health, Education, and Welfare
Division of Facilities Development
John N. Cameron, Director
Office of Construction Services
Washington, D.C. 20402

Index